The European Business Environment: UK

Volume Editor: Stephen Fox

INTERNATIONAL THOMSON BUSINESS PRESS

An International Thomson Publishing Company

London ● Bonn ● Boston ● Johannesburg ● Madrid ● Melbourne ● Mexico City ● New York ● Paris
Singapore ● Tokyo ● Toronto ● Albany, NY ● Belmont, CA ● Cincinnati, OH ● Detroit, MI

The European Business Environment: UK

Copyright individual chapters © 1998 individual authors
selection and editorial comment © 1998 Stephen Fox

First published 1998 by International Thomson Business Press

I(T)P® A division of International Thomson Publishing Inc.
The ITP logo is a trademark under licence

British Library Cataloguing-in-Publication Data
A catalogue record for this book is available from the British Library

Library of Congress Cataloguing in Publication Data
A catalogue record for this book has been requested

First Edition 1998

Typeset by LaserScript, Mitcham, Surrey
Printed in the UK by TJ International Ltd, Padstow, Cornwall

ISBN 1–861–52190–1

International Thomson Business Press

Berkshire House
168–173 High Holborn
London WC1V 7AA
UK

20 Park Plaza
14th Floor
Boston MA 02116
USA

Contents

List of tables and figures	vi
List of contributors	x
Series editors' introduction	xi
Volume editor's introduction	xv
Acknowledgements	xxii
1 The UK economy, business and technology *Peter Ingram*	1
2 The UK market environment *Michael Thomas*	46
3 The UK financial sector *Jenifer Piesse*	100
4 Accounting, financial reporting and corporate governance *Robert Perks*	122
5 The legal and institutional framework *Anne Ruff*	141
6 The legal framework *Anne Ruff*	162
7 UK management and human resource management *Stephen Fox*	190
8 UK vocational education and training *Ewart Keep and Ken Mayhew*	219
9 Industrial relations in the UK *Alan Whitaker*	242
10 Volume editor's conclusion *Stephen Fox*	257
Glossary	263
Bibliography	266
Index	276

List of tables and figures

TABLES

0.1	Five-phase development model of management education	xviii
1.1	Relative annual GDP growth rates, 1960–93	3
1.2	International comparisons of consumer price inflation, 1960–93	5
1.3	North Sea oil annual revenue and production, 1976–91	9
1.4	Proportions of total UK imports and exports, 1975–92	10
1.5	UK balance of payments, 1974–93	10
1.6	UK trade with EC, 1972–93	11
1.7	UK trade with non-EC countries, 1974–92	12
1.8	Structural change in employment, 1972–93	14
1.9	UK and Japanese manufacturing sectors, 1975–92	17
1.10	UK manpower demography in 1979, 1988 and 1991	18
1.11	Privatisation: major asset sales, 1981–91	20
1.12	Privatisation proceeds, 1984–93	20
1.13	Privatisation proceeds as a share of GDP, 1984–93	20
1.14	Public sector borrowing requirement as a percentage of GDP, 1979–93	21
1.15	The UK labour market, 1970–93	22
1.16	The UK business environment, 1970–92	30
1.17	Plant size and employment, 1979–89	31
1.18	Research and development expenditure, 1975–91	33
1.19	Composition of government-funded research and development expenditure in the UK, 1990–91	33
1.20	Share ownership in Britain, 1963–93	36
1.21	UK finance and capital markets, 1970–92	37
1.22	International comparisons of hourly compensation costs in manufacturing, 1992	43
1.23	Labour costs, 1992	43
2.1	CACI ACORN profile of Great Britain	47
2.2	National Readership Survey social grade definitions	48
2.3	Distribution of the population by social grade main shoppers	48

2.4 Main shoppers 48
2.5 ACORN categories 49
2.6 Distribution of personal incomes before and after tax in the UK in 1990–91 53
2.7 Distribution of marketable wealth of individuals in the UK in 1991 (range of net wealth) 53
2.8 Distribution of marketable wealth of individuals in the UK in 1989 (percentage of wealth owned) 54
2.9 Characteristics of household population 55
2.10 UK household expenditure in 1992 56
2.11 UK household expenditure on food in 1992 57
2.12 Regional variations in domestic food consumption in Great Britain 58
2.13 Household penetration of consumer durables in Great Britain 59
2.14 Equipment for leisure, hobbies and personal care 60
2.15 Clubs 61
2.16 Leisure activities 62
2.17 DIY 63
2.18 Gardening 64
2.19 Holidays taken by British people in 1991 65
2.20 Overseas travel and tourism in 1990 66
2.21 Grocery shopping habits: housewives 66
2.22 The structure of the retail grocery trade in Great Britain 67
2.23 Some multiple retailers 67
2.24 Large grocery stores and grocery superstores 68
2.25 Clothing: men's 68
2.26 Clothing: women's, children's, families' 69
2.27 Footwear 69
2.28 The retail trades in Great Britain 70
2.29 Total advertising expenditure, including direct mail (£m) 71
2.30 Total advertising expenditure, including direct mail (% of total) 71
2.31 Total advertising expenditure and its relation to consumers' expenditure and gross national product 73
2.32 Breakdown of national advertising by type of publication 73
2.33 Breakdown of regional advertising by type of publication 74
2.34 Readership of press groups by percentage of GB adults in an average period 74
2.35 Press: women's magazines 74
2.36 Press: some consumer specialised journals 75
2.37 Current developments in television 78
2.38 Television establishment data 80
2.39 Cable and satellite universe 80
2.40 Television reach data 81
2.41 Direct mail 82
2.42 Expenditure on market research 83

2.43 Top holding companies' advertising expenditure, 1991   84
2.44 The top 100 advertisers, 1991   85
2.45 Population and per capita gross national product of some
      countries, 1991   87
2.46 Civilian employment by main sectors, 1990   88
2.47 Machine tool production: world shares, 1990   88
2.48 Machine tool exports: percentage of world trade, 1991   88
2.49 Satellite communications: projected shares of value added services
      in Europe 1994   88
2.50 Origins of European cross-border acquisitions shares by country,
      June 1989–June 1990   88
3.1   UK clearing banks   109
3.2   Stocks of personal sector savings held with banks and
      building societies   110
3.3   Total assets of British financial institutions in 1990   112
3.4   Comparison of major international stock exchanges, 1990   114
3.5   Share ownership in Britain: percentage distribution by sector,
      1963–92   115
7.1   Members of the Consultative Council of Professional Management
      Organisation   194
9.1   Trade union membership in the UK   245
9.2   Union presence, membership density and collective bargaining
      coverage in 1984 and 1990   247
9.3   Strike trends in the United Kingdom, 1946–93   251

FIGURES

1.1   UK inflation rate, 1960–93   4
1.2   Total exchequer receipts from North Sea oil, 1969–93   9
1.3   Employment in manufacturing and services, 1972–93   15
1.4   International comparisons of added value per employee in
      manufacturing, 1980   16
1.5   International comparisons of added value per employee in
      government services, 1980   16
1.6a Industrial relations in a non-zero sum game   28
1.6b 'Prisoner's dilemma' pay-off matrix   28
1.7   Investment in innovation in the UK, 1989–94   35
1.8   Comparison of company insolvencies and price–earnings ratios for
      the FT-500, 1975–93   41
1.9   Advertisement promoting low wage costs in the UK   44
2.1   Sagacity Life Cycle groupings   52
2.2   Advertising as a percentage of gross national product, 1907–92 72
2.3   Television viewing patterns   82

2.4	Relationship marketing orientation: bringing together customer service, quality and marketing	89
2.5	Grocery brands and new products	91
2.6	Private label groceries and grocery value in Europe	91
2.7	Value delivery sequence	98
3.1	Flow of funds in a two-sector economy	103
3.2	Flow of funds in an economy with public and international sectors	104
3.3	Financial intermediation	105
5.1	Civil courts	153
5.2	Magistrates' courts	154
5.3	Legislative sources of UK law	157
6.1	Legal forms of limited company	165
7.1	How many managers are there in the UK?	191
7.2	Levels of managers in the UK	192
7.3	The new architecture	205
7.4	Ladder of progression	206
8.1	Training system in England and Wales	235

List of contributors

Stephen Fox is a senior lecturer and research director in the Department of Management Learning at the Management School, Lancaster University.

Peter Ingram is a lecturer in economics in the Department of Economics at the University of Surrey.

Ewart Keep is a senior research fellow in the Industrial Relations Research Unit at the School of Industrial and Business Studies, University of Warwick.

Ken Mayhew is a lecturer in economics at Pembroke College, Oxford University.

Robert Perks was a professor in the Department of Management and Business Studies at Birkbeck College, University of London. He is now retired.

Jenifer Piesse is a lecturer in management and Chair of the Department of Management and Business Studies at Birkbeck College, University of London.

Anne Ruff LL B (Hons), LL M, Barrister at Law is a principal lecturer in law at Middlesex University and Head of the postgraduate diploma in law programmes (CPE).

Michael Thomas is professor of marketing at the Department of Marketing at the University of Strathclyde in Glasgow, and Senior Vice-Chairman, Chartered Institute of Marketing.

Alan Whitaker is a senior lecturer in the Department of Behaviour in Organisations at the Management School, Lancaster University.

Series editors' introduction

European Business Environments

Robert Crawshaw and Stephen Fox

This book, the first part of a series which includes separate publications on the business environments of France, Germany and the UK, appears at a moment when the future of European union is being widely called into question. The belief that closer trans-European integration in education and training is required in order to respond to an increasingly international business environment is being undermined by pressures to reduce public spending. On a larger scale, the debate on European Monetary Union has raised questions as to whether the sacrifice of national economic control by individual member states will be outweighed by the advantages of a single currency area, doubts which public discussion on the subject has done little to dispel and less to inform. The relationship between economic cooperation within Europe and that between states on an international scale is increasingly under review. It is argued by some that the 'global marketplace' has overtaken the concept of a European Community in terms of its economic importance. Countries are better able to respond to the challenge of world competition on an individual basis than if they carry the collective burden of regional disparities within a wider Europe.

Yet the concept of European unity will not go away. The importance of maintaining political and economic equilibrium in the face of new national configurations on the Eastern borders of the continent is all the more pressing as a consequence of the high level of unemployment which is dogging the Western nations. The interdependency of European economies means that companies must continue to increase their capacity to operate across national boundaries. At the level of multinational groups, this implies regarding West Europe as a unitary field of operations. For small and medium-sized enterprises, it means facilitating expansion and export to other member states in the Union as well as more widely afield. In short, the importance of the single European market has not been diminished by the shrinking boundaries of global trade. On the contrary, the improvement of communications and the growing efficiency of distribution have enhanced Europe's identity as a discrete region of the world.

It is incontrovertible, however, that the struggle between the different models of global capitalism is vividly illustrated by the different approaches to national economic management current in France, Germany and the United Kingdom.

These differences are explored most cogently by Michel Albert in his now classic book *Capitalisme contre Capitalisme* and are reflected in the study for the Royal Institute of International Affairs, *Britain, Germany and 1992: the Limits of Deregulation* by Woolcock, Hodges and Schreiber. Both analyses date from the year 1991. Following the Rhodes summit of 1988, that year appears in retrospect to signal a heightened sense that a fundamental choice had to be made if the Europe of the post-1992 era was to be based on a common social and economic foundation. In both studies, the option of convergence between the three main West European economies was opposed to that of accepting their differences in economic principles and management practices.

From a primarily economic standpoint, one view was that Europe could be cast in the mould of a free trade area characterised by a lack of government involvement in corporate affairs and most public services – an unlikely scenario, given the traditional belief of the French in the civic responsibility of the state and the commitment on the part of the Germans to the *Ordnungspolitik* which formed the strength of their economy. On the other hand, from a more *dirigiste* perspective, a socially regulated community might emerge in which the German model of controlled intervention would dominate – by regional government in the management of local affairs and by banks and trade unions in corporate decision-making. To a greater or lesser extent, other states would be satisfied to compromise with German hegemony whilst preserving their cultural and political identities within a reconstituted political structure.

In fact, as Woolcock *et al.* saw it, a compromise between these two political and economic philosophies was the likely outcome, not out of respect for consensus, but as the result of a common reluctance to accept federal regulation of work practices at the European level. Within this context, the principle of the strongest European economy – that of Germany – would dominate. In Albert's eyes, this would be a positive development. France was faced with a choice between the law of the corporate jungle marked by low public investment and short-termism which characterised what he termed the 'Anglo-Saxon' model and the stability, social purpose and cost-effectiveness which he saw as the prerogative of the 'rhenan' system. He hoped that France would opt to maintain her long-standing tradition of forward planning and state regulation which he saw as complementary to *Ordnungspolitik*. He could not have reckoned on the extent to which his native country's balance of payments deficit and the *franc fort* policy of alignment with the Deutschmark would threaten her own institutions by inducing a more monetarist and hence *laissez-faire* approach to economic management.

Even in a climate of compromise, both Albert and Woolcock not surprisingly portray Britain as lying at the liberal end of the political–economic continuum against the background of a Franco-German alliance. Neither analysis took account of the potential consequences of victory by a socialist government in the UK. Britain sought both further deregulation and increased competition within Europe, having unilaterally made its own markets more open than those of other member states. For the sake of free market principles, the country was apparently unconcerned about sacrificing corporate sovereignty to foreign investors even to the extent of allowing its public utilities to be taken over by its European partners. However, in those countries where competition was still regulated through state intervention, it was not clear that UK firms found corporate success so easy.

Whatever the outcome, national differences continue to run deep and permeate every aspect of corporate and national life. It remains to be seen exactly what this means in terms of the social and economic structures which will shape the business environments of the different European countries and regulate managers' behaviour in the European organisations of the new millennium. If European unity means anything in terms of business administration, it must be the ability on the part of citizens generally and in particular on the part of managers to cope with diversity and difference, and to turn these factors to commercial advantage. Whatever the economic pressures for convergence and compromise and however uneven the pace of progression towards closer European union, the essential importance of understanding the fabric of national business environments remains undiminished. The objective of the *European Business Environments* series is to make this field of knowledge more accessible to students of management and practising businessmen.

Much has been written about the most appropriate form of education and training required to develop qualities of cultural adaptability alongside the fundamental technical and professional knowledge demanded of international managers. There is a growing literature on European management culture, much of which takes a comparative perspective and includes an analysis of behaviour in organisations in a number of different European countries. Equally, there have been a number of publications which attempt to provide an overview of business practice on a country-by-country basis, either as an everyday practical guide for the businessman or woman or in order to provide more 'in-depth' analyses of the countries concerned. Others too approach the topic of Europeanisation from the perspective of a single management 'discipline'. This is particularly true of the more 'technical' or professional fields such as accounting and marketing.

The *European Business Environments* series seeks to combine these approaches. Acknowledging the profound cultural differences already referred to between France, Germany and the UK, the series devotes a single volume to each of the three countries concerned. All three volumes, however, follow a common template based on the academic disciplines which together constitute the field of management studies. The aim of the series is not simply to provide a business person's guide to each individual country, but to offer an accessible introduction to the business environments of the countries concerned from a series of academic perspectives.

An original feature of the series is the fact that, although it is published in English with the editors of each volume being British nationals, each book is written by a team of academics who are natives of the country concerned, the academics being specialists in the disciplines which they represent. Thus, the perspective on, for example, business law in Germany will be that of a German academic and will reflect the style and analytical approach which is characteristic of that academic culture. In this respect, the series is not designed to replace or directly to compete with existing publications which seek to describe and compare European management practices. It aims to complement these texts and to fulfil a need which is not so far being met for the benefit of students following courses in European management at undergraduate, postgraduate or post-experience levels.

In so far as each volume covers five more or less discrete areas of academic specialisation, the series is intended as much as a source of reference as a collection of individual studies to read in their entirety. For example, the non-specialist student of management in France may have a particular interest in French business law but may not need to have a complete overview of the French accounting system. It is hoped that the series will be used eclectically in response to the different needs of individual programmes. Explanatory tables are provided in the text and each chapter includes recommendations for further reading within the specialist field concerned as well as useful sources of documentation. In addition to an index, each volume also contains a glossary of technical and specialist terms designed to enable non-native students to familiarise themselves with essential vocabulary as well as abbreviations and acronyms in current usage.

The series as a whole has been a joint enterprise between the publishers, International Thomson Business Press, the series and volume editors and the teams of academics in the three countries so far covered. It has involved extensive translation and editorial work over a three-year period and has enhanced the working relationships between the partner institutions engaged on the project. It is our hope that the series makes a worthwhile contribution to the available educational literature in the field and that, within its own limited sphere, it furthers the cause of European cooperation in the area of European management education.

Lancaster
July 1996

Volume editor's introduction

The UK Business Environment

Stephen Fox

The United Kingdom's business environment, is complex and multifaceted with a long history, not all of which can be described and analysed here. This book aims to introduce students to five key aspects of the UK business environment:

- the contemporary UK business world seen from a general economic viewpoint: examining the role of government and its macro-economic objectives, and its relations with big business and the unions who represent the UK workforce;
- the contemporary UK marketplace from a marketing perspective: how are UK citizens socially, economically and geographically classified, what do they buy and sell and how do retail and advertising businesses target them;
- contemporary UK capital markets and city institutions: how are UK firms financed, what pressures to perform are they under, and how are the capital markets regulated. Also, how do UK accountants operate, how is the profession structured, what are the links between accountancy and the city institutions, what rules cover financial reporting, auditing and the work of the Cadbury commission on corporate governance in the UK;
- contemporary UK legal institutions: the legislative bodies and the various courts, tribunals and legal professionals through which business disputes of various kinds may be resolved. Also what is the legal framework, the main areas of law relating to different types of business organisation, contracts, product liability, the workplace and the environment, employment and industrial relations, and competition;
- human resources in the UK: how are managers and business people educated, trained and developed, how are they managed at work, how does this affect the business culture, what is the adequacy of their education, training and development, and how are these processes changing? How are people more generally educated and trained in the UK before and after they join the workforce, what is the adequacy of such education and training and how are these processes changing? How are non-managerial employees managed at work, what is the nature of UK industrial relations (IR) and how is it changing?

These five areas are seldom brought together in one book, being usually left to more specialised books. The reason for bringing them together here is to provide an overview of the main aspects of the business environment which any manager or business person needs to know about in order to operate within the UK. Each of the five main sections provides a broad and informative account of a major area of the UK business environment. In each case, questions are raised which the professionals in the area are currently grappling with, such as the codes of practice covering advertising standards, auditing and accounting standards, or the most appropriate way in which to educate and develop senior managers. The technology and operational management of business enterprises differ enormously from sector to sector and it would take another book entirely to chart the production and operations management aspects of the UK business world. The present book focuses upon the more general aspects of the business environment as they effect firms in all sectors of the economy.

In selecting the five broad areas chosen here (the economy, the marketplace, the framework of law, the financial and accounting institutions and the managerial and working population or human resources) we are making a statement not only about the UK business environment, but about the nature of business administration or management studies as a 'discipline'. The word 'discipline' requires some qualification. The area of university study which sheds most light on the business environment of any country, is increasingly called 'business administration' or 'management studies', but this is not a universally agreed formulation; for instance this subject is not even taught at university level in Japan; and in Germany the term 'business economics', does not mean the same thing as 'business administration' in, say, the USA. The latter includes more social-psychological and organisation theory than is common in the German university curricula, which is dominated by technical economics and quantitative analysis, although private schools such as Koblenz have a syllabus closer to the US model. Also, within Germany's two tier higher education system, many of the *Fachhochschulen* curricula are modelled more closely on US lines, whereas the higher status universities are not. As a result it is sometimes claimed that the *Fachhochschulen* are gradually supplanting the universities in training the coming generation of German managers. As many top European business and management schools seek student and academic credit exchange schemes with each other and the USA, a gradual curriculum development process is under way and a certain homogenisation. The UK, France and most Scandinavian countries' business and management curricula are already more closely modelled upon the US syllabus, although there are differences of approach, especially in the teaching of social-psychology and organisational behaviour and theory, which tends to be more political, critical and radical in the EU, perhaps reflecting the social democratic traditions of corporatist Scandinavia, Germany, France and the European Commission (this is discussed at some length in Fox 1992).

It has been suggested that the American curriculum is gradually spreading globally, as internationalism and globalism become increasingly hot topics in business and management schools. For instance, Tanton and Easterby-Smith (1989) present a five-phase developmental model of management education (see Table 0.1), which follows the developing shape of the business systems, as different countries develop economically.

There are many problems with such 'developmental' models, since not all economies 'develop' along the same lines; there are different and equally valid ideas of being 'fully developed', adopted by different peoples, and cultures, a point emphasised in Davies *et al.* (1989). Yet, as the world shrinks, national differences of culture, political-economy and business environment become clearer and more relevant to the nations' managers and business communities on a day-to-day basis; while only twenty years ago these differences were mainly of interest to political élites, diplomats, foreign correspondents and students of international relations and anthropology. This gives more reason for students of business and management to start to look at their own cultures' ways of doing business and ways of managing from the viewpoint of the anthropological stranger, and to examine in detail how business environments differ from nation to nation. The present volume has been written to assist in that attempt.

The UK is in many ways an idiosyncratic nation in contrast to its peers in Europe, the Organisation for Economic Cooperation and Development (OECD) and the Group of Seven (G7). In some ways it resembles America, in its current emphasis upon free market economics, for example, in other ways it is closer to the other major countries of the European Union (EU), in its shared history and membership of that common market, for example. However, its position within the EU sometimes appears to be at odds with the seemingly common Franco-German vision of political and economic union. To understand the UK's idiosyncratic position, it is necessary to examine some of the key aspects of its existing business environment and to compare these with those of other countries.

As Ingram says in Chapter 1, Britain was the first democracy and the first industrialised nation, its wealth rooted in trade, empire and a liberal capitalist political–economic system. However, it is widely acknowledged that Britain is in long-term political–economic decline although this was scarcely recognised by the UK's political élite until the 1960s since, after the Second World War, it was the strongest economy in Europe. Economic reconstruction on the continental mainland, followed by thirty glorious years of sustained economic growth, soon left Britain behind, suffering from two main economic problems – slow growth and chronic inflation. As Ingram discusses, these were the problems which successive governments have tried to tackle since the 1960s, the most sustained attempt being the last seventeen years of Conservative party rule.

After the Thatcher government was elected in 1979 the Government ceased pursuing full employment as a direct economic policy objective, instead in accordance with monetarist theory, it concentrated on the objectives of price

Table 0.1 Five-phase development model of management education (ME)

	National context	Start of management education	Institutional teaching methods and approaches to training of teachers
Phase 1 Starting-up	Family businesses dominate. Management based on family values and networks. Lack of recognition of ME.	Few institutions exist, but pioneers founded at undergraduate level.	Lecture method dominates. Subjects restricted (e.g. a/c and finance). Staff transferred from industry. No formal training. Visiting experts advise on how to get started.
Phase 2 Growing	Development from smaller to larger industries. Poor administrative systems. Short-term goals. Complexity and growth leads to awareness of need for competition and improved methods.	Increasing demand for ME. New institutions open, many private, non-academic. Reliance on training skills and differentiated subjects, particularly those seen as having immediate application. Foreign materials imported from more developed countries.	Emphasis on quantitative rational methods. Experts from abroad introduced as teachers. Practitioners transferred to ME (ex-managers, no formal teacher training). Young teachers sent abroad to study.
Phase 3 Establishing	Public/Govt funding becomes available. Industries question relevance of ME. High priority given to facilities, funding and resources.	Universities establish ME. Increased dominance of subject divisions. Local academic material developed. Recognition for existing institutions. Mushrooming of number of courses overall although some courses still omitted or insufficient.	Overseas methods, especially case methods, brought back by externally qualified young academics. Development of research. Recognition of complexity and non-rationality in teaching methods. Difficulties between original and newly trained staff.
Phase 4 Consolidating	Governments pull out of funding. Cost-effectiveness questioned. Small companies recognise ME.	Demand for evaluation. Search for new methods. Split between management education and management training. Courses offered exceed demand, leading to sophistication and improved courses.	Experience-based methods. Demand for local materials. Demand for abstract analysis. Executive courses increase. Local staff developed.
Phase 5	Industries support ME, particularly senior executive management courses. Global competition. Technology and speed of change input on economy.	Collaboration between industries and academics. Networking internationally. Tailor-made programmes. High-quality students attracted. Employment of ME in alternative areas, i.e. trade unions, co-ops. Pluralistic approach. Generalised view of organisational problems rather than subject framework.	Consultancy skills. Local materials, programmes, teachers and research. Indigenous staff development policies. Development of 'whole person' approach to teaching. Integration across disciplines.

Source: Davies *et al.*, 1989: 16–17

stability to combat inflation, economic growth via supply-side reforms in the labour market and the public sector, and balance of payments equilibrium, leaving employment to find its 'natural' level. Prior to this, all post-war governments had pursued full employment and had adopted various versions of Keynesian discretionary demand management, including fifteen periods of incomes policy from 1965–1979, leading to the UK's infamous 'stop–go' business cycles, which eventually damaged the UK's ability to maintain balance of payments equilibrium in the late 1970s and forced its government to seek aid from the International Monetary Fund (IMF).

The role of government in the 1960s and 1970s was to be the most active agent of economic management in the economy. Together with big business and big trade unions, big government sought to 'manage' economic growth, price stability and national debt, and to deliver full employment to the electors. This concerted approach of the three most powerful stakeholder groups in the political economy was called 'tripartism' or 'corporatism'. When its attempts to manage began to fail seriously in the 1970s, it found that it could only attain one objective at the price of missing another. For example, growth was coupled with acute inflation, price stability with rising unemployment, and full employment with rising national debt.

By letting go of the objective of full employment in the 1980s and 1990s, the Government found that it could meet most of the other three objectives most of the time. However, Ingram shows that this was a difficult and unsteady achievement, benefiting from certain one-off 'windfall' factors, which can no longer be counted on for the future. For example, the discovery and sale of North Sea oil in the mid-1980s, the one-off benefits to the exchequer of privatisation proceeds from the sale of former public utilities, and the one-off wave of cost-cutting which led the private sector to shed jobs at an unheard of rate in the early 1980s (unemployment trebled from 1979 to 1982, from 1 million to over 3 million). On the other hand Britain also suffered several one-off losses, such as the run on the currency which precipitated Britain's exit from the Exchange Rate Mechanism. But the Conservative government also redefined the nature of British government in the process. It stopped seeking to 'manage' the economy in the previous corporatist sense of concerted demand management and dismantled many of the tripartite links between big government, big employers and big unions, such as the National Economic Development Office (NEDO). It continued to pay attention to the business community which lobbied effectively through the offices of the Confederation of British Industry (CBI) and Institute of Directors (IOD), but introduced legislation and labour market reforms which decimated the power of the unions, which lost over 4 million members (30 per cent of the 1979 13.3 million membership) between 1979 and 1992, as Whitaker discusses in Chapter 9.

Instead of actively seeking to 'manage' the economy, the Government sought to 'regulate' it, leaving the objective of economic growth to the managers and business people of the private sector. This placed a new burden on the UK's 2.4

million managers, as it did upon the rest of the British population, which they were not necessarily sufficiently well equipped to bear. As I discuss in Chapter 7, many UK managers have very little higher education and even less education relevant to business life and their entrepreneurial tasks. The process of reducing government responsibility and the size and expense of the welfare state necessarily left a vacuum, and placed a strain on many non-governmental private, professional and voluntary institutions which found themselves responsible for more than they ever had been to date. It would take a different book to explore the impact on the charities and voluntary organisations of the closure of the mental hospitals, the housing reforms and gradual removal of other social services. In this volume we explore the impact upon the business environment and the legal, accounting institutions which regulate it and the managers and workers responsible for its prosperity. It is, after all, the business community, especially the private sector, which must take up most of the strain of managing the economy when a government adopts a free market approach.

As Ruff points out in Chapter 5, the UK has a long tradition of voluntarism, and a suspicion of written rules and regulations; it has no written constitution and wherever possible professional and private matters are left to the self-appointed bodies concerned. Voluntary codes of practice predominate in the area of advertising standards (see Thomas's Chapter 2), corporate governance, and accounting standards. Although the various accounting professional bodies are producing a common body of accounting standards, nevertheless when companies are audited, much of the process is left to the judgement and discretion of the firm of accountants involved, (see Perks's Chapter 4). In effect, the UK has a highly oral and informal business culture based on trust and informal contacts, cultivated in public schools and gentlemen's clubs. The courts, for instance, still place great importance on the plaintiffs and defendants being present in court for 'hearings', even in minor matters, as Ruff illustrates in Chapter 6, a cultural fact that adds to the great cost of the British legal system.

In the UK, the 'public interest' is in practice, entrusted to the government of the day although debated hotly in Parliament, which has been televised since the 1980s in a relatively recent concession to 'freedom of information'. The British people receive less educational opportunities than in many other developed countries, as Keep and Mayhew, explain in Chapter 8; as late as 1988, only about 15 per cent of the nation's children entered higher education (HE), in contrast to over 30 per cent in France, Germany, the USA and Japan (Handy *et al.* 1988). The traditional explanation for this was that the HE system emphasised quality, not quantity, and that most of those who were selected successfully completed their degrees, whereas drop-out rates were higher in the other countries mentioned; and in Germany and the USA, for example, it could take much longer to complete studies, as students could resit courses they failed over and over again. Since a report in 1989 (Training Agency 1989) showed that there were 3.2 million professionals and 0.3 million senior managers in the UK, roughly 15 per cent of the working population of 24 million, it might appear that higher education was distributed on a 'need to know' basis in the UK, for most of the post-war period, rather than as a public good. The educational and cultural gap between the 15 per cent educated at higher level and the majority (85 per cent) who left school when aged either 16 (70 per cent) or 18 (15 per cent), has been a wide one and has perhaps been partly responsible for the adversarial industrial relations culture between employers and employees noted by both Ingram (Chapter 1) and Whitaker (Chapter 9).

One of the consequences of the free market approach of government is that managers and workers are not obliged to undergo relevant education, training and development, at the same time companies are under pressure to produce short-term results and dividend pay-outs or face the prospect of hostile takeover, as Ingram points out. Accordingly there is little incentive for firms to invest in the long-term education and development of their managers and workforce, especially in the smaller firms, since such expenditure is liable to be seen as a cost to be cut by a hostile takeover management team (see Fox and McLeay 1992 for a detailed discussion and case study of this phenomenon). Wary senior managers of such firms, cut such costs in advance to prevent takeover, but in the process potentially lock their company into a vicious downward spiral of underdeveloping their staff and missing any entrepreneurial pay-offs that might accrue from such investment. In such circumstances, as Ingram suggests, the only reliable way a small firm can grow is by taking over other firms itself, thus perpetuating the business culture of merger, acquisition and divestment. Meanwhile only the larger companies can manage to pass the costs of staff development on to either their customers or their shareholders, especially in complex industries such as pharmaceuticals where high margins are based on long track records of such investments.

City analysts argue that the takeover culture is a natural consequence of free market conditions, approximating to perfect competition, i.e. a form of evolutionary 'natural selection' which weeds out poor performers and guarantees efficient producers offering low prices to the customer as well as high returns to shareholders. However, this business culture is unlikely to take over the role of government in providing the financial resources to enable the UK workforce to catch up to the educational standards of comparable nations. Also, since even small UK firms are now competing in world markets, and can no longer rely on the domestic market to make their living, UK managers find themselves competing with firms in Europe and internationally, which benefit from managers and workforces which are educated and vocationally trained to a much higher level by the national authorities. Outside the UK, in both developed and some developing nations, managers speak several languages, and higher percentages of the workforces are educated to higher levels, and firms do not have to pay such high returns to investors immediately. In these circumstances the British government appears to be counting on the possibility that the costs of sustaining 'Fortress Europe's' social and welfare bills will eventually expand so much that the walls will crack and level the competitive playing field down to the

UK's low cost economy. In the long run this might happen, but in the short run Britain risks being frozen out of the fast lane to European political and economic union.

The question is whether in the long run, the world economy will tend to the Anglo-America 'free market' approach and break the high social spending of corporatist economies, such as Germany's, France's, Sweden's and Japan's, or will tend to the 'social market' approach of the latter creating a two-tier developed world with some nations inside a virtuous circle, producing high quality, high margin, sophisticated products and spending the proceeds on maintaining the knowledge gap (spending on research and education) between themselves and the rest, leaving other nations to produce lower margin, less sophisticated goods and services.

Such questions cannot be resolved by this book, or even the series as whole, but by beginning to describe and raise practical and critical questions over the business environments of different nations, a future generation of managers and business people will perhaps see the options more clearly and take less for granted about national ways of doing business.

ACKNOWLEDGEMENTS

I would like to thank Julian Thomas at International Thomson Business Press for carefully directing this volume, and the series of which it is a part, towards eventual publication. Rosemary Nixon was the original commissioning editor and she deserves special thanks for all of her ideas and suggestions in the early stages of the project.

I am grateful too to each of the contributors who worked very hard to produce the chapters of this book, amending drafts willingly and carefully. My co-editor in regard to the *European Business Environments* series is Robert Crawshaw whose commitment, energy and enthusiasm for the project kept us all on track and finally pushed us passed the finishing post.

1   The UK economy, business and technology

Peter Ingram

INTRODUCTION

Economic success in the United Kingdom has, historically, stemmed from trade, empire and a liberal capitalist political system. Following the Industrial Revolution the economic power these attributes bestowed on the UK, created a pre-eminent position of global influence and wealth. During the second half of the twentieth century however, Britain's economic prospects have been widely viewed as being in long-term decline. Some historians trace this relative decline back to the period following the Great Exhibition in 1851 when the UK economy was at the height of its global power and influence (Hobsbawm 1968). Notwithstanding this, even today, Britain's economic antecedents continue to influence the psyche of the nation: its attitude to trade liberalisation, the internal debate about further European integration and the enduring scale of its overseas defence commitments all stem from Britain's history as an island trading nation. This background is important to bear in mind in the context of a view of the UK's current economic and business environment.

In more recent years a perception of transformation in the UK's economic fortunes has emerged. The objective of this chapter is to explore the evidence of this transition, reviewing, in the process, an extensive series of economic statistics intended to convey an understanding of where the UK stands as an economic power within Europe and the world economy today. The discussion will explore the course and development of the UK's economic and business environment over this period of change. Although particular emphasis will be given to events over recent years, 1975 has been specifically identified as a starting-point as it marks a perceptible break of trend in the country's economic evolution.

The purpose of the argument is therefore to provide a detailed analysis of the extent of adjustment in the UK economy and the forces that have influenced both change and, in some instances, continuity in the features of economic life. The institutions which broadly make up the economy have undergone considerable transition: government, the city, management, the unions, employees and employers have all been profoundly affected. A major cause of this structural shift lies in the increased presence of competitive pressures in the economy.

Over the last two decades the British economy has been increasingly exposed to international competition as almost all indigenous industries have become increasingly exposed to international trade. The opening-up of the UK economy, the removal of domestic trade barriers, increased European trade flows and increased exposure to product market competition have all exercised a dramatic effect on the economic and commercial life of the nation. These shocks were reinforced by Britain's rapid emergence as a major oil producer in the early 1980s which gave sterling a role as a petro-currency which, in turn, made the value of the pound prone to fluctuations in the price of oil. The average value of sterling appreciated by 10 per cent against the dollar between 1979 and 1980 with a dramatic impact on Britain's traded manufacturing sector. As demand was depressed through economic recession in the domestic economy, international markets became fiercely cost competitive to UK producers as the value of the pound increased. Firms engaged in manufacturing were forced to cut costs and increase productivity to remain in business. Many less efficient producers were wound up prompting a surge in manufacturing redundancies and business failures through the early years of the decade.

As a consequence of increased product market competition, managements in the private sector introduced increasingly innovative forms of technical and managerial practice. Manufacturing productivity growth accelerated, the climate of industrial relations appeared to undergo a transition towards a more harmonious regime and the Government, as employer to the public sector, attempted, through budgetary control and privatisation, to introduce competitive pressures to this previously protected area of economic activity. Despite this pervasive force for change and adaptation, in other spheres evidence of continuity endured. As a result, despite these more favourable trends, the economy also witnessed worsening visible trade balances, further concern about the presence of inflation, deteriorating competitiveness and a continuing shift in the composition of employment. Change, adjustment and adaptation, have therefore, run parallel with continuity to represent pervasive features of economic life over the period since 1980.

The objective of this chapter is to present detailed evidence on the extent of these events. How have these developments influenced economic performance and the pattern of investment? How, by the mid-1990s, with the single European market a reality, have these trends shaped the UK as a European partner? Indeed, has the UK been able to achieve sufficient economic progress to allow convergence with the other main European economies so enabling full participation in an integrated monetary union and, if not, why not and what further developments are required to achieve these objectives?

Developments in the corporate sector have been pronounced as the economy has evolved. The discussion of the business environment seeks to identify and consider the implications of these trends. What impact has the changing structure of the corporate sector had on the economy, what evidence exists for the emergence of an enterprise economy in the UK and are allegations of short-termism among City investors justified?

BACKGROUND AND CONTEXT: ECONOMIC GROWTH, PRODUCTIVITY LEVELS AND INFLATION

Two main concerns have dominated UK economic management during the latter half of the twentieth century. The importance of these issues has profoundly influenced policy-makers across a range of different offices of state and governments of different political complexion. The two issues in question are first, the UK's high relative rate of indigenous inflation and second, its poor productivity performance relative to its trading partners. The significance of these two factors for the UK economy needs to be seen in context. Much of the economic policy response that has unfolded since 1975, indeed since 1960, has, at least implicitly, been inspired by a desire to address these enduring economic problems.

Economic growth and levels of gross domestic product per capita have been the subject of concern to policy-makers throughout the last thirty years. The level of UK manufacturing productivity immediately following the Second World War, was thought to be second only to the United States. Faster rates of growth elsewhere were seen as inevitable as these economies caught up with the level of productivity witnessed in the UK. Growing concern about the level of economic activity, however, began to emerge in the early 1960s as the level of gross domestic product (GDP) per capita in Britain became progressively superseded by the defeated powers of the Second World War. The cumulative effect of lower growth rates had caused Britain to lose its pre-eminent position in the league table of economic powers. Economic growth was seen as the means to economic advancement and prosperity. The cumulative impact of slow growth therefore prompted emerging concern. The attention of domestic policy then turned to the issue of why, despite intentions to the contrary, the UK was a slow growing economy. Table 1.1 contrasts relative growth rates from 1960 through to 1989. Throughout the period to 1979 the average annual rate of growth in the UK lagged behind those of other major trading nations. Even during the relatively high growth years of the 1980s the UK still fell behind the OECD average.

The identification of the causes of this slow relative growth performance became the major whodunit of policy-makers in the 1960s and 1970s. Almost any conceivable source of the growth problem became the subject of intense scrutiny: the structure of industry, the composition of output, the level of

Table 1.1: Relative annual GDP growth rates, 1960–93

	1960–68	*1968–73*	*1973–79*	*1979–89*	*1990–93*
UK	3.0	3.4	1.5	2.3	−0.1
France	5.4	3.4	2.8	2.1	0.9
Germany	4.1	2.8	2.3	1.8	2.5
OECD	5.1	2.1	2.7	2.1	1.6

Source: OECD

research and development expenditure, the nature of management and the trade unions all became, in turn, the focus of concern. The Labour administration of 1964 came to power pledged to promote the 'white heat of technology' in an attempt to improve the UK's growth performance. During the latter half of the 1960s the policy response was intense. The establishment of the National Plan, the Industrial Re-Organisation Corporation, the National Economic Development ment Council, the Department of Employment and Productivity, Selective Employment Tax and the Donovan Commission all sprang out of the desire to increase growth rates; even a flourishing anti-growth movement began to emerge as the preoccupation intensified (see, for example, Mishan 1967; Hirsch 1977). A more detached view of the issue was also provided when the Brookings Institution in Washington turned their attention to the conundrum (see Caves and Associates 1968). Solutions however, proved more elusive, the UK remained slow growing, with the country's growth record deteriorating in the 1970s.

The further tendency for the UK to be relatively prone to inflation again gave rise to a host of policy responses designed to ameliorate the problem. Figure 1.1 shows the profile of annual percentage changes in the Retail Price Index since January 1975 while Table 1.2 contrasts the UK inflation experience with other major economies since 1960. At its peak in 1975, price inflation in the UK was over three times the corresponding rate in West Germany. Throughout the last twenty-five years the inflationary record of the UK has been more pronounced than the average rate throughout the OECD. UK policy-makers again responded to this problem through a variety of means. The National Board on Prices and

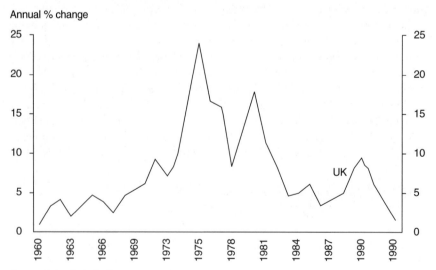

Figure 1.1 UK inflation rate, 1960–93

Source: IMF, International Financial Statistics

Table 1.2: International comparisons of consumer price inflation, 1960–93 (percentage increase per year)

	1960–68	1968–73	1973–79	1979–84	1984–88	1989–92	1993
UK	3.6	7.5	15.6	9.5	4.6	6.8	1.6
OECD average	2.9	5.7	9.9	8.3	3.8	4.4*	2.8*
West Germany	2.7	4.6	4.7	4.5	0.9	3.2	4.2
France	3.6	6.1	10.7	11.1	3.6	3.1	2.0
UK – OECD	0.7	1.8	5.7	0.8	0.8	2.4	−1.2
UK – West Germany	0.9	2.9	10.9	5.0	3.7	3.6	−2.6
UK – France	0.0	1.4	4.9	−2.6	1.0	3.7	−0.4

Source: OECD
Note: *excludes Turkey

Incomes, which operated during the late 1960s and 1970s represented the mostcomprehensive statutory attempt to contain inflation. The Board's function was to determine allowable, largely cost-plus, rates of increase in prices and correspondingly earnings in an effort to prevent inflationary wage–price spirals from emerging. As inflation intensified the scheme became progressively less easy to administer and more politically unpopular; the Board lost influence and power, and was subsequently replaced by the Price Commission which eventually was discontinued in 1980.

Incomes policies were a much more pervasive feature of the period up to 1979. Raw material and other factor costs are normally traded at internationally prevailing prices. Since, however, the escalating costs of these commodities, particularly oil, appeared to have less of an inflationary impact on other industrial economies, the indigenous resource of labour, and domestic increases in its price, seemed to offer a plausible source of the UK's relatively poor inflationary record. Between 1965 and 1979 fifteen periods of incomes policy were introduced and subsequently abandoned (see Fallick and Elliott 1981 for a chronological list of these policies). The purpose of these initiatives was to contain, by statute and occasionally voluntarily, the rate of growth in earnings to a prescribed limit. With one exception these provided for allowable percentage increases in pay over a given period. Effectively however, the result was to restrict the flexibility of companies in their wage-setting behaviour as, too frequently, any specified increase became both a ceiling and a floor for negotiators. This inevitably gave rise to marketdistortions in wage rates and increasing political dissatisfaction with explicit policies to contain the growth in earnings.

With the possible exception of the Social Contract during the late 1970s, these policies proved unsuccessful in their objective of containing inflation. As successive policies were abandoned, the rate of growth in prices and earnings resumed its trend level of increase. Escalating inflation, currency devaluations and balance of payments crises usually prompted a Keynesian demand management, macro-economic response to the problem. A period of demand deflation would be instigated to curb increasing prices, causing increases in unemployment and giving rise to the infamous 'stop–go' cycles of economic growth.

The problems of inflation and economic growth were therefore mutually reinforcing: as growth and consumer demand increased in the economy, inflationary wage and price spirals were triggered, which in turn required the level of demand to be subdued to offset emerging balance of payments difficulties. The perennial problem of the UK economy became the tendency for the rate of growth in wages to outstrip the rate of growth in productivity. Wage and price inflation therefore compromised the economy's capacity for growth while the inability to achieve faster growth constrained the rate of improvement in standards of living. During the 1960s and 1970s the UK economy appeared to be trapped in a vicious cycle of causation whereby each potential cause of slow growth, such as poor workplace relations, appeared to be the consequence of slow growth (see Caves and Associates 1968: 16).

Disillusion with the capacity of standard demand management to provide solutions to the UK's apparent malaise intensified through the later 1970s. The experience of inflation during 1975 convinced the then Labour Chancellor of the Exchequer, Denis Healy, to begin the process of embracing monetarist economics. Among the right wing of the Conservative opposition the case for the monetarist doctrine appeared to be overwhelmingly supported by the evidence of the recent past. The 1975 peak in inflation at nearly 27 per cent corresponded very closely with the rate of growth in the money supply eighteen to twenty-four months previously when the Conservative Chancellor, Anthony Barber, expanded the money supply in an effort to keep unemployment beneath the then politically sensitive 1 million mark.

After 1975 the capacity of governments to spend their way out of recession without spiralling inflation was effectively removed from the menu of economic policy choice. In the words of James Callaghan, the Prime Minister in 1976, as he addressed the Labour Party conference:

> We used to think that you could spend your way out of a recession, and increase employment by cutting taxes and boosting Government spending. I tell you in all candour that such an option no longer exists, and in so far that it ever did exist, it only worked on each occasion since the war by injecting a bigger dose of inflation into the economy. (Callaghan 1976)

At the same time domestic markets became progressively more open to international competition. Meanwhile on the political right, the Conservative opposition – with its right wing in increasing ascendancy – was embracing supply-side, monetarist economics wholeheartedly. From this perspective, Britain's poor economic performance could be traced to restrictions on the supply-side of the economy. The freeing up of factor markets was seen as the best prospect of achieving the rates of economic growth enjoyed in other industrialised economies. Likewise the idiosyncratic British tendency to inflation could be traced to market restrictions, particularly in the market for labour, where trade unions were allegedly able to hold wages above their market clearing level by applying monopoly power over the price of their labour. The economic ideology of the new right therefore placed great emphasis on the effectiveness of free market mechanisms and the control of trade unions to deliver economic benefit.

Through the late 1970s these views intensified as trade unions were seen to wield excessive power. Membership of trade unions reached an all time high in 1979 while Jack Jones, the leader of the influential Transport and General Workers Union (TGWU) was seen by public opinion to be more powerful than the Prime Minister. A Gallup survey in 1976 showed that 53 per cent of respondents thought Jack Jones had 'most power and influence in the country today', as against 25 per cent for the Prime Minister, and 69 per cent of respondents were 'dissatisfied' with the way this influence was used. The so-called strike prone 'winter of discontent' sealed the public's antipathy to trade unions. The following spring the Conservative Party was returned to power in the 1979 general election. On coming to power, the Government abolished all remaining restraints on international trade. Exchange controls and state subsidies to inefficient private sector producers were also removed. Since 1979 the determination of factor prices, not least incomes, has been left to the operation of the market.

By the mid-1990s a Conservative administration had been in power for four successive terms of office. Despite a change in Prime Minister in 1990 an appearance of consistency of economic policy remained a feature over this period. The Government that arrived in 1979 sought to redress what it saw as excessive union power in the economy and streamline the public sector, which it viewed as a collection of inefficient, loss-making monopolies dominated by high levels of union membership, reducing the level of public expenditure in the process. Market mechanisms were seen as the necessary means to improve both the efficiency and operation of the public and private sectors of the economy.

In the next section the success of these objectives will be considered. Despite the shift in economic direction taken in 1979, the ideological emphasis of the new right remained the search for a solution to the apparent British malaise of poor productivity and high inflation. With the twin policy objectives of reduced inflation and higher productivity remaining predominant in economic policy-making, a comprehensive picture of the development and success of the policies pursued in the UK economy in the 1980s and 1990s can be developed: though the policy response was superficially different, the direction of emphasis remained the same.

DEVELOPMENTS IN THE UK ECONOMY SINCE 1979

The period since 1979 marks a watershed in the UK's economic history. Although the force of product market competition had been increasing in evidence since the middle of the decade, 1979 saw the election of a Conservative administration committed to a free market doctrine in economic management. The macro-economic policy objectives of economic growth, price stability and balance of payments equilibrium were to be pursued by allowing market forces to regulate the economy. The fourth policy objective of attempting to maintain full employment was explicitly abandoned in the belief that the non-accelerating inflation rate of unemployment (NAIRU) could only be reduced by gradually removing the restrictions to the effective operation of the labour market. To attempt to reduce unemployment through deficit spending would only promote inflation. Unemployment was therefore allowed to rise while monetary targets were pursued in an attempt to contain inflation. The following section will address the record of the Government's main policy objectives subsequent to 1979. In considering this period of contemporary economic history, five related themes will be addressed: the role of North Sea oil; the balance of payments and European trade; the experience of privatisation and the management of the public sector; the changing structure of employment; the change in industrial relations and the growth in manufacturing productivity.

The emergence of North Sea oil and the growth in European and world trade

Perhaps the most notable exogenous feature of the UK economy in the 1980s was the arrival of North Sea oil. Oil made the UK unique as virtually the only industrialised economy in the developed world to be self-sufficient in this vital resource. It also provided considerable revenue. Oil-related tax revenues alone netted the Exchequer an income of over £8 billion per annum during the first half of the 1980s. The equivalent income at 1990 constant prices would amount to over £12 billion per annum (source: Treasury Financial Statements and Budget Reports, 1979–1994). Table 1.3 and Figure 1.2 set out the total North Sea oil annual production and revenue statistics from 1976. From having to import its entire oil needs a decade earlier, by 1985 the UK had emerged to become the fifth largest producer in the world. Oil production and receipts peaked in 1985 at 123 million tonnes and $23 billion respectively. The presence of oil is indeed significant. Prior to 1979 successive governments were totally dependent on imported supplies of oil. Interruptions to supply and inflationary hikes in its price were not unknown. Although supplies of certain forms of crude still had to be obtained from external sources, the effective removal of this commodity from the balance of payments accounts increased the manoeuvrability and scope of policy-makers from what had hitherto represented the greatest external constraint to domestic economic management. In 1975, (Table 1.4), fuel and oil-based imports made up 17.7 per cent of total imports. By 1988 this figure had fallen to 4.7 per cent while exports of oil products emerged to make up around 20 per cent of total exports from negligible levels in the mid-1970s. Moreover, from 1981 the total value of fuel-based exports exceeded the annual value of imports. This shift in the pattern of trade away from dependence on oil combined

Table 1.3: North Sea oil annual revenue and production, 1976–91

Year	North Sea oil production* '000 tonnes	Crude oil spot price average* US$bn	Estimated revenue* US$m	North Sea oil income* £m	North Sea oil income in 1985 prices** £m
1976	12,466	12.80	1,117	527	1,276
1977	38,512	13.92	3,753	1,971	4,185
1978	53,475	14.02	5,248	2,614	4,989
1979	77,116	31.61	17,063	5,255	8,758
1980	78,917	36.83	20,346	8,056	11,236
1981	87,946	35.93	22,119	10,864	13,614
1982	100,311	32.97	23,151	12,725	14,814
1983	110,839	29.55	22,927	15,683	17,348
1984	121,180	28.66	24,311	19,009	20,094
1985	122,492	27.51	23,588	18,514	18,514
1986	121,238	14.38	12,204	8,421	8,136
1987	117,613	18.43	15,173	9,511	8,758
1988	109,455	14.96	11,462	6,990	6,036
1989	87,404	18.20	11,135	6,763	5,454
1990	87,990	23.81	14,665	7,036	5,342
1991	86,827	20.05	12,186	6,413	4,564

Source: *IEA; **CSO *Blue Book*

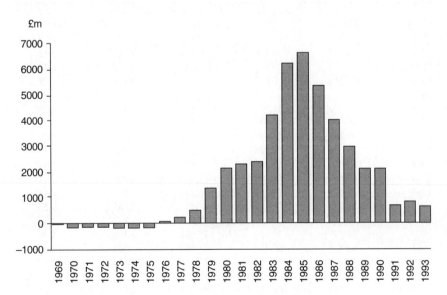

Figure 1.2 Total exchequer receipts from North Sea oil, 1969–93

Source: HM Treasury

Table 1.4: Proportions of total UK Imports and Exports 1975–92

| | Exports | Exported fuel | Exported manufactures | Imports | Imported fuel | Imported manufactures |
	% of GDP	% of exports	% of GDP	% of GDP	% of imports	% of GDP
1975	19.0	4.1	17.4	23.1	17.7	13.6
1980	20.4	13.6	15.8	21.5	13.8	15.5
1985	21.8	21.4	15.9	22.8	12.5	17.9
1988	17.0	7.6	16.5	21.6	4.7	20.1
1989	17.9	6.5	17.3	22.6	5.2	21.7
1990	18.5	7.6	17.6	21.9	6.2	20.5
1991	18.0	6.8	17.4	19.8	6.3	18.6
1992	18.0	6.4	17.2	20.2	5.5	18.2

Source: CSO Balance of Payments Service

with the revenues that the North Sea generated gave the Thatcher government an exogenous benefit unprecedented in the UK's post-war economic management.

Despite this favourable position the UK balance of trade, excluding oil, began to deteriorate markedly in the latter half of the 1980s. Table 1.5 shows that the UK's visible trade balance fell into sharp deficit in 1988 and 1989 with the size

Table 1.5: UK balance of payments, 1974–93

Year	Total value of imports £m	Total value of exports £m	Visible trade balance £m	Invisible trade balance £m	Current trade balance £m
1974	23,492	16,820	−5,229	2,047	−3,184
1975	24,423	20,111	−3,256	1,731	−1,524
1976	31,569	26,024	−3,961	3,189	−772
1977	36,996	33,308	−2,322	2,375	53
1978	39,533	35,386	−1,592	2,715	1,123
1979	46,925	40,637	−3,343	2,890	−453
1980	49,886	47,339	1,357	1,487	2,841
1981	51,348	50,786	3,252	3,496	6,748
1982	56,624	55,314	1,910	2,741	4,648
1983	65,581	60,590	−1,537	5,066	3,529
1984	75,601	70,265	−5,336	6,817	1,482
1985	81,336	77,991	−3,345	5,583	2,238
1986	82,186	72,627	−9,559	8,688	−871
1987	90,735	79,153	−11,582	6,599	−4,983
1988	101,826	80,346	−21,480	4,863	−16,617
1989	116,837	92,154	−24,683	2,171	−22,512
1990	120,527	101,718	−18,809	541	−18,268
1991	113,697	103,413	−10,284	2,632	−7,652
1992	120,458	107,047	−13,406	3,439	−9,967
1993	134,519	120,839	−13,680	2,753	−10,670

Source: CSO

of the deficit exceeding £20 billion in each of these years. Even with the onset of recession in the early 1990s and diminishing domestic demand for imported goods, the current balance of trade (visible and invisible trade) remained heavily in the red. When the effects of inflation are controlled for by expressing the trade deficit as a percentage of GDP, the average size of the deficit between 1984 and 1990 when domestic oil production was robust showed no improvement on the years 1972 to 1978 when the bulk of domestic oil consumption was met by imports. The effect of oil was effectively concealing the continuing decline in UK manufactured exports. Even including the growing trade in international financial services the current balance began to deteriorate markedly after 1986. By 1992 with continuing recession in the UK this measure remained in deficit by £11.5 billion.

Total UK trade with the European Community (EC) up to the completion of the single market in 1992 had experienced a secular increase since the UK joined the Common Market in 1973 (Table 1.6). Imports and exports with the European Community began to grow as percentage of GDP from the late 1970s onwards. Despite the growth in intra-European trade, consistently over the period 1972 to 1990, imports from the EC have been in excess of exports. This

Table 1.6: UK trade with EC, 1972–92

Year	Value of imports from EC £m	Value of exports to EC £m	GDP at current prices £m	Value of imports from EC % of GDP	Value of exports to EC % of GDP
1972	3,586.7	2,999.2	64,663	5.55	4.64
1973	5,261.7	3,926.5	74,257	7.09	5.29
1974	7,799.6	5,467.2	83,862	9.30	6.52
1975	8,871.8	6,390.5	105,852	8.38	6.04
1976	11,503.5	9,101.0	125,247	9.18	7.26
1977	14,160.4	11,848.6	145,938	9.70	8.12
1978	16,547.1	13,620.8	168,526	9.82	8.08
1979	20,887.6	17,479.4	198,221	10.54	8.82
1980	20,574.2	20,542.6	231,772	8.88	8.86
1981	21,718.0	21,119.1	254,927	8.52	8.28
1982	25,269.0	23,123.6	279,041	9.06	8.29
1983	30,104.1	26,508.8	304,456	9.89	8.71
1984	35,159.3	31,506.7	325,852	10.79	9.67
1985	39,004.8	36,223.8	357,344	10.92	10.14
1986	44,576.8	34,996.3	384,843	11.58	9.09
1987	49,555.4	39,414.9	423,381	11.70	9.31
1988	55,807.0	40,937.5	471,430	11.84	8.68
1989	63,495.0	47,140.2	515,957	12.31	9.14
1990	65,885.5	55,024.7	551,118	11.95	9.98
1991	61,328.0	59,280.2	573,645	10.69	10.33
1992	65,609.3	60,702.3	595,258	11.02	10.20

Source: CSO

pattern is repeated for trade flows with the rest of the world. In 1975 (Table 1.7) the total value of UK exports amounted to 21 per cent of GDP while the value of imports accounted for 25.6 per cent. These proportions remained virtually unchanged over the period to the early 1990s. Over this period the value of exported fuel products increased slightly from 4.1 per cent of exports to 6.4 per cent (Table 1.4). Correspondingly, the value of fuel-based imports fell from 17.7 per cent to 5.5 per cent.

The improvement in traded primary fuel products, however, conceals a deterioration in the shares of trade made up by secondary sector, manufactured goods. Although between 1975 and 1992 the value of manufactured goods remained around 80 per cent of total exports, the value of manufactured imports increased from 53 per cent of total imports in 1975 to 74.4 per cent of imports by 1992. The same picture emerges when the trade in manufactured goods is expressed as a percentage of GDP. Manufactured exports remained steady at about 17 per cent of GDP between 1975 and 1992 while manufactured imports increased from 13.6 per cent of GDP to 18.2 per cent over the same period. Therefore, even when controlling for the growth in trade, imported manufactures emerged to dominate exported manufactures as a proportion of UK economic activity.

These trends reflect a structural imbalance in the nature of UK production. The long-run *domestic income elasticity of demand* for goods imported into the

Table 1.7: UK trade with non-EEC countries, 1974–92

Year	Value of imports to non-EC £m	Value of exports to non-EC £m	GDP at current prices £m	Imports to non-EC % of GDP	Exports to non-EC % of GDP
1974	13,711.4	10,814.8	83,862	16.35	12.90
1975	13,569.2	12,794.5	105,852	12.82	12.09
1976	17,537.5	15,979.0	125,247	14.00	12.76
1977	19,844.6	19,834.4	145,983	13.59	13.59
1978	20,025.9	21,360.2	168,526	11.88	12.67
1979	22,926.4	22,991.6	198,221	11.57	11.60
1980	25,217.8	26,606.4	231,772	10.88	11.48
1981	25,698.0	29,548.9	254,927	10.08	11.59
1982	28,152.0	32,207.4	279,041	10.09	11.54
1983	32,096.9	34,191.2	304,456	10.54	11.23
1984	40,441.7	38,758.3	325,852	12.41	11.89
1985	42,331.2	41,767.2	357,344	11.85	11.69
1986	37,609.2	37,630.7	384,843	9.77	9.78
1987	41,179.6	39,738.1	423,381	9.73	9.39
1988	46,019.0	39,408.5	471,430	9.76	8.36
1989	53,342.0	45,013.8	515,957	10.34	8.72
1990	54,641.5	46,693.3	551,118	9.91	8.47
1991	52,369.0	44,132.8	573,645	9.13	7.69
1992	54,823.7	46,344.3	595,258	9.21	7.79

Source: CSO

UK has been estimated to exceed the long-run *world income elasticity of demand* for UK produced goods. Bairam (1988), has estimated the average income elasticity of demand in the UK for a typical portfolio of imported goods to be 2.14 per cent. This means that as domestic incomes grow, UK consumers spend proportionately more disposable income on imported items. A 1 per cent increase in income involves an increase in expenditure on imported goods of over 2 per cent. As a result, as domestic real incomes increase so more imported manufactures are demanded. Correspondingly, Bairam estimates the world income elasticity of demand for UK manufactured goods to equal 1.31 per cent. This implies that as world incomes increase, the increase in demand for UK manufactured goods is slightly in excess of unity, but considerably less than UK consumers' income elasticity of demand for imported goods.

Thirlwall (1992) points out that this imbalance between import and export income elasticities will constrain the rate of growth in GDP in the UK, if balance of payments difficulties are to be avoided. Although estimates of the world income elasticity of demand for UK production have improved over the last twenty years, (Thirlwall 1992: 281), the balance of payments is likely to continue as a constraint on sustainable growth rates until the industrialised world chooses to spend a higher proportion of its increasing income on UK goods. This necessity will become more apparent when the current contribution of North Sea oil to the balance of payments reduces. The solution to the imbalance between domestic and world income elasticities of demand requires an aggregate boost in the attractiveness of UK production to global consumers. This in turn depends on the traded sector producing superior goods that trade on quality rather than inferior goods that trade on price. The instance of the Japanese economy highlights the growth rates that are achievable without balance of payments constraints through the production of superior quality, high income elasticity of demand goods.

The structural shift in employment

Throughout the period since 1980 the process known as deindustrialisation has continued in the UK. This process describes the contraction of employment in the secondary or manufacturing sector of the economy, usually combined with a corresponding growth in employment in the tertiary or service sector. For an economy like the UK, built on a tradition of trade, this process has, in the past, been viewed with some alarm (see Bacon and Eltis 1976). More realistically however the process of the relative decline of the manufacturing sector can be seen as representing an inevitable phase in economic development. On the supply side a sectoral shift in employment from manufacturing to services can arise as productivity inevitably increases faster in the manufacturing sector of the economy: manufacturing can more easily embrace technological change, greater economies of scale and increase its capital intensity. On the demand side the consumption of output of manufactured goods is again likely to experience a relative decline as individuals' and society's income grows. This process follows since the income elasticity of demand for service sector output tends to be higher than for manufactured goods. As a result, as incomes grow, individual's spend proportionately more on service sector goods. At a national level this effect is demonstrated by increasing levels of expenditure, as a proportion of GDP directed to areas such as education and health as the total income of the economy increases.

The evidence in Table 1.8 and Figure 1.3 shows that in absolute terms employment in manufacturing in the UK stood at just over 7 million in 1975 or just over 30 per cent of employment. By 1992 however the manufacturing sector employed 4.46 million individuals or 21 per cent of employment. Correspondingly, employment in the service sector had increased by about 2 million employees taking the share of employment in the tertiary sector from 58 to 71 per cent. Despite this contraction, as the data in Table 1.15 show, manufacturing output experienced a slow, consistent increase during the 1980s. Moreover manufacturing productivity increased at an average rate of 4.5 per cent per annum between 1980 and 1992. Both these trends place the

Table 1.8: Structural change in employment, 1972–93

Year	Seasonally adjusted employment '000	Employment in mfg sector '000	Employment in service sector '000	% in mfg sector	% in service sector	% change on last year in mfg sector	% change on last year in service sector
1972	21,648	7,621	11,667	35.20	53.89		
1973	22,182	7,673	12,096	34.59	54.53	0.68	3.68
1974	22,296	7,722	12,240	34.63	54.90	0.64	1.19
1975	22,209	7,351	12,545	33.10	56.49	−4.80	2.49
1976	22,039	7,118	12,624	32.30	57.28	−3.17	0.63
1977	22,124	7,172	12,698	32.42	57.39	0.76	0.59
1978	22,246	7,143	12,859	32.11	57.80	−0.40	1.27
1979	22,611	7,113	13,222	31.46	58.48	−0.42	2.82
1980	22,432	6,808	13,345	30.35	59.49	−4.29	0.93
1981	21,362	6,107	13,102	28.59	61.33	−10.30	−1.82
1982	20,896	5,761	13,078	27.57	62.59	−5.67	−0.18
1983	20,557	5,431	13,130	26.42	63.87	−5.73	0.40
1984	20,731	5,316	13,465	25.64	64.95	−2.12	2.55
1985	20,910	5,269	13,731	25.20	65.67	−0.88	1.98
1986	20,876	5,138	13,918	24.61	66.67	−2.49	1.36
1987	21,081	5,068	14,220	24.04	67.45	−1.36	2.17
1988	21,748	5,109	14,841	23.49	68.24	0.81	4.37
1989	22,143	5,101	15,242	23.04	68.83	−0.16	2.70
1990	22,353	5,014	15,557	22.43	69.60	−1.71	2.07
1991	21,677	4,614	15,345	21.29	70.79	−7.98	−1.36
1992	21,307	4,419	15,343	20.74	72.01	−4.23	−0.01
1993	20,945	4,270	15,254	20.39	72.83	−3.37	−0.58

Source: *Department of Employment Gazette, June 1994*

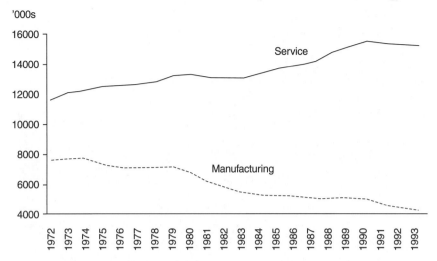

Figure 1.3 Employment in manufacturing and services, 1972–93

Source: Department of Employment Gazette, June 1994

concern over the contraction of the manufacturing sector in the UK into context.

Concerns emerge, however, about the size and efficiency of the secondary sector in the UK when comparisons are made with the experience of other industrialised countries over the same period (CBI 1991). Figure 1.4 contrasts the levels of real value added per employee, or value productivity, in manufacturing across six G7 economies including the UK in 1980. These figures show the performance of UK manufacturing to be about 66 per cent of the average of the other economies. Over the next five years, UK manufacturing productivity increased by an average of over 5 per cent per annum. Although the UK's productivity growth experience will be discussed below, this surge in productivity made little impression on closing the productivity gap with the other main industrialised countries. By 1985, the most recent reputable statistical evidence available suggests that the level of manufacturing output per employee in the UK still lagged its main trading partners by around two-thirds (Roy 1989).

Although problems exist with obtaining consistent quality of data between bench-mark years when comparing productivity levels across economies the results in Figure 1.5 imply that even an excess productivity growth in the UK of the order of 2 per cent per annum would require many years for the UK to close the productivity gap from this relatively low base. Coupled with the persistence of the manufacturing productivity gap has been concern about the size of UK manufacturing relative to that of competitor economies. As Table 1.9 demonstrates, while in Britain, manufacturing output as a proportion of GDP

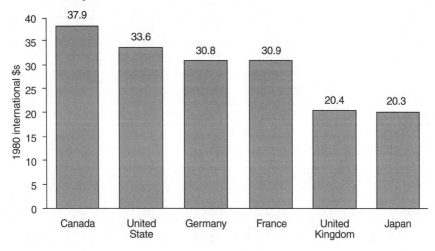

Figure 1.4 International comparisons of added value per employee in manufacturing, 1980

Source: Roy (1987), *Economic Trends*

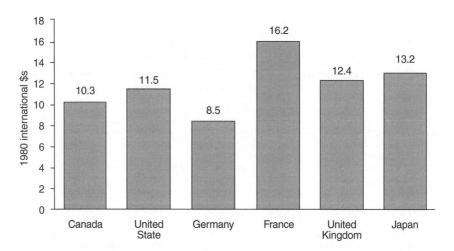

Figure 1.5 International comparisons of added value per employee in government services, 1980

Source: Roy (1987), *Economic Trends*

has declined from 28.3 per cent in 1975 to 23.7 per cent in 1990, in Japan the corresponding contraction is from 30.2 per cent in 1975 to 28.9 per cent by 1990. In addition, notwithstanding strong productivity growth, the percentage of employees in Japanese manufacturing has fallen by only 2 per cent to 24.3 per

Table 1.9: UK and Japanese manufacturing sectors, 1975–92

	Manufacturing employment as a % of total		Manufacturing sector as a % of GDP	
	Japan	*UK*	*Japan*	*UK*
1975	23.6	33.1	10.3	28.3
1980	24.7	30.4	29.2	26.9
1985	25.0	25.2	29.5	25.3
1988	24.3	23.5	28.7	24.2
1989	24.2	23.0	28.8	24.7
1990	24.0	22.6	28.9	23.7
1991	24.3	21.4	—	22.8
1992	—	21.1	—	22.3

Source: *Japan Statistical Yearbook 1992*, Statistics Bureau, Management and Coordination Agency and Central Statistical Office

cent of total employment, while in the UK manufacturing employment declined from 33.1 per cent of total employment in 1975 to 21.4 per cent by 1991 (source: Anglo-Japanese Economic Institute).

These statistics emphasise the potential concerns over the future of the manufacturing sector in the UK. Although considerable improvements in the health of the manufacturing sector have taken place through the doubling of manufacturing labour productivity in the 1980s, the need for further reforms are necessary for the UK to continue to converge towards the performance of its trading partners. The Confederation of British Industry's (CBI) Manufacturing Advisory Group advocate four steps 'to address the current challenges faced by UK manufacturing':

1 Best world practice must be applied and understood more effectively throughout manufacturing industry by companies of all sizes. New mechanisms must be developed to achieve this.
2 Government must play its full part by creating a climate which supports long-term investment in manufacturing industry. To achieve this, relationships between government and industry need to be more productive; changes to the machinery of government are required.
3 A stronger relationship must be built between industry and the financial community so that financial engineering is not so readily confused with the real thing.
4 Industry, collectively, must be more effective in dispelling the out of date image among young people and opinion formers. A more effective voice for manufacturing can help to achieve this (CBI 1991: 38).

Although aspects of the issues raised here by the CBI will be discussed later in this chapter, they demonstrate the continued perceived importance of manufacturing industry in the UK despite the view held by the Government during the 1980s that Britain's comparative advantage had shifted to the private services sector of the economy where invisible earnings were buoyant. Within this context there was an implicit, if not explicit, belief that the fate of manufacturing was of less direct concern. The fact that these issues remain of considerable importance today but as yet are unresolved, suggests that the success of the experience of the 1980s in regenerating the UK economy needs to be qualified. As the CBI argues 'it is no coincidence that the world's most successful economies, Germany and Japan, also have the strongest manufacturing industries' (CBI 1991: 4). In the UK however, what economic progress there was in manufacturing industry over this period was achieved 'against a backdrop of relatively benign neglect by all except those directly concerned with running the country's manufacturing companies' (CBI 1991: 38). A retrospective view might now suggest that more might have been done by government, with the benefit of North Sea oil revenues, for the good of the manufacturing sector in the UK.

Privatisation and the public sector

In 1979 the public sector in the UK employed about 6.9 million people (Table 1.10). This meant that the Government was effectively the employer of about 28 per cent of civilian employment. According to the market-driven philosophy of the new right, the public sector was regarded as being essentially protected from the commercial discipline of the marketplace and, as a consequence of this, it had become both expensive and overrun with institutional sclerosis. In addition the public sector represented a series of natural monopolies with high levels of unionisation that compounded its inefficiency. As competitive change swept the private sector, so the new Conservative government sought to exercise closer control over those areas for which it was direct paymaster.

The public sector in the UK can be divided into two principal elements. These are the nationalised industries, covering those areas of the economy under public ownership which effectively produce traded output and the non-traded public sector. In 1979 the nationalised industries engaged 1.8 million employees

Table 1.10: UK manpower demography in 1979, 1988 and 1991 (thousands)

	1979	1988	1991
Employed labour force	25,375	25,404	26,052
Civilian employment	25,061	25,088	25,754
Employees in employment	23,158	22,104	22,268
Non-traded public sector	5,038	5,087	4,828
Nationalised industries	1,849	798	747
Private manufacturing	6,806	5,005	4,075
Private services	7,742	9,769	10,915
Trade unions	13,498	10,475	9,947*

Source: *Department of Employment Gazette*, March 1993; CSO, *Blue Book 1992*
Note: *December 1990

covering telecommunications, transport and power. The non-traded or public services sector employed over 5 million employees throughout the range of social, educational, health, police and civil services. Although the public sector as a whole in the UK was perceived as being inefficient, Figure 1.5 suggests that in comparison with other industrialised countries, the level of real value added per employee in government services was second only to France and Japan in 1980 (Roy 1989). Despite this, the public sector was highlighted as an area for reform, not least to contain the size of total public expenditure in the country. This was initially achieved through the use of cash limits whereby constrained budgetary increases were determined annually for each constituent element of the public sector. Since the wage bill takes up a large share of public expenditure, particularly in the non-traded sector where it accounts for around 80 per cent of the annual budget, cash limits effectively required public sector managers to contain wages, control costs and increase efficiency. The traded public sector gained some room for cost manoeuvrability through their ability to increase productivity and therefore improve their 'ability to pay' (for a discussion of the use of cash limits in the public sector through the early 1980s see Pliatsky 1982).

Though budgetary control has remained the principal means by which the non-traded public sector has been regulated, from 1981 the process of privatisation has incrementally shifted sections of the former nationalised industries into private sector ownership. As budgetary controls assisted each nationalised concern to return to profit so the process of privatisation followed. Table 1.11 outlines the major elements of the process of privatisation in the British economy since 1981. The flotation of British Telecommunications (BT) in 1984, however, represented the first large-scale sale of public assets bringing the Exchequer £3.9 billion. This sale initiated the series of large stock exchange flotations designed to encourage the public to become individual shareholders; the proportion of the adult population owning shares increased as a result of subsequent privatisation from 6 per cent in 1984 to 25 per cent by 1990. Up to the end of 1992 the proceeds from privatisation had brought the Exchequer an average income of over £5 billion a year, see Table 1.12. As Table 1.13 illustrates, this was equivalent to more than 1 per cent of GDP per annum (HMSO 1992).

In addition to the financial benefits that privatisation has provided for the Treasury and the exercise in social engineering that increased individual shareholdings implied, the benefit of privatisation's overall contribution to the economy is perhaps more equivocal. A further objective of privatisation was to introduce competition into previously state-run monopolies. The takeover by private ownership was suggested to offer the prospect of improved management and efficiency to former loss-making nationalised concerns to the benefit of the economy as a whole. While these private utilities are answerable to their shareholders and required to operate at a profit in the face of quite stringent price regulation, it is a matter of debate as to whether private monopoly is inherently more efficient than public. Further and more comprehensive research is required on this contentious issue, as Robinson (1992) argues.

Table 1.11: Privatisation: major public asset sales, 1981–91

Year	Company	Sale Proceeds £m	Employees
1981	British Aerospace	40	23,000
	Cable & Wireless	180	25,000
1982	National Freight	5	3,000
	Britoil	630	14,000
1983	Associated British Ports	50	9,000
	British Rail Hotels	50	—
1984	British Gas onshore oil	80	—
	Sealink Ferries	65	—
	Enterprise Oil	380	48
	Jaguar Cars	300	9,500
	British Telecom	3,900	250,000
	British Technology Group	700	—
1986	British Gas	4,500	89,000
1987	British Airways	900	36,000
	Rolls Royce	1,400	38,995
	British Airport Authority	1,200	7,200
1988	British Steel	2,500	54,900
1989	Regional water companies	5,240	40,000
1990	Giro Bank	112	6,700
	Electricity authority	5,180	119,000
	National Power and Powergen	–	26,400
1991	Scottish Hydro-Electric and Scottish Power	1,105	13,300

Table 1.12: Privatisation proceeds 1984–93 (£m)

Year	Privatisation proceeds
1984	2,050
1985	2,706
1986	4,441
1987	5,178
1988	7,063
1989	4,138
1990	5,379
1991	7,923
1992	6,465
1993	8,116

Source: Bank of England

Table 1.13: Privatisation proceeds as a share of GDP, 1984–93

Year	Privatisation proceeds % of money GDP
1984	0.63
1985	0.76
1986	1.15
1987	1.22
1988	1.50
1989	0.80
1990	0.98
1991	1.37
1992	1.09
1993	1.29

Source: Bank of England

The objective of reducing the size of the State since 1979 achieved a measure of success. The combined effect of North Sea oil and privatisation proceeds assisted the reduction of the size of the public sector borrowing requirement (PSBR) which, in 1979 exceeded 6 per cent of GDP or an average of over £10

Table 1.14: Public sector borrowing requirement as a percentage of GDP, 1979–93

Year	PSBR % of money GDP
1979	6.33
1980	6.09
1981	4.12
1982	1.75
1983	3.80
1984	3.16
1985	2.08
1986	0.65
1987	−0.34
1988	−2.52
1989	−1.80
1990	−0.39
1991	1.32
1992	4.86
1993	6.87

Source: CSO

billion per annum, Table 1.14. This figure was reduced annually enabling the Government to achieve a public sector debt repayment (PSDR) by 1987. The PSDR peaked in 1988 at around £14 billion or 3 per cent of GDP. This surplus enabled the Government to repay its outstanding debt and reduce the immediate concern of financing the remaining public sector. Although debt repayment continued through 1989 and 1990, by 1991 recession in the economy and continuing public sector liabilities caused the PSBR to re-emerge and caused growing concern about the management of public sector debt and the enduring size of the public sector. Although privatisation had reduced the size of the remaining nationalised industries to 747,000 employees by 1991 (Table 1.10), the headcount in the public service sector had proved more resistant to government attempts at control. By 1991 the number of employees in the non-traded public sector had reduced by about 4 per cent of its 1979 level, largely through the impact of 'contracting-out' of previously direct labour services. By 1993–94 the PSBR increased to £50 billion or nearly 8 per cent of GDP.

The change in the conduct of industrial relations and productivity growth

During the 1960s and 1970s the conduct of industrial relations in the UK became an increasing source of economic concern. The apparent transformation of the conduct of workplace relations following 1979 represents one of the most dramatic features of the UK economy over the last fifteen years. Among the factors of production, the efficiency of labour represents the resource that is indigenous to an economy. Table 1.15 provides a composite statistical

Table 1.15: The UK labour market, 1970–93

Year	Gross domestic product[1]	Mfg output[1]	Output per person-hour in mfg[1]	Weekly earnings in mfg[2]	Wage cost per unit of output in mfg[1]	Competitiveness (index)	Real earnings[2]	Total mfg employment	Skills shortages % of companies*	Unemployment % of total labour	Inflation annual average %	Import penetration %	Trade union density %	Number of strikes	Days lost in strikes '000
1970	64.3	85.6	51.7	23.7	18.1	—	85.3	122.5	27	2.6	6.3	—	49.8	3,906	10,980
1971	65.3	84.8	53.8	26.4	19.7	—	86.6	118.3	12	3.4	9.4	—	50.3	2,228	13,551
1972	67.1	86.6	57.1	29.7	—	—	91.4	114.2	12	3.7	7.1	—	51.1	2,497	23,909
1973	72.2	94.6	61.2	33.8	21.8	—	95.2	115.0	37	2.6	9.2	23.5	50.5	2,873	7,197
1974	71.1	93.4	61.5	39.8	26.0	—	96.3	115.6	36	2.6	16.1	22.2	51.6	2,922	14,750
1975	70.6	87.0	60.4	50.4	33.7	85.9	98.0	111.0	16	3.9	24.2	23.2	53.7	2,282	6,012
1976	72.5	88.6	63.5	58.2	37.3	—	98.6	106.5	13	5.3	16.5	24.2	53.3	2,016	3,284
1977	74.4	90.3	64.1	63.5	40.5	—	93.9	107.2	20	5.5	15.8	26.0	54.7	2,703	10,142
1978	76.4	90.3	64.9	71.7	46.0	—	98.4	106.7	22	6.1	8.3	26.9	57.4	2,471	9,405
1979	78.5	90.6	65.2	82.9	52.9	98.8	100.5	106.2	21	5.7	13.4	26.2	57.4	2,080	29,474
1980	76.9	82.8	64.2	100.0	64.9	119.9	100.0	101.6	8	7.4	17.8	27.8	56.8	1,330	11,964
1981	76.0	77.7	67.3	112.9	71.1	123.0	101.3	91.1	3	10.6	12.0	29.2	55.5	1,338	4,266
1982	77.4	77.6	70.9	123.5	74.3	114.9	103.7	85.9	3	12.3	8.6	31.1	54.4	1,528	5,313
1983	80.3	79.2	76.3	113.9	75.0	103.4	107.9	81.0	5	13.1	4.5	33.4	53.3	1,352	3,754
1984	81.9	82.2	79.4	142.0	77.4	99.1	112.1	79.2	8	11.7	5.0	34.3	51.7	1,206	27,135
1985	85.2	84.5	81.6	153.8	81.8	100.0	115.0	78.7	13	11.2	6.1	34.3	50.5	887	6,402
1986	88.6	85.6	84.7	163.4	85.1	92.4	119.8	77.0	12	11.2	3.4	35.2	49.3	1,053	1,920
1987	92.7	89.6	88.8	177.1	87.1	90.4	124.0	76.3	15	11.0	4.2	35.6	48.3	1,004	3,546
1988	97.3	95.9	93.7	191.0	89.4	96.3	128.3	77.3	22	9.9	4.9	36.7	45.8	770	3,702
1989	99.4	100.2	97.9	207.3	93.2	95.0	129.8	77.5	23	6.3	7.8	—	44.4	693	4,128
1990	100.0	100.0	100.0	225.9	100.0	99.1	130.0	76.7	14	5.8	9.5	—	43.5	620	1,903
1991	97.7	94.7	102.2	245.0	107.0	101.4	132.7	72.1	6	7.9	5.9	—	—	357	761
1992	97.2	93.9	106.5	260.9	109.2	97.0	—	67.4	4	9.7	3.7	—	—	240	528
1993	99.0	95.5	112.3	—	109.4	—	—	65.3	6	10.3	1.6	—	—	203	649

Source: CSO except* CBI, *Industrial Trends Survey*
Notes: [1]1990 = 100; [2]1980 = 100; [3]1980 = 100

perspective of the main trends that have affected the evolution and development of the UK labour market and domestic economy from 1970. This table includes statistical series that will be referred to throughout this section.

Since 1979 the conduct of UK workplace relations has changed considerably. Strike activity has declined sharply, labour productivity growth has experienced a pronounced increase, real wages have grown strongly and trade union membership has been in secular decline. Of all the developments common to most industrialised economies of the world over recent years – the liberalisation of markets, the growth in trade and the increased flow of capital – the change in the conduct of industrial relations in the UK has served to exert a unique and pervasive impact of the microeconomic efficiency of the domestic workplace. The particular importance of the labour market is therefore crucial to the development of the British economy in recent times.

The system of industrial relations in the UK during the 1960s was considered to be largely adversarial in nature and the potential source of widespread inefficiency. The nature of workplace relations was believed to restrict the scope for productivity growth: the structure of trade unions in Britain was believed to engender widespread restrictive practices and 'make-work' rules as skills and work operations were duplicated under so called multi-unionism. The traditional craft structure of Britain's trade unions and the growth in the number of separate unions within the workplace were contrasted enviably with the 'industrial' and 'enterprise' styles of unionisation common in the more successful economies of the industrialised world. The apparent 'two-tier' structure of workplace collective bargaining also became a source of economic concern. Two-tier bargaining described the fissure between the formal structure of industry-wide collective agreements and the informal and fragmented nature of workplace negotiations over pay. This decentralised, workplace-level, tier of bargaining became associated with factional plant-level arrangements which prompted widespread inflationary wage 'leap-frogging', an absence of considerations of productivity or efficiency and the emergence of 'wild-cat' strikes (for a discussion of these issues see Ullman 1968). This latter feature contributed to the notion of the 'British disease'; the idea that the UK economy was particularly strike prone. The UK, during this period, was in fact fourth in the international league table of most strike-prone nations; only Italy, Spain and Ireland lost more days per 1,000 employees. The decentralised system of collective bargaining itself represented a further peculiarity of the British system of industrial relations by affording considerable power to workplace-level union organisation in the form of the shop steward.

The response to these apparent problems was the establishment of the Royal Commission on Trade Unions and Employers' Associations in 1965. The commission, headed by Lord Donovan, reported in 1968; its recommendations were designed to address Britain's poor workplace productivity record. For a recent discussion and appraisal of the Donovan Commission's recommendations, see Metcalf (1989). Formal single-employer bargaining was to be encouraged as a means of controlling wage inflation, boosting productivity and curbing industrial action. The decade that followed, however, further compounded Britain's poor industrial relations record. Productivity growth dropped, wage inflation escalated and strikes became more widespread.

Further attempts at reform were thwarted by union strength. The Labour government's attempt at reform of the 'British disease', 'In Place of Strife', was aborted before reaching the statute books in 1969, while the Conservatives' response, the 'Industrial Relations Act' was effectively defeated by union opposition in 1971. Meanwhile over the decade to 1979 trade union membership grew consistently.

In response, successive governments attempted to engender economic responsibility in the conduct of industrial relations through a process of industrial corporatism or tripartism. This system sought to engage trade unions, employers and the government in the process of economic management. Though the system was not without success, its principal failing stemmed from the inability of the trade unions nationally to control local level union organisation, particularly over considerations of pay and efficiency. With union membership at a numerical peak of over 13 million in 1979, almost paradoxically, public opinion returned a Conservative government with a platform of widespread union reform. As the Conservative Party manifesto (Conservative Party 1979: 7) said: 'Our ... tasks are: 1) To restore the health of our economic and social life, by controlling inflation and striking a fair balance between the rights and duties of the union movement ...'. The Conservatives' belief in free market, neoclassical economics led them to depart from what had been a post-war consensus and the commitment to full employment: real jobs, according to this doctrine, would only follow where real demand existed for them; jobs could not be created.

This shift in emphasis effectively removed from the trade unions the security of a government committed to preserve full employment and job security. Within thirty-six months of the end of 1979 the number of people unemployed increased by 250 per cent. Between 1980 and 1982 the average annual rate of redundancy jumped to 59 per 1,000 employees from 17 per 1,000 between 1977 and 1979. Average recorded unemployment throughout the 1980s was three times the average level in the 1970s. The growth in unemployment therefore reduced the sense of strength among trade unionists. The level of redundancies particularly, engendered a sense of vulnerability among employees in the workplace. During the early 1980s this growth in unemployment effectively shifted the balance of power in collective bargaining away from trade unions towards management and gave rise to the notion of a sense of employee compliance or fear in the workplace. Trade unions therefore, effectively lost their power to resist the series of legislative reforms that followed. During the 1970s, legal reform had proved inadequate in the face of union opposition. By the early 1980s however, this resistance was effectively emasculated by growing unemployment and fear of job loss. An iterative process of union reform was set in motion (Dorey 1993).

The ideology behind this platform of legislation was the promotion of individual freedom. Individual rights were therefore promoted at the expense of collective rights in a desire to foster individual responsibility through the provision of 'voice' and 'exit' to individual trade unionists. Most crucial, however, for the trade unions were the 1982 and 1984 legal reforms, which gave, respectively, trade unions a legal personality which removed their immunity from civil action, and the requirement of statutory balloting of union members on a series of internal decisions (see Metcalf 1990 for a detailed discussion of the trade union and employment legislation from an economic perspective).

In the early 1980s, growing unemployment therefore reinforced the legislation with a power that it lacked during earlier attempts at legal reform. The condoning of the increase in unemployment was not, however, an explicit aspect of policy. Rather, the growth in unemployment was largely a consequence of the free market policy and emphasis on product market competition adopted by the government. Following the 1979 election economic policy involved the removal of all remaining industrial subsidies provided by the State, the removal of any remaining protection of domestic industry from import substitutes through the elimination of exchange controls and any remaining tariff barriers, and the exposure of domestic industry to a harsh exchange rate regime. This latter feature, which was a direct consequence of the arrival of North Sea oil, (discussed above), was seen as beneficial to the Government's counter-inflation strategy, with a strong exchange rate providing cheaper imports. This counter-inflationary stance also prompted a tightening of monetary discipline in an effort to control domestic inflation which exceeded 20 per cent in the second quarter of 1980. With tightening recession in the domestic economy, UK producers were increasingly forced to look towards overseas markets to sell their output. However, to be successful in these markets UK exporters had to absorb the loss of cost-competitiveness in their prices caused by the appreciation in the value of sterling. Meanwhile in home markets, import competing companies faced a similar need to contain their costs and prices to maintain market share.

As a result of the influence of increased product market competition, UK exporters and import competing companies sought to control costs from the early 1980s onwards. In this context, in order to survive, businesses in the UK had to become more productive by improving their capital and labour utilisation or risk going out of business. This involved a process of firms shedding their least productive resources giving rise to plant closure, redundancy and unemployment. The impact of product market competition therefore intensified cost disciplines on employers and their concern with the efficient use of capital and labour. To do otherwise was to risk going out of business. These pressures effectively exerted their greatest impact on the traded sector of the economy, in manufacturing, employment fell by nearly 20 per cent between 1979 and 1982 while the number of manufacturing plants employing over 200 people fell by 15 per cent between 1979 and 1982 (source: PA 1003 Business Monitor, Business Statistics Office, 1979 and 1982). The response in the private sector to increasing competition in turn reflected itself in the so called 'managerial revolution' (Purcell 1991) and the emergence of the notion of management as a factor of production.

The result of increased competitive pressure, therefore, forced companies, particularly, at first, those in the manufacturing sector, to increase output per person, or productivity. This pressure manifested itself in the so-called manufacturing productivity miracle of the 1980s. Table 1.15 shows that output per person hour in manufacturing increased by over 50 per cent in the decade as a whole, or a growth of nearly 5 per cent per annum. With the exception of the impact of early stages of the 1990–92 recession this productivity performance shows some indications of enduring into the 1990s. The UK productivity record in the 1980s compares with an equivalent average rate of growth of 3 per cent per annum during the 1960s and 1 per cent per annum in the 1970s. The notion of a 'productivity miracle' stemmed from the fact that this rate of increase in the UK exceeded both the standards of the past and contemporaneous international comparison. The implication of this increased growth was that the UK had apparently shed its long run tendency to be slow growing.

Although a number of studies have undertaken detailed analyses of the reasons for the acceleration in productivity growth a series of common themes emerge:

1 **The improvement in the average quality of productive resources**   This route to increased productivity is frequently referred to as the *batting average effect*. Plant closures, capital scrapping and improved labour utilisation effectively involves shedding the least productive resources and improving the utilisation of the remaining productive capacity. These combined effects obviously exerted an impact in the early 1980s during the contraction in manufacturing sector (and have probably been partly responsible for boosting productivity during the 1990s recession). However, their impact represents only a once and for all effect, consistent with the shake-out in manufacturing in the early 1980s; they do not amount to an explanation of dynamic productivity growth throughout the last decade.

2 **Improved rates of innovation and research and development**   This route to improved productivity growth, through labour to capital substitution involving the microchip, computer controlled machine tools and design, and increased investment offers the potential for dynamic productivity growth with improving output per employee generating the circumstances whereby further investment and the prospect of innovation might follow. The likely impact of this source on productivity over the period since 1980 will be discussed in the business and technology section below.

3 **Improvements in the quality of labour**   This involves the potential combination of improved education and training, better workplace organisation and an improvement in the quality of management. Again such a route would offer the prospect of a dynamic productivity improvement with the

improvement in human capital corresponding closely to technical change on the capital side. Although there is little evidence of general improvement in education and training making a pronounced contribution to the improvement in productivity performance, changes in workplace organisation and an improvement in the nature of management have been more in evidence (Purcell 1991). The size of the impact of this route to increased productivity growth, however, depends crucially on the conduct and climate of the workplace environment. A virtuous circle of improving human capital is only likely where the return on the investment is likely to be realised. The climate of industrial relations is therefore critical to increased investment in both capital and labour.

4 **The transformation of industrial relations** As mentioned previously the impact of this factor is not independent of 2 and 3 above. If the nature of the industrial relations environment has changed to embrace the introduction of new technology and more flexible working practices, then permanently higher productivity can follow. The distinction needs to made however, between workplace change through cooperation or, alternatively, compliance. Compliance with workplace change due to the reduced power of employees can only endure while the balance of power remains in management's favour.

Though the possibility of workplace compliance is consistent with the rate of productivity growth in the first half of the 1980s and early 1990s, it is less likely to provide a robust explanation of the continued strong productivity growth performance in the latter half of the 1980s. During this period, as Table 1.15 shows, manufacturing output was rising, employment had stabilised, unemployment was falling and manufacturing skill shortages had increased to levels not seen since the early 1970s. These trends suggest a position of increased employee security in the workplace and a reduced role for compliance in workplace change. An increased role for cooperation between management and employees – serving to boost productivity growth – seems to be in evidence, at least over this period.

Industrial relations are not a zero-sum game. If employees and management can cooperate over workplace organisation they can increase the total sum of their joint product. If the improved productivity growth in the UK is derived through this route then it offers the potential – subject to the cyclical fluctuations in economic activity – of enduring productivity growth in the future. This hypothesis implies that if the climate of British industrial relations has changed – permanently – for the better, then a virtuous circle of higher growth may be attained. The argument runs that if relations between management and employees become more harmonious as opposed to adversarial, then improved investment in plant, innovation and human capital might follow. These in turn give rise to increased output per employee, improved working conditions and a higher growth rate of real earnings. Figures 1.6(a) and (b) illustrate the potential benefits from cooperative industrial relations in a 'prisoner's dilemma' context.

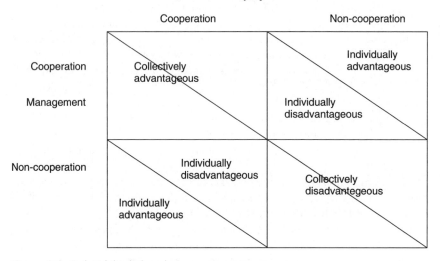

Figure 1.6a Industrial relations in a non-zero sum game

Employees

	Cooperation	Non-cooperation
Cooperation	7 / 7	10 / −1
Management		
Non-cooperation	−1 / 10	2 / 2

Figure 1.6b 'Prisoner's dilemma' pay-off matrix

If both parties in the workplace cooperate, the sum product is Pareto superior to adversarial, non-cooperative interaction.

The evidence that the British economy has achieved the Pareto optimum position is, however, inconclusive (see Metcalf 1990). The experience of the late 1980s, where manufacturing productivity growth remained robust in a tight labour market, offers some plausible endorsement of this view. The experience of the 1990s however has seen a re-emergence of high unemployment, further contractions in the manufacturing sector and a growth in the use of short-term, temporary employment in insecure, low productivity jobs. This ostensible flexibility, whereby individuals are hired on short-term contracts, on market clearing wage rates is unlikely to contribute to renewed, vigorous, enduring productivity improvement. Robust productivity growth in the UK economy requires functionally flexible, highly skilled employees on longer-term contracts of employment where employers can realise their returns on human capital. Where the supply-side response effectively diminishes human capital, compliance, as a means to efficiency improvement becomes more likely. Only as the UK economy recovers, unemployment reduces and the sense of insecurity in the workplace abates will the consequences for the long-term productivity prospects become clearer.

THE BUSINESS ENVIRONMENT AND TECHNOLOGY IN THE 1980s AND 1990s

Transition in the corporate sector

Alongside the widespread change that has occurred in the economy, the nature of the business environment in the UK has also been the subject of transition. The emergence of increased product market competition after 1979 and the impact of the recession in the early 1980s had, in turn, a profound impact on the conduct of the corporate sector in the UK. Increased exposure to competition required the private sector in the UK to increase efficiency in order to contain costs and retain market share. Between 1980 and 1982 the profitability, or pre-tax, real rate of return on capital employed in non-North Sea oil industrial and commercial companies in the UK fell to a post-war low of just 2.5 per cent. This represented a rate of return approximately equivalent to the risk-free opportunity cost of capital that could be earned in a bank. By late 1988 average pre-tax, real rates of return among industrial and commercial companies had exceeded 10 per cent. Table 1.16 provides a composite picture of the corporate sector in the UK over the period since 1980 which will be referred to throughout this section.

Increased international trade and exposure to product market competition progressively sharpened the immediate disciplines faced by the traded sector of the economy. In this climate the very culture and conduct of the corporate sector as a whole appeared to undergo a transition towards improved efficiency. The increased discipline provided by capital markets in the UK appeared to be acting in parallel with the constraints imposed by the economy. The notion of the emergence of an enterprise culture in the UK has been advanced while the change in the climate of industrial relations and the so-called 'managerial renaissance' have appeared to reinforce the vitality of corporate life since 1980. Concrete evidence of these events however is more nebulous. Self-employment has certainly been increasing. Between 1979 and 1990 the number of self-

Table 1.16: The UK business environment 1970–92

Year	(1) Company starts	(2) Company stops	(3) Company stock	(4) ICC's profitability %	(5) Investment: all industries £bn	(6) ICC capital formation* % of GDP	(7) Japanese investment $m	(8) Share ownership % of population	(9) Labour productivity (mfg) index	(10) Unit labour costs (mfg)	(11) Capacity utilisation* % of Cos	(12) GDP index	(13) R&D expenditure % of GDP
1970	—	—	—	9.2	50.1	6.4	—	—	62.6	22.5	51	75.1	—
1975	—	—	—	4.3	42.4	6.3	—	—	78.8	41.9	30	82.9	2.03
1979	158	—	1289	5.6	43.6	7.1	—	7.0	79.4	65.5	43	92.8	—
1980	152	142	1305	3.8	41.3	6.4	—	7.0	78.2	80.1	27	90.8	2.32
1981	166	120	1337	2.5	37.5	5.7	176	7.5	82.0	87.5	20	89.6	—
1982	180	145	1357	3.8	39.6	5.4	152	7.0	86.3	91.2	24	91.2	2.29
1983	182	145	1392	4.8	41.6	5.0	318	6.0	93.0	91.7	30	94.7	2.32
1984	182	152	1422	5.3	44.9	6.0	375	6.0	97.2	94.5	42	96.3	2.23
1985	191	163	1441	6.8	45.5	7.0	984	12.0	100.0	100.0	49	100.0	2.19
1986	209	164	1486	7.7	45.6	6.9	2,473	14.0	103.5	104.0	48	103.6	2.22
1987	237	167	1510	8.0	51.0	7.6	3,956	19.0	109.8	105.9	54	108.6	2.21
1988	255	171	1576	9.7	58.3	8.4	5,239	20.0	116.2	108.6	68	113.5	2.19
1989	239	172	1659	8.9	65.1	8.9	6,806	22.0	120.8	113.6	62	115.8	2.22
1990	192	184	1709	7.5	64.5	9.2	3,588	25.0	121.9	123.2	51	116.6	2.21
1991	N.A.	244	1646	7.2	59.2	7.3	2,948	25.0	122.5	132.6	30	113.9	—
1992	N.A.	N.A.	N.A.	6.9	49.6	7.0		23.0	128.2	135.0	37	113.1	

Source: CSO except *CBI, *Industrial Trends Survey*
Note: All indices 1985 = 100

employed people, with or without employees, increased by 71 per cent to 3.2 million at an average annual growth rate of over 5 per cent. After 1990 however, with increasing company closures, the number of self-employed individuals fell to 2.9 million by 1992. Some of this early growth could therefore be explained by the growth in unemployment and the relatively generous benefits available for unemployed individuals on the Enterprise Allowance Scheme. Alternatively, proponents of the notion of the *enterprise economy* argue that the number of self-employed will also tend to increase when unemployment is low or falling. In such circumstances, the possibility of alternative, paid employment is readily available, prompting individuals to become more likely to venture into self-employment.

Following this reasoning, the growth in the proportion of self-employed individuals in Britain in the 1980s provides evidence of an increased entrepreneurial spirit in society. Additional evidence of increased entrepreneurial behaviour is provided by a recorded 14 per cent increase in the annual average number of patent registrations between 1980 and 1988 as compared with the period 1974 to 1979. The evidence, however, for the existence of an enterprise economy in Britain following the experience of the 1980s is weak and unconvincing. The alternative source of work provided by the possibility of self-employment by the late 1980s was perceived by employees to represent an unattractive proposition. In 1989 the British Social Attitudes Survey reported that between 1983 and 1989, taking the level of unemployment into account, 'there was no increase in the proportion of employees who were tempted to consider self employment' (Blanchflower and Oswald 1989: 127–43). The growth in self-employment in Britain in the 1980s, on the strength of this evidence, appeared to be more the product of the trebling of the average level of unemployment, than the emergence of a new spirit of enterprise in British society.

These facts notwithstanding, columns 1, 2 and 3 in Table 1.16, covering company VAT registrations, deregistrations and stock, show an increase of nearly a third in the total stock of firms, to 1.7 million, over the 1980s as a whole. This growth reflects the more pronounced performance of *company starts* over company closures for the period. This growth of new businesses concurrent with a period of increased labour shedding among existing businesses caused a substantial reduction in the average size of employing units after 1980. As Table 1.17 shows, there was a 15 per cent increase in the proportion of firms employing up to 499 employees between 1979 and 1989: the average size of industrial units in the UK had become smaller and, by implication, were less likely to be unionised.

Table 1.17: Plant size and employment 1979–89 (percentages)

Share of employment	1979	1986	1989	% change
Up to 49 employees	33.6	42.1	42.3	26
Up to 499 employees	57.3	64.7	65.8	15

Source: *DEG, February 1992: 47–51*

Column 4 of Table 1.16 provides detail on the UK profits renaissance. Throughout the period 1981 to 1988 the real rate of return on capital employed in the corporate sector consistently increased. Encouragingly, despite the recurrence of economic recession in the early 1990s, the rate of return on capital employed remained relatively buoyant, dipping to 6.9 per cent in 1992 as compared to 2.5 per cent in 1981. By the first half of 1993, profitability had recovered to 8 per cent. This relatively robust profitability record, in the face of prolonged recession, suggests that in the 1990s the corporate sector had become leaner, cost-conscious, more efficient and better equipped to withstand the economic climate.

This position is also reflected by the investment record of UK companies. Column 5 provides statistics on investment across all industries at 1985 constant prices, while column 6 expresses industrial and commercial companies' (ICC) formation as a per cent of GDP. Throughout the 1990's recession, although levels of investment declined, they remained similar to average investment levels during the latter half of the 1980s and well above the levels of investment recorded during the 1980–82 recession. This relative investment record in the 1990's recession, despite a similar depth and duration to the 1980–82 recession, is reflected in responses to the CBI's Industrial Trends Survey (ITS). Consistently, over the period between 1990 and 1992, expected capital expenditure authorisations to 'expand capacity' were twice as high as during the period 1981 to 1982. Although the average proportion of manufacturers reporting an expansion in capacity was only around one in five in the early 1990s, compared to one in three during the late 1980's boom, this relatively high proportion of respondents to the ITS compares well with the one in ten respondents recorded during the early 1980's recession.

Although substantially reduced, this readiness to invest, despite recession, probably reflected the improved rates of return in industry. These in turn could reflect improved investment opportunities, particularly in information technology or a greater potential to realise the return on investment following the change in the UK industrial relations environment. Increased flexibility of operation enabled companies to control their costs more effectively during the 1990s recession allowing a greater return on investment to be realised.

A major feature of the UK commercial environment since the early 1980s was the increased presence of Japanese direct investment into the economy. Column 7 provides statistics on annual direct investment in billions of dollars at current prices. Japanese direct investment increase sharply towards the end of 1980s and subsequently declined to 1992. The influence of this investment on the corporate sector in the UK, however, goes well beyond the scale of the expenditure. The presence of Japanese investment brought a widespread cultural shift in the conduct of management and industrial relations. Working practices and production systems in the UK sought to emulate Japanese management practice through the adoption of team-based organisation, 'just in time' production, quality circles and statistical process control. Emulation became widespread. Oliver and Wilkingson (1989: 80) report on the extent of emulation of Japanese production techniques among the *Times 1000* companies in 1987; they found over 80 per cent of companies employing group and flexible working and over 60 per cent used statistical process and total quality control. However, in the absence of personnel policies commensurate with the production system, Oliver and Wilkingson found that a 'strategic mismatch' could qualify the commercial benefits available from adopting Japanese practices in the UK. They cited the example of the Ford Motor Company which introduced just in time manufacture enabling the subsequent 1990 strike by Ford employees in the UK to shut down the whole of the company's European operations. The reasons for this increased Japanese investment are likely to be a combination of the desire to locate direct investment in Europe prior to the single European market, low relative UK labour costs, an improved industrial relations record and a preference for the English language. The completion of the European single market could well account for the reduced investment levels in recent years.

Research and development (R&D) expenditure in the UK remained at fairly constant levels throughout the 1980s and early 1990s at about 2.2 per cent of GDP, (see Table 1.16 column 14, and Tables 1.18 and 1.19), which is consistent with expenditure in the USA and EC. Much of this expenditure, however, has

Table 1.18: Research and development expenditure, 1975–91

Year	R&D expenditure £m	Money GDP £m	R&D expenditure as a % of GDP
1975	2,151	105,852	2.03
1978	3,510	168,526	2.08
1981	5,921	254,927	2.32
1983	6,583	304,456	2.16
1985	8,198	357,344	2.29
1986	8,945	384,843	2.32
1987	9,448	423,381	2.23
1988	10,227	471,430	2.17
1989	11,288	515,957	2.19
1990	12,019	551,118	2.18
1991	11,.906	573,645	2.08

Source: CSO

Table 1.19: Composition of government-funded research and development expenditure in the UK, 1990–91

	Civil	Defence	Total
Basic	46.1	—	25.8
Strategic	26.0	1.8	15.3
Applied	24.6	15.5	20.6
Development	3.4	82.7	38.4

Source: Cabinet Office, *Annual Review of Government Funded Research and Development*

been defence related. Although the role of innovation and R&D doubtless served to reinforce the improvement in manufacturing productivity through the 1980s, the route from levels of R&D expenditure through to commercial utilisation is more complex. The rate of innovation in the UK has, from the days of the intense scrutiny of the 1960s, remained high. The commercial realisation of innovation is, however, key to its economic success. In recent years UK companies, particularly in the pharmaceutical industry, have prospered on their innovative success. The record of the British company Glaxo, one of the most profitable in the world, represents an illustration of success through the realisation of research and development.

Consistent evidence on research expenditure and technological development is limited. The development of office and information technology (IT) in the UK has been widespread since 1980. The financial service and the banking industry have undergone a considerable technological revolution since the late 1970s. Developments in micro-electronic technology have been fundamental to the development of banking and international trading. Decision-making in banking and finance depends on rapid and accurate information. The importance of the financial services sector and the role of the City of London have been dependent on such technological advances. Technology has made the expansion and diversification of financial services possible. Although, on aggregate, service sector output as a proportion of GDP has increased only slightly, from 61 per cent in 1979 to 64 per cent by 1994, the contribution of the financial services sector to output and employment has been more pronounced. The role of financial services, and therefore technological implementation, in Britain's trade performance has clearly been of vital importance in maintaining London's pre-eminent position.

The telecommunications industry has also undergone a considerable evolution in technology following the privatisation of BT, the introduction of the Cable and Wireless/Mercury duopoly competitor, and tight regulation of the sector by the Office of Telecommunications (OFTEL). In signalling and communications equipment, the private sector financed Eurotunnel venture provides a classic illustration of a new technology providing a new product, in this case one that ends Britain's geographical isolation. With the exception, however, of Britain's chemical and pharmaceutical industry, domestic manufacturing industry has benefited less from technological implementation. The connection between technical innovation, technology implementation and the structure of Britain's international trade has been apparent. Manufactures have declined: the domestic motor industry has virtually disappeared; electronics have experienced considerable decline; and the shipbuilding industry, although assisted by construction for North Sea oil exploration and development has also been greatly reduced. While increased product market competition has represented a spur to technological adaptation and development in services, its impact in manufacturing has been, on balance, detrimental.

British manufactured goods have suffered for this lack of technological investment. The relatively poor income elasticity of demand for UK exports, discussed in 'Background and context' above, reflects this lack of investment. Japanese direct investment into the UK, in industries such as electronic equipment and motor vehicles, has benefited from technological superiority allowing Japanese-owned companies to command markets throughout the European Union (EU). Aware of the importance of development expenditure on product and process innovation the CBI Industrial Trends Survey, a survey confined to manufacturers, has included a question seeking details on firms' investment intentions on innovation. Figure 1.7 shows the balance of firms expecting to spend 'more' on product and process innovation since 1989. Although the series dipped, in line with the pronounced recession in the domestic economy, expenditure on innovation, a crucial area of investment throughout recession, maintained a positive balance of firms, far in excess of those investing in plant and machinery. Throughout the course of the 1990's recession, the relative readiness to invest in innovation was seen as encouraging for the future of domestic manufacturing. The problem, however, is that the question merely seeks details on whether 'more' or 'less' expenditure is expected to be authorised over the next twelve months; nothing is known of the actual level of expenditure in the case of either series.

Capital markets and corporate ownership

Although less than 1 per cent of all UK owned companies are publicly quoted firms, these firms make up the vast majority of domestic corporate output. In

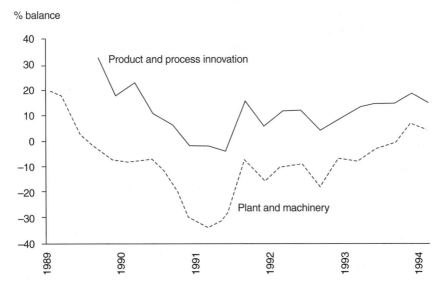

Figure 1.7 Investment in innovation in the UK, 1989–94

Source: CBI Industrial Trends Survey

addition to their importance to the economy, their relationship with domestic capital markets is the most intense. Ownership in the corporate sector has become progressively more concentrated since the late 1970s. Table 1.20 shows that over 50 per cent of shares in British publicly quoted companies are effectively owned by the insurance companies and pension fund managers while the constituent members of the Institutional Shareholders Committee (Association of British Insurers; Association of Investment Trust Companies; British Merchant Banking and Securities Houses Association; The National Association of Pension Funds Ltd; Unit Trust Association) control over 60 per cent of UK equities.

This concentration of corporate control gives tremendous implicit power over the function of UK managers. The increased importance of yardstick competition, the threat of takeover and acquisition and the role of capital market discipline on internal corporate control have exerted a considerable influence over the domestically owned corporate sector. With the exception of perhaps the United States, few industrial economies exhibit such a pattern of corporate ownership. In such circumstances, the expectations of institutional shareholders assume a considerable role over the conduct of the UK capital markets. In other industrial economies, in particular in the cases of Japan and Germany, where the banking sector plays a pronounced role in corporate ownership, the pressures created through concentrated equity ownership exert less influence on the immediate performance of firms. In the UK, the concentration of corporate ownership has led to allegations of short-termism in industry. This view maintains that shareholder expectations for higher returns places a burden on UK managers to produce short-run, high returns to the detriment of longer-term investment opportunities.

Table 1.21 provides a statistical perspective on the financial side of the UK corporate sector since 1975. Columns 1 to 6 in Table 1.21 will be referred to

Table 1.20: Share ownership in Britain, 1963–92 (percentages)

	1963	1969	1976	1981	1989	1992
Individuals and unincorporated businesses	54.0	47.4	37.5	28.2	20.8	20.0
Non-profit-making bodies	2.1	2.1	2.3	2.2	2.1	2.2
Public sector	1.6	2.6	3.6	3.0	2.0	1.2
Banks	1.3	1.7	0.7	0.3	0.7	0.2
Insurance companies	10.0	12.2	15.9	20.5	18.5	20.7
Pension funds	6.4	9.0	16.8	26.7	30.5	31.1
Unit trusts	1.3	2.9	4.1	3.6	5.9	5.7
Other financial institutions	11.3	10.1	10.5	6.8	3.1	2.8
Industrial and commercial companies	5.1	5.4	3.0	5.1	3.8	3.3
Overseas	7.0	6.6	5.6	3.6	12.7	12.8
Total	100.0	100.0	100.0	100.0	100.0	100.0

Source: CSO, *Share Register Surveys*

Table 1.21: UK finance and capital markets, 1970–92

	(1) ICC financial surplus	(2) ICC expenditures on acquisitions	(3) ICC capital gearing	(4) ICC income gearing	(5) Dividend payout ratio	(6) FT-500 P/E ratio
	% of GDP	% of GDP			%	
1970	−0.3	2.1	20.0	14.1	29.8	—
1975	0.2	0.3	16.8	26.4	24.5	7.77
1979	−0.5	0.8	8.6	18.0	14.2	7.76
1980	0.2	0.6	9.3	25.3	21.4	6.02
1981	0.9	0.4	8.1	26.2	25.7	8.53
1982	1.3	0.7	9.1	26.4	32.0	9.90
1983	1.8	0.7	9.4	21.3	17.8	12.28
1984	1.8	1.7	9.0	14.6	14.0	11.69
1985	1.2	2.0	10.3	19.6	15.4	11.74
1986	0.2	4.0	11.8	16.0	20.0	14.13
1987	0.1	3.9	12.7	13.5	24.0	17.10
1988	−1.7	4.9	14.9	13.8	29.0	12.20
1989	−4.2	4.5	19.1	19.7	37.6	12.69
1990	−5.0	1.5	20.0	28.7	40.2	10.77
1991	−2.4	3.8	21.0	26.4	41.4	13.49
1992	−2.5	1.3	21.0	29.8	42.8	15.87

Source: Bank of England

throughout this section. The issue to address here is the connection between the financial or speculative side of the economy and the real side of the economy in the UK. How does the economic climate affect speculative investment expectations and vice versa? The notion of confidence, and what influences it, will always remain an elusive element in economics. The recent aggregate history of the UK industrial and commercial sector, however, may shed some light on the record of transition in the economy. Column 1 shows the financial surplus of industrial and commercial companies as a percentage of GDP. Negative values here express the extent of indebtedness of the corporate sector: essentially this amounts to an excess of bank borrowing over retained earnings. The statistics show that the corporate sector moved heavily into debt after 1988 following a financial surplus over the previous eight years. The fact that this debt emerged in 1988 when trading conditions were very strong, suggests that the debt was voluntarily entered into on the strength of contemporary economic activity. The subsequent growth in debt to 5 per cent of GDP in 1990 indicates that the recession that followed was unanticipated, as was the rise in interest rates. Retained profits fell, the Bank of England's Minimum Lending Rate increased to 15 per cent by the end of 1989 from a low of 7.5 per cent in 1988 resulting in an increase in debt repayments.

Corporate spending on acquisitions, shown in column 2, provides an indication of why corporate borrowing increased so dramatically in the late

1980s. Corporate expenditure on acquisitions as a percentage of GDP began to increase from 1985, reaching a peak of 4.9 per cent of GDP in 1988. Meanwhile capital gearing, (debt at book value as a percentage of net capital stock at replacement cost) and income gearing (interest payments as a percentage of post tax income), shown in columns 3 and 4, increased. These figures provide confirmation that the dramatic increase in company acquisitions in the late 1980s was largely financed through increased borrowing. This suggests that companies were seeking to expand and increase profitability through cash-financed acquisition rather than firm-specific investment. These developments contributed to the belief that the capital market in the UK suffered from so-called short-termism.

Acquisitions offered shareholders more immediate returns on their investments. Supposedly weak companies were targeted for takeover with the prospect that a new management team might increase its profit performance and, therefore, the dividend payable to the acquiring company's shareholders. In this respect the growth in company acquisitions exercised a considerable capital market discipline over the possibility of managerial slack. Managerial teams not perceived as maximising shareholder wealth risked the prospect of a hostile takeover and new ownership. This pressure is very likely to have contributed to an increased pressure on management to maximise short-run profits, increase share valuations and boost dividends. Concerns that the financial institutions might be placing excessive emphasis on more immediate investment horizons began to emerge. In this context, acquisitions offered investors the prospect of short-term returns unavailable through longer-term investments. The potential damage that this activity might be causing the UK economy led the CBI to establish the City–Industry Task Force to investigate allegations of a potential schism between companies and investors (CBI 1987). As the CBI stated in the introduction to its report:

> While the need for British industry to invest has never been more apparent, it is alleged that industrial logic and the need for international competitiveness – within the manufacturing sector in particular – has been sacrificed on the alter of short-term financial gains; while the interests of other stake-holders in the future of the business, including the workforce, suppliers and the local community have effectively been ignored by the market (CBI 1987: 9).

Although the CBI task force found no evidence of this allegation, concerns that capital markets in both the UK and the USA place more immediate emphasis on company profitability than in Germany and Japan still enjoys widespread currency. The dividend pay-out ratio of publicly quoted companies offers some plausible endorsement of this belief. Column 5 shows the dividend paid to shareholders as a proportion of net profit.

During the 1980s the dividend pay-out ratio nearly doubled. Despite the stagnation of company profitability during the early 1990s, the growth in dividend pay-outs continued. The demands of shareholders for increasing dividend returns can threaten to place inevitable constraints on the reinvestment of company profits. A recent survey of finance directors conducted by *3i* on factors influencing company dividend policy indicated that half the respondents in the sample regarded the long-term growth in profits to be the most important determining factor (*3i* Group Plc 1993). The expectations of shareholders was cited by nearly a fifth of all respondents. Shareholder expectations were important inasmuch that the emphasis given to the firm's relative dividend performance served as a sign of the relative prospects of the company. Over 55 per cent of finance directors in the *3i* survey agreed with the statement: 'Any cut in the dividend pay-out sends adverse signals to markets and should be avoided'.

These results suggest that publicly quoted firms seek to maintain a balance between factors internal and external to the firm. Certainly, the evidence of the late 1980s and early 1990s suggests that UK firms which deviated from shareholder objectives tended to suffer from lower market valuations, making them more vulnerable to takeover bids, hence the pressure to maintain high dividend yields.

Companies issue equity since pure debt finance can result in high financial gearing and sensitivity to interest rate changes. As a result, an attractive consequence for firms of high market valuations is the ability to acquire inexpensive finance for expansion or new investment. Correspondingly, lower share valuations can increase the cost of fresh capital issues. The importance of maintaining a high dividend policy to this potential source of investment funding was substantiated by respondents to the *3i* survey; over 10 per cent of financial directors regarded the need to maintain access to sources of capital as the most important factor determining their company's dividend payments.

The potential adverse affects of high dividend policy in UK capital markets is regarded by City analysts and some financial economists as being overstated. In their view, share prices will reflect company profitability regardless of how the surplus is distributed. In this respect, a share's valuation will represent profits paid back into the business for future growth on an equal basis with those profits distributed in dividend pay-outs. This view, though widespread among financiers, is not shared in industry. Instead, industrialists see shareholder expectations as evidence of the short-termism of the UK capital market. Contrasts with the lower expectations made of German and Japanese companies is frequently cited as supporting evidence for this view.

While comparisons with the expectations of overseas capital markets provide powerful endorsement for the short-termist allegation, higher inflationary expectations in the UK – discussed in 'Background and context' above – may also provide a rationale for international yield differentials. Unlike bonds, equities are closely related to real asset values. As a result, many institutions use them as a hedge against inflation. Since pension funds represent inter-temporal transfers of money, returns on these holdings are required to maintain their real value. If returns do not rise in line with pension liabilities the deficit must be funded from company profits. As a result, the expectations of institutional owners of UK equities will require higher, differential returns from UK stock to allow for nominal price movements.

Allegations of short-termism stem from the mismatch between the views of industrialists and the expectations of financiers. The existence of short-termism implies that investment projects are required to produce high and rapid returns. Longer-term investment projects and expenditure on research and development for speculative returns are allegedly undervalued in favour of short-run, high return, ventures and dividend pay-outs. This view of UK capital markets is contradicted by the contention that companies' market valuations, or share prices, will reflect all the known information likely to influence the long-run value of the firm. Longer-term projects are inherently more uncertain while R&D is speculative and until recently has remained unaudited and therefore unknown.

In such circumstances, the presence of uncertainty will increase the rate at which the institutions will discount the value of such investments in assessing their net present values. In an open, speculative, capital market however, excessive concentration on the short term, or an undervaluation of longer-term initiatives, would imply that institutions prefer to hold unbalanced investment portfolios. Competition between alternative investment opportunities would ensure that this imbalance would be inefficient and therefore would not exist. Plausible evidence of this is provided by the experience of the pharmaceutical sector in the UK. In this sector, heavy investment in speculative research has been financed out of retained profitability, yet share valuations in pharmaceutical companies have remained high relative to net assets. Meanwhile, on the strength of this research record, pharmaceutical has represented one the most internationally successful sectors for British firms. This success, and the capital market's willingness to sustain high research expenditures, reflects the proven track record of the sector in capitalising the fruits of research and development.

Column 6 in Table 1.21 shows the annual average P/E or price–earnings ratio while Figure 1.8 plots the P/E ratio alongside the rate of company insolvencies. The objective here is to contrast directly, the real and the speculative sides of the company sector. The price–earnings ratio reflects the equity market's valuation of a stock. Expressed for each individual company, the price is the current share price of the stock while earnings are the earnings per share calculated at the time of the last company accounts. The P/E ratio therefore reflects the market's confidence in a company. High P/E ratios are the result of a high current share price relative to known earnings: a high P/E value is reflective of the perception that future earnings per share will be higher. The anticipatory nature of the stock market therefore bids up the share in anticipation of higher future earnings.

Figure 1.8 shows the average P/E ratio for the FT-500 from 1975 to 1993. This shows a trend growth in the P/E ratio throughout the 1980s – peaking in 1986–87 – with 1990's levels continuing to increase. This series reflects the boost in the level of confidence present in UK capital markets since 1980. By the

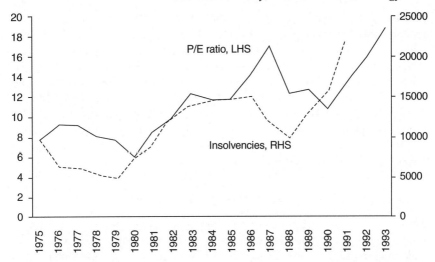

Figure 1.8 Comparison of company insolvencies and price–earnings ratios for the FT-500, 1975–93

Source: CSO *Annual Abstract of Statistics*, FT Business Service

early 1990s, investors were willing to sustain a price, relative to earnings, nearly twice as high as in 1979–80. This to a great extent reflects a level of speculative confidence in the growth, and profitability prospects, of domestic joint stock companies. This evidence is reflective of a clear change in the more nebulous notions of confidence and the perceptions of investors in the domestic capital market over this period.

The inclusion of the level of insolvencies in Figure 1.8 is intended to display a concurrent measure of the real vibrancy of the corporate sector. Insolvencies and business start-ups typically track each other. As more firms are set up, so the greater the likelihood becomes that marginal firms will go out of business. Although superficially a negative indicator, the level of insolvencies can, paradoxically, reflect a healthy and competitive corporate sector. To this extent Figure 1.8 provides evidence of a correspondence between confidence and reality. The two series in Figure 1.8 also reflect, to some extent, the anticipatory role of the speculative side of the economy. As a result, in times of recession, such as the early 1990s, insolvencies increase as the P/E ratio takes off. Although the 1990's recession exceeded most market expectations in its duration, throughout much of the early 1990s, the stock market bid-up share values in anticipation of economic recovery. Correspondingly, during the late 1980s, towards the end of the notorious Lawson boom, share values started to fall in anticipation of impending recession.

The objective of this section has been to attempt to illustrate many of the key features of the transition in the business environment in the UK since 1980.

Much of the change in the climate and attitude in the business environment probably owed as much to market deregulation, the growth in world trade, more benign tax regimes, the abundance of wealth from the North Sea and a sympathetic government as any change in Britain's real productive base. The alleged transition of the British economy remained largely illusory: the evidence of Britain's particular economic difficulties among the industrialised world in the first half of the 1990s provides testament to the lack of a sea-change in British productive potential. This is endorsed by the failure to use the opportunity provided by the 1980s to embrace more widespread implementation of technology change in industry.

PROSPECTS FOR THE FUTURE: CONCLUSIONS

The UK economy and business and commerce have undergone a series of pronounced changes over the period since 1979. The twin problems of growth and inflation have been addressed by introducing greater flexibility to changing market circumstances into the economy through a combination of economic and legislative reforms. However, this solution is yet to provide conclusive evidence that a lasting accommodation – or indeed, panacea – to these difficulties has been reached. Despite faster average productivity growth in manufacturing throughout the period following 1980, the growth in GDP still lagged the OECD average. By the end of the first half of the 1990s the level of GDP per capita remained below the G7 average. Inflation has been subdued at the cost of recession in the domestic economy and increased unemployment. A recurrence of inflation in a more buoyant economy would, under present policies, be greeted with further attempts at promoting flexibility in the labour market through further decentralisation and deregulation of pay determination in an attempt to suppress wage inflation. Although adjustment has taken place the essential structural weakness of the UK labour market remains in place. This is the tendency for the system of wage-setting to exacerbate inflation through its uncoordinated character. Only with far-reaching reforms to promote increased flexibility, which could involve doubtful implications for increased productivity, might the renewed increase in inflation be stemmed.

Concomitant to lower levels of productivity in the UK economy are lower levels of labour costs. Table 1.22 contrasts the level of hourly compensation costs in manufacturing in 1992 with those of other developed industrialised economies. Manufacturing is shown here as its definition is fairly consistent across countries, it is not dissimilar to the whole economy and it corresponds with the international comparisons of productivity levels. These figures from the Bureau of Labor Statistics in Washington show UK hourly compensation costs at around 75 per cent of the average level of other G7 economies. Low relative labour costs in the UK have been highlighted as a potential attraction for direct investment and the movement of capital into the UK. In an attempt

Table 1.22: International comparisons of hourly compensation
costs in manufacturing, 1992

Country	Hourly compensation costs index
United Kingdom	100
Canada	115
France	114
Germany	176
Italy	132
Japan	110
United States	110

Source: Bureau of Labor Statistics, Washington

to retain this labour cost competitiveness the UK government has been anxious to retain its opt-out from the European Social Chapter. Figure 1.9 depicts an advertisement, placed by the British Consulate in Dusseldorf, that appeared in 1993 in Germany's leading business paper, *Handelsblatt*, promoting low wage costs in the UK. Table 1.23 however suggests that UK labour costs have a long way to fall against the newly industrialising countries of the world to compete effectively on low labour costs. Rather than seeking to embrace new skills and technology, the future agenda for policy-makers has become one of highlighting the need for labour market deregulation and the reduction of wages as the remedy for future competitiveness.

The goal of a prosperous, high productivity, high wage economy has long been the objective of economic policy-makers from both sides of the political divide in the UK. The transition of the UK economic and business environment since 1979 has been considerable. The political culture has changed, the climate of industrial relations has been transformed, the process of privatisation is either complete or its effects largely discounted. The average annual level of unemployment has been three times the average of the 1960s and 1970s while the control of inflation has proved a stubborn objective: the annual increase in prices exceeded 10 per cent as recently as the early 1990s. The effective self-sufficiency in oil has represented an unparalleled benefit for the UK. Nevertheless the underlying balance of payments position remains parlous,

Table 1.23: Labour costs, 1992

Country	Hourly compensation costs index
United Kingdom	100
Korea	33
Mexico	16
Taiwan	35

Source: Bureau of Labor Statistics, Washington

Figure 1.9 Advertisement promoting low wage costs in the UK
Source: *Handelsblatt*

while again, as recently as 1992, devaluation has had to restore the UK's international competitiveness. While change, transition and evolution have undoubtably occurred in the UK since 1979, continuity also deserves its place as a theme of the age.

ACKNOWLEDGEMENTS

The author would like to acknowledge the help and assistance provided in the preparation of this chapter from the Government Statistical Service, the Bank of England, the SCPR and the Anglo-Japanese Economic Institute. Thanks are also due to Esmond Lindop and Donald Roy.

David Martin and Andrew Pipe provided valuable research assistance with the compilation of the statistical evidence.

This chapter was written in 1993 but the key issues and scope of research make it highly relevant to this text and Peter Ingram has kindly given permission to include it in this work. More up-dated information on this topic can be found in the relevant government statistical publications.

SELECTED READING

Bairam, E. (1988)
Caves, R. E. and Associates (1968)
Caves, R. E. and Lawence, B. K. (1980)
Oliver, N. and Wilkingson, B. (1989)
Thirlwall, A. P. (1992)

2 The UK market environment

Michael Thomas

Marketing, the marketing concept. Much has been written about its meaning, and definitions could be mustered that would occupy much of this chapter. Peter Drucker, a management guru who has remained in fashion for at least three decades, stated in 1954 that the marketing concept was *the whole business seen from the point of view of its end result, that is from the point of view of the consumer* (Drucker 1954: 37). I propose, therefore, to discuss the marketing environment in the United Kingdom from the point of view of the consumer, because it is the profile of British consumers that will differentiate any discussion of marketing in the United Kingdom from any other.

PROFILE OF BRITISH CONSUMERS

CACI Information Services is a company that provides very sophisticated analysis of demographic data. I begin by examining the CACI ACORN classification profile of Great Britain. ACORN stands for 'A Classification of Residential Neighbourhoods'. The system was developed by CACI. Table 2.1 shows ACORN's thirty-eight neighbourhood types, the eleven groups they form, and their share of the GB population of 54,680,920 in 1991. ACORN is based on the Government's Census of Great Britain conducted in 1981. The 1991 populations of neighbourhoods are derived from CACI's proprietary demographic model of Great Britain. The most recent data available are for 1991.

The ACORN profile uses an alphabetic and numeric classification, namely A1, G22, U39. This may cause some confusion because an older classification, and one generally more familiar, derives from the National Readership Survey (Table 2.2). This latter classification is simpler than ACORN, deriving from a classification of occupations. These social grades are in widespread use, and the data in Tables 2.3 and 2.4, July 1991 to June 1992, show the population profile by social grade.

CACI, the company that generates the ACORN profiles, has recently developed a more sophisticated classification system – its targeting classification. Table 2.5 combines ACORN types with a behavioural classification scheme A, B, C, D, E and F. This table also cross-refers to the National Readership

Table 2.1 CACI ACORN profile of Great Britain

ACORN types		% of 1991 Population		ACORN groups	
A 1	Agricultural villages	2.6			
A 2	Areas of farms and smallholdings	0.7	3.3	Agricultural areas	A
B 3	Post-war functional private housing	4.4			
B 4	Modern private housing, young families	3.7			
B 5	Established private family housing	6.0	17.6	Modern family housing, higher incomes	B
B 6	New detached houses, young families	2.9			
B 7	Military basis	0.7			
C 8	Mixed owner occ'd & council estates	3.5			
C 9	Small town centres & flats above shops	4.1	17.9	Older housing of intermediate status	C
C10	Villages with non-farm employment	4.9			
C11	Older private housing, skilled workers	5.5			
D12	Unmodernised terraces, older people	2.4			
D13	Older terraces, lower income families	1.4	4.2	Older terraced housing	D
D14	Tenement flats lacking amenities	0.4			
E15	Council estates, well-off older workers	3.4			
E16	Recent council estates	2.8	13.2	Council estates category I	E
E17	Better council estates, younger workers	5.0			
E18	Small council houses, often Scottish	1.9			
F19	Low rise estates in industrial towns	4.6			
F20	Inter-war council estates, older people	2.8	8.8	Council estates category II	F
F21	Council housing, elderly people	1.4			
G22	New council estates in inner cities	2.0			
G23	Overspill estates, higher unemployment	3.0	7.0	Council estates category III	G
G24	Council estates with some overcrowding	1.5			
G25	Council estates with greatest hardship	0.6			
H26	Multi-occupied older housing	0.4			
H27	Cosmopolitan owner-occupied terraces	1.0	3.8	Mixed inner metropolitan areas	H
H28	Multi-let housing in cosmopolitan areas	0.7			
H29	Better-off cosmopolitan areas	1.7			
I30	High status non-family areas	2.1			
I31	Multi-let big old houses and flats	1.5	4.1	High status non-family areas	I
I32	Furnished flats, mostly single people	0.5			
J33	Inter-war semis, white collar workers	5.7			
J34	Spacious inter-war semis, big gardens	5.0	15.8	Affluent suburban housing	J
J35	Villages with wealthy older commuters	2.9			
J36	Detached houses, exclusive suburbs	2.3			
K37	Private houses, well-off older residents	2.3	3 8	Better-off retirement areas	K
K38	Private flats, older single people	1.5			
U39	Unclassified	0.5	0.5	Unclassified	U
			100.0		

Table 2.2: National Readership Survey social grade definitions*

Social grade	Social status	Occupation
A	Upper middle class	Higher managerial, administrative or professional
B	Middle class	Intermediate managerial, administrative or professional
C1	Lower middle class	Supervisory or clerical, and junior managerial, administrative or professional
C2	Skilled working class	Skilled manual workers
D	Working class	Semi and unskilled manual workers
E	Those at lowest level of subsistence	State pensioners or widows (no other earner), casual or lowest-grade workers

Source: National Readership Survey
Note: *These are the standard social grade classifications using definitions agreed between Research Services Ltd, and JICNARS. A JICNARS publication "Social Grading on the National Readership Survey" and National Readership Survey Appendix E describes the definitions and methodology used

Table 2.3: Distribution of the population by social grade*

Social grade	All adults 15+		Men		Women		Main shoppers* (female)	
	'000s	%	'000s	%	'000s	%	'000s	%
A	1,391	3.1	714	3.3	677	2.9	554	2.8
B	7,106	15.7	3,617	16.5	3,489	14.9	2,949	14.9
C1	11,654	25.7	5,316	24.3	6,338	27.0	5,280	26.7
C2	11,756	26.0	6,192	28.3	5,564	23.7	4,656	23.5
D	7,689	17.0	3,775	17.3	3,913	16.7	3,305	16.7
E	5,705	12.6	2,248	10.3	3,456	14.7	3,047	15.4
Total	**45,300**	**100.0**	**21,863**	**100.0**	**23,437**	**100.0**	**19,791**	**100.0**

Source: National Readership Survey, July 1991–June 1992
Note: These social grades are based on grades of head of household
*Main shoppers are identified as those who personally select half or more of the items bought for their household from supermarkets and food shops. This member may be male or female

Table 2.4: Main shoppers

	'000	%
Female main shopper	19,791	70.6
Male main shopper	8,229	29.4
All main shoppers	28,020	100.0

Source: National Readership Survey, July 1992–June 1993

Table 2.5: ACORN categories

	ACORN groups		ACORN types			
A THRIVING	1 Wealthy achievers, suburban areas	1.1	Wealthy suburbs, large detached homes	2.5%	ABC1	
		1.2	Villages with wealthy commuters	3.2%	ABC1	
		1.3	Mature affluent home-owning areas	2.7%	ABC1	
		1.4	Affluent suburbs, older families	1.0%	ABC1	B6, 114
		1.4	Mature, well off suburbs	2.0%	ABC1	B14, 133
	2 Affluent greys, rural communities	2.6	Agricultural villagers, home based workers	1.5%	ABC2D	A1, A2
		2.7	Holiday retreat's, older people, home based workers	0.7%	ABC2D	K37, A1
	3 Prosperous pensioners retirement areas	3.8	Home owning areas, well-off older residents	1.5%	ABC1	K37, J33
		3.9	Private flats, elderly people	1.3%	ABC1	K38, K37
B EXPANDING	4 Affluent executives, family areas	4.10	Affluent working families with mortgages	1.8%	ABC1	B6, B4
		4.11	Affluent working couples with mortgages, new homes	1.3%	ABC1	B4, B5
		4.12	Transient workforces, living of their place of work	0.3%	–	B7
	5 Well-off workers, family areas	5.13	Home owning family areas	2.5%	ABC1	B4, B3
		5.14	Home owning family areas, older children	2.6%	C1C2	B3, B5
		5.15	Families with mortgages, younger children	1.9%	C1C2	B4, B3
C RISING	6 Affluent urbanites, town & city areas	6.16	Well-off town & city areas	1.1%	AB	I30, J34
		6.17	Flats & mortgages, single & young working couples	0.9&	ABC1	K38, C9
		6.18	Furnished flats & bedsits, younger single people	0.5%	ABC1	I32, I31
	7 Prosperous professionals, metropolitan areas	7.19	Apartments, young professional single & couples	1.4%	ABC1	I30, K38
		7.20	Gentrified multi-ethnic areas	1.0%	ABC1	H29, I30
	8 Better-off relatives, inner city areas	8.21	Prosperous enclaves, highly qualified executives	0.9%	ABC1	I31, I32
		8.22	Academic centres, students & young professionals	0.6%	ABC1	I30, I31
		8.23	Affluent city centre areas, tenements & flats	0.7%	ABC1	K38, I31
		8.24	Partially gentrified multi-ethnic areas	0.8%	ABC1	I31, H28
		8.25	Converted flats & bedsits, single people	1.0%	–	I31, K38

Table 2.5: (Continued) ACORN categories

ACORN groups		ACORN types			
D SETTLING	9 Comfortable middle agers, mature home owning areas				
	9.26	Mature established home owning areas	3.4%	ABC1	J33, B5
	9.27	Rural areas, mixed occupations	3.4%	–	C10, A1
	9.28	Established home owning areas	3.9%	C1	J33, B5
	9.29	Home owning areas, council tenants, retired people	3.0%	ABC1	C8, J33
	10 Skilled workers, home owning areas				
	10.30	Established home owning areas, skilled workers	4/3%	C2	C11, B3
	10.31	Home owners in older properties, younger workers	3.2%	C1C2	C11, C9
	10.32	Home owning areas with skilled workers	3.3%	C2DE	C11, D12
E ASPIRING	11 New homes owners, mature communities				
	11.33	Council areas, some new home owners	3.7%	C2DE	E17, E15
	11.34	Mature home owning areas, skilled workers	3.3%	C2DE	E15, C8
	11.35	Low rise estates, older workers, new home owners	2.9%	C2DE	E19, E15
	12 White collar workers, better-off multi ethnic areas				
	12.36	Home owning multi-ethnic areas, young families	1.0%	C1	H29, J33
	12.37	Multi-occupied town centres, mixed occupations	2.0%	–	C9, D12
	12.38	Multi-ethnic areas, white collar workers	1.0%	C1	H29, D12
F STRIVING	13 Older people, less prosperous areas				
	13.39	Home owners, small council flats, single pensioners	2.9%	C2DE	C8, C9
	13.40	Council areas, older people, health problems	2.8%	C2DE	E20, C8
	14 Council estate residents, better off homes				
	14.41	Better-off council areas, new home owners	2.0%	C2DE	E16, E17
	14.42	Council areas, young families, some new home owners	2.2%	C2DE	E19, G23
	14.43	Council areas, young families, many lone parents	1.6%	C2DE	E16, E19
	14.44	Multi-occupied terraces, multi ethnic areas	0.7%	C2DE	H27, D13
	14.45	Low rise council housing, less well off families	1.8%	C2DE	E19, E20
	14.46	Council areas, residents with health problems	2.1%	C2DE	E19, E20
	15 Council estate residents, high unemployment				
	15.47	Estates with high unemployment	1.3%	DE	G22, E20
	15.48	Council flats, elderly people, health problems	1.1%	C2DE	E21, E20
	15.49	Council flats, very high unemployment singles	1.2%	DE	E21, G22
	16 Council estate residents, greatest hardship				
	16.50	Council areas, high unemployment, lone parents	1.5%	DE	G23, E16
	16.51	Council flats, greatest hardship, many lone parents	0.8%	DE	G25, G23
	17 People in multi-ethnic, low income areas				
	17.52	Multi-ethnic, large families, overcrowding	0.5%	DE	H27, H29
	17.53	Multi-ethnic, severe unemployment, lone parents	1.0%	DE	G22, H28
	17.54	Multi-ethnic, high unemployment, overcrowding	0.5%	DE	H26, H27

Source: CACI Information Services

Survey classification (penultimate column), therefore providing a substantial profile of British consumers. All the data are derived from the 1991 census of population. These data need no comment from me, other than to observe that the ACORN profile provides marketers with a powerful targeting tool, since housing type and location tell us a great deal about their occupiers, and can be related to broad behavioural characteristics.

Let me briefly illustrate why this is so. The 1991 census of population provides marketers with an extremely rich database. The census provides information on owner-occupancy (split by 'owned outright' and 'buying' an indicator of affluence and, alas, negative equity); multiple car ownership, a key indicator of affluence; ethnic origin; industry or occupation; travel to work, the kind of transport used in going to work; socio-economic group; and unemployment. Manipulation of this data has enabled ACORN to develop its targeting classification.

The concept of the family life cycle is well known to students of marketing, and this concept has been operationalised in the UK. The 'Sagacity Life Cycle' groupings (Figure 2.1), developed by Research Services Ltd, provide a valuable insight into the life cycles.

Data on real wealth in the UK is relatively limited, deriving from Inland Revenue statistics. Examination of the data in Table 2.6 suggests that over half the UK population derives income in the range £6,000–£19,999 per annum. Tables 2.7 and 2.8 shows that wealth is, however, less modestly distributed, with 10 per cent of the population owning half of the marketable wealth (marketable wealth is defined as cash, liquid assets, houses, land, shares and personal chattels, but excludes pension rights).

HOUSEHOLD EXPENDITURES

I now turn to the household, the central purchasing unit of the consumer. The data in Table 2.9 provides a good platform for understanding the behaviour of the family. Great Britain excludes Northern Ireland, hence the population of the UK is larger than that of Great Britain. In all of the data that follow, we shall use the UK household as the basic unit of account.

Anyone wishing to understand the UK as a market, particularly on a comparative basis, must be prepared to investigate the wealth of statistical material available. In my experience (including many years in the USA) the UK has the richest and probably the most accurate data on many aspects of household behaviour and expenditure. I have had to be somewhat selective in my selection of representative data, but the following pages will give some insights into how and what we as a nation consume. Much of the following data is reproduced and annually updated in *The Marketing Pocket Book* published by the Advertising Association and NTC Publications Ltd.

Table 2.10, based on 1990 data, shows the breakdown of household expenditure on a weekly basis, and as a percentage of total expenditure. It is

The basic thesis of the SAGACITY grouping is that people have different aspirations and behaviour patterns as they go through their life cycle. Four main stages of life cycle are defined which are sub-divided by income and occupation groups.

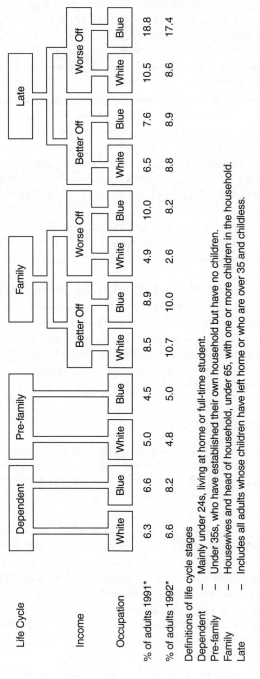

Life Cycle	Dependent		Pre-family		Family				Late			
Income					Better Off		Worse Off		Better Off		Worse Off	
Occupation	White	Blue	White	Blue	White	Blue	White	Blue	White	Blue	White	Blue
% of adults 1991*	6.3	6.6	5.0	4.5	8.5	8.9	4.9	10.0	6.5	7.6	10.5	18.8
% of adults 1992*	6.6	8.2	4.8	5.0	10.7	10.0	2.6	8.2	8.8	8.9	8.6	17.4

Definitions of life cycle stages
Dependent – Mainly under 24s, living at home or full-time student.
Pre-family – Under 35s, who have established their own household but have no children.
Family – Housewives and head of household, under 65, with one or more children in the household.
Late – Includes all adults whose children have left home or who are over 35 and childless.

Definitions of occupation groups
White – Head of household is in the ABC1 occupation group.
Blue – Head of household is in the C2DE occupation group.

*Year to June

Figure 2.1 Sagacity Life Cycle groupings

Source: Research Services Ltd

Table 2.6: Distribution of personal incomes* before and after tax in the UK in 1990–91

Income ranges £	Number before tax '000	%	Number after tax '000	%	Value after tax '000
3,005– 4,999	4,750	16.6	5,680	19.9	7.3
5,000– 7,499	4,980	17.4	6,000	21.0	12.1
7,500– 9,999	4,430	15.5	4,810	16.8	13.5
10,000–14,999	6.620	23.1	6,730	23.5	26.7
15,000–19,999	3,810	13.3	3,050	10.7	16.9
20,000–29,999	2,660	9.3	1,640	5.7	12.6
30,000–49,999	993	3.5	511	1.8	6.0
50,000 +	369	1.3	172	0.6	4.9
All incomes over £2,785	28,600	100.0	28,600	100.0	100.0

Source: Inland Revenue Survey of Personal Incomes 1990–91. Please see this source for definitions and methods of estimation.
Notes: *After deduction of superannuation contributions.

Table 2.7: Distribution of marketable wealth* of individuals in the UK in 1991 (range of net wealth)

£	Number of owners** '000	%	Marketable wealth £'000m	%
nil– 4,999	14,034	31.8	40	2.5
5,000–14,999	9,210	20.9	96	6.1
15,000–24,999	4,852	11.0	97	6.1
25,000–49,999	8,825	20.0	345	21.9
50,000–99,999	3,928	8.9	289	18.3
100,000+	3,231	7.3	711	45.1
Total	**44,080**	**100.0**	**1,578**	**100.0**

Source: Inland Revenue Statistics 1993. See this source for definition and methods of estimation.
Notes: *Marketable wealth includes cash, liquid assets, houses, land, shares and personal chattels but excludes occupational and State pension rights.
**Adults aged 18 and over.

worth noting that the largest item, 12.7 per cent of all expenditure is Income Tax payments (but only 12.71 per cent it should be noted, by those who argue we are overtaxed as a nation), the second largest is food (12.0 per cent). Because food is a major item of expenditure, it is of interest to analyse how the £44.81 per week is actually spent (see Table 2.11).

The *Family Expenditure Survey* from which both of the above sets of data are taken is a major statistical source for anyone wishing to know more about the UK consumer. It is published annually.

As any visitor to the UK will quickly discover, we are a nation as heterogeneous as any nation four times our size, hardly speaking the same language (I speak as a local resident of Glasgow). Regional variations are

Table 2.8: Distribution of marketable wealth* of individuals in the UK in 1989 (percentage of wealth owned)

% owned by	Marketable wealth		Marketable wealth plus occupational and state pension rights	
	1976	*1989*	*1976*	*1989*
Most wealthy 1% of population	21	18	13	11
Most wealthy 10% of population	50	53	36	38
Most wealthy 25% of population	71	75	57	62
Most wealthy 50% of population	92	94	80	83

Source: Inland Revenue statistics 1991. See this source for definitions and methods of estimation
Notes: *Marketable wealth includes cash, liquid assets, houses, land shares and personal chattels but excludes occupational and State pension rights

important in Great Britain as the data in Table 2.12 demonstrate. The table shows variations from the figure for average consumption in Great Britain. It is interesting to observe that in some aspects of food consumption, variations are reducing over time, though surprisingly in others the regional variation is increasing. Compare for example prepared fish in the North, and fresh fish in Scotland; and mutton and lamb in Greater London and Scotland.

Food consumption – you can tell what a man or woman is by what (s)he eats – will be returned to later in this analysis when I discuss distribution patterns in this country, for food retailing has gone through an extraordinary transformation in recent years, and anyone trying to market food to the UK must understand the structural transformation of food retailing that has taken place. Man or woman cannot, however, live by bread alone.

Although the comparative consumption of mutton and lamb may be an indicator of the quality of life, other more penetrating measures are available. Table 2.13 shows the penetration of durables in GB households from 1987 to 1991. Over the period covered, the increase of dishwasher ownership is notable, as is microwave oven ownership. One per cent of households exist without refrigeration, 18 per cent of households are without central heating, 96 per cent of households have colour television, over half have two or more TV sets. All that double glazing advertising has had its effect, since almost half of all households have it. Eighty-nine per cent of all households have a telephone (99 per cent in the USA).

A further glimpse of the quality of life may be derived from leisure, hobbies and personal care products. By March 1992 it would appear that 29 per cent of all British householders had a home computer, driven no doubt by children wanting to do battle with mutant turtles rather than an innate British disposition towards computing. Leisure activities are an interesting indicator of a nation's inclinations and eccentricities.

Club membership (the data in Table 2.15 are not cast iron but indicative) tells us quite a lot about ourselves. If you are a stand-up comedian and

Table 2.9: Characteristics of household population

(a) Number of h'holds March 1992:

	Great Britain	UK
	21,885,000	22,471,000

(b) Size of h/h 1991 (%)

1 person	26
2 persons	35
3 persons	17
4 persons	16
5 persons	6
6 or more persons	2
	100

Average (mean) h/h size	1991	2.48
	1971	2.91

(c) Sex of head of h/h 1991 (%)

Male	74
Female	26
	100

49% of the female heads of household are over 60 and living alone.

(d) Marital status by sex 1990 (%)

16 and over	Men	Women
Married	63	57
Cohabiting	5	4
Single	24	18
Widowed/divorced etc.	8	21
	100	100

(e) Female h/wives with/without children (%)

With children		
0–23 months	6.8	
0–4 years	17.4	
0–15 years		46.5
Without children		52.2
		100

(f) Working status of h/wives (female)^2 (%)

Working full-time		
30+ hours per week	24.4	
Working part-time		
8–29 hours per week	20.8	
Working full- or part-time		45.2
Not working; and part-time		
under 8 hours per week		54.8

(g) Number of economically active persons in h/h (%)

No persons	31.5
1 person	29.0
2 persons	30.7
3 or more persons	8.9
	100.0

(h) Retired/non-retired h/h^3 (%)

Retired, mainly dependent on state pensions	13.0
Retired, other	21.1
Non-retired	65.8
	100.0

(i) Static/non-static h/h in Q1 1992 (%)

Static		90
Non-static		
newly weds h/h	2	
Movers into		
new homes	1	
other movers	7	10
		100

Sources: (a), (i): GIK Marketing Services Ltd
(b), (c), (d): General Household Survey
(e), (f): National Readership Survey, July 1991–June 1992
(g), (h): Family Expenditure Survey, 1990

Notes: ^{1}(g), (h) refer to the UK; (b), (c), (d), (e), (f), (i) to Great Britain.
^{2}According to the Family Expenditure Survey 1986, 16% of households have working married women with dependent children.
^{3}Households consisting of one adult or one man and one woman only.

masochist, note that working men's clubs have a membership of 5 million. Association football (soccer) has 2.6 million members (many more weekly spectators of course), golf 1.1 million, and billiards and snooker 1.5 million. In this compendium, hang-gliding is the minority sport (3,150 members),

Table 2.10: UK household expenditure in 1992

Commodity or service	£	£	%
		Average weekly expenditure	
Housing (rent, rates and maintenance) (net)*		44.42	11.9
Mortgage and other payments for dwellings		43.67	11.7
Food		44.81	12.0
Alcoholic drink		10.01	2.7
Tobacco/cigarettes/cigars		4.82	1.3
Clothing and footwear		16.03	4.3
Household goods		20.00	5.4
Household services		12.28	3.3
Personal goods and services		9.47	2.5
Leisure goods		11.38	3.0
Motoring expenditure and other travel costs		40.02	10.7
Fares (railway, bus and coach)	2.32		
Purchase, maintenance, running of motor vehicles	33.83		
Other	3.87		
Fuel, light and power		11.11	3.0
Gas	4.27		
Electricity	5.59		
Coal, coke, etc.	0.66		
Fuel, oil and other	0.59		
Entertainments, inc. TV licences		4.72	1.3
Educational and training expenses		3.03	0.8
Hotel and holiday expenses		10.26	2.8
Miscellaneous other services		3.54	1.0
Income tax payments less refunds		47.14	12.7
National Insurance contributions		12.25	3.3
Insurances		16.90	4.5
Savings		4.00	1.1
Betting payments less winnings		0.81	0.2
Miscellaneous		1.95	0.5
Total		**372.52**	**100.0**

Source: *Family Expenditure Survey*, HMSO 1992
Note: *Net of all receipts of rent and rent rebates, rent allowances and housing benefits

though I am surprised that 45,000 people are dedicated to an underwater existence, a similar number (45,500) preferring to go up (parachuting) rather than down.

Although only 77,000 people belong to a rambling club, rambling as such is the major leisure activity, as Table 2.16 indicates. Walking is the Great British leisure occupation it would seem. For males it is occupying three and a half times as many people as watching football. Cultural activities are in general more 'in use' than spectator sports.

The major occupation of most British households is however less exotic than the above list suggests. Do-it-yourself (DIY) (Table 2.17) and gardening (Table

Table 2.11: UK household expenditure on food in 1992

Commodity	Average weekly expenditure		
	£	%	Index 1980=100
Bread	1.78	4.0	144
Flour	0.09	0.2	82
Biscuits/cakes	2.09	4.7	171
Breakfast and other cereals	0.92	2.1	256
Meat poultry	7.75	17.3	135
Fish/fish and chips	1.80	4.0	180
Butter	0.34	0.8	71
Margarine	0.20	0.4	87
Lard/fat	0.37	0.8	218
Milk/cream	3.35	7.5	156
Cheese	1.02	2.3	176
Eggs	0.49	1.1	100
Potatoes	1.45	3.2	207
Vegetables	2.60	5.8	194
Fruit	2.53	5.6	220
Sugar	0.29	0.6	94
Jam/syrup, etc.	0.20	0.4	143
Sweets/chocolate	1.14	2.5	158
Tea	0.54	1.2	154
Coffee	0.50	1.1	156
Cocoa/drinking chocolate, etc.	0.11	0.2	275
Soft drinks	1.19	2.7	248
Ice cream	0.33	0.7	194
Other foods	4.32	9.6	322
All food consumed at home	35.39	79.0	170
Meals out	9.42	21.0	219
Total*	**44.81**	**100.0**	**178**

Source: *Family Expenditure Survey*, HMSO 1992
Note: *12.0% of total weekly household expenditure as shown alongside

2.18) are major leisure activities. In these respects, the UK is unique in its dedication to home and garden improvements.

All of this activity is clearly exhausting, and in 1991, 54 per cent of adults took at least one holiday of 4+ nights (Table 2.19). Using this definition of 'a holiday', 54.25 million holidays were taken, 34 million in the UK, 20 million abroad.

Data from 1990 regarding overseas travel and tourism (Table 2.20) reveal that 21.3 million visits abroad were for holidays, a further 4.0 million were overseas visits to friends and relatives, and 5.0 million were overseas business visits. The UK has an unfavourable balance of trade in respect of holidays, since only 7.7 million holiday visits were made to this country – tourist boards please note.

I now turn to distribution in the UK, particularly to food distribution. The link is housewives' shopping habits, particularly in respect of grocery shopping.

Table 2.12: Regional variations in domestic food consumption in Great Britain

Regions	Percentage deviations from average consumption for GB			
Main food groups*	1970–75	1975–80	1989	1990
North				
Prepared fish	+44	+41	+34	+22
Flour	+50	+44	+38	+62
Yorkshire/Humberside				
Prepared fish	+76	+59	+56	+55
Cooking fats	+42	+35	+42	+58
Other fats, i.e excluding butter, margarine, lard	−18	−35	−18	−19
Wholewheat & wholemeal bread	−37	−47	−10	−15
Flour	+42	+31	+41	+55
North West				
Pork	-29	−23	−18	−19
East Midlands				
Cooking fats	+31	+30	+8	−8
West Midlands				
Poultry	+31	+26	+17	+12
Processed fish	−33	−31	−24	−33
South West				
Fresh green vegetabes	+23	+30	+26	+21
Wholewheat & wholemeal bread	+33	+69	+9	+15
Greater London				
Mutton & lamb	+47	+43	+48	+45
Poultry	+30	+32	+12	+10
Processed fish	+44	+56	+69	+12
Margarine	−33	−29	−36	−27
Other fats, i.e. excluding butter, margarine, lard	+39	+67	+24	+12
Fresh fruit	+30	+25	+16	+16
Wales				
Butter	+31	+22	+17	+14
Coffee	−27	−23	−23	−16
Scotland				
Beef & veal	+28	+40	+32	+34
Mutton & lamb	−56	−53	−50	−61
Pork	−57	−51	−17	−35
Poultry	−31	−28	−23	−20
Fresh fish	+61	+65	+51	+35
Prepared fish	−43	-49	−36	−27
Frozen fish	−54	-47	−43	−27
Fresh green vegetables	−54	−50	−40	−35
Wholewheat & wholemeal bread	−69	−38	−14	−10
Other bread, i.e. excl. standard white & brown	+115	+93	+29	+41
Flour	−47	−44	−27	−24
Oatmeal & oat products	+169	+138	+80	+92

Source: National Food Survey of the Ministry of Agriculture, Fisheries & Food, 1980 Report for
1970–80 data; 1989 Compendium of Results for 1989 data; 1990 Compendium of Results
for 1991 data

Note: *See original source for definitions

Table 2.13: Household penetration of consumer durables in Great Britain (percentage)

Measurement month in 1991		1987	1988	1989	1990	1991
Washing machine	Dec.	87	88	88	89	89
Clothes dryer	Dec.	45	45	44	44	43
Dishwasher	Dec.	8	9	11	13	14
Gas cooker, freestanding	Dec.	47	45	43	43	42
Electric cooker, freestanding	Dec.	37	37	37	36	37
Microwave oven	Dec.	36	44	48	52	55
Refrigerator, incl. fridge/freezers	Dec.	99	99	99	99	99
Separate freezer	Dec.	37	38	37	38	37
Fridge freezer	Dec.	44	47	49	50	52
Vacuum cleaner	June	98	98	98	98	97
Central heating system	March	73	75	78	80	82
Electric space heating	March	55	51	51	43	41
Gas space heating[1]	March	44	47	49	50	52
Oil/paraffin heater	March	6	5	5	3	3
Water heating	March	99	99	99	99	99
Shower fitment	March	40	41	43	46	46
Colour and/or monochrome television	June	98	98	98	98	98
Colour television	June	91	92	94	94	96
Television sets, two or more	June	50	50	52	55	55
Video recorder	June	49	51	58	62	69
Kitchen gadgets						
Coffee maker		35	–	–	–	–
Deep fat fryer		24	–	–	–	–
Electric toaster		55	–	–	–	–
Food mixer		52	–	–	–	–
Sandwich maker		37	–	–	–	–
Slow cooker		15	–	–	–	–
Loft insulation	Dec.	74	73	73	75	75
Cavity wall insulation	Dec.	12	13	14	15	16
Double glazed windows	Dec.	40	42	42	45	48
Power lawnmower	Sept.	62	63	64	64	62
Hand lawnmower	Sept.	14	14	11	10	9
Powered tool (saw/sander)	Sept.	32	47	33	34	35
Electric drill	Sept.	63	58	65	65	65
Car, one only		44	44	44	44[2]	–
Car, two or more		19	21	23	22[2]	–
Car, one or more		63	65	67	66[2]	–
Telephone	31st June	84	85	87	90	89

Sources: GfK Marketing Services Ltd ©; except Birds Eye Wall's/MAS Omnimas for kitchen gadgets, Dept. of Transport for cars, British Telecom for telephone (data refer to BT lines only)

Notes: [1]80% of households had a gas meter in 1991
[2]Estimate

Table 2.14: Equipment for leisure, hobbies and personal care

Portable Audio	% adults owning	Cameras	% adults owning
Radio	33.6	Still camera:	
Radio/Cassette recorder	32.5	110/126 instamatic cartridge	16.4
Cassette recorder	15.5	Instant Picture (Polaroid)	6.1
Headphone cassette player (no CD)	19.3	Compact	18.8
Headphone CD player	3.0	SLR with removable lens	13.8
		Other 35mm/roll	
Car Audio	*% households owning*	film cameras	30.1
Car radio, fixed	27.5	medium/large format cameras	1.1
Car cassette player	12.3	Video camera	5.2
Combined car radio/cassette player	38.2		
		Boats & caravans	*% households owning*
Computers, calculators,		Power boat	0.8
typewriters	*% adults owning*	Sailing boat	1.1
Home computer	29.1	Caravan, stationary or towable	4.9
Electric calculator	42.3	Motor caravan, camping vehicle, etc	0.8
Typewriter	24.5		
		Personal care	*% adults owning*
Sewing and knitting		Electric hairdryer	60.6
machines	*% adults owning*	Electric shaver, men's	34.5
Sewing machine	37.4	Electric shaver, ladies	14.8
Knitting machine	4.3		

Source: TGI April 1991–March 1992 (British Market Research Bureau)

Table 2.21 (April 1991–March 1992) reveals how eight institutions have come to dominate the retailing of food products.

DISTRIBUTION

The data In Table 2.22 show the number of shops and turnover by type of organisation. The multiples (defined as companies that have shops in many high streets or shopping centres) dominate food retailing, in 1990 having 75.7 per cent of all commodity turnover, having had only 44 per cent in 1971. This dominance is achieved using fewer shops than in 1971 (4,439 vs 10,973). Thus supermarketing has come to dominate the lives of British consumers, particularly in food, but as subsequent data will reveal, there are many other factors as well.

The ownership and relative strength of the grocery multiples are shown in Table 2.23. The fact that Britain has a grocery distributive system dominated by large supermarkets is illustrated in Table 2.24. The major supermarket chains have significant numbers of superstores.

Outside the field of grocery retailing, concentration is less marked, but in some sectors it is significant. In men's clothing (Table 2.25), the Burton Group (Burton, Top Man, Principles for Men) dominates. In women's and children's clothing (Table 2.26), the Burton Group again dominates (Evans, Top Shop, Dorothy Perkins, Principles, all belonging to that group). Thus the high street

Table 2.15: Clubs*

	Approx. no. of clubs, branches, units	Approx. no. of members
Working men's	3,480	5,000,000
Conservative	1,300	600,000
Liberal	150	60,000
Royal British Legion	3,500	735,500
Women's Institutes	9,000	310,000
Youth clubs	7,000	750,000
Scouts	10,500	700,000
Girl Guides	34,830	730,000
Chess	2,000	50,000
Bridge	1,240	42,300
Photographic	1,140	45,000
Operatic & dramatic	3,000	75,000
Folk, dance & song	600	46,500
Angling	1,665	435,000
Archery	1,200	20,000
Association football	45,650	2,650,000
Athletic	3,550	315,000
Badminton	4,225	87,300
Basketball	1,065	21,200
Billiards & snooker	8,000	1,500,000
Bowls	10,075	455,600
Boxing	990	35,000
Canoeing	460	15,900
Cricket	7,040	150,000
Cycling (racing & touring)	1,395	61,000
Fox-hunting	195	48,000
Gliding (excl. hang gliding)	85	10,000
Golf	5,620	1,140,000
Hang gliding	48	3,150
Hockey	2,035	90,000
Judo	1,000	50,000
Lawn tennis	2,800	253,000
Martial Arts (inc. karate)	5,000	61,600
Motor car sport	750	27,000
Mountaineering	260	18,750
Parachuting & parascending	140	45,500
Rambling	800	77,000
Rowing	525	28,600
Rugby union	2,810	283,500
Sailing (incl. yachting)	1,460	350,000
Skiing	195	21,750
Squash	1,730	315,000
Sub-aqua	1,300	45,000
Swimming	1,935	262,000
Table tennis	5,840	63,500
Waterskiing	168	14,300

Source: Associations concerned, July 1992
Note: *The reader is advised to regard these figures as informed estimates only.

Table 2.16: Leisure activities (percentage)

	All	Males	Females
Active sports, games & physical activities, 1986			
Outdoor			
Walking (2 miles or more) incl. rambling/hiking	19	21	18
Swimming (incl. public pools)	2	3	2
Football	3	6	—
Golf	3	5	1
Athletics field (incl. jogging) & track	3	4	1
Fishing	2	3	Ø
Cycling	2	2	1
Tennis	1	2	1
Bowls	1	1	1
Camping/caravanning	1	1	1
Horse riding	1	—	1
Cricket	1	1	—
Field sports	Ø	1	—
Sailing	Ø	1	—
Rugby	Ø	1	—
Motor sports	Ø	1	—
Indoor			
Snooker/billiards/pool	9	17	3
Swimming	9	9	10
Darts	6	9	3
Keep fit/yoga	3	1	5
Squash	2	4	1
Badminton	2	2	2
Table tennis	1	2	1
Bowls/tenpin	2	2	1
Gymnastics/athletics	2	3	1
Spectator sports,* 1986			
Outdoor			
Football	3	5	1
Rugby	1	1	—
Horse racing	1	1	1
Cricket	1	1	—
Motor sports	—	1	—
Entertainment, cultural, 1987			
Films	11	12	10
Theatre/ballet/opera	9	8	10
Classical music	2	2	3
Jazz, blues, soul, reggae	2	2	1
Other music shows	7	7	7
Museum/art galleries	8	9	8
Stately homes, castles, cathedrals etc.	8	8	8

Source: *General Household Survey*, published by HMSO
Notes: *Spectating excludes watching on television
          Ø Less than 0.5%

Table 2.17: DIY

DIY jobs done in last 12 months	% of adults 15+
Painted inside	56.9
Painted exterior woodwork	24.8
Painted exterior walls	10.8
Hung wallpaper	37.1
Put up shelves	21.8
Renovated furniture	7.6
Making and putting up cupboards	11.9
Stripping paint/varnish from furniture/furnishings	10.9
Hired DIY/gardening equipment	12.5

Source: TGI April 1991 – March 1992 (British Market Research Bureau).

Who chose materials/colours for last DIY task?	Total %	Men %	Women %
Respondent alone	31	11	48
Partner alone	15	28	3
Respondent & partner jointly	49	56	43
Respondent & someone else	2	1	2
Someone else alone	1	1	1
Daughter/son	2	1	2

Source: The Polycell 1987 Report on the Home Improvement Market (survey by Taylor Nelson).

shopper sees shops with many different names, but the ownership reality (and the buying power) lies with the Burton Group.

The same applies to footware retailing (Table 2.27), where the British Shoe Corporation owns Freeman Hardy Willis, Saxone, Dolcis, Cable, Manfield, Shoe City and Truform. Very few consumers are aware that all these shoe shops belong in fact to the same group.

The general situation is summarised in Table 2.28.

ADVERTISING

I want now to turn to the non-distributive aspects of marketing, and in particular to the marketing activity that many people see as the public face of the marketing business, namely advertising. The trends in expenditure on advertising are shown in Table 2.29. Advertising expenditures are expressed as percentages of the total in Table 2.30.

Figure 2.2 reveals a potential problem for the advertising industry in general, namely a decline in advertising expenditure as a percentage of gross national product (GNP) since 1990. We shall return to this 'problem' in a later section. Is it simply recession related, or is some more fundamental trend showing? The raw data behind this graph is shown in Table 2.31. Expenditures in 1992 were

Table 2.18: Gardening

Ownership of	% of adults 15+
Garden	85.2
Allotment	2.7
Grass	77.8
Flowers	77.0
Fruit	27.9
Vegetables	23.8

	% of households
Lawnmower, manual	11.4
Lawnmower, power – hover rotary	26.1
Lawnmower, power – other rotary	19.3
Greenhouse	14.7

Buying of	% of adults 15+ with garden
Seeds	42.7
Bulbs	40.9
Fertilisers	40.5
Weedkillers	34.1
Plants/trees/shrubs	43.6

Responsibility for upkeep	% of men	% of women
Main gardener	40.8	31.4
Equal main gardener	20.4	21.1
Not main gardener	23.0	31.7
Do not own garden/don't know	15.4	14.2

Source: TGI April 1991 – March 1982 (British Market Research Bureau).
Note: According to TGI in April 1991 – March 1992, size of garden and/or allotment among
             adults was as follows: under 2,000 sq. ft. 53.1%; 2,000–3,999 sq. ft. 17.7%; 4,000–9,999
             sq. ft. 6.5%; 10,000 or more sq. ft. 2.5%

1.52 per cent of GNP, just above the 1985 figure. These are deflated figures, so the inflationary element has been removed.

We may now examine some different media in a little more detail. National and regional newspapers are the most important press advertising vehicles. Trends in national newspaper advertising are shown in Table 2.32.

Trends in regional newspaper advertising are also available (Table 2.33). It should be noted that the amount of regional newspaper advertising is greater than national newspaper advertising. Compared with many other countries (particularly the USA) we tend to think that national newspapers dominate, but the figures reveal that the regional press is very healthy indeed, and a powerful vehicle for carrying advertising.

Readership of newspapers is an indicator of their power as vehicles for carrying advertising. The data in Table 2.34 show that 69 per cent of adults read

Table 2.19: Holidays taken by British people in 1991

	Total	Taken in Britain	Taken abroad[4]
Number of holidays[1][2]	54.25m	34.0m	20.0m
		%	%
Holiday arrangements[3]			
Inclusive		11	54
Independent		89	54
Holiday began in[3]			
May		10	9
June		12	11
July		18	15
August		23	13
September		14	15
Other months		23	37
Transport to reach destination[3]			
Car		78	—
Coach or bus		12	—
Train		6	—
Other		4	—
Plane		—	73
Boat		—	26
Hovercraft		—	1
Estimated expenditure, incl. cost of travel[1]	£15,980m	£ 4,670m	£11,310m
Average cost of holiday per person[3]		£137	£550

Source: BTA's British National Travel Survey (*BTNS*) 1991
Notes: [1]Four+ night holidays of adults and children accompanying them
[2]In 1991, 60% of adults (16+ years) took at least one holiday of 4+ nights (36%) took one, 24% two or more, 40% none)
[3]Holidays in Britain of 4+ nights, holidays abroad of 1+ nights
[4]74% of all overseas holidays were spent in Europe (Spain 23%, France 15%, Greece 7%, Italy 4%, Portugal 4%, West Germany 3%), 11% in North America (USA 9%, Canada 2%) and 18% elsewhere

a Sunday national, that the types of regional newspapers are complex and that free weeklies are the most powerful vehicle.

A British phenomenon is the proliferation of magazines. Britain must have the most varied fare of women's magazines in the world, as Table 2.35 illustrates. Even more astonishing is the variety of specialised journals (Table 2.36) – the British are catered to by magazine publishers to an extraordinary degree.

TELEVISION

National and regional newspaper advertising amounted to £2,749 million in 1991, television advertising amounted to £2,313 million. Readers may need to be reminded of the structure of the television industry in the UK, for which see Table 2.37.

Table 2.20: Overseas travel and tourism in 1990

	Overseas visitors to UK		Visits abroad by UK residents	
	'000	%	'000	%
Total all visits	18,021	100.0	31,182	100.0
Area of residence (inward) or visited (outward)				
Europe EC	9,222	51.2	22,535	72.3
W. Europe non-EC	1,658	9.2	2,849	9.1
N. America	2,772	15.4	2,321	7.4
Other countries	3,013	16.7	2,775	8.9
Mode of travel				
Air	12,814	71.1	21,474	68.9
Sea	5,207	28.9	9,708	31.1
Purpose of visit				
Holiday	7,700	42.7	21,255	68.2
Business	4,494	24.9	4,807	15.4
Visits to friends & relatives	3,616	20.1	3,963	12.7
Miscellaneous	2,211	12.3	1,157	3.7

Source: *Employment Gazette*, July 1992, published by HMSO. The tables are drawn from the results of the International Passenger Survey

Table 2.21: Grocery shopping habits: housewives (percentage)

Grocers shopped at for regular major shopping*		Frequency of regular major grocery shopping	
Sainsburys	27.2	Every day	4.1
Tesco	21.0	4–5 days a week	2.8
Asda	13.9	2–3 days a week	16.8
Safeway	12.4	Once a week	16.8
Kwik Save	11.3	Less often	13.1
Co-op	10.9		
Marks & Spencer	9.6	*Day(s) of regular major grocery*	
Gateway	9.0	*shopping**	
Milk delivery roundsman	8.0	Monday	6.6
Morrisons	4.2	Tuesday	9.4
Waitrose	3.6	Wednesday	9.5
Leos	2.7	Thursday	20.7
Lo-Cost	1.8	Friday	27.2
Wm Low	1.6	Saturday	15.5
Presto	1.3		
Spar/Vivo	1.3		
Cash & carry warehouse	1.0		
Budgens	0.7		
VG	0.7		
Grandways	0.6		
Any Mace line	0.3		

Source: TGI April 1991 – March 1992 (British Market Research Bureau)
Notes: *Some housewives named several grocers
         **Some housewives named several days

Table 2.22: The structure of the retail grocery trade in Great Britain

| | Number of shops | | % shares of all commodity turnover | |
	1971	1991	1971	1990
Co-operatives	7,745	2,545	13.2	10.3
Multiples	10,973	4,439	44.3	75.7
Independents	86,565	41,223	42.5	13.9
All Grocers	105,283	48,207	100.0	100.0

Source. A.C. Nielsen, Nielsen House, London Road, Oxford (1990)

Concentration:

Share of all commodity turnover – 1990	%
Top 2% of shops	53.6
Top 5% of shops	75.3
Top 10% of shops	85.2
Top 20% of shops	90.3

Source: A.C. Nielsen, Nielsen House, London Road, Oxford (1990)

Table 2.23: Some multiple retailers

Trade	Retailer	Approx. no. of branches
Grocers	Co-op (incl. 88 superstores and 1,549 supermarkets)	2,594
	Kwik Save Group; Kwik Save Stores (incl. Best of Cellars off-licences located within these stores) 780; free-standing Tates Late Shopper 75	855
	Argyll Group; Safeway 334; Presto, incl. Galbraith 215; Lo-Cost incl. Cordon Bleu 292	841
	Gateway Foodmarkets 502; Somerfield 62; Gateway Village 20; Food Giant 21; David Greig 4; Solo 64; Wellworth 33 (all Isosceles)	706
	Tesco Supermarkets & Superstores, incl. Home 'n' Wear	400
	Cost cutter, (incl. franchised)	380
	J. Sainsbury, (incl. 9 Savecentres)	328
	Asda Stores, (incl. 9 Savacentres)	206
	Waitrose (John Lewis Partnership)	102
	Budgens Stores (Barker & Dobson)	97
	Wm Low (52 in Scotland; 12 in England)	64
	Wm Morrison	60
	Grandways 29; Jacksons (convenience stores) 27 (William Jackson & Son)	56
	Walter Wilson	55
	Aldi	47
	Netto	31
	Betta Superettes	11

Source: AA/NTC (1993)

Table 2.24: Large grocery stores and grocery Superstores (Estimated number in Great Britain, March 1992)

	Large stores *10,000–24,999 sq. ft.*	*Superstores* *25,000 sq. ft. & over*
Asda	11	188
Budgens	12	—
Gateway	220	29
Wm. Jackson	11	1
Wm. Low	34	5
Wm. Morrison	9	47
Normans Superwarehouses	9	6
Safeway/Presto	245	76
J. Sainsbury	147	154
Savacentre*	—	9
Tesco	116	199
Waitrose**	85	—
Co-op (all societies)	195	75
Independents	13	6

Sources: Institute of Grocery Distribution Research Services
Notes: *Savacentre is now solely owned by Sainsbury; **Waitrose belongs to the John Lewis
         Partnership

Table 2.25: Clothing: men's

Retailer	No. of branches
Burton 439; Top Man 247; Principles for Men 180 (all Burton Group); the figures incl. 162 shops-in-shops	866
Fosters; Your Price (Fosters Menswear)	338
Greenwoods	232
Dunns/Hodges (Hodges)	151
Moss Bros 10; Cecil Gee 14; Suit Co 51; Savoy Taylors Guild 17; Beale & Inman 1; Dormie 8 (all Moss Bros) (excl. 8 concessions)	101
John Cheatle, incl. Juston, Rudge, Flex, Jeans Stations, Ellis of Burton	48
Horne Bros	38
Austin Reed (women's clothing also available in all stores)	36
Blazer (Storehouse)	24
Peter Brown (Etam), incl. shops-in-shops	22
Alexon excl. 167 concessions (Alexon International)	17
Co-op	5

Source: AA/NTC 1993

Television ownership is almost universal (96 per cent of households have colour TV) and Tables 2.38 and 2.39 show how both set ownership and broadcast vehicles are proliferating. The other data that are of interest relate to research data and hourly viewing data. The data in Table 2.40 and Figure 2.3 show conventional and satellite viewing.

Table 2.26: Clothing, women's, children's families

Retailer	No. of branches
Evans 257; Top Shop 237; Dorothy Perkins 533; Principles 216; (all Burton Group); the figures include 283 shops-in-shops	1,243
Miss Selfridge 97; Wallis 149; Adams 261; Warehouse 46 (all Sears)	553
Mothercare 259; Richards 223 (both Storehouse)	482
Etam, incl. 194 Etam; 60 SNOB; 181 Tammy (incl. shops-in-shops)	435
Benetton 230 incl. shops-in-shops, duty free etc; O–12 158, incl. concessions, Sisley 35, incl. concessions (all Benetton, all franchised)	423
Next (mainline stores 268; Directory Stores 44)	312
River Island Clothing Co (Lewis Trusts)	260
Mackay's Stores	215
Laura Ashley, incl. 59 shops-in-shops in Sainsbury's Homebase	178
Country Casuals, incl. shops-in-shops	155
Contessa (Courtaulds)	134
New Look	120
C&A	115
Ethel Austin	110
Dash 70; Sale Shops 38 (Alexon International); excl. concessions; 160 Dash; 16 Sale Shops; 207 Eastex	108
Bewise for All the Family	105
Qs Familywear	77
Jaeger 57; company-owned; 6 independent; Viyella 8 (all Coats Viyella), excl. 83 Jaeger; 84 Viyella shops-in-shops	71
Co-op	54

Sources: AA/NTC 1993

Table 2.27: Footwear

Retailer	No. of branches
British Shoe Corporation, incl. Freeman Hardy Willis; Saxone; Dolcis; Cable, Manfield; Shoe City, Truform etc.	1,837
Clarks International, incl. Clarks Shoes 395 (50 concessions); K Shoe Shops 226; Ravel 82 (3 concessions); Rohan 14	717
Olivers; Timpson (Olivers Group Plc)	447
Stead & Simpson	302
Barratts (Stylo Barratt Shoes), excl. 109 concessions and 66 Stylo Instep sports shoe outlets	242
Shoefayre, excl. shops-in-shops (Co-op)	235
A. Jones & Sons, incl. Jones Bootmaker; James Allen (in Scotland) and other trading names, excl. 59 Church shops-in-shops	103
Milwards	84
Shoesave 47; Terminus 2; Shoe Attraction (superstores) 4 (all British Bata)	53

Sources: AA/NTC 1993

Table 2.28: The retail trades in Great Britain (Analysis by broad business and form of organisation in 1989)

Kind of business and form of organisation*	Businesses Number	Outlets Number	Retail turnover[1] £m
Total retail trade	242,356	350,015	123,556
Single outlet retailers	215,736	215,736	33,551
Small multiple retailers	25,726	67,760	14,541
Large multiple retailers	894	66,520	75,464
Of which co-operative societies accounted for	89	4,207	5,248
Food retailers[2]	67,849	90,075	43,562
Single outlet retailers	61,469	61,469	7,546
Small multiple retailers	6,188	16,367	2,912
Large multiple retailers	191	12,238	33,104
Drink, confectionery and tobacco retailers	48,744	61,641	12,061
Single outlet retailers	46,382	46,382	7,076
Small multiple retailers	2,284	5,486	1,031
Large multiple retailers	78	9,773	3,954
Clothing, footwear and leather goods retailers	31,429	58,538	12,252
Single outlet retailers	26,393	26,393	2,898
Small multiple retailers	4,783	12,909	2,259
Large multiple retailers	253	19,236	7,095
Household goods retailers	48,735	69,599	20,371
Single outlet retailers	41,585	41,585	7,066
Small multiple retailers	6,978	18,030	4,126
Large multiple retailers	172	9,984	9,180
Other non-food retailers	39,156	52,543	11,323
Single outlet retailers	34,416	34,416	5,499
Small multiple retailers } Large multiple retailers }	4,739	18,126	5,824
Mixed retail businesses[2]	4,149	11,542	22,704
Single outlet retailers	3,429	3,429	3,301
Small multiple retailers	661	1,747	1,092
Large multiple retailers	58	6,365	18,311
Hire and repair businesses	2,294	6,079	1,283
Single outlet retailers	2,062	2,062	165
Small multiple retailers } Large multiple retailers }	233	4,018	1,118

Source: Business Statistics Office
Notes: [1]Inclusive of VAT.
      *Form of organisation: Small multiples have 2–9 outlets, large ones 10 or more.
      **Large retail business: 'Large' denotes businesses with retail turnover of £12m or more in 1989 £11m or more in 1988).
      [2]Mixed retail business: Where less than 80% of a business's sales, or 50% in the case of food retailing or hire and repair, fall into the main broad kinds of business, the business is classified as a mixed retail business.

Table 2.29: Total advertising expenditure, including direct mail, (£m)

	1991		1992
National newspapers	1,121		1,155
Regional newspapers	1,628		1,640
Consumer magazines	438		432
Business & professional	708		688
Directories	504		523
Press production costs	417		427
Total press		4,816	4,864
Television		2,313	2,478
Direct mail		895	945
Outdoor & transport		267	284
Radio		149	154
Cinema		42	45
Total		8,481	8,769

Source: The Advertising Association news release, London

Table 2.30: Total advertising expenditure, including direct mail, (% of total)

	1991		1992
National newspapers	13.2		13.2
Regional newspapers	19.2		18.7
Consumer magazines	5.2		4.9
Business & professional	8.3		7.8
Directories	5.9		6.0
Press production costs	4.9		4.9
Total press		56.8	55.5
Television		27.3	28.3
Direct mail		10.5	10.8
Outdoor & transport		3.1	3.2
Radio		1.8	1.8
Cinema		0.5	0.5
Total		100.0	100.0

Source: The Advertising Association news release, London

DIRECT MAIL

In 1992 £945 million was spent on direct mail advertising, a significant amount of money, and with the improvement of databases it would appear very likely that targeted mailings will become more powerful, with the corresponding possibility that television advertising will become less so. See also Table 2.41.

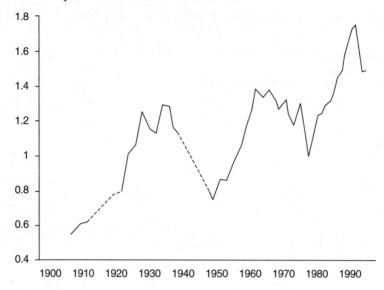

Figure 2.2 Advertising as a percentage of gross national product, 1907–92

Source: The Advertising Association News Release

MARKET RESEARCH

The reader may ask where much of the data that have been exposed to this point are generated. The UK has an extremely professional market research industry, indeed it is probably the world leader in the quality and professionalism of those engaged in it.

Table 2.42 shows how much is spent on commissioning market research – £266 million in 1991 (Association of Market Survey Organisations members spend approximately two-thirds of the total spend), together with the fields that are the focus of market research. Finally, the data reveal that personal interviewing remains the central plank of data and information gathering.

THE TOP ADVERTISERS

Having reviewed advertising expenditures, the vehicles that carry advertising and the commercial intelligence gathering industry, we can now look at who spends the money on advertising. The effectiveness of this advertising spend is, of course, the subject of considerable interest. Companies do not usually spend money without asking whether it is producing some sort of return. Market research is used to ascertain brand and advertising awareness, so, in a list of the top 100 advertisers, we are looking at companies that spend the large amounts of money that support the advertising industry. We must ask whether they spend this money with no concern for what that money is bringing them

Table 2.31: Total advertising expenditure and its relation to consumers' expenditure and gross national product

Year	Total expenditure in 1985 prices *a* £m	Total expenditure in current prices £m	Total expenditure as a percentage of:	
			consumers expenditure *b* at market prices	gross national product *b* at factor cost
1975	2,704	976	1.48	1.01
1976	2,862	1,205	1.57	1.06
1977	3,123	1,524	1.73	1.17
1978	3,540	1,869	1.85	1.24
1979	3,651	2,187	1.82	1.25
1980	3,683	2,604	1.87	1.30
1981	3,646	2,884	1.86	1.31
1982	3,740	3,211	1.88	1.34
1984	4,108	3,689	1.97	1.40
1984	3,332	4,188	2.10	1.47
1985	4,608	4,608	2.12	1.49
1986	5,145	5,321	2.21	1.61
1987	5,622	6,055	2.29	1.67
1988	6,235	7,044	2.36	1.75
1989	6,426	7,827	2.39	1.77
1990	5,914	7,885	2.26	1.64
1991	5,368	7,577	2.06	1.52

Source: Advertising Association's *Advertising Statistics Yearbook 1992*, tables 2.1; 3.1.1; 3.1.2. See this source for definitions

Notes: *a*Figures in this column are obtained by deflating the current price figures by the Retail Price Index

*b*Due to revisions made by the Central Statistical Office to GNP and consumer's' expenditure data – often going back many years – the ratios given in this table may differ slightly from ratios given in previous years

Table 2.32: Breakdown of national newspaper advertising by type of publication (£m)

	1986	1987	1988	1989	1990	1991
Daily	499	560	639	704	688	650
Sunday	345	399	460	518	500	471
Popular	412	455	521	589	591	595
Quality	433	504	579	633	596	526
Newsprint sections	702	794	903	992	969	918
Colour supplements	142	165	196	230	218	203
Total	**844**	**959**	**1,099**	**1,222**	**1,187**	**1,121**

Source: The Advertising Association's *Advertising Statistics Yearbook 1992*, table 5.6.1

Table 2.33: Breakdown of regional newspaper advertising by type of publication (£m)

	1986	1987	1988	1989	1990	1991
Daily and Sunday	544	605	701	781	781	720
Weekly paid for	243	270	321	339	334	325
Weekly free	314	405	522	587	601	584
Total	**1,101**	**1,280**	**1,544**	**1,707**	**1,715**	**1,628**

Source: The Advertising Association's *Advertising Statistics Yearbook 1992*, table 5.7.1

Table 2.34: Readership of press groups

Newspapers	Av period	%	Magazines	Av period	%
Any national morning	weekday	60	Any general weekly	Week	41*
Any national Sunday	week	70	Any general monthly	month	42
Any regional evening	weekday	28	Any women's weekly	week	47 (women)
Any regional morning	weekday	11[#]	Any women's monthly	month	47 (women)
Any regional weekly (paid)	week	39[#]			
Any regional weekly (free)	week	79[#]			

Sources: National Readership Survey, July 1991–June 1992; [#]TGI 1992
Note: *Includes listings magazines

Table 2.35: Press: women's titles

Title	Issue frequency	circulation (,000)	Title	Issue frequency	circulation (,000)
Take a Break	w	3,792	Family Circle	m	1,039
Woman's Own	w	3,092	Sugar	m	1,024
Bella	w	2,641	Elle	m	935
Woman	w	2,388	She	m	935
Woman's Weekly	w	1,930	Essentials	m	906
Best	w	1,891	House and Garden	m	863
Hello!	w	1,877	Clothes Show Mag	m	762
Chat	w	1,608	Country Living	m	594
My Weekly	w	1,306	Needlecraft	m	507
The People's Friend	w	1,086	Practical Parenting	m	481
Woman's Realm	w	1,007	Country Homes and Interiors	m	466
That's Life	w	733	Slimming	m	462
OK!	w	293	BBC Homes and Antiques	m	434
The Lady	w	201	Woman's Journal	m	417
More!	f	1,049	Health and Fitness Mag	m	385
Inside Soap	f	513	Harpers and Queen	m	375
Mizz	f	420	Options	m	334
A Taste of Safeway	m	1,848	Perfect Home	m	321
Good Housekeeping	m	1,811	BBC Veg Good Food	m	311
Cosmopolitan	m	1,690	Home and Country	m	304
Prima	m	1,533	Pregnancy and Birth	m	293
The Somerfield Mag	m	1,475	Vanity Fair	m	277
Marie Claire	m	1,468	Tatler	m	269
Vogue	m	1,375	Parents	m	240
Ideal Home	m	1,338	Inspirations	m	237
BBC Good Food	m	1,144	Elle Decoration	m	201
Woman and Home	m	1,082	World of Interiors	m	197
Just Seventeen	m	1,060	Here's Health	m	127

Source: National Readership Survey July 1996–June 1997
Note: This table is merely representative of the market and does not contain every available title.

Table 2.36: Press: Some consumer specialised journals

	Issue frequency	Circulation[1]	Adult readership[2] '000	%	Page rates[3] £	£
Angling & Fishing						
Angler's Man	W	81,535	429	1	1,590	2,500
Angling Times	W	100,389	696	2	3,644	4,410
Sea Angler	M	50,016	—	—	826	1,532
Trout & Salmon	M	50,404	286	1	1,130	2,007
Boating, Yachting, Nautical						
Motor Boat & Yachting	M	24,858	182	—	1,090	2,290
Practical Boat Owner	M	59,246	313	1	1,112	1,960
Yachting Monthly	M	42,752	260	1	1,134	2,120
Yachting World	M	28,758	192	—	1,164	2,175
Camping & Caravanning						
Camping & Caravanning	M	96,804**	—	—	893	1,434
Caravan Magazine	M	27,512**	—	—	835	1,425
En Route	8 pa	283,921**	—	—	2,700	3,885
Children's Comics						
Bunty	W	—#	—	—	400	600
Care Bears	F	16,392	—	—	—	680
Look-in	W	84,898	—	—	1,340	1,900
Thunderbirds	F	94,468	—	—	1,800	2,000
2000 AD	W	81,989	—	—	1,800	2,000
Cinema, Film & Theatre						
Empire	M	98,185	266	1	2,520	3,950
Film Monthly	M	—#	—	—	648	837
Film Review	M	23,846**	—	—	1,080	1,560
Flicks	M	—#	560	1	2,270	2,700
Current Affairs & Politics						
Business Magazine	M	—#	—	—	975	1,225
The Economist	W	282,003	459	1	3,450	6,100
Investors Chronicle	W	47,061	152	—	2,950	4,100
New Scientist	W	195,449	410	1	2,700	3,885
New Statesman & Society	W	22,613**	—	—	1,200	1,600
D.I.Y.						
Do It Yourself	M	37,538**	486	1	2,095	2,778
Practical Householder	M	39,017**	261	1	2,129	2,821
Practical Woodworking	M	41,807	249	1	1,060	1,570
Gardening						
Amateur Gardening	W	91,347	544	1	1,670	2,585
BBC Gardener's World	M	371,524	1,662	4	2,300	4,000
Garden News	W	106,702	403	1	3,633	5,586
Practical Gardening	M	111,181	1,121	3	1,644	2,860
Health						
Here's Health	M	28,753**	—	—	1,395	1,870
The Vitamin Connection	BM	21,925**	—	—	1,250	1,800

Table 2.36: (Continued) Press: Some consumer specialised journals

	Issue frequency	Circulation [1]	Adult readership [2]		Page rates [3]	
			'000	%	£	£
Hi-Fi						
Gramophone	M	72,487**	—	—	896	2,106
Hi-Fi Choice	M	28,619	—	—	976	1,951
Hi-Fi News & Record Review	M	30,013**	276	1	1,055	2,606
What Hi-Fi?	M	68,395	664	2	1,820	4,060
Home Computing						
Computer & Video Games	M	96,846	—	—	1,100	1,650
Crash	M	—#	—	—	885	1,200
Mean Machines	M	122,854	—	—	1,200	1,620
Micro User	M	17,303	—	—	800	1,030
Men's Magazines						
Escort	M	—#	—	—	2,650	2,650
Fiesta	M	257,268	594	1	3,375	3,375
Knave	M	97,427	296	1	2,200	2,200
Mayfair	M	—#	510	1	2,500	2,500
Men Only	M	—#	—	—	2,500	2,500
Penthouse	M	—#	436	1	2,000	2,750
Motor Cycling						
Bike	M	63,915	316	1	1,040	1,965
Classic Bike	M	60,931**	433	1	945	1,760
Motorcycle International	M	38,577**	—	—	785	1,560
Motorcycle News	W	128,007	685	2	2,664	3,443
Performance Bikes	M	78,343	519	1	1,150	2,070
Superbike	M	39,971**	380	1	835	1,292
Motoring						
Autocar & Motor	W	90,015**	554	1	2,090	4,350
Car	M	132,248**	720	2	2,642	5,937
Car Mechanics	M	33,839**	368	1	995	1,995
Classic & Sportscar	M	88,710	521	1	1,500	2,950
Classic Cars	M	90,029	1,252	3	1,375	3,025
Custom Car	M	34,079**	506	1	1,130	2,533
Motor Sport	M	38,319	808	2	605	1,575
Performance Car	M	55,059	806	2	1,265	2,849
Practical Motorist	M	—*	—	—	917	1,680
Street Machine	M	56,290**	557	1	1,100	2,420
What Car?	M	144,442	2,085	5	2,850	5,900
Personal Finance						
Money Observer	M	31,892	—	—	1,700	2,500
Moneywise	M	81,314	227	1	2,715	3,360
What Investment?	M	—#	—	—	1,947	2,172
Photography						
Amateur Photographer	W	48,331	376	1	1,130	2,250
Photo Answers	M	65,149	167	—	958	1,920
Practical Photography	M	111,295	714	2	1,355	2,695

Table 2.36: (Continued) Press: Some consumer specialised journals

	Issue frequency	Circulation[1]	Adult readership[2]		Page rates[3]	
			'000	%	£	£
Sport						
Athletics	W	16,500**	—	—	542	741
Cricketer International	M	34,544**	—	—	886	1,295
Cycling Weekly	W	36,902**	—	—	880	1,350
Golf Monthly	M	95,632	1,080	2	1,685	2,825
Golf World	M	89,923	662	2	1,865	3,065
Horse & Hound	W	79,436	351	1	1,480	2,700
Rugby World and Post	M	43,556**	—	—	825	1,390
Running Magazine	M	45,340**	219	1	1,395	1,995
Shoot	W	145,020	505	1	1,270	2,025
Sporting Gun	M	34,182	310	1	694	1,412
Sporting Life Weekender	W	24,065	—	—	1,200	—
Tennis World	M	11,545	—	—	675	1,150
Teenage & Pop Music						
The Face	M	80,517	327	1	2,090	3,600
I-D	M	—#	—	—	1,000	1,600
Kerrang	W	45,504	280	1	1,450	2,050
Melody Maker	W	68,596	407	1	1,985	3,925
New Musical Express	W	116,415	646	1	2,285	4,950
Q	M	161,104	627	1	3,550	5,700
Smash Hits	F	368,258	1,195	3	7,780	13,300
Sky Magazine	M	125,055	1,063	2	4,100	5,100
Vox	M	114,213	431	1	1,600	2,500
Video						
Video World	M	22,871**	—	—	1,000	1,400
What Video?	M	42,616	—	—	995	1,535

Sources: (1) ABC data January–June 1992
(2) National Readership Survey, July 1991–July 1992
(3) British Rate and Data August 1992, r.o.m./single insertion rate
*No figures supplied for audit period
**January–December 1991
#Uncertified

Note: The space available allows us to show only a small proportion of existing titles. Inclusion of a title does not imply any preference over those not shown

by way of a return on advertising investment. The top ten advertisers' expenditures in the UK appear in Table 2.43. Some of their subsidiaries are also listed in Table 2.44. It is worth noting that HM Government is the third largest advertiser.

The top 100 advertisers' expenditures in the UK are shown in Table 2.44. Unilever (see Table 2.43) is a holding company involved in a wide range of products – food, cosmetics, cleaning products. Procter and Gamble are primarily in cleaning and personal care products. (HM Government is, of course, into

Table 2.37: Current developments in television

| ITC | Since 1st January 1991 the Independent Television Commission has been responsible for controlling all aspects of independent commercial TV in the UK, taking over the previous responsibilities of the IBA and the Cable Authority. The ITC is located at 70, Brompton Road, London SW3 1EY. Tel. 0171-584 7011. |

Terrestrial television

Channel 3 (ITV)	Channel 3 is split into 14 regions, in each of which one contractor has the sole right to broadcast TV programmes, and sell advertising between 9.25am and 5.59am the following day. The sole exception to this is London, which is shared between two contractors one of which has the weekday (Mon–Fri) contract and the other the weekend (Friday evening–Sunday).
	Each contractor holds his licence for around 10 years. The last re-allocation was in 1991, when licences were awarded on a tender basis to the highest bidder, subject to a quality threshold. 10 licences remained with their existing contractors and 4 changed hands, those for the South and South-east (from TVS to Meridian), the South-west (from TSW to Westcountry TV), the London weekday service (from Thames to Carlton), and the breakfast service (6.00–9.24am).
	Programme schedules on Channel 3 stations are broadly similar at present, with about 70% of programming being the same for all stations at the same time, particularly in peak-time. From January 1993 this situation will be consolidated, with the appointment of a network scheduler.
	Most areas broadcast for the full 20.5 hours a day to which they are entitled. Advertising minutage is an average of seven minutes an hour, with a maximum of seven-and-a-half minutes in peak time.

| Channel 4 | Channel 4 is a statutory corporation operating under licence from the ITC with a remit to be complementary to (and different from) Channel 3. It is responsible for commissioning its own programming (it has no product facilities of its own) and (from January 1993) for selling its own advertising. If its advertising revenue falls below 14% of total terrestrial advertising, Channel 3 is responsible for contributing up to 2% more, and if it rises above 14%, C4 has to pay 50% of the surplus to Channel 3. In 1991 C4 took 14.9% of ITV advertising revenue, and 18.7% of ITV audiences. |

| Channel 5 | Channel 5 is a new commercial terrestrial channel which is scheduled to start broadcasting in 1993. The licence for the channel was advertised in 1992, but only one application was received, from Channel 5 Holdings, and so far no licence has been awarded. Potential obstacles to the new channel include the obligation to re-tune all VCRs, incomplete cover of the UK, and financial uncertainty. |

| S4C | The Welsh language channel, S4C, is broadcast on the C4 frequency in Wales (part of the Wales and West area). It started at the same time as C4, and differs from that channel in that it carries a high proportion of Welsh language programming. Programmes carried by both C4 and S4C are often broadcast at different times. |

| Breakfast TV | The licence for the national breakfast TV service on Channel 3 was awarded to GMTV in 1991 (previously held by TV-am) and will take effect in January 1993. From this date, C4 will take responsibility for its own breakfast-time service and advertising sales. |

| Teletext | Teletext UK Ltd were awarded the franchise for teletext services on ITV. The service will take over from Oracle Teletext on 1st January 1993. |

Cable television

| | Cable penetration in the UK is still low, although growing fast. In July 1992, 2.4% of all homes were connected to cable systems (23% of homes passed) of which over half (15% of all homes) were connected to new broadband systems. There are now 32 franchises with more than 2,500 subscribers (19 in 1991), and licences have been issued for areas which cover more than half the country. |

Table 2.37: (Continued) Current developments in television

The largest operators are:

| Operator | Homes | | Penetration |
	Passed	Connected	%
Videotron	263,853	62,728	23.8
Telewest	229,350	53,712	23.4
Comcast	119,211	37,417	31.4
CUC Cablevision	99,917	34,920	34.9

Advertising and sponsorship — Advertising and sponsorship on all TV channels in the UK are controlled by the ITC, under codes of Advertising Standards, Programme Sponsorship, and Rules on Advertising Breaks published in January 1991. These codes apply to both ITV and satellite broadcasters, and incorporate elements of previous rules established by the IBA and the Cable Authority, as well as the European Directive on Television Broadcasting.

Direct broadcasting by satellite

DBS is the name given to television transmissions via medium-to-high-powered satellites which can be received on dishes of less than 1 metre diameter, suitable for private homes. It has been available in the UK since February 1989, when SKY TV started broadcasting on the Astra satellite.

There are currently 3 direct-to-home (DTH) satellites providing English-language programmes: Astra 1a, Astra 1b and Marcopolo 1, Marcopolo provides a duplicate service of the 6 BSkyB channels for homes with squarial receivers.

	Astra 1a	*Astra 1b*
BSkyB channels	Sky One	Sky Sports
	Sky News	The Movie Channel
	Sky Movies Plus	Sky Movies Gold
Other English language	Children's Channel	Adult Channel
	Eurosport	Children's Channel
	Lifestyle	CNN
	MTV Europe	MTV Europe
	Satellite Juke-box	
	Screensport	

Source: AA/NTC 1993

everything and is not included in Table 2.44). The list in Table 2.44 is a mirror to our behaviour as consumers.

Perhaps lost in the detail of the statistics that have been presented thus far, is the reality of the UK's comparative standing *vis-à-vis* our European, trans-Atlantic and trans-Pacific neighbours. Measures of comparative well-being are generally unsatisfactory. Nevertheless, and to complete the record, the per capita GNP for the first seventeen rank ordered countries is shown in Table 2.45. Average Britons may take small comfort from knowing that they had in 1991 almost exactly half the per capita income of Switzerland and Luxembourg.

The source of this *relative* poverty would have to be the subject of an extensive analysis of economic trends in the last thirty years. The figures in Table 2.46 are however worthy of attention.

Table 2.38: Television establishment data

	1987	1988	1989	1990	1991	1992
TV ownership & reception capabilities						
TV households penetration (%)						
2 sets	34	33	34	32	34	35
3+ sets	11	12	13	13	13	15
Colour TV	88	89	90	95	92	96
Teletext	18	21	27	32	34	40
Remote control	42	47	54	59	63	69
VCR	41	48	54	59	62	65

Source: BARB Establishment Survey, March each year

All cable (%)						
Homes passed	5.87	6.59	6.96	7.73	9.29	10.78
Homes connected	0.97	1.24	1.32	1.57	1.90	2.45
Broadband cable (%)						
Homes passed	0.99	1.60	2.32	3.03	4.51	6.95
Homes connected	0.12	0.23	0.32	0.48	0.85	1.47

Sources: JICCAR/ITC. July each year

All direct to home satellite system (%)						
Direct to Home Satellite dishes/SMATV				4.25	7.2	11.13

Source: Continental Research, July each year

Table 2.39: Cable and satellite universe

	DtH '000	Cable '000	DtH & Cable penetration % of households
Astra			
Sky One	2,511	541	13.5
Sky News	2,511	441	13.0
Sky Movies	1,990	262	9.9
Sky Sports	2,511	433	13.0
The Movie Channel	1,430	161	7.0
Eurosport	2,511	330	12.5
Screensport	2,511	313	12.4
Lifestyle	2,511	321	12.2
Childrens Channel	2,511	399	12.8
MTV	2,511	399	12.8
CNN	2,240	295	11.2
Others			
Super Channel	—	333	1.5
Discovery	—	340	1.5
Bravo	—	277	1.2
Landscape	—	230	1.0

Sources: Y&R estimates/ITC. September 1992
Note: All figures refer to domestic reception, and exclude hotels, offices etc

Table 2.40: Television reach data

All TV Homes	Daily reach (%)				Weekly reach (%)			
	Men	Women	H'wives	Children*	Men	Women	H'wives	Children*
All TV	74.8	77.9	79.9	69.5	91.9	93.3	93.6	92.6
BBC1	60.6	63.9	66.1	53.1	89.1	90.4	91.1	88.0
BBC2	35.0	30.9	33.7	17.7	78.4	76.3	78.8	60.4
ITV (inc. TV-am)	62.1	66.6	68.1	56.2	89.6	90.7	91.1	89.8
C4/S4C	33.0	34.0	35.7	26.6	74.5	76.1	77.3	71.9

Source: BARB. Week ending 14th June 1992

Astra Receiving Homes	Daily reach (%)				Weekly reach (%)			
	Men	Women	H'wives	Children*	Men	Women	H'wives	Children*
All TV	78.6	79.8	83.8	70.1	94.9	94.6	95.4	92.1
BBC1	58.0	60.7	64.6	40.8	91.3	89.7	92.0	84.2
BBC2	29.4	25.6	28.1	12.2	71.9	70.7	72.7	44.7
Total BBC	62.6	54.7	68.6	44.1	92.5	90.8	92.7	85.8
ITV (inc. TV-am)	60.8	64.7	68.5	43.5	92.7	89.2	91.6	86.0
C4\S4C	28.6	28.6	31.6	15.0	72.6	71.0	76.9	52.6
Total ITV/C4	64.9	67.8	71.7	47.7	93.5	90.3	82.8	89.7
Sky One	19.4	22.3	23.7	35.2	52.5	54.2	54.4	69.8
Sky News	12.2	8.9	10.5	2.5	33.7	28.3	30.4	12.1
Sky Movies	18.0	15.0	16.2	10.4	44.7	40.2	41.6	36.4
The Movie Channel	12.1	11.1	11.5	7.9	33.3	34.0	32.7	25.2
Sky Sports	15.9	9.4	11.3	7.0	46.3	34.2	37.0	31.9
Comedy Channel	1.6	0.3	1.7	2.4	8.4	8.3	8.5	9.1
Childrens Channel	3.3	4.0	4.5	15.4	11.1	11.3	11.9	36.6
MTV	9.1	7.9	6.8	5.9	27.7	26.3	23.7	23.1
Lifestyle	8.5	7.1	7.4	3.2	29.5	24.6	26.8	14.5
Screensport	8.4	4.7	5.3	2.2	28.7	21.7	24.7	12.7
Others	21.6	13.6	15.6	7.4	53.4	41.2	45.6	28.2

Source: BARB. Week ending 14th June 1992
Note: *Individuals aged 4–13

The data in Table 2.46 suggest that in respect of industrial employment, the UK is very like Ireland, and very unlike Germany with a much higher percentage of employment in this sector. In respect of agriculture, the UK is very efficient in the sense that the low level of employment in the sector is a reflection of the modernisation and mechanisation of British agriculture, compared particularly with Ireland. Of the five countries examined, the UK has the highest employment in services, primarily white-collar rather than blue-collar employment. Although tourism and servicing of visitors is significant in the UK, those who would argue that we are still a nation of shopkeepers could arm themselves with these data. Manufacturing has had a continuously declining importance in the UK's economic life over the last decade. I do not rush to judge in these

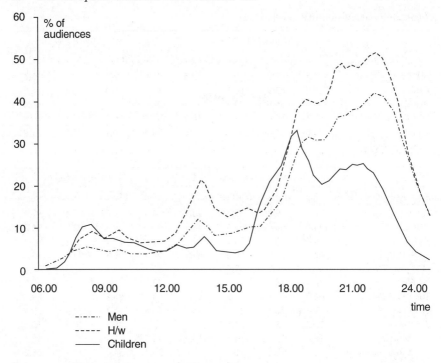

Figure 2.3 Television viewing patterns

Source: BARB. Average weekday May 1992 all channels

Table 2.41: Direct mail

The average British Household receives just under six items of direct mail per month. Direct mail is defined as personally addressed advertising that is delivered through the post. Direct mail suppliers will provide quotations on request. Prices can vary dramatically with volume and type of material. Specimen charges range as follows

Service	Cost per '000
List rental cost by type:	
• Consumer list (responders/purchasers)	£70+
• Consumer lifestyle database	£75+
• Electoral register – geodemographic selection	£50+
• Named subscribers to business magazines	£80+
• Companies classified by SIC code	£80+
Laser printing	£12–£30
Inserting 1–2 items by machine	£10–£12
3–4 items by machine	£12–£16

Source: Direct Mail Information Service

Table 2.42: Expenditure on market research

Value of GB commissioned market research:

	1986	1987	1988	1989	1990	1991
AMSO members' turnover (£m)	152	177	207	230	265	266

The AMSO accounts for more than two-thirds of all market research conducted in the UK.

AMSO members' source of income by client's business 1991:

	£m	%		£m	%
Food/soft drinks	51.7	+2	Advertising agencies	9.8	−8
Media	24.3	−1	Retailers	7.7	−12
Public services and utilities	21.6	+6	Household products	7.7	+74
Alcoholic drinks	21.0	+9	Travel land tourism	6.8	−9
Health and beauty aids	19.0	+7	Oil	3.8	+32
Financial services	14.3	+1	Tobacco	3.5	+5
Vehicle manufacturers	13.9	−13	Household durables/hardware	2.9	+8
Government (central and local)	13.2	+21	Other direct clients	19.3	−11
Pharmaceutical companies	12.4	−7	Other AMSO companies (mainly		
Business and industrial	11.4	−4	subcontracted fieldwork)	1.5	−7

Nature of AMSO members' fieldwork (%):

	1990	1991		1990	1991
Personal interview	55	55	Hall test	10	12
Telephone interview	17	15	Group discussion	10	10
Self-completion survey	8	8			

Source: Association of Market Survey Organisations, 1992

matters however. The creation of services can add value quite as effectively as manufacturing. The UK remains a major international capital investor, which means that UK companies manufacture all over the world.

It is, however, a cause for concern that our domestic industrial base is significantly smaller than that in the Federal Republic of Germany. It is a statement about the UK's international competitiveness.

Great care must be exercised in making judgements about relative industrial decline. The interested reader is directed to Newman and Foster (1993) in the bibliography. Some indicative data are provided in Tables 2.47, 2.48, 2.49 and 2.50.

THE MARKETING PROCESS

Current trends

Analysis of trends is an attempt to foresee pattern. However, trends are by definition transitory (a contradiction in terms?). What may seem today to be a significant trend may, within months, seem to be nothing of the sort. That is the

Table 2.43: Top holding companies' advertising expenditure, 1991

Holding company	Subsidiaries expenditure, £'000	Total expenditure TV, press & radio £'000
1 Unilever	Lever Brothers 63,045; Elida Gibbs 31,177; Birds Eye Wall's 26,491; Brooke Bond Foods 25,640; Van den Berghs & Jurgens 19,367; Rimmel International 2,578; John West Foods 1,439; Parfums International 1,333; Mattessons Wall's 1,207; Elizabeth Arden 638; Unipath 552	173,469
2 Procter & Gamble	Procter & Gamble 62,494; Procter & Gamble (Health & Beauty Care) 41,207; Max Factor 3,535; Hair Care 10	107,245
3 HM Government	Dept. of Employment 15,670; Dept. for National Savings 8,823; Home Offices 6,578; Ministry of Defence 6,3440; Health Education Authority 5,860; Dept. of Health 5,609; Board of Inland Revenue 5,082; Dept. of Education and Science 3,480; Dept. of Transport 2,622; English Tourist Board 1,953; Dept. of Trade and Industry 1,457; Scottish Information Office 1,168; Office of Population Censuses and Surveys 800; Welsh Development Agency 800	75,518
4 Nestlé Holdings (UK)	Nestlé Company 39,830; Rowntree Mackintosh 29,928	69,758
5 Mars (GB)	Mars Confectionery 32,801; Pedigree Petfoods 25,679; Master Foods 6,843	65,324
6 Kingfisher Plc	B&Q 20,677. Woolworths 15,849; Comet Group 14,835; Superdrug Stores 3,995; Charlie Browns Autocentres 455; Kingfisher 11	55,821
7 Kellogg	Kellogg Company of Great Britain 52,506	52,506
8 Ford Motor Company	Ford Motor Company 47,130; Jaguar Cars 2,802; Ford New Holland 4	49,937
9 British Telecommunications	British Telecommunications 46,653; Mitel Telecom 8	46,662
10 Boots Company	Boots Company 22,516; Crookes Healthcare 11,450; Childrens World 1,242	35,208

Source: Register-MEAL

nature of marketing dynamics. It is with this caveat that I comment on current trends in marketing in the United Kingdom.

The marketing concept

The marketing concept has been around for thirty years, at least it was in the early 1960s that many sales directors decided it was time to call themselves marketing directors, although that act alone made little difference to their behaviour and attitudes.

Table 2.44: The top 100 advertisers, 1991

			Advertising expenditure		
Rank	Advertiser*	Total £'000	TV %	Radio %	Press %
1	Lever Brothers	63,045	81.1	0.5	18.4
2	Procter & Gamble	62,494	98.2	0.5	1.3
3	Kellogg Company of GB	52,506	96.0	0.8	3.2
4	Ford	47,130	54.2	2.4	43.4
5	British Telecommunications	46,653	69.1	2.7	28.2
6	Procter & Gamble (Health & Beauty Care)	41,207	96.5	1.0	2.5
7	Nestlé	39,830	87.5	0.9	11.6
8	Vauxhall (General Motors)	34,339	39.5	1.3	59.3
9	Mars Confectionery	32,801	94.0	0.4	5.7
10	Kraft General Foods	32,188	91.3	0.1	8.6
11	Elida Gibbs (Unilever)	31,177	75.5	0.1	24.4
12	Rowntree Mackintosh (Nestlé)	29,928	96.3	0.3	3.4
13	Citroën (UK)	28,172	22.7	0.3	77.0
14	British Gas	27,729	59.8	1.0	39.2
15	Gallaher Tobacco (American Brands)	27,348	11.9	0.2	87.9
16	Rover Group (BAE)	27,109	46.2	1.3	52.5
17	Birds Eye Wall's (Unilever)	26,491	87.5	—	12.5
18	Peugeot Talbot	25,774	30.0	0.1	69.9
19	Pedigree Petfoods (Mars)	25,679	98.2	—	1.8
20	Brooke Bond Foods (Unilever)	25,640	69.2	0.4	30.4
21	Dixons	25,541	11.8	0.1	88.1
22	Cadbury (Cadbury-Schweppes)	24,703	98.9	0.7	0.4
23	Renault (UK)	24,354	51.2	2.7	46.1
24	National Westminster Bank	24,173	61.8	0.8	37.4
25	Halifax Building Society	23,820	29.6	0.2	70.2
26	Bass Brewers (Bass)	22,635	85.0	1.5	13.4
27	Boots	22,516	28.0	—	72.0
28	Imperial Tobacco	21,266	31.7	—	68.3
29	Tesco	21,139	49.3	0.2	50.4
30	B&Q (Kingfisher)	20,677	27.3	0.4	72.2
31	VAG (UK)	20,649	42.2	0.7	57.1
32	McDonald's	20,304	91.5	8.4	0.1
33	Abbey National	19,848	31.1	1.6	67.3
34	Van de Berghs & Jurgens (Unilever)	19,367	66.2	—	33.8
35	Nationwide Building Society	18,620	23.7	5.1	71.2
36	MFI Furniture	17,603	6.5	—	93.5
37	Barclays Bank	16,920	48.9	0.3	50.8
38	Post Office	16,726	73.4	2.5	24.1
39	Texas Homecare (Ladbroke)	16,555	14.6	2.0	83.5
40	Book Club Associates	16,228	—	—	100.0
41	Woolworths (Kingfisher)	15,849	56.0	0.1	43.8
42	Co-operative Retail Services	15,759	10.8	4.4	84.8
43	Department of Employment	15,670	42.5	0.6	56.9
44	Fiat Auto (UK)	15,589	12.6	1.4	85.9
45	British Railways Board	15,466	49.3	5.6	45.1

Table 2.44: (Continued) The top 100 advertisers, 1991

Rank	Advertiser*	Total £'000	Advertising expenditure		
			TV %	Radio %	Press %
46	Panasonic (UK) (Matsushita)	14,955	23.0	0.5	76.4
47	Comet (Kingfisher)	14,835	42.8	0.6	56.5
48	J Sainsbury	14,102	43.3	0.3	56.4
49	Toyota (GB)	13,970	0.9	1.0	98.1
50	Reckitt & Colman	13,962	75.4	0.7	23.9
51	Asda Stores	13,380	43.4	1.1	55.5
52	Courage (Fosters)	12,614	87.4	3.1	9.5
53	Midland Bank (HSBC)	12,551	64.6	1.0	34.4
54	Great Universal Catalogue Order (GUS)	12,439	0.2	—	99.8
55	Scottish Power	12,275	41.6	0.1	58.3
56	Guinness Brewing (GB) (Guinness)	11,892	78.7	7.1	14.1
57	National Dairy Council	11,818	82.9	0.5	16.6
58	BMW (GB)	11,661	49.1	0.4	50.5
59	Crookes Healthcare (Boots)	11,450	80.9	1.6	17.5
60	St Ivel (Eden Vale)	11,172	86.4	—	13.6
61	Colgate Palmolive	11,124	54.3	0.3	45.4
62	ICI Plant Division	11,110	82.8	—	17.2
63	News Group Newspapers	11,056	92.3	5.5	2.2
64	Volvo Concessionaires	10,953	30.5	0.3	69.1
65	Franklin Mint	10,942	1.0	—	99.0
66	Debenhams	10,895	18.5	1.3	80.2
67	American Airlines	10,826	24.0	0.3	75.7
68	Gillette (UK)	10,647	83.2	—	16.8
69	Whitbread	10,471	88.8	2.5	8.8
70	CPC (UK)	10,421	86.4	0.8	12.8
71	Express Newspapers (United Newspapers)	10,125	75.9	22.5	1.7
72	H J Heinz	10,054	73.7	—	26.3
73	Electricity Association	10,035	70.6	—	29.4
74	Prudential Assurance	9,910	95.1	2.1	2.8
75	W H Smith	9,834	12.9	—	87.1
76	Lyons Tetley (Allied Lyons)	9,814	88.2	0.5	11.3
77	British Sky Broadcasting	9,607	57.2	3.0	39.8
78	Mirror Group Newspapers	9,548	92.3	4.0	3.7
79	Scott	9,371	83.1	—	16.9
80	Coca Cola (GB)	9,342	90.8	7.1	2.1
81	Britannia Music	9,256	—	—	100.0
82	Allied Maples	9,017	41.8	0.2	58.0
83	Rothmans (UK)	9,008	—	0.1	99.9
84	Automobile Association	8,998	50.3	0.2	49.5
85	Allied Breweries (Allied Lyons)	8,996	91.6	0.5	7.9
86	Shell UK	8,884	61.6	4.9	33.5
87	Department for National Savings	8,823	53.1	—	46.9
88	Associated Newspapers	8,803	91.7	3.9	4.4
89	Proton Cars (UK)	8,797	40.7	—	59.3
90	IPC Magazines	8,730	37.7	1.1	61.1

Table 2.44: (Continued) The top 100 advertisers, 1991

			Advertising expenditure		
Rank	Advertiser*	Total £'000	TV %	Radio %	Press %
91	Bernard Matthews Food	8,691	96.4	—	3.6
92	Mazda Cars (UK)	8,690	4.9	0.7	94.4
93	Mercedes Benz (UK)	8,690	10.4	3.3	86.2
94	Golden (L'Oreal)	8,682	75.2	—	24.8
95	Alliance & Leicester Building Society	8,596	54.8	1.2	44.0
96	Lunn Poly (International Thomson Organisation)	8,522	56.8	0.1	43.2
97	Premier Brands (UK)	8,374	88.5	—	11.5
98	National & Provincial Building Society	8,262	40.8	—	59.2
99	Lloyds Bank	8,186	59.1	—	40.9
100	Walkers Crisps	8,166	97.0	3.0	—

Source: Register-MEAL
Notes: *Some company names have been abbreviated
Outdoor, cinema, industrial and overseas publications are excluded. TV expenditure reflects an average discount of 1.3%. Comparisons with previous years should be made with caution

Table 2.45: Population and per capita gross national product* of some countries, 1991

		GNP per capita	
Country	Population millions	US$	World Rank
Switzerland	6.7	33,510	1
Luxembourg	0.4	31,080	2
Japan	124.0	26,920	3
Sweden	8.6	25,490	4
Finland	5.0	24,400	5
Norway	4.3	24,160	6
Denmark	5.1	23,660	7
Germany[1]	79.6	23,650	8
Iceland	0.3	22,580	9
United States	252.0	22,560	10
Canada	26.8	21,260	11
France	56.7	20,600	12
Austria	7.7	20,380	13
Belgium	1.0	19,300	14
Italy	57.7	18,580	15
Netherlands	15.0	18,560	16
United Kingdom	57.7	16,750	17

Source: World Bank, *World Tables 1992 Update*, September 1992
Note: *GNP is calculated at market prices
[1]Population figure for unified Germany, GNP for GDR only
All countries with less than 1 million people and, of necessity, those countries (mostly in the Soviet bloc or at war or civil war) for which GNP data are not available have been excluded. The above table shows all industrial countries and selected other countries

Table 2.46: Civilian employment by main sectors, 1990 (%)

	France	Germany (FR)	Ireland	Switzerland	UK
Agriculture	6.1	3.4	15.0	5.6	2.1
Industry	29.9	39.8	28.6	35.0	29.0
Services	64.0	56.8	56.4	59.3	68.9
Gross fixed capital formation, 1990 (proportion of GDP)	22.2	22.2	19.1	27.1	19.2

Source: OECD Economic Surveys, 1993

Table 2.47: Machine tool production: world shares, 1990 (percentage)

Japan	23.2
Germany	22.2
Switzerland	6.8
UK	3.7
France	2.9

Source: *Financial Times*, 9 May 1991

Table 2.48: Machine tool exports: percentage of world trade, 1991

Germany	26.5
Switzerland	11.4
UK	3.9
France	2.3

Source: *Financial Times*, 6 May 1992

Table 2.49: Satellite communications: projected shares of value added services in Europe 1994 (percentage)

UK	41
France	20
Germany	14

Source: *Funkschau*, 8 March 1991

Table 2.50: Origins of European cross-border acquisitions shares by country, June 1989–June 1990 (percentage)

UK	26
France	25
Germany	6

Source: *The Grocer*, 9 March 1991

In the interval there has, I believe, been an increasing awareness of what the implications of the marketing concept are. Those implications, baldly stated, are that the purpose of business is to capture and satisfy customers, and to do so profitably over the long term. The evidence, drawn from those businesses who succeed appears to be that customer satisfaction is built on providing better added value than your competitors, and that product and service quality are powerful ingredients in adding value. 'Relationship marketing' (see Figure 2.4) is the current term for leading edge marketing behaviour. As the diagram clearly suggests, it is the combining of marketing with quality and customer services that defines relationship marketing.

It is ironic that relationship marketing best practice is more frequently found in Japanese companies than it is in British or American companies. We have, however, absorbed the concept, and the current concern with quality standards (BS5750 and ISO9000) shows that action is following understanding.

Figure 2.4 Relationship marketing orientation: bringing together customer service, quality and marketing

Quality now brings production and marketing together. What goes on in the factory provides manufacturers with a role in marketing, because we now understand that consumers understand and value quality. Hence you cannot for long sell low quality at high prices. If consumers are getting value for money, they will tend to stay with the same suppliers. Total quality management is a means of ensuring that the factory understands that dissatisfaction with the product they make will be a major determinant of the consumer's loyalty to the brand and to the company.

Good quality and good marketing will, however, no longer seal the relationship. Most products are now sold with a service component – the right to a refund, the expectation that the retailer will honour any manufacturers guarantee, the long-term relationship that exists when capital items are purchased, such as automobiles or personal computers. Customers now expect a high level of customer service and getting the delivery of that service right is the third element in relationship marketing.

The marketing system has in a sense become a victim of its own success. If you deal with a company that provides 'good value for money' products, along with high levels of service, effective and efficient marketing, then every other supplier is tested against that norm. We tend to beatify St Michael, but virtually every Briton has shopped in Marks and Spencer and has learnt what first-class marketing is all about. The Sainsbury, Safeway and British Airways experiences add to that knowledge.

Relationship marketing holds out much promise but, that said, marketing is having a mid-life crisis. Three themes permeate discussion of this crisis. One relates to brand proliferation. The 1960s, 1970s and 1980s saw a marketing bonanza, partly as a result of an expansionary zeal (among politicians) that resulted in marketing budgets that were largely unconstrained. Those thirty years saw the maturing of the marketing concept, both as a business philosophy and as a set of specific business activities. There were, and are, many success stories – Britain can claim some world players and excellence by any international standard – Marks and Spencer, Safeway, Sainsbury, British Airways, Jaguar. But recession has tolled the knell and dampened this euphoria, and fundamental questions are being asked.

Consumers have become more sophisticated, better informed and recession has caused them to become more protective of their disposable personal income. The result is the emergence of the concept of relationship marketing. Securing customers is not enough, retaining customers is the name of the game. Building an ongoing relationship with customers requires not simple marketing skills, and not just the right product at the right price, in the right place, at the right time. The successful marketer wants a relationship that is based on more than a single positive response to an advertising burst. The evidence appears to be that people buy product *and service*, and that quality is the cement of the relationship. People showing increasing care about spending are much better informed about value for money. In business-to-business marketing, relationship marketing takes the form of joint product development and co-makership and of course the recognition by production that, if quality is paramount, then every factory line worker becomes *de facto* part of the marketing team.

It is perhaps an irony that the very understanding of the concept of relationship marketing is drawing marketing into every corner of the enterprise. The marketing system, it can be argued, is now seen to be descriptive of the total system of economic activity – from production of goods and services to their final distribution to ultimate consumers, and embracing a feedback loop that keeps ultimate consumers in close touch with the suppliers of goods and services. The question then arises, if marketing is central to an enterprise, is it sensible to leave it to the marketing team? Do we need a separate marketing department?

What will determine the future of marketing as a function and, indeed, as a profession will be the ability of marketing personnel to demonstrate that they have a better understanding of the customer, or the consumer, than anyone else. Beyond that, marketing personnel must be prepared to demonstrate that money spent on marketing is an investment and not a cost.

In an earlier section, I commented that advertising expenditures were not looking as buoyant as they did in the 1980s and that significant behavioural and structural change might be at work. Without wishing to nail my colours to the mast, and brands being what they are (see Figures 2.5 and 2.6), one or two observations are necessary.

Information technology has permeated the marketing business. The large expanse of data to which the reader has already been exposed, demonstrates both a high level of number-crunching and a level of associated strategic thinking. In

Percentage of food expenditure, UK   Percentage of top fifty brands

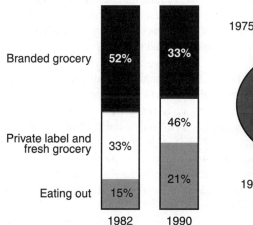 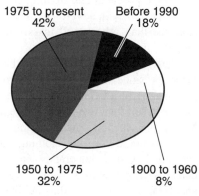

Figure 2.5 Grocery brands and new products
Source: *Guardian*, 10 August 1993

Product category	% share
Wine	75
Cheese	65
Prepared poultry meals	63
Fruit juice	60
Dessert and yogurt	56
Frozen	56
Pasta	51
Canned vegetables	50
Bakery	46
Fish (frozen and other)	46

Percentage of total grocery value, 1991

Figure 2.6 Private label groceries and grocery value in Europe
Source: *Guardian*, 10 August 1993

other words we have already entered the era of targeted marketing. The rise and rise of direct marketing stems from a combination of demographic and economic analysis (in the ACORN tradition) and the ability of the computer to assemble data in a user-friendly form. Personalised letters and addresses for virtually everyone in the United Kingdom is within the reach of any business. The proliferation of media vehicles compounds the problem of targeting customers, as does the structural change that has occurred in much of retail distribution.

What we may be observing is a significant change from mass advertising to targeted advertising, reflecting both the perceived advantages of speaking more directly to potential and existing consumers, but also the desire to secure better value for money in advertising. It is easier to measure some types of advertising response than others, and mass television advertising effectiveness is hard to measure in the short term.

These developments must also be put in the context of changes in retailing. We know, since the data are unequivocal, that the power of large-scale retailers is growing – we all shop in stores belonging to fewer and fewer owners. These incline to sell their own brands. One paragon of effective and profitable retailing, Marks and Spencer, makes nothing and sells only its St Michael brand, an umbrella brand covering clothing, furnishings and food. In food retailing you can still buy national brands, but own-label brands belonging to the grocery chain itself appear to be taking larger and larger market share. Data from 1982 and 1990 in Figure 2.5 illustrate the point.

Private- or own-label brands do not require zero advertising, for the retail outlets are not against advertising, though Marks and Spencer is known to spend very little on media advertising. What we do know is that the retail outlet builds a relationship with the customer, and national brands are fighting for shelf space in retail outlets where private label is used.

In some respects the consumer has been a major beneficiary of recent developments in marketing. I say 'in some respects' because the distribution of wealth and income determines the extent to which the consumer is able to engage in the marketing game. The affluent middle class in this country have never had it so good, though many continue to demand further income tax reductions.

You may recall (Table 2.8) that the most wealthy 10 per cent of the UK population own 50 per cent of the marketable wealth and the most wealthy 25 per cent of the population own 71 per cent of the marketable wealth. Thus 75 per cent of the population share the remaining 29 per cent of the marketable wealth.

The benefits (some may say spoils) of the marketing system are not evenly distributed hence the marketing system has not yet spread its benefits to all who observe and deserve it. Hence good economic management and the generation of real wealth remains a priority for politicians. The marketing system, the variety of choice it offers, the information it provides, the opportunities to spend that it offers, require only that more people have more disposable income.

CONSUMER PROTECTION

Protection of the consumer takes a number of forms. The consumer is protected in law, both in UK law and by the laws of the European Community. In this chapter I cannot discuss law in detail, but the following legislation impinges directly on the relationship between marketers and the customer:

- Monopolies and Restrictive Practices Act 1948;
- Restrictive Practices Act 1956 (set up the Register of Restrictive Practices and the Restrictive Practices Court) and 1968;
- Fair Trading Act 1973 (set up a Director of Fair Trading);
- Consumer Credit Act 1974;
- Unfair Contract Terms Act 1977;
- Consumer Protection Act 1978;
- Competition Act 1979;
- Resale Prices Act 1977;
- Consumer Protection Act 1961 and 1971;
- Sale of Goods Act 1892;
- Supply of Goods (Implied Terms) Act 1972;
- Trade Descriptions Act 1968–72.

Articles 85 and 86 of the Treaty of Rome deal respectively with agreement and practices which hinder the free play of competition, and the abuse of dominant market position.

Total quality is now defined by a British Standard (BS5750) and by the international standard ISO9000. In so far as these standards are designed to underwrite and guarantee quality, they assist the consumer. A rapidly increasing number of UK companies are registering for the standard BS5750 (ISO9000), as a means of communicating to their customers that they adhere to high quality standards.

In the area of advertising, the UK is governed primarily by voluntary codes of practice. The British Code of Advertising practice is published by the Committee of Advertising Practice, which itself represents all of the associations representing the media. The code is under the supervision of the Advertising Standards Authority. The essence and the spirit of the code are defined thus:

The essence of good advertising
All advertisements should be legal, decent, honest and truthful.
All advertisements should be prepared with a sense of responsibility both to the consumer and to society.
All advertisements should conform to the principles of fair competition generally accepted in business.

The essence of the Code
The Code is applied in the spirit as well as in the letter.

Commencement
This edition of the Code came into force on 1st December 1988. It replaced all previous editions. (ITC 1991)

The Advertising Standards Authority was set up in 1962. The authority is responsible for the active promotion of high advertising standards, and issue a case report in which it expresses its opinions about advertising which fall below the standard the public has a right to expect. The code which the Authority supervises, is not merely general. It deals in detail with acceptable practice in a number of fields:

- health claims;
- vitamins and minerals;
- cosmetics;
- financial advertising;
- limited editions;
- media requirements;
- cigarettes;
- hair and scalp;
- slimming;
- mail order;
- employment and business opportunities;
- children;
- advertisements for alcoholic drinks.

Because television is such a persuasive medium, the Independent Television Commission issues a Code of Advertising Standards and Practice. The general principles are worth quoting.

General Principles

1. Television advertising should be legal, decent, honest and truthful.
2. Advertisements must comply in every respect with the law, common or statute, and licensees must make it a condition of acceptance that advertisements do so comply.
3. The detailed rules set out below are intended to be applied in the spirit as well as the letter.
4. The standards in this Code apply to any item of publicity inserted in breaks in or between programmes, whether in return for payment or not, including publicity by licensees themselves; and the term 'advertisement' is to be so construed for the purposes of this Code. (ITC 1991)

The Code itself covers forty-four rules stretching from (i) 'appeals to fear', (ii) 'inertia selling' and (iii) 'animals' to (iv) 'matrimonial and introduction agencies'.

For example:

(i) 'Advertising must not, without justifyable reason, play on fear.' That rule does admit fear appeals in respect of road safety advertising.
(ii) 'Inertia selling' – no advertisement must be accepted from advertisers who send the goods advertised, or additional goods, without authority from the recipient.
(iii) Licensees must satisfy themselves that no animal is caused pain or distress in the course of making any commercial and no advertisement

may contain anything that might reasonably be thought to encourage or condone cruelty or irresponsible behaviour towards animals.

(iv) Matrimonial and introduction agencies – the code is precise in this matter 'until further notice, advertising for this sector is not acceptable on ITV, TV-am or Channel Four'. (ITC 1991)

Broadcasting standards are subject to the same detailed treatment.

It must be said that in general the voluntary codes of practice in the UK have worked extraordinarily well and no political party has felt an urgent need to legislate at this level of concern. The advertisers themselves clearly would not wish to be legislated against, so it is in their own best interests to police themselves. That having been said, the public interest is, from time to time, determined by the political process as requiring interference with the freedom to advertise – clearly cigarettes as a product are the subject of this type of debate.

The umbrella of legislation, and the codes of practice lying beneath this umbrella, might suggest that consumers have no need for further help, assistance or protection. This view is not shared by all consumers, and in the UK the public as consumer supports one organisation that for many years has acted as a watchdog and lobbyist on behalf of the consumer interest, namely the Consumers Association founded in 1957. Its influence is far greater than its primarily middle-class membership would suggest, and its publishing operation is very extensive – its current titles include:

- *Which* (primarily product test reports);
- *Gardening Which*;
- *Motoring Which*;
- *Holiday Which*;
- *Money Which*;
- *Handyman Which*.

The 700,000 membership of the association may represent only about a tenth of *Which* magazine's readership, as anyone who has visited a public library will attest.

Local and central government are both involved in consumer protection, at one level implementing the law referred to earlier, at another level serving as watchdogs of marketing behaviour and the marketplace. Indeed, the role of local government dates back to the Weights and Measures Act of 1878 which has now evolved into enforcement departments in local government called Trading Standards or Consumer Protection. The legal framework for much of their activity consists of the Consumer Credit Act 1974, the Home Purchase Acts, Food and Drink Acts, the Consumer Protection Act and the Trade Descriptions Act.

Although it would appear that consumers have extensive legal protection, the fact is that in the UK most consumers do not regard the law as particularly user-friendly, and this observation is attested to by the continuing workload undertaken by the Citizens Advice Bureau. They were first developed in 1938 and, because they are staffed by volunteers, it has suited central government to encourage their expansion. For a modest grant from central government, and with some additional help from local government, they handle millions of enquiries a year. Most of the problems they handle relate to post-shopping matters. As described earlier, the Consumers Association performs an important service in providing pre-shopping advice, through its product testing and product recommendation activities.

Before completing this section, mention should be made of what used to be called Nationalised Industry Consumers Councils. Since the denationalisation policies of successive Thatcher Governments have placed many of these natural monopolies into the private sector, the future of their consumer councils is unclear. The last Conservative Government addressed this issue with the publication of a series of consumer charters. It would be impossible at this moment in time to make a judgement as to whether these charters will satisfy the new Labour Government, which is likely to be more proactive in forcing natural monopolies operating outside the public sector to improve their performance. At worst, the charters will be seen as pious invocations to deal fairly with the customer.

I have already referred to the voluntarism that characterises much of the field of marketing. Having observed that in the media world it works well, I now turn to professional associations in marketing. As Past Chairman (1995) of the Chartered Institute of Marketing, I subscribe proactively to the view that professional managers, that is, all professional managers, not just marketing managers, fully versed in their understanding of the concept of marketing and understanding what relationship marketing means, will by the very act of managing, develop a marketing system that results in satisfaction to both buyer and seller. Paradoxically, the ideal marketing relationship is one where the customer sees no need to change his or her allegiance to the supplier – reliable brand loyalty. A market-driven system encourages all suppliers to try to seduce rival brand loyal customers to change to the proactive marketer, hoping to deliver better value than the competition. We have yet to invent a better system if you accept the fundamental premise that welfare is maximised if true consumer sovereignty exists.

There are a number of professional associations in the UK that between them cover a wide spectrum of marketing activities, and knowledge of them will permit any observer to judge the quality of management in the field.

Modesty requires me to look first at the Chartered Institute of Marketing (CIM). Twenty-six thousand marketing directors and managers belong to it. Thirty thousand students, the majority of whom are practising marketing professionals in over seventy countries study for its Certificate and Diploma. It has a training division offering a full range of marketing courses, and an Institute of Sales, representing sales professionals. The CIM is a founder member of the European Marketing Confederation and received a Royal Charter in 1989 in recognition of the qualifications and the quality of its members.

The Institute of Practitioners in Advertising represents the major advertising agencies in the UK; the Advertising Association is a federation of thirty-six trade associations and professional bodies representing all aspects of advertising, media and supporting services; the Marketing Society represents very senior marketing professionals, its annual conference being its major showcase. The Market Research Society is the professional society for market researchers, and has a membership of about 6,000.

All of the above organisations have defined codes of practice for their members, and mechanisms for dealing with breaches of the code. *The Marketing Managers Handbook*, published annually, provides an exhaustive list of all organisations connected with the marketing industry.

THE FUTURE OF MARKETING IN THE UNITED KINGDOM

The role and function of marketing to the United Kingdom is well understood, though its implementation is far from complete. Marketing is generally understood to be of concern not just to people who work in the marketing department of a company, but to all who are involved in any activity where future success depends on establishing a long-term relationship with customers. Art galleries, theatres, local government, the National Health Service, the gas industry, the local window-cleaner, all are in the marketing business, and that view is widely accepted. What you then do to implement the marketing concept is of course another matter, and many companies and organisations are still travelling up the learning curve.

The future will undoubtedly see the most successful companies and organisations embracing the concept so that it becomes a corporate function rather than a specialist function. Once the telephone operator and the assembly-line worker understand that they are part of their organisation's marketing effort we shall be some way to establishing an effective marketing system. Such a system will require a high level of marketing professionalism, and it is the responsibility of marketing directors and managers to enlighten their colleagues – in finance, in research and development, in production, in personal and human resources development – that the relationship between the organisation or the company and its publics is critical to future success. The value chain (Figure 2.7) is a critically important concept, and it is the marketing professional who should most clearly see its implications.

The only purpose of production is consumption, and the challenge in the UK is to provide consumption goods and services that contribute to the 'good life' as defined by the market concept. The market does not always want conspicuous consumption, for the good life may be defined in terms of environmentally friendly products and services – culture may take precedence over consumables, information may be preferred to propaganda. At the end of the day it is only marketing that generates revenue, either in the form of profits or taxable income. Marketing is thus at the heart of wealth creation.

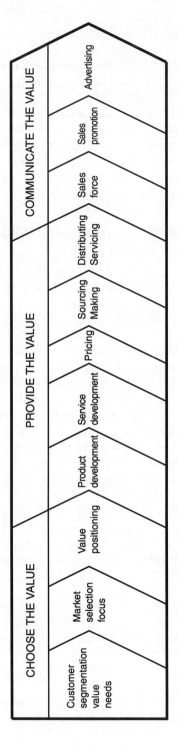

Figure 2.7 Value delivery sequence

SELECTED READING

Advertising Association (1993)
Advertising Association (1997)
AP Information Services (1993)
Baker, M. (1994)
Christopher, N., Payne, A. and Ballantyne, D. (1993)
Newman, D. and Foster, A. (1993)
Thomas, M.J. (1989)
Thomas, M.J. (1995)
Thomas, M.J. (1994)
Thomas, M.J. (1996)

Market data erodes very quickly, the data in this chapter is illustrative of the quality and variety of market data available. I recommend as a source of reasonably current data, the *Marketing Pocket Book*, (1997), Advertising Association in association with NTC Publications Ltd, Henley on Thames (fax: 01491 571188).

3 The UK financial sector

Jenifer Piesse

INTRODUCTION

This chapter begins by describing the need for a financial system in the allocation of funds, including a brief outline of the movement of capital throughout the economy. Then we shall consider the process which matches surpluses and deficits, and introduce the concept of financial markets.

Having provided a rationale for such a financial sector, we consider in more detail some of the major participants. First, we shall briefly consider the role of the central bank and the way in which government policy is implemented. Then we shall discuss the deposit-taking and non-deposit taking intermediaries, and those involved in trading instruments related to direct financing, including securities based on claims to real assets and those whose value is derived from an underlying asset.

Finally, we shall look at the position of the UK financial sector as part of a larger European system, and conclude with a discussion of some possible future developments which may affect the future of financial markets and institutions in the United Kingdom.

THE INSTITUTIONAL FABRIC

The UK financial sector is a collection of institutions and markets which exist to ensure the movement of monetary flows between those wishing to borrow funds and those wishing to lend. In some cases, the transfer of financial claims is straightforward, and sometimes there is a process of intermediation to adapt one to the needs of the other. This chapter covers both the direct financial markets and the intermediaries in the UK.

The structure of the UK financial system has developed differently from those in other European countries. One major difference is the relationship between the financial and the corporate sector. The UK model is that of a security-based system, where the providers of funds and the users of funds are separate. In other countries, e.g. Germany and Japan, and to some extent, France, banks collect deposits from savers and undertake the same intermediation process, but they also actively participate in the management of the firm. This takes the form of performance monitoring of management and if necessary, the initiation of a change of ownership of the firm, although in a less contentious environment than a strictly market-oriented system entails. Other countries are moving towards a more security-based system, although their regulatory and institutional arrangements impede introduction of the hostile takeover culture that exists here. For this reason the capital markets are particularly well developed in the UK.

The British financial environment is a dynamic one. Changes in technology relating to the provision of products and processes mean that the sector is constantly evolving, as it responds to the changing needs of the market, as well as interacting with other financial centres abroad. The present international nature of financial markets is largely a new phenomenon, since while London has always been the centre for foreign exchange dealing, commodity, Eurocurrency and Eurobond markets, prior to the 1980s the domestic markets of most countries were relatively independent of those elsewhere. However, the world is now a quite different place. Products are frequently traded across national borders and markets have become internationally integrated. Therefore while this chapter is primarily about financial institutions and practice in the UK, it is necessary to consider these in the wider framework of global financial markets. This is particularly true in the corporate sector, where many of the major participants are themselves operating internationally, but also in the retail market which is also becoming increasingly catholic in its tastes for products and services.

The UK financial sector is made up of a number of different products and markets. It includes investment banks, merchant banks, and universal and commercial banks, insurance companies, pension funds, unit trusts and mutual fund companies, building societies and savings and loan associations, as well as money brokers and traders in various kinds of securities. There are a number of financial and commodity futures and options markets, including the International Petroleum Exchange, the Agricultural Futures Exchange, the London Gold Market, the London Silver Market, the Baltic International Freight Futures Exchange, and the London Commodity Exchange. It also contains one of the largest markets for risk insurance and reinsurance. Frequently, financial institutions overlap, and many of the same products and services are offered by a number of institutions, albeit to different segments of the market. Increasingly nowadays, non-financial firms such as the major retail stores also offer financial services, which were previously the domain of the mainstream deposit-taking organisations. It is not possible, or probably useful, to give details of the activities of all of these, but rather to provide some general guidelines in terms of the structure and function of the major participants and their markets.

In common with many UK institutions, the financial markets function in an environment of adaptation and innovation. They have been allowed, and even encouraged, to respond to changes in demand, which is itself a reaction to the cyclical nature of the economy, both domestically and globally. This highly market-driven approach has brought benefits to the City in terms of its perceived importance as a financial centre which is sufficiently flexible to respond quickly. However, clearly there are costs to this, one of which is a reluctance of the financial community to commit to lengthy investment projects on the part of both the corporate and the financial sectors and prompting the current debate on short-termism.

If we examine the factors which have contributed to the change in the financial markets during the last decade, it is clear that two in particular have had a major impact. The first is the introduction of new technology. Increased use of computers to store and analyse data, and improvements in communication and the transfer of information have resulted in changes in the way business is carried out, and in the introduction of new products and processes to the market. The second is deregulation, both specific to the UK, and as a result of closer integration with other European Union (EU) member states via EU harmonisation directives. This has allowed a greater degree of competitiveness, but at the expense of concerns about accountability and supervision. Issues of regulation and its affect on trading systems will be returned to throughout this chapter.

THE FLOW OF FUNDS AND THE MATCHING OF SURPLUSES AND DEFICITS

Before looking at how the financial sector is structured, it may be useful to question why there is a need for one at all. If all the resources in the economy were allocated in a perfectly efficient way, there would be no need for a complex set of institutions and markets, and the private and the social needs of the society would be met costlessly. However, in a mature economy such as in the UK, this is not so, and systems have to be put in place to transfer resources from where they are in surplus to where they are in deficit.

If we divide the economy into two sectors, one made up of households, and the other firms, we can see that the household sector exchanges the resources under its control, essentially labour and property, for the goods and services provided by firms. Thus there is a group who are in surplus and able to save. This group is made up predominantly of households who earn more than they wish to currently spend, but also includes some firms who are unable to find a suitable investment project at any point in time, and sometimes the Government, if they have a budget surplus. This group in aggregate are the ultimate lenders. There is also a group who are in deficit. These are generally firms who wish to increase productivity and require additional physical assets in place to do so, but also some households requiring loanable funds, e.g. a mortgage, and sometimes the Government. This group in aggregate are the ultimate borrowers.

The interaction between these groups can be explained in the following way. The savings of the households are made available to firms who use them to fund investment. In return, firms issue securities, which are contingent claims on future benefits. These can be either a promise of regular interest payment, and the repayment of the loan at maturity, i.e. debt, or a claim on future profits, either in the form of dividends or capital gains which result from investment funded by the loan, i.e. equity.

These areas of activity are illustrated in Figure 3.1. The trade of goods and services takes place in the real sector of the economy. It begins with the factor markets on the left of the figure, and results in the production and exchange of goods and services. This market functions through monetary exchange, in the form of the flows of income and expenditure, which enables a system of interaction between the factor and the goods markets. This is shown in the centre of Figure 3.1. The right of the figure incorporates the source of investment funds, or the capital markets. The intermediary role of the financial institutions is shown by the communicating links between the sectors which completes the system.

Thus far, we have only considered households and firms, and so have a two-sector economy in Figure 3.1, but the public sector should also be included. The

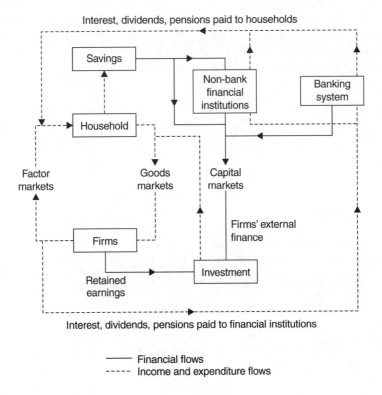

Figure 3.1 Flow of funds in a two-sector economy

Government is both a consumer and an investor, and frequently these aspects are hard to separate. Another simplification is that we have assumed that this movement of funds is confined to the domestic economy, although implicitly, the capital markets are global. Obviously we cannot neglect the general international dimension, particularly since this is a major aspect of the UK financial sector activity. The inclusion of both the government and the international sector is necessary to truly equate ultimate investment and ultimate saving. The more comprehensive flow of funds, Figure 3.2, includes both of these.

The simplification of the factor and goods markets centred around the households and firms in the economy, allows the introduction of central and local government as well as the international aspects into the figure. However, the connecting mechanisms between sectors are again the financial institutions, and this is what we shall address in the next section.

FINANCIAL INTERMEDIATION

Having introduced the borrowers and lenders of funds in the economy, we have to address the mechanism for reconciling these two groups. The action of simply bringing together buyers and sellers can best be described as brokerage. However, just providing information about the supply and demand for funds can be achieved in many ways, and increased communication makes this an easy process. The difficulty is that the funds may not be in a suitable form. The financial institutions exist to transform the funds supplied to match the funds

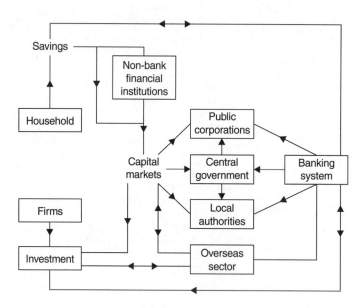

Figure 3.2 Flow of funds in an economy with public and international sectors

demanded. This is known as intermediation, and the main features of this process are the following:

1 **Maturity transformation** Since borrowers frequently require long-term funds, while lenders need short-term liquidity, the maturity of the liabilities will not be equal to that of the assets. An example of this is a building society which provides mortgages (long-term loans) while the savers make constant deposits and withdrawals. It is the responsibility of the financial institution to match these such that they can meet their commitments.

2 **Risk transformation** Individual lenders are not able to assess the risk associated with a particular borrower. A financial institution is able to spread the risk over a number of borrowers in different sectors of the economy, and frequently has the benefit of access to superior credit assessment techniques.

3 **Volume transformation** Generally lenders tend to save in small amounts compared to the amounts the borrowers wish to borrow. The deposit-taking institutions are able to collect the individual savings and make these available to firms in the denominations they require.

The kinds of institutions undertaking this financial intermediation, or repackaging of funds between lenders and borrowers, are shown in Figure 3.3. The first group are the deposit-taking institutions, where the largest group are the commercial banks and the building societies. They perform all of the intermediary functions discussed above, resulting in an indirect financing of firms by lenders. Another group undertake direct financing, which is facilitated by brokers and investment banks in a more straightforward series of transactions. Finally, the investment institutions, such as the pension funds, insurance companies and mutual funds are intermediaries, although they differ from banks

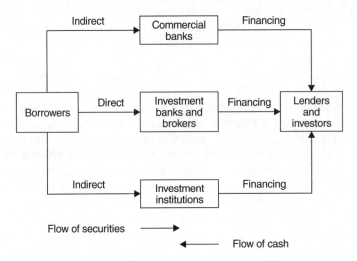

Figure 3.3 Financial intermediation

in that they do not provide a payments system, i.e. they do not clear cheques nor provide instant liquidity. In return for the use of these funds, firms issue securities, or claims on future cash flows.

THE STRUCTURE OF FINANCIAL MARKETS

As has been explained in the section on intermediation, the existence of financial markets can smooth the process of changing deposits into financial claims. Furthermore, traders (or 'market makers') who simply ensure the market is active, can maintain competitive conditions even when it is rather slow.

There are two divisions within the financial markets. First, the primary market which deals in new issues of loanable funds, either equity or debt. This can be by an initial public offering, as is the case with the flotation of new companies. This aspect of the primary market has increased enormously in the past decade, following the privatisation of a number of nationalised industries, and the creation of an equity-owning subset of the population who had not previously actively participated in the stock market. Also included in the primary market are firms which are already listed on the exchange and wish to increase their capitalisation, either by appealing to existing shareholders, by a rights issue, or to new shareholders on the open market.

However, by far the largest proportion of the total transactions take place in the secondary market. In this case, neither the ultimate borrower nor lender is affected, as the security is simply transferred from one owner to another. The existence of the secondary market is very important. If there were only a small chance of selling a security, assets would be very illiquid, and investors would be discouraged from entering the market. Therefore the presence of an active secondary market supports the primary one. Secondary markets also contribute to the efficiency of the primary market, by providing pricing information, and giving an indication of a starting price. Efficiency in the secondary market gives confidence to investors that the price reflects all information about the future value of the asset, and thus gives information which enables investors to make decisions about which security, out of all those available, best meets their needs.

Markets can be in a physical location, but it is obviously not essential, since there are examples of computer-based and trading-room based markets in the UK financial sector. For example, prior to October 1986 trading in stocks and shares took place on the London Stock Exchange trading floor, but now takes place in dealing rooms. Some of the London commodity markets are still in a single location, for example, the options and futures trading takes place on a trading floor. However, if electronic trading systems, conducted on a twenty-four hour basis, are introduced in the USA, then London could well follow.

So far, we have looked at the role of the financial system in intermediating between borrowers and lenders, and have also introduced the concept of a market for financial products and services. Now we shall consider some of the major participants in the UK system.

THE FINANCIAL INSTITUTIONS

Before considering the individual commercial institutions in more detail, we should first look at the role and impact of the central bank, since that is at the centre of the UK financial system. Then we shall consider the main groups of institutions which comprise the financial sector.

The Bank of England

The Bank of England is one of the oldest central banks in the world, founded in 1694, and established in its present form in 1948. The powers of the bank to exert influence over the financial markets, and the behaviour of the institutions within it, is considerable. There are four main areas of responsibility for the bank: to act as supervisor to UK institutions and to monitor non-UK organisation, to undertake management of the national debt, to be banker to the Government and the instrument for implementation of Government monetary policy, and to act as banker to the other UK banks.

Monetary supervision

Under the Banking Act 1987, the bank is responsible for the supervision of those institutions which make up the monetary sector. Prior to the 1987 Act, this took the form of granting a licence to the deposit-taking institutions and requiring them to submit regular statements of accounts so that liquidity, capital adequacy and the spread of risk could be monitored. However, bank failures led to questions being raised about the effectiveness of this level of supervision, and the 1987 Act extended the power of the bank to control shareholding and to intervene if there is any doubt about the legality of operations. It also demanded more regular and more rigorous reporting.

In terms of the supervision of foreign banks, the banking directives of the EU give central banks a responsibility to domestic investors, but ultimate supervisory control lies with the home country central bank. We return to this in more detail in the section entitled 'The UK and European monetary union'.

Management of the national debt

Since tax revenues are rarely sufficient to cover government expenditure, the bank issues debt instruments. Decisions relating to the type and maturity of this debt lie with the Bank of England authorities. For example, they may decide to issue marketable debt, such as Treasury Bills for short-term financing, or government securities for long-term financing. The bank is also responsible for issuing replacement for maturing debt instruments to ensure the continued refinancing of the debt.

Banker to the Government

The central bank has to control the flow of expenditure and taxes. These flows may be the result of transactions between the Government and the private or public sector, or could result from the sale or purchase of government stock.

Another component of the role of banker to the Government is the implementation of monetary policy. Monetary control can be divided into market intervention through open market operations or intervention in the foreign exchange market, or through portfolio controls which are mainly in the form of directives or reserve requirements.

Banker to UK banks

In terms of the relationship with other banks, particularly the clearing banks, the central bank maintains liquidity and acts as lender of last resort for retail banks who have suffered an unexpectedly high number of withdrawals by customers, or some other irregular pattern of payments. One situation which can result in this event occurring is the mass demand for cash by the new share-owning public who wish to benefit from the Government's privatisation programme. Another is the consequence of bank failures. Following the collapse of BCCI, lack of confidence in banks generally led nervous customers to withdraw their deposits from other totally secure banks.

Finally, clearing banks which have to transfer payments from one to another, may have some level of short-term indebtedness or illiquidity, and need to initiate overnight borrowings to make these inter-bank settlements. This provision is also a responsibility of the bank.

The deposit-taking institutions

This group is composed of the commercial banks and the building societies. These institutions were quite different historically, but now are becoming increasingly similar. There has been some discussion about building societies changing their status to become clearing banks, but at the time of writing, only the Abbey National has done this.

The Bank of England recognises a bank, as set down by the Banking Act 1979, as an authorised institution which meets specific criteria including a capitalisation of at least £5 million. There are approximately 500 authorised banks in the UK, although more than half of these are branches or subsidiaries of foreign banks. Since deregulation in the UK, many more foreign banks are operating in London. This is made attractive by the EU Directive which allows member banks to offer products and services which reflect those in their home institutions. The subsequent increasingly competitive environment has put considerable pressure on the domestic banks in the UK financial sector.

There are a number of broad categories of banks in the UK: clearing banks, savings banks, a group covered by the British Merchant Banking and Securities Houses Association, and those authorised institutions under the Banking Act 1987 which include all other banks, divided into British and non-British. This latter group includes the foreign subsidiaries of overseas banks, many of which may actually be retail banks in their home country.

Historically in the UK, there was a clear distinction between retail and wholesale institutions, but this is becoming increasingly blurred. For our purposes, there is some advantage to considering them separately, since the strategy and risk management of a retail bank differs from the wholesale institutions, largely determined by the retail banks clearing function. The retail sector, therefore, comprises the clearing and savings banks, while wholesale business is generally the speciality of the remaining institutions. Thus while in total they make up the banking sector, they are not all deposit-taking, although they all are indirect financing intermediaries.

Clearing banks

This group have retail and commercial business divisions, with many branches throughout the UK and some overseas. Their clearing status is granted by the Bank of England, and they undertake to clear or process cheques for those institutions in the banking sector which do not have clearing provision. These are among the largest banks in the world, in terms of market capitalisation and, in the UK, in terms of assets. This is shown in Table 3.1.

The clearing banks, like other multi-product corporations, have become financial conglomerates engaged in almost every field of financial activity. The traditional banking trade centred around taking deposits from savers, making loans to investors and providing a payment mechanism, but they now offer a number of services formerly provided by other organisations.

Table 3.1: UK clearing banks

Bank	Asset value (£m)	Market capitalization (£m)
Barclays	138,108	8,769
National Westminster	122,569	7,844
Midland	59,408	13,521[*]
Abbey National	57,405	6,292
Lloyds	51,306	7,478
Royal Bank of Scotland	32,166	3,438
Trustee Savings Bank	25,138	3,501
Standard Chartered	23,407	2,697
Bank of Scotland	22,095	2,223

Source: *Bankers Almanac*, January 1994 and *Financial Times*, 25 January 1994
Note: [*]Hongkong Shanghai Bank

Within the retail banking category, most of the following products and services are offered to personal customers: savings and current accounts, mortgages and other loans, administration of estates, private trusts, investment services, unit trusts, life assurance, insurance broking, credit cards, hire purchase and consumer credit, personal advisory and agency services, foreign exchange and travellers cheques.

In the commercial banking area, they provide most of the services offered by the merchant banks, as well as their traditional lending activity, often with specialist divisions dealing with small businesses, the medium-sized corporate client, or specific industrial sectors where they have built up a particular expertise. Recent acquisitions have taken the banks still further from their traditional business activities, illustrated by their move into ownership of travel agencies, life assurance brokerage firms, estate agencies, and leasing companies.

Building societies

Some distinctions still exist between the banks and building societies, and although this is not generally an issue for the customer, it is for the institution. Traditionally, building societies have been mutually owned, that is, they do not issue equity, but all of their customers, both borrowers and lenders, have a share in ownership. In common with other mutual organisations, building societies do not distribute any surplus profits as dividends, but add it to reserves. The vast majority of their borrowings are from households and they are specialist lenders to the personal sector, mostly those requiring mortgages. They compete with the banks for deposits, and now have overtaken the retail banks in this respect, as seen in Table 3.2.

Another factor which differentiates them from retail banks is their restricted access to the wholesale markets, although this has now been considerably relaxed, following the Building Societies Act 1986. However, given the high level of deposits, many societies are cash rich and would like the freedom to expand their capital market operations still further.

Table 3.2: Stocks of personal sector savings held with banks and building societies (£m)

Year	Bank deposits	Building society deposits
1963	6,232	4,057
1965	7,210	5,211
1970	10,036	10,194
1975	19,206	22,748
1980	36,598	50,002
1985	61,488	104,922
1988	94,129	152,700

Source: CSO, Financial Statistics

Non-deposit taking wholesale banks

Although they do not fit under the title of deposit-takers, other institutions are included in the banking sector, and are under the supervisory control of the Bank of England. They are intermediaries which deal mainly in sizable deposits (minimum sums involved tend to be from £50,000 upwards) and undertake inter-bank lending via the parallel money markets on a large scale.

Merchant banks

The merchant banks, or acceptance houses, as they were known when first created, originated in the nineteenth century. They operated by first establishing a good name and reputation which they could then use to back bills of exchange for merchants engaged in international trade. Their role was to provide guarantees of payment at a time when delivery dates and capital transfers were much more lengthy and uncertain procedures than they are now. This business still continues, but they have extended their range of activities to advising on, arranging, placing and underwriting new capital issues, acting as intermediary between companies involved in mergers and acquisitions and acting as consultants with expertise in investments and portfolio management. Many of the clearing banks have merchant bank subsidiaries.

Other wholesale banks are included in this group which are similar to merchant banks but are slightly different in structure. While providing many similar services, the real differences are cultural rather than practical. In particular, merchant banks have a deal-making culture in which the objective is to get the deal concluded before the market realises it is happening. Their aim is to minimise market risk, whereas commercial banking is a business where the objective is to acquire assets for the balance sheet while minimising credit risk. This difference in approach will probably mean the overlap between the institutions will never be eradicated.

Finally, a number of institutions in the wholesale banking sector have developed largely as a result of the importance of London in the Eurocurrency, and in particular, the Eurodollar markets.

Private banks

There are a small number of private banks still practising. They take the form of small limited companies with a few branches or they are the subsidiary of a major clearing bank. One example of these is Coutts & Co, who are now a subsidiary of National Westminster.

Investment institutions

These are the group of financial intermediaries engaged in indirect financing, which enable small investors to participate in collective investment funds. These contributions are combined and invested in a portfolio of assets. They are indirect financing institutions, specialising in long-term liabilities. Examples of these institutions are the pension funds, insurance companies, investment trusts and unit trusts. They have become dominant in recent years, due to the sheer size of their portfolios. The volume of assets of these institutions are given in Table 3.3, with the comparable statistics for banks and building societies included for comparative purposes.

Table 3.3: Total assets of British financial institutions in 1990 (£b)

Life insurance and pension funds	498
Retail banks	391
Building societies	190
Other British banks	113
Unit trusts	57
General insurance funds	40
Investment trusts	24

Source: Bank of England, *Quarterly Bulletin and Financial Statistics*, 1991

- **Pension funds**

  Pensions in the UK are either provided from the State, an occupational scheme or a personal pension, or currently some combination of these. The first is a flat rate pension. The second is a fund which receives contributions from employers and employees in the public and private sector. The third is a voluntary contribution by individuals which is often in addition to the others. The nature of these funds is that the liabilities are long term, and generally need to perform better than the inflation rate. Typically they are index linked.

- **Unit trusts and investment trusts**

  A unit trust is a fund to which individuals and companies may contribute in order to obtain a share in the returns generated by the fund. Investors purchase a number of units, which do not represent any particular security, but are a share of the total portfolio.

  Although similar to unit trusts, investment trusts are firms who invest funds in financial assets. They raise their finance like any other company, through the issue of equity and debt.

- **Insurance companies**

  The insurance business is divided into non-life and life, or general and long term. The former includes all kinds of provision against contingencies, i.e. accident, motor, property, etc., and is usually a series of short-period contracts, i.e. one year. They have to be able to pay when claims are made against reserves.

  Long-term insurance is managed differently. Premiums are generally less than the claims, although there is a considerable period of time before payment is due, and the shortfall has to be made up from earnings on the deposits.

To comment briefly on the influence of investment institutions on the UK economy generally, there are claims that the frequency of performance assessment of the managers of institutional investors has contributed to the short-termism mentioned earlier. Certainly they have generally performed better than the deposit-taking institutions, and some measure of this may be due to government policy of offering tax incentives, and changes in the state pension scheme which has encouraged private provision. Thus the situation exists where the household sector is encouraged to use the institutional investors for their long-term investment, while the institutions themselves take little interest in the use of their funds, but only their short-term profitability. This is increasingly important as they have taken a large share of the securities market, as can be seen in Table 3.4.

The market for securities

This section discusses the markets for securities, including equity, debt and derivative instruments. This is the means of direct financing, either between individuals, companies or financial institutions. There is no intermediation involved other than of a purely broking nature, i.e. the bringing together of buyers and sellers, and the provision of pricing information.

The International Stock Exchange

The International Stock Exchange is at the centre of the UK's highly integrated security industry and provides the mechanism for the issue of new securities, both public sector and corporate equity, and the trading of existing ones.

The London Stock Exchange originated in the seventeenth century in the coffee-houses around the City of London. These were expanded and developed in the eighteenth century when funds were raised by the Government to finance the wars in Europe. The fashion for speculation in highly risky business ventures continued and was only checked by the South Sea Bubble scandal in 1772. At this time it was realised that in order to act as a reliable market and encourage investors to continue to provide funds, certain standards had to be set and complied with by market participants. This resulted in a concentration of trading in one place, both for the exchange of information and for purposes of easy monitoring. Thus, in 1773, New Johnathan's Coffee House was established as the London Stock Exchange, and a formal set of rules for members was introduced in 1802.

The Stock Exchange has undergone many changes since its foundation, the most recent being the general restructuring in October 1986, known as the 'Big Bang'. These reforms substantially altered the trading practices of the market and arose out of the inadequacy of the existing Stock Exchange to cope with future requirements. A number of texts give details of this reorganisation, (see, for example, Thomas 1986) and therefore only a brief discussion will be undertaken here as an attempt to put the current trading system into context.

The need for a programme of reform was identified by the Royal Commission set up to review the functioning of the financial institutions. These findings were published in the Wilson Report (1980) and the results highlighted two major shifts in the financial system which had a bearing on the effective functioning of the Stock Exchange. The first was an increase in the ownership of government and company securities by the financial institutions, especially the pension funds and insurance companies. The growth of these institutions put a huge strain on the existing system, and some of the implications are discussed in the conclusion to this chapter.

The second major factor identified in the Wilson Report was the growth of foreign and other banks resident in the UK, and in particular, the Euro-currency markets. The UK had abolished exchange controls in 1979 and introduced an environment of deregulation, which many other countries have now followed. The move by London to provide an international financial centre, prompted by the removal of much of the regulatory constraint, was made possible by the rapid diffusion of technology in communication and the mechanisms of trading.

Therefore, in a relatively brief period, trading changed not just in terms of the role of individual participants, but also in the form of exchange, since the physical marketplace was no longer the floor of the exchange, and is now conducted in individual dealing rooms. The market is a continuous one, and dealers use screens to display prices, although the actual trading is done by telephone. Currently, buyers and sellers use the Stock Exchange Automated Quotation system (SEAQ) disseminated through the Stock Exchange's TOPIC (Teletext Output of Price Information by Computer) screens where each potential client has a screen giving competing quotes from the intermediaries.

As shown in Table 3.4, London is the largest of the European exchanges in terms of total turnover and has the highest level of foreign business in the world.

Table 3.4: Comparison of major international stock exchanges, 1990

	Market value of domestic equity (£bn)	No. of companies		Turnover (£bn)	
		Domestic	Foreign	Domestic	Foreign
Tokyo	2,639	1,597	119	1,436	12
New York	1,800	1,634	87	957	n.a.
London	507	2,015	544	198	85
NASDA Q*	241	4,026	267	249	14
German Fed Exchanges	227	628	535	218	11
Paris	227	462	223	69	3
Zurich	107	117	229	n.a.	n.a.
Milan	106	211	0	27	0

Source: International Stock Exchange, *Quality of Markets Quarterly*, 1990
Note: *National Association of Securities Dealers Automated Quotations – the over-the-counter market in the USA

This table also gives some comparisons of market size and level of activity of the major exchanges.

The main market for companies and government securities in the UK is the International Stock Exchange. As shown in Table 3.4, there are over 2,000 domestic companies on the Official List, and they have a combined market valuation of about £500 billion. The Unlisted Securities Market was established in 1980 to allow smaller companies to enter the market, but at a lower listing price. There is also an informal market that consists of trading in small business shares, undertaken by a group of brokers and licensed dealers to the public. This is sometimes referred to as the 'over-the-counter' (OTC) trading, although this term is now more often used to differentiate screen-based trading, as in London, from that carried out on the trading floor, such as the New York Stock Exchange.

Equity markets

Share ownership is divided among several groups. As seen in Table 3.5, the financial institutions have control of the majority of equity, approximately 60 per cent of the total. Therefore, despite claims that direct shareholding by households has increased following the recent government privatisations, the proportion of securities held directly by individuals has fallen considerably over time.

Thus the institutional investors have enormous bargaining power in the form of indirect shareholding for individuals, and we have raised some questions about the effects this may have. But they do allow households to invest in diversified portfolios of securities, that they could not manage on their own, due to lack of information and specialist knowledge of the markets. In addition, technology has made this type of intermediation easier and cheaper, since the volumes of securities traded make the transaction costs much lower for the intermediary than for an individual investor.

Table 3.5: Share ownership in Britain: percentage distribution by sector, 1963–92

Sector of owner	1963	1969	1975	1981	1989	1990	1992
Individuals and firms (Ltd)	54.0	47.4	37.5	28.2	20.8	20.5	20.0
Non-profit organisations	2.1	2.1	2.3	2.2	2.1	1.6	2.2
Public sector	1.5	2.6	3.6	3.0	2.0	2.0	1.2
Banks	1.3	1.7	0.7	0.3	0.7	0.7	0.2
Insurance companies	10.0	12.2	15.9	20.5	18.5	20.4	20.7
Pension funds	6.4	9.0	16.8	26.7	30.5	31.4	31.1
Unit trusts	1.3	2.9	4.1	3.6	5.9	6.1	5.7
Other financial institutions	11.3	10.1	10.5	6.8	3.1	2.7	2.8
Firms (industrial and commercial) (Plc)	5.1	5.4	3.0	5.1	3.8	2.8	3.3
Foreign investors	7.0	6.6	5.6	3.6	12.7	11.8	12.8
Total	100	100	100	100	100	100	100

Source: Share Register Surveys

Fixed interest securities

One group of fixed interest securities are domestic bonds, which are issued by both firms and governments. There is less demand nowadays for corporate bonds in the UK, probably due to the tax and administrative complexities and the growing number of more attractive instruments, particularly in the Euro-markets, and commercial paper. Debentures, which are bonds secured on corporate assets, represent an alternative form of finance for firms, but again are faced with competition.

The UK government issues gilt-edged fixed income securities, and these make up a large proportion of the funds traded on the Stock Exchange. There are two distinct markets for gilts, the short market – stocks with less than five years to maturity – and medium and long gilts – sometimes up to thirty years to maturity. They are often index linked (retail price index) and ownership is registered.

The other fixed interest security is the Eurobond. This is a bond issued in markets other than that of the currency of issue and is sold internationally. They are generally issued 'off-shore' which means that the issue is not subject to the rules and regulations governing foreign bonds issued in that currency, and therefore avoid tax and other obligations.

Eurobonds should be differentiated from foreign bonds. Foreign bonds are issued to a non-resident borrower on the market of a country in the domestic currency. Both Eurobonds and foreign bonds are bearer denominated, that is, not registered in the owners name.

Trading takes place on the International Stock Exchange (or in Luxembourg for Eurobonds), and the system of trading matches that of equities. The market structure is also similar to that of equities and experienced the same reorganisation and reform during 1986.

New instruments and derivatives

There has been a rapid increase in corporate new issue activity in the United Kingdom in the past few years, and this has encouraged the development of innovative types of securities. Some of these are hybrids of existing financial forms of asset, such as convertible loan stock, which are a mix of equity and debt, and combine the best qualities of both.

In addition, the volatility of securities and currency markets, and interest rates over recent years has led to the growth of financial instruments, which can be used to hedge risk and thus reduce uncertainty. These are collectively known as 'derivatives', and are financial instruments whose value is 'derived' from an underlying asset, but which does not give the owner a claim on the underlying asset. Examples of these are 'options' and 'futures'. Options can be written on a variety of underlying entities, including: equities, stock indices, commodities, currencies, interest rates, and other contracts including futures. Option contracts are traded internationally, and this has certainly been encouraged by agreements with other trading centres, particularly in the USA. Futures contracts began based on physical commodities, but are now also written on equity, interest rates, bonds, stock indices and currencies.

The traded options market began operations on the floor of the Stock Exchange in 1978, and then at the London Traded Options Market. Futures trading has traditionally taken place at the London International Financial Futures Exchange, which was opened in 1981. These two merged in March 1992 and are now the London Derivatives Market. The clearing mechanism for these derivatives is managed by the International Commodities Clearing House, which is owned by the six largest clearing banks.

The foreign exchange market

The foreign exchange market provides a means of buying and selling the currencies required for transactions in international goods and assets markets. Retail transactions are carried out by local financial institutions, but these obtain their currency from the London market. Unlike the securities markets, trading is screen based, and carried out by dealers trading in specific currencies. Of the total foreign exchange contracts, the majority are 'spot' and 'forward' prices and only a small proportion are options and futures. The bulk of the options and futures market is in the UK.

Measurement of market performance

For many years, the performance of equity on the International Stock Exchange had been measured in terms of either the FT-Actuaries or FT-30 indices. These were indices constructed from the prices of a number of financial assets. However, when the derivative markets were developed, and many of the contracts were to be based on equities, neither of these seemed to be appropriate for an index which had to be constantly updated. Therefore, the Financial Times Stock Exchange 100 (FT-SE 100) index was created in 1984. This is small enough to be updated regularly and yet reflects the actual movement in a sufficiently large number of active securities. The FT-SE 100 is an index comprising the largest listed UK companies, weighted by market capitalization. It is based at 1,000 and recalculated every minute during market trading hours.

Much of the corporate financing in the UK is done by retained earnings rather than through the Stock Exchange. Therefore the underlying economic performance is reflected in the amount of capital investment, whether reliance is on the stock market or earnings.

REGULATION AND SUPERVISION

We have already noted that supervision for the banking sector is carried out by the Bank of England. Most of the present regulation for the control of investment business, is a result of the 1986 Financial Services Act (Gower Report 1986). This includes securities issues by companies, public corporations and central and local government, as well as the derivatives, insurance and investment and unit trusts. It was centred around obtaining authorisation before trading, and some compensation after a legitimate complaint by the public. The overall regulatory body is the Securities and Investment Board (SIB), and a number of self-regulatory organisations (SROs), so the industry is expected to exert pressure by its own members to regulate itself. The aim is to achieve investor protection with a minimum of government intervention, which ensures a systems of fair rewards without fraud.

The obligation to provide a fair and efficient market for trading is the responsibility of the International Stock Exchange. At the same time as the reorganisation of the trading mechanisms and the redefinition of the market participants (i.e. the abolition of the single capacity separation between brokers and market makers), the old Stock Exchange and the International Securities Regulatory Organisation merged to form the International Stock Exchange (ISE). Their overall remit now includes:

1 The provision of a market for the trading of foreign and domestic fixed interest and company securities and traded options.
2 The choice of stocks to be traded on the London Stock Exchange.
3 The publication of price information about individual stocks and other instruments.
4 The organisation of payment and other settlement.
5 A guarantee that the ISE members comply with the established rules, and thus the maintenance of a good secondary market.

The financial institutions, as intermediaries, are positioned between borrowers and lenders, and therefore need to gain the confidence of both. However, the balance between prudence and competitiveness is a fine one. Investments carry a certain level of risk, and excessive constraints may be costly and may discourage innovation in the sector.

THE UK AND EUROPEAN MONETARY UNION

Most of the discussion up to now has considered the UK financial system independent of any interaction with the rest of world, apart from the very general inclusion of the international sector in the flow of funds (Figure 3.2). However, not only are there numerous transactions involving non-UK nationals and non-UK economic systems, but increasingly, institutional structures are being developed to bring the economies of a number of countries closer together. This is especially true of the member states of the European Union and therefore we should include in this section some comments about the nature of economic and financial integration, particularly with respect to the trade in financial services and to economic and monetary union.

The general concept of a single market for Europe has existed since the Treaty of Rome in 1957. From its inception, the underlying objective has been to benefit consumers and producers in all sectors of the economy by the removal of non-tariff barriers to trade, and the creation of an increasingly competitive environment, based on the advantages to be gained from economies of scale. There are three main non-tariff barriers in the financial services sector: the requirements for market entry; variations in the levels of regulation, especially differences in prudential requirements; and differences in the rules of acceptable conduct in the market.

A number of Directives to address these issues, which refer specifically to each area of financial activity, (i.e. banking, investment services, insurance, etc.) have been agreed by all the member states. The Directives allow a basic right of establishment for the providers of financial services to operate in other host countries and compete on an equal basis with the home state firms, provided they establish local offices and conform with the regulations of the host country. Regulation is harmonised at the level of fundamental prudential standards, but overall supervision is the responsibility of the home country.

These Directives have had an important effect on the UK financial services industry. Already a highly deregulated sector for some time, the reciprocity agreements have resulted in making the establishment of operations in the UK by foreign firms very popular. Financial firms from other EU member states find the UK liberal market environment very attractive and those from outside the EU have gained entry via mergers with, and acquisition of, UK firms. In addition, the abolition of foreign exchange controls in the UK in 1979 encouraged foreign investment through UK intermediaries, although these controls have now been removed in all member states, or will be in the very near future.

Thus the only obstacle to the creation of a truly single market is the uncertainty created by fluctuations in the exchange rates between EU member states, which may inhibit cross-border trade. A way to achieve this degree of financial integration is through the introduction of an exchange rate mechanism, although this has not yet been resolved. However, the concept is fairly straightforward although the implementation is proving to be more difficult.

The first stage of European monetary union was begun in 1991 and largely involved the liberalisation of financial markets as has been already described. The second stage involves the creation of a European system of central banks, to operate in parallel with the individual central banks in the member states. The third is to fix exchange rates and at the same time, to introduce a single currency, essentially a simple task if parity between countries was determined.

The idea of allowing exchange rates to fluctuate within a narrow band is not new, and such an arrangement has been successfully used during a large part of the twentieth century. The Bretton Woods system (established in 1944) allowed the exchange rates of the participating currencies to vary within a small range of their initial value, set against the US dollar. This was replaced in 1972 with a similar system for EC countries, although again currencies were valued relative to the US dollar. With some refinements, this became the European monetary system (EMS).

The central feature of the present EMS is the exchange rate mechanism (ERM) which is constructed in the form of a parity grid that places an upper and lower limit on the possible movements of exchange rates between each pair of member countries. Therefore it is a matrix and each country's currency must be within the required bands with respect to every other country. When one currency threatens to leave its band, the central banks of all other affected countries must intervene to help it return to its place in the grid. Thus all have an equal responsibility to maintain parity, and the onus is not on the weakest currency only. The aim of this system is to reduce volatility and bring about convergence of some aspects of national economies. As well as providing aid in the single market for goods and services, it will maintain equivalent levels of inflation and economic growth in the member countries. This is discussed in detail in Haldane (1991).

The UK is not currently a member of the ERM, and follows a floating exchange rate, in common with several other EU countries. This will undoubtedly continue until there is a stable economic convergence between member states.

FUTURE DEVELOPMENTS

During the past decade, there has been a high level of innovation, both in the product markets and in the process of exchange, and the future will almost certainly incorporate a similar kind of activity. New instruments will undoubtedly continue to be introduced, and technology will remain a competitive necessity.

However, two issues which are expected to attract considerable debate in the near future, and which we should consider before concluding this chapter are the independence of the central bank, and the role of the City of London in the European financial community.

The independence of the Bank of England has been discussed for a number of years. Of the many areas of responsibility currently borne by the bank, it is the enactment of monetary policy which is the focus for independence, and this has gained importance after sterling's exit from the exchange rate mechanism of the European monetary system. Since one of the arguments in favour of European monetary integration was price stability, and this has now been abandoned, an independent Bank of England could provide a credible basis for low inflationary expectations. They could do this by controlling short-term interest rates, and, unlike the Treasury, the bank would not be tempted to create money.

The debate so far has implications for government rather than the financial sector, but the effects would be far-reaching. For example, if such a policy were undertaken this would imply a change in the Bank's other activities too. A more independent Bank of England would relinquish responsibility for debt management. It also would no longer be the banker to the Government, and would be under no obligation to provide government with automatic overdrafts or to buy government stock. In addition, supervision for the banking sector would be transferred elsewhere.

The other topic more directly affects the whole of the financial sector. The highly competitive and deregulated environment in the UK has given London a tremendous advantage over other potential financial centres in Europe. Historically, London has been differentiated from other financial centres by the international span of business it attracts. However, financial operations are now on a global level and other centres are moving from a more parochial view to encompass international trading, and they are doing this in an integrative way, possibly excluding London.

The location of the European central bank, and other EU financial institutions will be subject to strong competitive bidding in the near future, while the European Monetary Institute has already been established in Frankfurt.

CONCLUSION

This chapter has outlined the main areas of activity which make up the UK financial sector, and some of the major players within it. It is a very important part of the UK economy, accounting for 7 per cent of UK gross domestic product. It is also clearly a sophisticated and complex collection of markets, with no restrictions on the flow of funds and with a highly deregulated structure to encourage competition between institutions while maintaining a degree of prudential control. We have stressed the importance of technological innovation and the increasingly global nature of the financial markets. But it must not be forgotten that the success of a system depends on its ability to reconcile entrepreneurial freedom with effective accountability. Stability of the financial system in any country depends on the strength of financial institutions and markets globally.

SELECTED READING

Buckle, M. and Thompson, J. L. (1992)
Gilbody, J. (1991)
Piesse, J., Peasnell, K. and Ward, C. (1995)

4 Accounting, financial reporting and corporate governance

Robert Perks

INTRODUCTION

This chapter begins by outlining the different forms of business organisation, and the advantages of incorporating as a company. It then outlines the main requirements of the Companies Acts, particularly in relation to accounting and auditing. The development and role of the accountancy profession is then outlined and its role in relation to the setting of accounting and auditing standards is examined. The move towards relaxing the accounting and audit requirements for smaller companies is then discussed.

The final parts of the chapter deal with some of the more controversial areas of accountancy, and criticisms of its operation in practice. 'Creative accounting' is discussed, and there is a critical assessment of the role of auditing, particularly in relation to the 'expectations gap', and apparent lack of independence. Many of the problems of corporate governance were taken up by the Cadbury Committee, and their proposals for dealing with them are examined in the final part of the chapter.

TYPES OF BUSINESS ORGANISATION

Most businesses in the UK are established as companies; these are legal entities separate from their owners or shareholders. But smaller businesses are often 'unincorporated', i.e. not established as companies. Where there is just one proprietor or owner, the unincorporated business is called a sole trader. Where there are several partners or proprietors, the business is referred to as a partnership. There are relatively few formalities for establishing an unincorporated business, or regulations concerning the accounts that they produce, and there is no requirement that they should be audited. But unincorporated businesses often produce accounts in much the same way as companies, if only to be more credible in dealing with bankers and the tax authorities.

Most companies are formed by registration under the provisions of the Companies Acts and are either private limited companies (e.g. ABC Ltd) or public limited companies (e.g. ABC plc). Most private companies are very small, often with only two shareholders and directors (e.g. husband and wife). There are no restrictions on size, but private companies are not allowed to issue shares to the public by advertisement.

Public companies are usually larger, and their authorised capital must be at least £50,000. Many companies start off as private limited companies, and convert at a later stage to public limited companies, which means that, in due course, they may invite the public to subscribe for shares. When a company has made a public issue of shares, and those shares are listed on the stock market, it is known as a listed company. Many public, listed companies have tens or hundreds of thousands of shareholders.

An unincorporated business has the advantage of avoiding accounting and auditing requirements, and this arrangement is often satisfactory for businesses owned and controlled by one or a small number of proprietors. Administrative expenses are minimised, and there are no public rights of access to information about unincorporated businesses.

But there are advantages in incorporating, i.e. establishing the business as a company. The main advantages are as follows:

1 The company has a legal existence in its own right, separate from the individual owners, and can continue in existence indefinitely, even though individuals retire and die.
2 The liability of shareholders for the debts of the company is limited to the amount of their shareholdings. In an unincorporated business, the individual proprietors are personally liable for all of the debts of the business.
3 The assets, liabilities, expenses, income and taxation matters of the business are clearly and legally separate from those of the individuals running the business.
4 Once a company has become reasonably large, it is easier to raise substantial amounts of capital, for example through a public issue of shares, or by borrowing with a floating charge on company assets which does not restrict the company's freedom to continue to trade with those assets.

THE COMPANIES ACTS

There are substantial legal requirements regarding the conduct of the affairs of companies and the production and audit of their accounts or financial statements. These are contained in the Companies Acts 1985 and 1989.

Accounting and auditing requirements for companies have increased steadily since the Joint Stock Companies Act 1844. Originally companies were required only to produce balance sheets, little was specified about the content of balance sheets; and almost anyone could be an auditor. The Companies Act 1929 required the publication of profit and loss accounts. The Companies Act 1948 introduced substantial changes with new requirements for additional disclosure, the production of consolidated accounts, and the need for auditors to be qualified. The Companies Act 1967 required turnover to be disclosed for the first time, and additional information had to be disclosed in the directors' report, including political and charitable donations, market values of investments and property, and directors' interests. The Companies Act 1976 further strengthened disclosure provisions and the powers of auditors. The Companies Act 1980 laid down detailed requirements for determining the amount of profit that is available for distribution as dividends. The Companies Act 1981 implemented the EC's Fourth Directive: it required standard formats for accounts for the first time, specified fundamental accounting principles and valuation rules, and extended disclosure requirements. The Companies Act 1985 was a major consolidating piece of legislation, it integrated many previously diverse pieces of legislation. The Companies Act 1989 implemented the Seventh and Eighth Directives of the EC which deal with group accounts and the qualifications of auditors.

Auditing

Private sector

The main requirements of the Companies Acts in relation to auditing deal with the duties of the auditor: what is to be covered by the audit report, the qualifications of auditors, the powers of auditors, and the independence of auditors from directors.

Every company's annual report and accounts must include an audit report which states whether, in the auditor's opinion, the annual accounts have been properly prepared in accordance with the Companies Acts, and whether, in the opinion of the auditor, the balance sheet and profit and loss account give 'a true and fair view' of the state of affairs of the company at the end of the financial year, and of the profit or loss for the year. The UK has insisted on the right to retain the phrase 'a true and fair view', and that it can predominate over other requirements, although it has no very clear meaning. Compared with many other EU countries there seems to be a desire for UK accountants to assert that their professional judgement in specific circumstances is more valuable than a rigid set of accounting rules.

Auditors are required to carry out such investigations as will enable them to form an opinion on whether proper accounting records have been kept, and whether the accounts are in agreement with the accounting records. If this is not the case, or if they are unable to obtain all the information and explanations that they believe are necessary, this should be stated in their report.

In order to be appointed as an auditor a person must be a member of a recognised body. This usually means that they must be members of one of the three Institutes of Chartered Accountants (Scotland, England and Wales, Ireland), or of the Chartered Association of Certified Accountants. The Secretary of State may also recognise others such as those with overseas qualifications.

Auditors must also be independent from the directors of the company in specific ways. They cannot be directors or employees of the companies that they audit. They are appointed by the company (i.e. its shareholders) at a general meeting, and the way in which they are remunerated is also determined at a company general meeting. The auditor also has some security in the holding of the office. If it is decided to try to remove auditors before the year end, special procedures are prescribed for a motion at a general meeting, and auditors have the right to put their views to shareholders. If the auditor resigns there are also special provisions to ensure that the auditor's reasons for so doing can be put to shareholders, and the auditors can require a special general meeting to be called to hear their reasons for resigning.

In order to carry out their duties, auditors have the right of access to the books, accounts and vouchers of the company at all times; to require information and explanations from the company's officers; and to attend and be heard at all general meetings.

In view of the powerful position of auditors, directors would be ill-advised to alienate them; difficulties between the directors of companies and their auditors rarely become apparent.

There are often criticisms of audit reports and of the auditor's independence, particularly when a company gets into financial difficulties, or some financial scandal or abuse becomes public. A company's annual report may give the impression that the financial position is sound, and the auditor's report may reveal nothing to cause concern. When a financial crisis becomes apparent some months later, it is easy for politicians, journalists and aggrieved shareholders or creditors to blame the auditors. This sometimes happens when one company takes over another, accepting that company's financial statements at face value, and believing that they have made a sound purchase; if it then turns out that their acquisition was a mistake, attempts are sometimes made to blame the auditors. Auditors may be accused of producing audit reports that reveal little or nothing; and they may be seen as identifying too closely with directors, accepting directors' versions of events too readily, and exhibiting little or no real independence.

Where the audit report includes reservations about whether the accounts show a true and fair view it is said to be 'qualified'. Most audit reports in practice are 'unqualified': they use standard wording and provide a bland reassurance that all is well. It would be almost unknown for auditors to state that accounts are untrue or unfair, or that the company is about to collapse. There is a need to pay careful attention to any unusual wording in auditors' reports. They may state that they have relied on directors' explanations for certain figures; they may draw attention to the fact that the accounts have been drawn upon the going concern assumption; or that it is assumed that particular financial support (such as overdraft facilities) will continue. Although such wording is cautious it may be a sign of potentially serious problems.

The independence of auditors from directors is in some respects questionable. When the first appointment is made, or when a casual vacancy arises, it is the directors not the shareholders who make the appointment, and directors' decisions or recommendations are rarely challenged. Similarly, the directors in effect decide the remuneration of auditors. Most large firms of auditors also undertake substantial taxation and consultancy work for clients, leaving auditors open to the criticism that their independence may be compromised in negotiations for such work.

Public sector

Auditing in the public sector is the responsibility of two bodies:

1 **The National Audit Office** (NAO), headed by the Controller and Auditor General, carries out the audits of all central government departments and works closely with Parliament's Public Accounts Committee in ensuring the regularity and propriety of government expenditure. In recent years increasing emphasis has been given to 'value for money' investigations designed to ensure that government programmes and activities are economical, efficient, and effective in achieving their objectives. NAO reports are published and are often extensive and controversial. The NAO undertakes the audit work of all government executive agencies, and a range of other organisations such as the Fire Service College and the Central Statistical Office. The audit work of privatised public utilities and other companies is undertaken in the private sector.
2 **The Audit Commission** was established in 1982 and is responsible for appointing the external auditors of local authorities. These auditors may be from the Commission's own staff, or from a private sector firm of accountants. Prior to the 1972 Local Government Act, local authority audits were undertaken by the district audit service. Between 1971 and 1982 local authorities were able to choose between the district audit service, and appointing private sector auditors from an approved list.

Although the nature of accountability in the public sector is different from that in the private sector, with a responsibility to the public, private sector approaches have become increasingly prevalent in the public sector. The emphasis on professional qualifications for auditors has increased, and an increasing amount of audit work previously undertaken in the public sector is now undertaken by the private sector.

Accounting

The directors of a company are responsible for ensuring that proper accounting records are kept sufficient to show and explain the company's transactions; to record all sums of money received and expended; to maintain a record of assets and liabilities; to enable disclosure with reasonable accuracy of the company's financial position at any time; to provide a statement of stock at the end of the financial year; and to enable a profit and loss account and balance sheet to be prepared when required.

The directors of a company are responsible for the preparation of the annual financial statements. These have to be audited, and the financial statements together with the auditor's report and a directors report have to be laid before the company's shareholders in a general meeting and, when adopted, delivered to the Registrar of Companies where they are available for inspection by members of the public.

The overriding requirement of the Act is that the accounts should show 'a true and fair view', but this concept is undefined, and relies as much on convention and tradition and 'generally accepted accounting practice' as it does on principles, or clear-cut accounting rules. But the Companies Act 1985 lays down the required form and content of balance sheets and profit and loss accounts much more specifically than has traditionally been the case in the UK. A number of standard formats are prescribed with more standardisation of terminology and layout than has previously applied.

The directors' report of a company must include the following: disclosure of the main activity of the company; a review of performance over the period and of the financial position at the year end; significant changes in asset values, and an open market valuation of land if this is significantly different from book value; names of directors and details of their shareholdings; details of any material events after the balance sheet date; political and charitable donations; information about any research and development activity; details about any acquisitions by the company of its own shares; information about employee involvement and policy regarding employment of disabled persons (where there are more than 250 employees); and (in some industries) arrangements for employees' well-being and safety.

Although the general trend of Companies Acts has been for a steady increase in reporting and auditing requirements there have been some reductions. Smaller companies may now file abbreviated or modified accounts with the Registrar; and listed companies are allowed to send summary financial statements to shareholders, rather than the full accounts, although shareholders retain the right to a full set of accounts if they wish. As the majority of shareholders appear to be content with summary statements, there can be substantial reductions in costs for companies with large numbers of shareholders.

THE ACCOUNTANCY PROFESSION

The term 'accountant' is interpreted very broadly in the United Kingdom, and 'accountants' are involved in many different types of work. This is why there appear to be more accountants per head of the population than in most other countries. Auditing continues to be the bread-and-butter work of professional accountancy firms, but even in these firms other related work, such as preparing accounts, dealing with taxation, insolvency work and consultancy generally are at least as important as auditing. Most accountants do not work in professional practice: they may be in industry and commerce or in the public sector, working as financial accountants, cost accountants, management accountants, financial managers, internal auditors, advisers, or in management positions more generally. For many years management education in the UK was poor or non-existent, and the tradition of the amateur manager lived on. In this situation, the professional accountant was well placed to move into powerful management positions.

Anyone in the UK may call themselves 'accountants', but the term is usually used for members of the six main professional accountancy bodies shown below that now have the status of being established by royal charter:

1 **The Institute of Chartered Accountants of Scotland** (ICAS), the first professional accountancy body in the world, began with separate bodies in Glasgow and in Edinburgh, established in 1854, and in Aberdeen in 1867. The three bodies formally merged in 1951.
2 **The Institute of Chartered Accountants in England and Wales** (ICAEW), traces its origins back to local societies of accountants in Liverpool (1870), London (The Institute of Accountants in London, 1870; The Society of Accountants in England, 1872), then Manchester (1872) and Sheffield (1877). The ICAEW came into being as a result of a series of mergers, the most recent being in 1957 with the Society of Incorporated Accountants (founded 1885).
3 **The Institute of Chartered Accountants in Ireland** (ICAI), which was founded in 1888, before the island of Ireland was partitioned, and which still operates both north and south of the border.

These first three bodies, the original 'chartered' bodies have comparable examination and training contracts, with an emphasis on auditing, and each operates mainly in its own part of the UK. Most entrants to the profession are university graduates but, especially in England and Wales, are likely to have taken subjects other than accountancy at university. It must seem strange to other professionals, and to accountants from outside the UK, that the major professional accountancy firms seem to prefer to recruit graduates in subjects such as History or English, especially if they went to Oxford or Cambridge, rather than those who have studied accountancy.

Until recently, all training took place within professional accountancy firms, but accountancy training in industry is now arranged. All three bodies arrange for their members to be qualified as auditors.

4 **The Chartered Association of Certified Accountants** (ACCA) can trace its origins back to the Corporation of Accountants founded in Glasgow in 1891. A series of mergers resulted in its establishment as the Association of Certified and Corporate Accountants in 1938, and it was joined by the Institute of Certified Public Accountants in 1941.

Members of these first four bodies are eligible to be auditors of companies, provided they have undertaken the right training. Unlike the first three bodies, many members of ACCA have not dealt with auditing. They are free to undertake accountancy training in almost any area of the public or private sector, or in professional practice. Although the ACCA is based in London, it recruits and trains accountants in many countries throughout the world.

5 **The Chartered Institute of Public Finance and Accountancy** (CIPFA) was established in 1885. It was previously known as the Institute of Municipal Treasurers and Accountants, and it specialises in public sector accounting work, particularly in local government. The CIPFA professional qualification is the normal expectation for senior local authority accountants, and has become more widespread in accounting and management positions in public sector organisations. Historically very few public sector auditors had professional qualifications, but both the National Audit Office (central government), and the Audit Commission (local government) are increasingly emphasising professional qualifications, but ICAEW qualification is now at least as likely as the CIPFA qualification.

6 **The Chartered Institute of Management Accountants** (CIMA) was originally known as the Institute of Cost and Works Accountants and was founded in 1919. Originally its members dealt mainly with costing in manufacturing organisations, but have now moved into management accounting more generally in all kinds of organisation.

The ICAEW, often known as 'the English Institute', is by far the largest, and probably the most powerful, of these six bodies, with over 100,000 members. The second largest body, in terms of membership, is the ACCA with less than half as many members as the ICAEW; and the CIMA is about one-third of the size of the ICAEW. The other three bodies are significantly smaller, each with memberships in the range 8,000–14,000.

With so many different bodies it is difficult for outsiders to know who should be considered a properly qualified accountant. Different qualifications are appropriate for different purposes. In order to avoid confusion, to reduce running costs, and perhaps to reduce competition between the different bodies there have been many proposals for mergers between two or more of the bodies. A 1970 proposal, that all six should merge, fell through because it did not have sufficient support from ICAEW members; more recently a proposed merger between ICAEW and ICAS fell through because it did not have sufficient support from ICAS members. The difficulty is made worse because there are a number of other professional bodies, with varying status and reputation, that have members working in accountancy. These include the Society of Company and Commercial Accountants, the Association of International Accountants, the Association of Cost and Executive Accountants, and the Institute of Financial Accountants.

ACCOUNTING STANDARDS

Companies Acts have been increasingly detailed in specifying the form and content of the financial statements and annual reports that companies are required to publish. But there is often a need for more detail, and for requirements to be made more specific, and the accountancy profession has taken on the responsibility for producing accounting standards to establish more detailed guidance on the content of published financial statements. The profession's 'accounting standards' deal with:

- definitions of terms that are used in financial statements;
- measurement rules to be applied in determining the amounts to be shown for assets, liabilities, reserves, income, expenditure and profit;
- information to be disclosed in published financial statements, sometimes in addition to that prescribed in Companies Acts, and sometimes providing more detailed guidance; the information may be in the form of additional data, or by way of explanation, such as specifying accounting policies adopted; and
- approved formats for the presentation of information.

The earliest versions of accounting standards (the ICAEW's 'Recommendations on Accounting Principles', 1942–69) proved inadequate in the face of accounting scandals in the late 1960s. The highly publicised cases of Robert Maxwell's Pergamon Press, and the takeover by GEC of AEI showed that when different accountants were brought in, substantial profits could be reinterpreted as substantial losses – all on the basis of 'principles' that in practice were largely a matter of opinion.

There is a case for government imposed, rigid uniformity in accounting standards and principles, but the British accountancy profession has always fought against this. They prefer to have some flexibility to adapt principles to meet the needs of particular circumstances and to retain the specification of accounting standards in its own hands rather than allow governments to take over the role. In response to criticisms of the profession, they established the Accounting Standards Committee which issued twenty-five Statements of Standard Accounting Practice (SSAP) during the period 1971 to 1990.

These SSAPs were intended to 'narrow the areas of difference and variety' in accounting practice, but often allowed a variety of different practices to continue. Accountants were theoretically required to follow these recommendations of their professional bodies, but there were no effective enforcement mechanisms, and the problems of lax accounting standards continued.

As a result of the Dearing Report (The Making of Accounting Standards, September 1988), the procedures for setting accounting standards were radically altered. The whole procedure is overseen by a Financial Reporting Council with a rather wider representation than the accountancy profession alone. A new Accounting Standards Board now issues accounting standards on its own authority, without approval of the six professional bodies being required. And a

Review Panel has been established to examine departures from standards. Accounting standards are now known as FRSs (Financial Reporting Standards); they are preceded by FREDs (Financial Reporting Exposure Drafts); and they are supplemented by UITF (Urgent Issues Task Force) Abstracts which deal with specific problems that have arisen in practice.

The whole procedure has been strengthened, but there are still doubts about the specification and enforcement of effective accounting standards, and it may be that more radical action is required to eliminate the practice of 'creative accounting'.

AUDITING STANDARDS

The accountancy profession also issues auditing standards and auditing guidelines. The *auditor's operational standard* is very brief and relies on auditing guidelines to be more specific. It requires that there should be adequate planning, control and recording of the audit work; that the adequacy of the enterprise's system of recording and processing transactions should be ascertained; that sufficient relevant and reliable evidence should be obtained; that if auditors place any reliance on internal control systems their adequacy should be tested; and that the auditor should carry out a review of the financial statements that is a 'sufficient' basis for an audit opinion.

The *audit report standard* states what should be included in an audit report and what circumstances give rise to various forms of qualifications. A typical audit report would be as follows:

We have audited the Accounts on pages (xx–xx) in accordance with Auditing Standards.

In our opinion the Accounts give a true and fair view of the state of the company's affairs at (date) and of its profit and cash flow for the year and have been properly prepared in accordance with the Companies Acts.

Various technical forms of wording are then outlined to draw attention to potential problems – or perhaps to protect auditors from the accusation that they failed to draw attention to such problems. An audit report may be qualified:

- because of uncertainty. In such a case the auditor will state that the report is 'subject to' a particular qualification. For example, the report may provide details about a particular transaction or situation, and then go on to say something like 'Subject to the effect of any adjustments to the financial statements that may be found to be necessary following determination of the matter referred to above, in our opinion the accounts . . .'. Such a qualification may also be because of an inability to carry out the necessary audit procedures, perhaps because accounting records are inadequate. Or it may be due to the inherent uncertainties of a situation, sometimes where the continuation of the business as a going concern is dependent on the continued, but uncertain, support of bankers or other creditors;

- because there is a disagreement with the directors. In this situation, the wording of the report will have an 'except for' qualification. For example, the report may state that the accounts show a true and fair view except that a particular accounting standard has not been followed, or that some items (perhaps stocks) have been included at directors' valuation.

Very occasionally, in more serious cases, a specifically adverse opinion may be expressed, saying that the accounts do not give a true and fair view. More frequently there may be a very minor comment or unusual reference in an auditor's report, and this may indicate particular concerns of the auditor. Before the financial difficulties of Queen's Moat Houses plc were made very public, the audit report stated, 'In our opinion these accounts, which have been prepared under the historical cost convention as modified by the revaluation of hotel and catering fixed assets, give a true and fair view...'. The inclusion of any information or unusual wording in an audit report that departs from the minimum in the typical audit report shown above should be interpreted as a potential danger signal.

The *auditing guidelines* include operational guidelines that provide detailed guidance on the operational standard; guidelines dealing with the special requirements of particular types of organisation; and detailed operational guidelines.

SMALLER COMPANIES

Until relatively recently the accounting and auditing requirements of small companies, even those with only two directors and no other employees, was much the same as for large companies, however large they were. As these requirements have steadily increased, the burden has been seen as too great for the very small businesses, and the accounting, reporting and auditing requirements of smaller companies are being reduced.

Most companies have 'limited liability', which means that directors and shareholders are personally liable only to the extent of any share capital that they have subscribed. If a company goes into liquidation, and there are insufficient assets to meet the claims of creditors, the shareholders cannot be required to make good any deficit. For creditors there is a risk in dealing with limited companies, and the traditional argument has been that there should be sufficient financial information available to them to enable them to assess the extent of that risk. In other words, the financial accounts of all companies should be available to the public. But there is also an argument that this is unduly burdensome for small companies, and that there is no public requirement for small companies to disclose much of the detailed information that is required from large companies.

The Companies Act 1985 allows some reductions in the information that has to be published by small and medium-sized companies. Full disclosure requirements apply to public limited companies and to information produced for shareholders. But limited companies which are below defined size criteria are exempt from making some of the information public.

A company is medium sized if two of the following apply:

• turnover does not exceed £8 million;
• gross assets do not exceed £3.9 million;
• the number of employees does not exceed 250.

A medium sized company is not required to make public its turnover.

A company is small if two of the following apply:

• turnover does not exceed £2 million;
• gross assets do not exceed £0.975 million;
• the number of employees does not exceed 50.

Small companies are required to file their balance sheets with the Registrar of Companies, but most items can be shown under broad headings without detailed analysis. No disclosure is required of the following:

• profit and loss account;
• directors' report;
• remuneration of directors and other highly paid staff.

Prior to 1994 all companies in the UK were required to have a full audit, but in autumn 1993 the Government announced its intention to abolish the requirement for small companies to be audited. This follows continuing pressure and debate over proposals to allow smaller companies to be exempt from the formal audit requirement completely, or to allow them to opt for a 'review', which might be cheaper and quicker, rather than a full audit. Even with exemption from audit requirements, many small companies will probably opt for full audits if they want their financial statements to be taken seriously by banks and other financial institutions, creditors and the tax authorities.

THE PROBLEMS OF CREATIVE ACCOUNTING

British accountants are concerned to demonstrate that theirs is a technically sophisticated art requiring the exercise of significant professional judgement in presenting financial statements, in determining what is a true and fair view, and defining and measuring assets, liabilities, income and expenses. It is not merely a matter of formal compliance with detailed, technical rules. There are many special circumstances where the exercise of judgement is necessary. Accountants are involved in determining such things as depreciation policies, the accounting life of fixed assets, the basis for stock valuation, assessing uncertainties, making provisions for future losses, and so on, all of which will affect the amounts of reported profits. There is always the danger that this 'professional judgement' will be used more to present the company's position and results in a favourable light, than to be 'true and fair'. Attempts, often successful, to interpret, bend and, even, flout generally accepted accounting standards in order to present a particular view of the financial position of a company are known as 'creative accounting'.

The term 'creative accounting' came into widespread usage in the late 1980s with the publication of two popular books on the subject (Griffiths 1987; Jameson 1988). They were critical of the accountancy profession and the apparent lack of standards to determine what should be disclosed in company accounts, and particularly the variability in the measurement of profits and assets. They drew attention to many examples of published accounts some of which seemed to have elevated creative accounting to an art form.

There are of course many controversial and difficult areas in accountancy, and it is unrealistic to expect too much certainty or 'truth' from accounting information. Concepts such as value and cost are difficult to define and measure, and although many might want to use published financial statements to predict the future viability of companies, predicting the future is notoriously difficult. There are always likely to be companies that appear to be healthy at one point in time, only to get into financial difficulties within a year or so. Auditors are sometimes then criticised for having given the company a clean bill of health at an earlier date. The accounting profession has tackled many of the difficult and controversial areas in accounting by issuing accounting and auditing standards and guidelines. But many of these have proved to be inadequate in application, and they are revised again and again.

In January 1991 Phillips and Drew produced a research report 'Accounting for Growth' which showed in detail a number of questionable accounting techniques that well-known companies had used and which had the effect of exaggerating their profits and/or making their financial position appear more favourable. They listed eleven items of evidence of such practices, as follows:

1   Creation and use of any significant balance sheet provisions, including any fair value adjustments in respect of acquisitions.
2   Significant reorganisation costs appearing as extraordinary items which affect cash flow, but are not charged against pre-tax profits.
3   Major debt that does not appear on the balance sheet.
4   Significant 'capitalization' of interest and other expenses. This is where costs have been incurred, but are shown on the balance sheet as assets, not charged against profit for the year like other expenses.
5   Significant non-trading profits (e.g. from asset disposals, or sale and leasebacks) that are credited to pretax profits.
6   Inclusion of brand names as assets on the balance sheet.
7   Significant changes in the lives of assets so that depreciation charges and profits are affected.
8   Reductions in pension fund contributions that have the effect of increasing profits.
9   Deferred payments on acquisitions, dependent on future profits.

10 Major currency mismatching, and the possibility of crediting high interest receivable to the profit and loss account, while reductions in the value of overseas investment are taken directly to reserves.

11 Unusually low tax charges in relation to published profit figures.

They then listed nearly 200 major companies, and showed how many of the above practices were used by each of the companies. Examples of companies using a significant number were British Aerospace (7), Maxwell (7), Burton (7). A few companies, such as Amstrad and Wellcome, used none of these practices. The list was presented as an accounting health check, the implication being that the more that a company resorted to questionable accounting practices, the more likely it is that profits are exaggerated, and the more likely it is that they will get into financial difficulties. Although attempts were made to ban it, Terry Smith, who had done the research with Phillips and Drew, subsequently published the information more fully in his book *Accounting for Growth: Stripping the Camouflage from Company Accounts* (Smith 1992).

The Accounting Standards Board (ASB) has attempted to stem the flood of creative accounting practices. Their first Financial Reporting Standard (September 1991) emphasised cash flows, addressing the problem that, where profit figures had been exaggerated, additional cash flow information can provide a more balanced picture. Their second standard cleared up some areas in consolidated accounts. Their third standard tackles the use of extraordinary items to avoid some items affecting earnings figures by requiring much more detail to be disclosed on the components of financial performance, including separate information regarding the performance of (a) continuing, and (b) discontinued operations, and any profits on the sale of properties. The ASB has also issued a number of pronouncements in the form of UITF Abstracts. But there seems to be no limit to the creativity of some companies and their accountants, and the ASB has a tough and unequal task in attempting to stop abuses.

THE EXPECTATIONS GAP AND THE PROBLEM OF AUDITOR INDEPENDENCE

There have been many criticisms of auditors in the UK, and it is often said that there is an 'expectations gap' between what is expected of them and what they do in practice. There are many examples of what auditors might regard as unreasonable expectations from auditing, some of which are listed below.

1 The financial statements are prepared by the auditors; they are correct, and the auditors agree with them and are responsible for what they contain. But it is the directors, not the auditors who are responsible for the accounts, and the accounts give the directors' view. The auditors merely state that this is '*a* true and fair view', not '*the* true and fair view'. The auditors do not state that they

agree with this view, and different accountants would probably form different views. There is no single 'correct' version of a company's financial performance and position.

2 The balance sheet shows what the company is worth, and the assets have been properly valued. But a balance sheet is not intended to show what the business is worth as a whole. It attaches a monetary value to each individual item, but this may be based on what the item originally cost, or on one of many different bases of valuation. The amount that a business is worth as a whole cannot be assumed to be a simple total of the value of each of its assets (less liabilities); a successful company ought to be worth much more than the value of its individual assets because it has a reputation, trained workforce, established customers and so on.

3 The auditors have checked that there is no significant fraud taking place. Historically auditors were more concerned with finding fraud, but they have gradually shed their responsibilities in this respect. Auditors ought to find out about any frauds that are so large that the accounts could not show a true and fair view. But a clean audit report is no guarantee that frauds are not taking place.

4 The business is a going concern: it is not likely to collapse in the foreseeable future. Again, a clean audit report is no guarantee of this. Accounts are usually prepared on the *assumption* that the business is a going concern, but auditors offer no reassurance that this is the case. Indeed, when auditors actually draw attention to the fact that the going concern assumption has been used it may indicate that there is some doubt about the company's future.

The expectations of users have been severely disappointed when companies have received a clean audit report but have collapsed shortly afterwards. The accounting profession recognised that there are serious concerns about the extent to which users of accounts can or should draw conclusions about the financial viability of a company, and whether the directors' or auditor's report should provide more useful information. The profession expected the Cadbury Committee to deal with this matter; the Cadbury Report recommended that guidance should be produced by the accounting profession.

5 The company is properly run by a board of competent and reputable directors. But auditors are not expected to check on the ability, competence or honesty of directors, or on the running of the company, and auditors are unlikely to wish to criticise management.

6 The auditors are independent, and their role, report and opinions would not be influenced by directors, especially when there appear to be irregularities. In fact there are serious doubts about the independence of auditors.

It sometimes seems that the auditors are responsible for very little, and we might reasonably question whether it is worth the expense and trouble of having auditors at all. But without auditors there would be even less restriction on the powers of directors and the auditors do check that proper accounting records have been kept; in the event of subsequent scandals this usually means that it is possible to find out what has happened. But the auditors 'opinion' that the accounts show 'a true and fair view' is probably not worth very much in practice.

The value of the audit function is likely to be reduced if auditors are not independent, and seen to be independent. There are both statutory provisions and professional guidance that provide for some measure of independence but, in the UK, there is still too much reliance on the idea that independence is 'a state of mind', as opposed to the result of specific arrangements and relationships. Although the auditor is in theory appointed by the shareholders to act as a check on directors, in practice the auditors are appointed as a result of the directors' nomination, and the auditors' remuneration is determined by the directors (and approved by the shareholders). As a result, auditors usually regard the directors as being their clients, not the shareholders. As long as the appointment of auditors, and the determination of their remuneration is *in effect* in the hands of the directors, auditor independence is very limited. It is difficult to see how this situation can be avoided unless the appointment and remuneration of auditors is determined by an independent body such as a State Auditing Board (see Perks 1993).

Almost all auditing of companies in the UK is undertaken by firms of professional accountants who are also in business to provide a range of services including accounting, taxation, insolvency and receivership, financial planning and advice, computing and systems work, recruitment services and consultancy generally. In spite of EC pressure, UK accounting firms have retained the right to undertake any additional work for audit clients that they wish. This must severely limit their independence. A firm of accountants may, with a particular client, be simultaneously trying to stand up to directors who are attempting to use dubious accounting practices to flatter their results, and persuading the client to make use of the accountancy firm's other services, and to earn substantial fees for so doing. It seems inevitable that the attempt to do the latter will compromise the effectiveness of the former.

Although UK accountants retain the right to do non-audit work for audit clients, it is now a requirement that the fees earned for such work are disclosed. The evidence so far suggests that this has not deterred accounting firms from undertaking such work, and there are examples of audit fees in excess of £1 million where the same accounting firm is paid even larger sums for non-audit work.

IMPROVING CORPORATE GOVERNANCE: THE CADBURY REPORT

There have been many criticisms of the ways in which some companies have been run in the UK, heightened by the scandals of Robert Maxwell and the BCCI, and many highly publicised examples of excessive directors pay, perks and compensation for loss of office. As a result a Committee on the Financial

Aspects of Corporate Governance (the Cadbury Committee) was established, jointly by the Financial Reporting Council, the Stock Exchange, and the accountancy profession in 1990. The objectives were to raise the standards of corporate governance, and the level of confidence in financial reporting and auditing. It is intended that this should be achieved through a voluntary code of best practice rather than through increased regulation. As such it may be seen as a typical piece of British self-regulation, intended to avert the threat of government action, and stricter regimes, in the face of serious scandals and abuses. 'Enforcement' is to be achieved through the Stock Exchange requiring the company to state that it has complied with the code and reasons for any non-compliance, and auditors should 'review' the statement of compliance.

Much of the Cadbury Report is concerned with avoiding the possibility of one or two people in a company becoming too powerful, so that the company in effect becomes their private empire, run for their own personal benefit. There have been cases where a single individual, who is both chairman and chief executive, appears to have unfettered power. In theory other directors, auditors and other professionals such as accountants and company secretaries could limit the personal excesses of such individuals; but in practice such an individual may be able to appoint his own friends and supporters to these positions, and get rid of any who oppose him. The Cadbury Report addresses this problem in a number of ways.

The report lays great stress on the role of *non-executive directors*, who are seen as being independent from the management of the company, and should be able to take a lead in potential conflicts of interest between management and the wider interests of the company. The report says that there should be at least three, and the majority of them should be 'independent' from the company. They would of course receive directors' fees, and they could have shareholdings in the company. But it should be regarded as good practice for them not to participate in share option schemes or in pension schemes. There should be a clear letter of appointment specifying their duties, their (limited) term of office, and their remuneration.

Considerable importance is also attached to the role of the *audit committee*. Such committees are now a requirement of the New York Stock Exchange, and about two-thirds of the UK's largest companies already have them. The code says that all UK listed companies should establish an audit committee of at least three non-executive directors and that it should have written terms of reference which deal clearly with its authority and duties. The external auditor and the head of the internal audit function (where there is one), and the finance director should normally attend audit committee meetings.

In many respects the audit committee has considerable independence. It should have explicit authority to investigate any matters within its terms of reference and the resources that it needs to do so, full access to information and the ability to obtain outside professional advice and to invite appropriate outsiders to its meetings. Its membership should be disclosed, and its chairman should be available to answer questions about its work at Annual General Meetings of the company. It should have a discussion at least once a year with the external auditor, without executive board members present, to ensure that there are no unresolved issues of concern. But the code also says that (presumably with that exception) other board members should also have the right to attend the committee's meetings; this provision has the potential to undermine the committee's independence and to expose it to the influence of a chairman and chief executive.

The scandals and abuses in relation to executive directors' remuneration is addressed by recommending that it should be subject to the recommendations of a *remuneration committee*, comprising wholly or mainly non-executive directors; that there should be fuller disclosure, including details of any performance related elements and how performance is measured; the membership of the committee should be disclosed, and its chairman should be available to answer questions at Annual General Meetings. To protect the independence of individual directors, especially where conflicts arise, directors should have access to appropriate professional advice and training at the company's expense.

In a number of important respects the Cadbury Report backs down from incorporating important reforms and recommendations into its code of practice. One of the problems of 'self-regulation' is that compliance is largely voluntary, and if there is widespread avoidance of any particular recommendation, then the whole system loses credibility.

The Cadbury Committee appears to be against a single individual holding the office of both chairman and chief executive in a company as it puts too much power into the hands of a single individual. But they did not make this part of their Code of Best Practice. Instead they said:

> There should be a clearly accepted division of responsibilities at the head of a company, which will ensure a balance of power and authority, such that no one individual has unfettered powers of decision. Where the chairman is also the chief executive, it is essential that there should be a strong independent element on the board, with a recognised senior member.

The Cadbury Committee also appears to be against the idea that the appointment of directors can, in effect, be determined by a single individual. Instead, they prefer the idea of a *nomination committee* which would make clear how these appointments are made, and assist boards in making them. It would have a majority of non-executive directors, and would have the responsibility of proposing to the board any new appointments. But this is included in the Cadbury Report as being only 'one approach to making board appointments'. It is not included in the Code of Best Practice.

The code contains a number of other items which in some ways ought not to be necessary. The fact that they have been included implies an acceptance that unacceptable practices and misinterpretations must have been widespread. It states that 'The board should ensure that an objective and professional relationship is maintained with the auditors'. This may be taken as implying that this is often not the case.

The code also states that: 'It is the board's duty to present a balanced and understandable assessment of the company's position'. This may be taken as implying that financial statements are often not balanced or understandable. The code states that directors' service contracts should not exceed three years without shareholders' approval. But as shareholders' approval would not usually be difficult to obtain, the effectiveness of this restriction may be limited.

The code includes a number of other items: there should be a formal schedule of matters that require a board decision; some strengthening of the position of company secretary; explanation of directors' responsibility for preparing the accounts; a report on the effectiveness of the company's system of internal control; and the directors should report that the business is a going concern, with supporting assumptions or qualifications as necessary.

SUMMARY AND CONCLUSIONS

Most business in the United Kingdom is conducted by companies. Many small, unincorporated businesses flourish, but there are advantages in being established as a company, and the formal accounting and auditing requirements for small companies are being reduced. Large parts of the public sector have been privatised so that, for example, gas, electricity, telephone services and most of the provision of bus services and water are now controlled by companies.

There are substantial, and sophisticated requirements for financial reporting by companies, for keeping financial records, for audits, and for the general control and governance of companies, all under the auspices of government legislation in the form of various Companies Acts. In practice not all of this lives up to expectations. Financial scandals have not been eliminated, and the accountancy profession is often in the firing line. Accounting standards are sometimes fairly flexible and may be overridden by what is presented as being 'a true and fair view', and creative accounting still flourishes. From time to time governments attempt to enforce stricter rules with a new Companies Act, but on a day-to-day basis responsibility for developing and enforcing accounting standards, and for providing guidance on current accounting problems and abuses, remains in the private sector, with the accountancy profession playing the most important role.

SELECTED READING

Perks, R. W. (1993)
Smith, T. (1992)

5   The legal and institutional framework

Anne Ruff

INTRODUCTION

Managers working in or trading with the United Kingdom will find knowledge of UK legal institutions and law invaluable to them and their employers. This should include knowledge of European Community institutions and law.

Businessmen and women in practice often concentrate on commercial factors when doing business and try to avoid becoming entangled with 'expensive' lawyers. However, ignoring the legal implications of a decision or action can often prove more expensive in the long run.

An understanding of the legal and institutional framework enables managers to understand the constitutional and legal context in which the business is operating and thereby helps to ensure that its operation runs smoothly and effectively. The legal dimensions of a management proposal or practice can be identified in advance and resolved before any major problem or dispute arises. When talking to the company's lawyers, or to central or local government officials, managers will be in a stronger position if they are familiar with the legal and institutional background to the discussion. Ignorance of the law is no defence.

This chapter concentrates on the constitutional framework of government, the institutions available for resolving legal disputes, and the legal profession. The following chapter introduces the key areas of law of importance to managers, such as company, contract and employment law. In both chapters current areas of debate and practical issues are emphasised.

The present chapter describes:

1 The institutional framework, including the constitutional framework of government and law-making, and the courts and tribunals which apply the law and resolve disputes.
2 The two main sources of UK law, that is, legislation and case-law.
3 The legal profession in the UK, which advises clients and handles litigation in the various courts and tribunals on behalf of clients.

The chapter concludes by pointing out some of the common criticisms levelled at the whole system.

THE INSTITUTIONAL FRAMEWORK

The constitutional framework of government

The United Kingdom has a unitary or centralised system of government rather than the federal or regional system which can be found, for example, in Germany or the USA. The UK has been a member of the European Community since 1973 and this means that certain areas of policy and law originate from Brussels. Apart from these areas of policy, UK government policies are normally formulated in London where most government departments are based. However, there is a Scottish Office in Edinburgh, a Welsh Office in Cardiff, and a Northern Ireland Office in Belfast.

Local government has primarily an administrative function, implementing central government policy. It has limited law-making powers and does have the power to make certain policy decisions, but in practice the latter are often curtailed by the financial controls exercised by central government. There are three tiers of local government: counties, districts and parishes, although in some areas there are unitary authorities. Currently, there are no regional assemblies.

In addition to central and local government many functions of government were carried out by public sector bodies such as area health authorities, or nationalised industries such as British Gas or British Coal (the National Coal Board). It has been government policy in recent years to devolve administrative functions to executive agencies and to privatise nationalised industries. These policies have had a considerable legal and constitutional impact. In addition to understanding how the various institutions work, it is important to note the constitutional and legal controls to which they are subject, as well as considering the influence which different groups can bring to bear on policy and legislation.

The European Union

When the United Kingdom joined the European Community (EC) at the beginning of 1973, it was in effect accepting that on certain matters the UK Government and Parliament would have to accept EC policies and laws. These matters included competition law, company law and certain aspects of employment law. During the last decade the EC has embarked on a determined attempt to harmonise the laws of member states not just in these areas but also, for example, in the areas of consumer protection, health and safety at work, and environmental law. The EC is now known as the European Union (EU).

Managers need to recognise the importance and potential of EU policies and laws for their business. The advantage for businesses which export goods is that products which comply with the requirements of UK law will normally comply with the law of other member states and that anti-competitive practices will not be permitted within any of the member states.

Since 1995 there have been 15 member states of the EU. The area of the single market also includes three member states of the European Free Trade Association (EFTA); Iceland, Liechtenstein and Norway. These countries form an European Economic Area with the EU.

There are three EU institutions which have an important role in policy and law-making. These are the Commission, the Council of Ministers and the European Parliament. The Commission is in effect the EU civil service. There are 20 Commissioners nominated by the member states including two nominated by the United Kingdom. Its province goes beyond that of the domestic civil service because it has a more central role in formulating and implementing policy. In particular it puts forward proposals to the Council of Ministers, drafts the budget proposals, is responsible for the implementation of policy and ensures that member states comply with their EU obligations.

The Council of Ministers is the main decision-making body of the EU. It is composed of ministers from each of the member states. Civil servants can also represent a member state on the council. The membership varies according to the subject under discussion. Therefore, if the subject is trade there will be a meeting of the trade ministers of all the member states. The Council is a part-time body and in practice much of its work is done by the Committee of Permanent Representatives which acts as a filter between the Commission and the Council. The Council normally acts on proposals put forward by the Commission and it has limited powers to amend those proposals. It is often required to consult the Parliament as well as the Economic and Social Committee before reaching a decision. However, the Council, can veto most proposed legislation.

The European Parliament has increased its powers over the budget in recent years. It is not a law-making body, although the Council of Ministers must consult it about certain proposed legislation. It mainly has a supervisory and advisory function. It has 567 members who are directly elected by the citizens of each member state.

In addition there is an Economic and Social Committee and a new Committee of the Regions which represent regional and sectional interests and which can advise the Council and the Committee on certain matters. Finally there is the European Court of Justice which is looked at in a later section of this chapter and a Court of Auditors which oversees and checks on the implementation of the budget.

The United Kingdom central government

Central government has a pivotal role in the formulation and implementation of new policies which may have a considerable effect on the aims and operation of a business. Managers need to know who has influence over the formulation, approval and implementation of such policies so that they can ensure that their voice is heard either individually or through a representative pressure group (such as the Confederation of British Industry).

The United Kingdom has a constitutional monarchy with the Queen as the Head of State rather than a president. Unusually among modern nation states, the UK has no written constitution. The monarch still has considerable constitutional powers in theory although in practice these powers are exercised on the advice of her ministers, usually the Prime Minister. Such powers include appointing and dismissing the Prime Minister as well as dissolving Parliament. Parliament is composed of the House of Lords and the House of Commons. The House of Lords is composed of hereditary peers, as well as life peers and senior bishops of the Church of England.

The Prime Minister is the leader of the political party with the majority of seats in the House of Commons and he or she is also a Member of the House of Commons. The Prime Minister is head of the government, which includes approximately 100 ministerial posts. Ministers are normally members of the House of Commons but occasionally are members of the House of Lords. The inner core of government is to be found in the Cabinet, whose twenty-plus members are usually heads of the important government departments such as the Home Office or the Department of Trade and Industry. Most government policy is formulated, or at least approved, in the Cabinet or in the Cabinet Committees. All members of the Cabinet are bound by its decisions and must not publicly dissent from those decisions unless they are prepared to resign.

In practice much of the background work is done by members of the Civil Service, who are permanent officials responsible for the implementation and administration of government policy. Civil servants are normally impartial and anonymous advisers. It is the Secretary of State or minister, as head of the government department, who is responsible to Parliament for the work of that department. In addition to civil servants some ministers, including the Prime Minister, appoint political advisers who only remain in post while the minister or the party is in power. These advisers can play an important role in the formulation of government policy.

Once the Cabinet has made a decision then it needs to be implemented. Often this requires legislation to be passed by Parliament. Draft legislation in the form of a 'bill' is published and is put before both Houses of Parliament. The issue of principle underlying the bill is debated at the second reading and the detailed provisions are scrutinised at the committee stage. Once the bill has been approved by a simple majority of the House of Commons and the House of Lords, it must receive the 'royal assent', which in practice is never refused, and it will then become an Act of Parliament. The House of Lords cannot veto a bill, it can only delay its progress for up to one year.

Apart from Acts of Parliament government departments frequently use 'subordinate legislation' to implement a policy. This can be done, for example, where there is an existing Act of Parliament giving the minister the power to introduce such provisions. An example of such delegated legislation is a statutory instrument. There are a variety of procedures for implementing statutory instruments. For example, the statutory instrument can be laid before

Parliament and members have the option of questioning the relevant minister about it.

The House of Commons has a potentially important role in the scrutinising of legislation. However, in the great majority of cases the principle of a Bill is accepted without much debate although there may be more argument over the detailed content of the Bill. This is because the government is selected from the party with the majority of seats in the House of Commons, and although members of the House of Commons are supposed to represent the views of their constituencies, in practice they do not usually diverge from their party's policy when voting. This system of government has been described as an 'elective dictatorship'(!) However, it is worth noting that there are a number of parliamentary committees which can influence government policy.

If legislation is not required, or even where it is, the detailed implementation of a proposal will often be supplemented by departmental circulars, or codes of practice, which although not 'law' in the sense of being legally binding are often of great practical importance and value, and should normally be complied with.

United Kingdom local government

In England, outside London there are two main types of authority: county councils and district councils. There are also 45 unitary authorities such as Bristol, Hull and Leicester. Wales and Scotland only have unitary authorities. County councils are normally responsible for, among other things, social services, education, aspects of planning control, refuse disposal and consumer protection. District councils are usually responsible for housing, aspects of planning control, local licensing and refuse collection. Parish councils are to be found in rural areas and have powers concerning rights of way and open spaces.

In London since the Greater London Council was abolished in 1985, there has been no London-wide local government authority. Local government rests in the hands of the London boroughs and the City of London corporation which exercise all local government functions.

Councillors are elected by British citizens who are resident or occupy land in the local government area. Councillors stand for election in the electoral area known as a 'ward', which is a relatively small area, with an electorate of several thousand voters. Councillors are not paid a salary for their work. They only receive an attendance allowance for time spent on council business. The most influential councillors are usually the Leader of the Council who is normally a member of the group which has the majority of seats on the council, and the chairmen/women of the council sub-committees. Councillors have recently tended to stand as a candidate for one of the national political parties, rather than purely on local issues.

Councils' duties and powers are usually granted to them by an Act of Parliament. These powers include policy-making powers, the extent of which varies according to the subject-matter but they are often circumscribed by central government controls. Major shifts in policy will normally have to be acceptable to central government. This is because the money which local government spends is only partly raised by the council tax. Business occupiers pay the non-domestic business rate which is set by central government. The majority of local government revenue comes from central government funding. Local government spending is a classic example of 'he who pays the piper calls the tune'. The council must not exceed the powers granted it by Parliament, and must exercise those powers lawfully. If the council is under a duty to provide a service then it is acting unlawfully if it fails to provide that service.

Local government policy is implemented by its full-time permanent staff, who also put forward proposals and give advice to the elected members. Most businesses find it useful to develop links with both these officials and with the local councillors for their ward. This is particularly true where the business needs the support of the council, for example, in certain licensing applications or planning developments, or where the business would like to be consulted about local authority proposals.

It is worth noting that the public and the press have the right not just to attend meetings of the council, but also meetings of its committees and sub-committees, as well as the right to examine council papers.

United Kingdom government agencies and other public sector bodies

During the last 150 years government has taken on more and more functions which were perceived as being its responsibility because the function benefited a large number, or a particular group of citizens. Since it was not practicable and arguably not necessary for all these functions to be carried out by central government departments, these departments set up agencies which were separate from themselves and run by a chief executive rather than by a minister. Since 1988 the Government has decided that this approach should be more widespread in order to improve the management and efficiency of the particular organisation.

These agencies implement rather than formulate government policy. They are normally established by an Act of Parliament, and are staffed by civil servants, but because there is a chief executive at their head rather than a minister their accountability to Parliament is less direct than that of a government department. Some agencies, such as the Benefit Agency, are departmental bodies. Others such as the Health and Safety Commission or the National Health Service are non-departmental.

In addition to these agencies governments have, for hundreds of years, given individuals or companies the right to carry out certain activities. Sometimes the right has not been exclusive, but often it has created a monopoly. Usually such rights have been granted by Act of Parliament such as those granted to the British Airways Corporation (BA), but occasionally they have been granted by royal charter, as in the case of the BBC. These bodies operate in much the same way as a private company (see Chapter 6), except that the members of the public cannot buy shares in them and the Government usually has some control over, for example, appointments to the board.

This has also been the main procedure used to nationalise particular industries which have been taken into public ownership particularly since 1945. Ministers usually are accountable to Parliament for how they exercise their powers (set out in the particular Act) in relation to the particular industry but not for the day-to-day running of the industry. The agency or industry did not usually consider its only purpose to be a profit-making concern. It was often felt that such an organisation should also take into account social factors, particularly where it was providing a service to the public.

However, due to a change in government policy, from 1979 onwards there has been and continues to be a spate of denationalisation and privatisation of both central and local government functions. The emphasis has been on encouraging efficiency and profit. However, it should be noted that removing functions from central or local government and placing them in private hands also reduces the legal and political accountability of the organisation to the citizens and to their elected representatives.

Privatisation and compulsory competitive tendering

These are two distinct techniques which have been introduced mainly with the aim of reducing the role of government in the provision of services to the public and ensuring that such ventures operate efficiently and on a commercial basis.

Many of the nationalised industries which are statutory corporations have been or may yet be turned into private companies. Examples are British Steel Corporation, British Telecom, British Gas, National Power, British Rail, the Post Office and London Underground. Normally as private companies their shares are then sold to members of the public on the Stock Exchange. The privatised companies are then subject to the ordinary rules of company law (see Chapter 6) rather than the rules of constitutional and administrative law. Sometimes the Government owns a percentage of the shares or has a 'golden share' which gives the Government additional rights; both of these options originally applied in the case of British Telecom, for example.

Local government and the National Health Service are now legally required to put out certain work to compulsory competitive tender. This can include cleaning and catering as well as building work, and legal services.

Accountability of government

Governments which are democratically elected are ultimately responsible to their electorate since the electors can decide not to vote for the party in power at the next election. Members of the Cabinet are jointly responsible to the House of Commons for its decisions. If the Cabinet does not have the support of the majority of the members of the House of Commons then it should resign. This is known as the 'doctrine of collective responsibility' which also requires Cabinet ministers to present a united front on policy matters.

Ministers are also personally responsible for the work of their department under the 'doctrine of individual responsibility'; this means that depending upon the circumstances they are accountable to the Prime Minister and their party, the House or Commons and to the courts. In addition the Government is the main UK institution involved in EU affairs, in particular through its membership of the Council of Ministers. The Foreign Secretary and other ministers report back to the House of Commons on EU developments.

Since the European Parliament, the House of Commons and local councils are elected bodies, the electors have some influence on the elected members of these institutions. The elected representatives can often provide useful information about the aims and objectives of, and the background to, a particular policy. In addition they may agree to support a business's view or proposal, or try to obtain redress for a grievance. Clearly in the case of the European Parliament and the House of Commons one member's influence and power may be limited but often their assistance is valuable. Therefore, the identity and interests of the particular members for the area in which a business is located should be known and, if appropriate, contacts made.

In addition members of elected bodies often work in committees. For example, the House of Commons has select committees shadowing most government departments including Trade and Industry, and the Environment. These committees are cross-party and they can interview and question ministers and other individuals on matters within the remit of the department. They produce reports which can have an influence on government policy. There are also two important select committees which scrutinise respectively EU legislation and more generally the work of the EU. In addition to these formal committees it is also useful to be aware of any relevant parliamentary groups which exist, such as the Scottish Whisky Distillers Association Group. These groups maintain links between, for example, a particular industry and members of both Houses of Parliament.

In practice most policy decisions in local government takes place not when voted upon in the full council but in discussions in the sub-committees of the council. The Finance sub-committee is particularly important in the decision-making process. In practice if one party has a clear majority on a council the decisions are often taken even earlier in private party meetings.

These traditional methods of making the government accountable were considered to be defective partly because of the great increase in administrative work undertaken by central and local governments. In particular members of the public did not always have complaints dealt with adequately, even where they were able to enlist the help of their Member of Parliament (MP) or local councillor. In 1967 a Parliamentary Ombudsman was introduced (formally known as the Parliamentary Commissioner for Administration). He or she is responsible for investigating complaints, by members of the public, of maladministration by a central government department or certain other authorities. Members of the public cannot approach the Ombudsman direct, they must go through their local MP. The Ombudsman reports back to the MP and can recommend but not enforce a remedy such as an award of compensation or administrative changes in the department concerned. The Parliamentary Ombudsman is also the National Health Service Ombudsman. In the mid-1970s Local Government Ombudsmen were introduced to investigate complaints, made to them by members of the public, of maladministration by local authorities.

Government accountability, however, is in effect reduced by making central government departments and local government responsible for fewer activities. This is a consequence of devolving functions to government agencies and public corporations, or privatising certain activities.

The Government has responded to this concern by extending the powers of the Parliamentary Ombudsmen to approximately 100 public bodies which carry out executive and administrative functions which are funded by government. These bodies include urban development corporations, the Environmental Agency (formerly the National Rivers Authority) and the Director General of Electricity Supply. However, nationalised industries are not within his jurisdiction.

Once a nationalised industry is privatised then even the limited accountability of the minister responsible to Parliament is removed. In effect monopolies are created which are not subject to the monopoly, takeover and merger controls to the same extent as large public companies. In the case of public services such as British Telecom, British Gas, and the electricity and water industries there has long been some form of public control and regulation. However, a common feature of these privatisations has been the introduction of independent bodies responsible for monitoring and scrutinising the new organisations. For example, OFTEL is responsible for regulating telecommunications in the UK and for ensuring that telecommunications operators comply with the obligations imposed by their licences. OFFER (Office of the Electricity Regulator) is concerned with monitoring the electricity supply industry's activities, promoting competition in the electricity industry, and protecting customers as well as controlling prices and issuing licences for generating, transmitting and supplying electricity. OFWAT (Office of Water Services) was set up to protect the interests of consumers of water and sewerage services. In particular the latter organisation is concerned with issuing licences to the appointed water companies as well as ensuring that water companies do not make excessive profits or unwise investments which result in increases in consumers' bills. This can be done, for example, by limiting the prices which companies can charge their customers. OFGAS (Office of Gas Supply) monitors the gas supply industry. Public gas suppliers have to comply with obligations imposed by the Government, the

Director General of Gas Supply and the Gas Consumers Council. In addition there are consumers committees for each of these industries.

The majority of powers exercised by government departments and by ministers as well as all those exercised by local government and public statutory bodies are granted by legislation, frequently an Act of Parliament. The legislation itself often provides for criminal or civil liability arising in certain circumstances. However, administrative law also imposes a general duty on public bodies to exercise their public law powers lawfully. This means that public bodies should act fairly when reaching a decision, hearing the views of interested parties before reaching the decision. In addition a public body should not exceed or abuse the powers granted to it by statute. If statute imposes a duty on a public body such as the obligation imposed on district councils to house the homeless, then they must perform that duty. If the court decides that the public body has acted unlawfully there are a variety of remedies available depending upon the particular situation. The court, for example, may quash the original decision or it may order the body to perform its legal duty.

It is worth noting that the UK government can challenge on similar grounds in the European Court of Justice, the validity of the decisions or actions of, for example, the Commission and Council of Ministers.

The distinction between a public body exercising its powers and a private body such as a club acting in pursuance of a contract is fairly clear. However, the distinction is not always so clear-cut when the work of government departments are devolved to government agencies, industries nationalised and nationalised industries privatised. Unlike French law, there is not a long tradition of administrative law based on the public/private distinction. For example, English law does not yet clearly distinguish between contracts made involving public bodies and those involving private individuals or organisations.

Pressure groups

So far this chapter has concentrated on the formal framework of government. However, other groups can have considerable influence on government policy at all levels.

In the context of the EU there are many national and international non-governmental organisations which lobby and attempt to influence the European Commission and the European Parliament. An example is ECRE (European Consultation on Refugees and Exiles) which was set up as a forum for collaboration between some forty-five non-governmental organisations in Europe concerned with refugees and the right of asylum. Another example is the Consumers Association which is not just concerned with lobbying the UK Parliament and government but also the appropriate EU institutions because much of consumer law now emanates from the EU rather than from the UK government. Other grous are represented by, for example, the Commission for Racial Equality (CRE) and the Equal Opportunities Commission (EOC).

Employers' associations such as the CBI and the Institute of Directors can also attempt to influence and comment upon UK government policy, as can trade associations, for example, the Society of Motor Manufacturers and Traders. Some MPs will speak on behalf of particular groups in the House of Commons. Some organisations employ professional lobbying companies to help them get their view across to MPs and Ministers.

Employees' interests are represented by trade unions, who sponsor some Labour Party MPs. The Police Federation also has a Conservative MP who will speak on its behalf. At local government level local chambers of commerce and professional groups can be influential.

Given this array of lobbying groups, policy-making procedures and mechanisms, the important thing for managers is to identify those groups which have similar interests to those of their own organisation and to join and participate in those groups. This should increase the information available to and the influence of the manager's own organisation. In conclusion, managers should be familiar with the formal framework, the extent of the powers of each institution, and find out who and where in practice decisions are made and influence lies.

Courts, tribunals and other forms of dispute resolution

The idea of the law conjures up to many people the idea of courts and bewigged barristers seeking justice in the courts on behalf of innocent defendants wrongly accused of crimes. Although going to court is one means of resolving legal disputes two points should be noted.

First, going to court is usually only done in the last resort in civil cases. Over 90 per cent of civil disputes are resolved without going to court. They are resolved by negotiation between the parties, by mediation or by arbitration. Not all disputes fall within the jurisdiction of the courts. Certain matters, for example claims for unfair dismissal, are heard by tribunals.

Second, the law should not just be regarded as a means of resolving disputes, it also has a *planning function* in that it can be used to reduce the risk of disputes or legal liability arising in the first place.

The United Kingdom has three different legal systems which have different court structures and administer slightly different laws. The three systems are those for England and Wales, Scotland, and Northern Ireland. This chapter and the next are based on the law applicable to England and Wales, although in the areas of law covered by this book there is little practical difference, in the content of the law, between the systems. The main differences are in the areas of land law and criminal law. The different court structures in Scotland will be briefly noted.

The *adversarial system* of justice prevails in the United Kingdom. This means each of the parties to the dispute has to present their case orally, with the help of documents and witnesses, to the court. Witnesses will be questioned by the barrister for each party with the aim of establishing the truth. The judge is concerned with managing the trial and hearing the evidence presented. Judges may ask questions of the witnesses but only to clarify a point. Once the evidence has been presented, the judge then gives a reasoned decision. Normally, juries are only used to decide serious criminal cases. This system contrasts with the *inquisitorial system* which is more common in the rest of Europe. This normally depends more heavily upon written rather than oral evidence and the judge can have a more active investigating role. It is also worth noting that other European countries often have a separate system of administrative courts or tribunals for reviewing government decisions and actions.

The courts

Courts have criminal and/or civil jurisdiction. Managers are likely to come across both civil and criminal law in their work. Civil law is concerned with imposing obligations on individuals, companies and government as well as with resolving disputes by, for example, awarding compensation to the injured party. The law of contract, employment law and company law are examples of civil law. Criminal law is more concerned with protecting people and their property from harm, preserving public order and punishing offenders. Managers would come into contact with criminal law where, for example, there has been a breach of health and safety or consumer protection regulations, or where there has been insider dealing in a company's shares.

Civil courts   Cases are heard in the County Court or one of the three divisions of the High Court (see Figure 5.1). The jurisdiction of the County Court is limited geographically and financially. Usually the County Court has jurisdiction if the defendant lives in its area. The County Court hears claims, for example, in contract and tort, for the recovery of debts as well as disputes over land and bankruptcy proceedings. In contract or tort cases the court has jurisdiction to hear claims up to £50,000. If the claim is for more than £50,000 then it would usually be heard in the Queen's Bench Division. Claims for less than £3,000 fall within the small claims jurisdiction of the County Court. An advantage of using the small claims jurisdiction is that claimants do not have to pay the other party's costs even if they lose the case. This jurisdiction is a form of arbitration and can also be available where the claim is for £3,000 or more, if both parties agree. Cases are heard by a single judge.

The Queen's Bench Division of the High Court hears many commercial cases and has a specialist Commercial Court, which hears, for example, international trade cases. The Chancery Division hears a variety of cases including those involving bankruptcy, partnership and intellectual property. There is a Patents' Court within this division. The Family Division hears matrimonial and child care cases. In all three divisions cases are usually heard by a single judge.

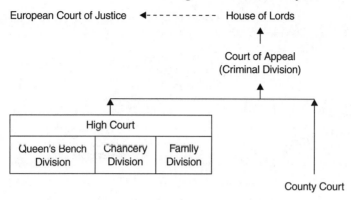

Figure 5.1 Civil courts

Appeals against the decision of the County Court or the High Court judge can be brought by a dissatisfied litigant. Such appeals would normally be heard by three lord justices in the Court of Appeal (Civil Division). In certain circumstances a further appeal can be made on a question of law to five law lords in the House of Lords. In Scotland the Sheriff Court deals with most civil litigation with any appeal being heard first by the Court of Session and then by the House of Lords.

If the case involves a question of interpretation of European Union law then the House of Lords must refer that question to the European Court of Justice. Lower courts have a discretion over whether or not to refer the case.

Criminal courts   Criminal cases, including prosecutions for breach of health and safety regulations, always start in the Magistrates Court (see Figure 5.2). If the offence is a summary offence then the trial will also take place in that court. There will be three lay magistrates or one stipendiary magistrate hearing the case. The former are not legally qualified and they are not paid for this work, which they do on a rota basis. Stipendiary magistrates are legally qualified, normally have full-time appointments and are paid a salary. Stipendiary magistrates are found in the larger cities such as London, Birmingham and Manchester.

If the offence is more serious and is classified as an indictable offence, then the trial will take place in the Crown Court. The case will be heard by a judge and a jury of twelve people. Certain intermediate offences can be tried in either court.

Appeals against the decision of a Magistrates Court are usually heard by the Crown Court which will then be composed of a judge and two lay magistrates. An appeal can be made against the finding of a Crown Court in either case, to three judges in the Court of Appeal. Appeals on questions of law can also be heard by two or three judges in the Queen's Bench Divisional Court. A final

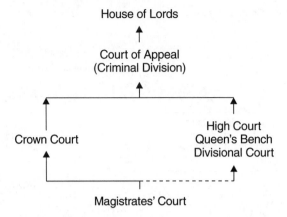

Figure 5.2 Magistrates' courts

avenue of appeal, on important questions of law, can be heard by five law lords in the House of Lords.

In Scotland, summary offences are tried in district courts, summary and solemn (similar to indictable) offences in the Sheriff Court or the High Court of Justiciary, and the High Court has exclusive jurisdiction over certain serious offences such as murder. The Court of Criminal Appeal is part of the High Court and hears criminal appeals from all three courts. There is no provision for an appeal to be made to the House of Lords.

Tribunals

Tribunals have been introduced, particularly in the last fifty years, as a means of resolving disputes between the citizen and the Government. The disputes are often over relatively small sums of money. Social security appeal tribunals are an example of such a tribunal. The advantages of tribunals over courts are supposed to be that they are quicker, cheaper, less formal and more specialized. These advantages are not apparent in all tribunals!

A tribunal is also the forum for resolving claims brought by employees against employers for unfair dismissal or redundancy, as well as for sex or race discrimination. Such industrial tribunals have proved very popular with employees. However, there are long delays in hearing the cases, employment law is complex, employers often use lawyers to represent them, and legal aid is not available for tribunal hearings. The hearings are usually more informal than in court. The tribunal is composed of a legally qualified chairman with an employers' representative and a trade union representative. It is usual in most tribunals to have a legally qualified chairman and two lay representatives providing specialist practical knowledge.

An appeal against an industrial tribunal decision can be made to the Employment Appeal Tribunal (EAT) and then to the Court to Appeal (Civil Division), and to the House of Lords. The EAT is composed of a judge and two lay representatives as in an industrial tribunal.

Other forms of dispute resolution

Litigation is stressful, time-consuming, expensive, confrontational and public. Managers and businesses have to remember that even if they win the case it can be costly psychologically as well as financially, and there can be long-term financial effects if the other party was, for example, a valued customer or supplier. It is becoming more and more common to attempt to resolve disputes without resort to litigation in order to avoid its disadvantages.

Arbitration has long been used as a means of resolving contract-based disputes, such as those arising in shipping and in the construction industries. Arbitration is agreed by the parties as the means of resolving any dispute. Legislation provides a statutory framework for such arbitration. The parties appoint the arbitrator and agree upon the arbitrator's terms of reference. The arbitrator is normally an expert in the subject-matter of the dispute as well as being familiar with the relevant law. The parties will be bound by the arbitrator's decision although it is possible to appeal to a court on a point of law.

London is an international centre for arbitration. For example, the Chartered Institute of Arbitrators has published rules for national arbitrations and has set up an International Arbitration Centre in London which provides arbitration services. Contracts or disputes with an international element can use the rules of the London Court of International Arbitration. The institute also provides conciliation and mediation services as well as a supervised settlement procedure.

Conciliation basically involves a conciliator trying to encourage the parties to reach a settlement themselves. *Mediation* is similar but the main difference is that the mediator will put forward proposals for settlement to the parties. If these procedures are used then it is not necessary to take account of the relevant law, nor are the parties bound by any recommendations made by the conciliator or the mediator. The *supervised settlement procedure* is more like a trial in that each of the parties nominate a management representative who has authority to negotiate on their behalf. They then give each other their written version of the facts before representing themselves at a formal meeting where their differences are clarified. An independent third party is also involved and present at the meeting, and tries to encourage them to reach a negotiated settlement after the formal meeting. If these procedures do not produce a resolution of the dispute then the parties can still refer the matter to arbitration.

In December 1993 the Commercial Court of the Queen's Bench Division issued a 'Practice Statement' encouraging parties to litigation and their advisers to consider using alternative dispute resolution such as mediation and conciliation, particularly in cases where the costs of litigation were likely to be wholly disproportionate to the amount at stake. A further Practice Statement was issued in June 1996.

SOURCES OF UNITED KINGDOM LAW

There are two main sources of law in the United Kingdom today. These are legislation and case law. Legislation has been the primary source of new law for about the last hundred years. Businesses need to know which rules are legally binding and must be complied with, and which are merely indicative of good practice.

Codes of practice whether issued by trade associations, the Office of Fair Trading or government departments are not law. Nor are self-regulatory guidelines such as the City Code on takeovers and mergers, or the Cadbury Code of best conduct and recommendations on corporate governance. However, it is advisable to be aware of and normally comply with any guidance contained in such documents as they can be produced in court as evidence of good practice. Government departments also issue circulars, guidance notes and policy statements which, while not strictly law, are of considerable practical importance and are often treated by the courts as indicative of, for example, how a particular piece of legislation should be interpreted.

Unlike most European countries the UK does not have a codified system of law. Therefore it is not possible to find the basic principles of law in a single code or series of codes. For example, in France the Code Civil or Napoleonic Code of 1804 and in Germany the Bürgerliches Gesetzbuch (BGB) or Civil Code of 1896 contain the basic principles of private law, that is the law which sets out the rights and duties which individual citizen and organisations owe each other.

Legislation

Both the UK Parliament and the European Union promulgate legislation. In the UK Acts of Parliament, also known as 'statutes', are the major source of new principles of domestic law. Subordinate legislation usually provides for the detailed implementation of an Act. By-laws are usually passed by local government or specific bodies, such as London Transport, to whom Parliament has delegated its law-making powers. In terms of quantity, more pages of subordinate legislation come into force each year.

An Act of Parliament becomes law once it receives the 'royal assent'. However, it does not necessarily come into force on that date. It is important to know the exact date when an Act or a piece of subordinate legislation comes into force because it is only then that it becomes part of the law and legally binding. Usually legislation does not have retrospective effect.

European Union law has been part of UK law since 1973. It is binding on all member states and takes priority over the domestic law of all the member states including that of the UK. However, only the treaties and regulations have 'direct effect', that is, are automatically part of UK law and enforceable in the UK courts as soon as they are part of EU law.

Directives and decisions are not automatically part of domestic law. However, numerous directives have been incorporated into UK law. They are the main method used by the EU for achieving harmonisation of specific areas of national law. Each member state must incorporate directives into their national law. In the UK this is normally done by UK 'regulations' – a form of UK subordinate legislation. If a member state fails to incorporate the directive properly, or at all, then the member state will be in breach of EU law and individuals will have a remedy in the domestic courts in certain circumstances. Decisions of the EU institutions are normally of limited importance because they are only binding on the parties to whom they are addressed.

The legislative sources of UK law are summarised in Figure 5.3.

Case-law

This is the second main source of UK law. It is also referred to as 'judicial precedent'. This concept is one of the chief distinguishing characteristics of the English legal system. It means that if an English court has made a decision on a particular point of law, such as the meaning of a word in an Act of Parliament, then that decision will be binding on another court if the same point comes before it, unless that court is of a higher status (see above). This is known as the 'doctrine of binding precedent'.

In practice it is the decisions of the House of Lords and the Court of Appeal which are most influential. Decisions of the High Court can be influential if there are no relevant decisions of the higher two courts. Most of the important decisions of these courts are reported in one of the sets of 'law reports'. The

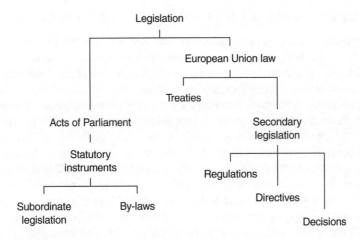

Figure 5.3 Legislative sources of UK law

whole decision is not binding, only the part which applies the principles of law to the facts found to be material by the court. This is called the *ratio decidendi* (reason for the decision). The courts tend to apply previous decisions and to interpret legislation restrictively. The judges claim that they are merely declaring what the law is and they deny that by their decisions they are making new law, although in reality sometimes they are doing so.

The European Court of Justice has not adopted the English doctrine of binding precedent, preferring to follow the European approach that previous decisions while influential are not binding. The Court of Justice has been fairly adventurous in its interpretation of European Union legislation, being prepared to fill in any gaps in that legislation rather than leave it to the EU institutions to amend the legislation.

The basic problem for managers among other litigants is being able to predict how a court will interpret and apply the law in a particular case. The traditional English approach is more predictable but favours certainty sometimes at the cost of flexibility and fairness. On the other hand, an approach which favours filling in gaps and looking at the purpose of the legislation can create considerable uncertainty.

As already indicated different legal systems operate in Scotland and Northern Ireland, but the content of the law discussed in this and the next chapter is very similar in all three jurisdictions. England and Wales comprise one jurisdiction. The increasing importance of European Union law as a source of United Kingdom law should not be underestimated. In theory this should make life easier for Europe-wide businesses because the same principles of law should apply in all member states of the EU. In practice, however, member states do not always implement EU law in the same way or at the same time. This can cause uncertainty which may only be resolved by a decision of the European Court of Justice.

THE LEGAL PROFESSION IN THE UNITED KINGDOM

Three points must be made at the outset. The first is that in the United Kingdom there is a split profession, the split being between lawyers who are primarily advocates or specialists and those who deal with the lay client. The former are known as barristers, except in Scotland where they are called advocates, the latter are called solicitors. Barristers are usually portrayed wearing wigs and gowns. Secondly, there are separate professional organisations for England and Wales, Northern Ireland and Scotland as well as some differences of organisation in Scotland. Thirdly the judiciary is selected from the members of the legal profession and usually from among senior barristers who have practised for at least twenty years. It is not uncommon for solicitors to be appointed as circuit or district judges who sit in Crown Courts and County Courts, but it is rare for a solicitor to be appointed as a High Court Judge. Unlike other European countries, such as France, academic lawyers are rarely appointed as judges and their views are less influential than in civil law systems.

Large and middle-sized companies and trade unions often employ solicitors and occasionally barristers in their own legal department. These lawyers deal with the legal aspects of the particular organisation and should ensure, for example, that the organisation's working practices comply with legal requirements such as health and safety at work and consumer protection regulations, as well as advising on employment and trading contracts. The legal department should be able to advise managers on the legal aspects of a particular problem. Smaller organisations tend to not have their own legal department but regularly use firms of solicitors to deal with legal matters. Legal departments may also refer specific matters to specialist firms of solicitors or to a barrister.

Barristers normally can only be sent work by a solicitor who may work for an organisation or for a firm of solicitors. An organisation which does not employ a solicitor cannot normally directly approach a barrister. A barrister will usually be sent a case because the barrister's expertise as an advocate or a specialist is needed, an independent view is useful, and because using a barrister can be cheaper than using a solicitor. Senior barristers can apply to the Lord Chancellor's department to be made a Queen's Counsel (QC), colloquially referred to as a 'silk' because their gown is made of silk. QCs normally appear with a junior barrister.

The division of work between barristers and solicitors is based on the principle that only barristers have the right to appear in the higher courts (Crown Court, High Court, Court of Appeal and House of Lords) and that only solicitors can deal with lay clients, whether organisations or individual members of the public. Until recently solicitors had a monopoly over conveyancing, which includes, for example, the sale of a house, and in practice most conveyancing is still carried out by them. Solicitors have frequently argued that they should have a right of audience in the higher courts. They can appear in the Magistrates Courts, the County Courts, and in industrial tribunals, but if the case goes to appeal they normally have to instruct a barrister to represent the client in the higher court. In 1990 the Courts and Legal Services Act permitted solicitors to become 'licensed advocates' and to appear in the higher courts. The first such advocates appeared in the Scottish courts in 1993.

In return barristers in limited circumstances are now allowed to be approached directly by members of other professions such as surveyors and accountants who no longer have to approach them through a solicitor. Barristers have considered pressing for the general public to have direct access to them. The cost of legal advice varies according to the status of the individual solicitor or barrister and the status of the solicitor's firm. Most solicitors work in firms which legally are partnerships rather than companies (see Chapter 6). The senior solicitors will be partners who will have a share in any profits made by the firm. Their hourly rate will vary but is unlikely to be less than £75 and could well be £500. Other solicitors will be salaried and will not have a share in the profits. When going to a firm of solicitors for advice it is becoming more common for the client to ask for and be given details of the fees which will be charged and, if appropriate, an estimate of the likely cost of the legal advice and assistance required. It is now possible but still unusual for solicitors to work in partnership with other professionals such as surveyors or accountants in order to provide a client with a package of services.

A practising barrister is self-employed and works with other barristers from offices known as 'chambers'. The great majority of barristers are based in central London in or around the four Inns of Court. Barristers' chambers are also to be found in the larger provincial cities such as Birmingham, Manchester, Cardiff and Newcastle. A barrister's fees are negotiated between the solicitor and the barrister's clerk.

It is difficult to give precise figures, but in commercial litigation with court hearings lasting weeks rather than days the legal costs can run into hundreds of thousands of pounds. Even for a relatively straightforward contract claim in the County Court one party's legal costs can reach £10,000. These costs do not take into account the cost of running the court itself, that is, the cost of the judge, the court staff and the buildings. The Lord Chancellor has unsuccessfully proposed that these costs should be borne by the parties to the litigation.

A system of civil and criminal 'legal aid' provides advice and assistance for the poorer sections of the community paid for out of central government funds. However, only the poorest people are not required to contribute some money towards the cost of their case. From the point of view of a business, one of the disadvantages of suing, or being sued by, a litigant on legal aid is that unlike a personally funded litigant there are fewer financial constraints on them pursuing the claim to the bitter end. In addition even if the business wins its case it is unlikely to recover its costs from the Legal Aid Board.

In conclusion, the legal profession is being hauled into the second half of the twentieth century. The division between solicitors and barristers remains but is less clear-cut. Solicitors will continue to deal with the vast majority of legal work. They are becoming more efficient and responsive to the needs and expectations of their clients. Fax machines and word processors are becoming the norm even in small firms. The Bar will survive as an independent profession, but it is likely to provide a specialist referral service with individual barristers providing expertise which would not normally be available in a solicitor's firm.

The very poor or the rich can afford to obtain legal advice and assistance. The people in the middle are often deterred by the cost. Either the Government has to expand the 'legal aid scheme', which is unlikely, or the fees charged by lawyers must be reduced. This could be done either by simplifying many of the procedures by, for example, reducing the number of oral hearings, or by ensuring that the legal profession allows everybody who is qualified, to train and practice as a lawyer. Neither of these proposals are likely to be implemented in the near future.

CONCLUSION

There are two major criticisms of the English legal system. First, that it is too expensive. Second that it is too slow. The question of expense usually refers to the cost of the lawyers. The adversarial system is in itself expensive requiring two sets of lawyers investigating and preparing the case for both the plaintiff and the defendant. The British system has always placed great emphasis on oral argument, but in recent years has also required written submissions to support the oral case.

The Conservative Government was considering requiring the parties to civil litigation to pay the real cost of court time rather than the nominal fees now required. This proposal may have reduced the amount of litigation and encouraged the use of cheaper alternative methods of resolving disputes, but it was successfully opposed by the legal profession.

Delays occur at all stages of the legal process. However, in civil litigation it is the parties and the lawyers who regulate the speed at which a dispute proceeds towards the courtroom, although they are dependent on the courts themselves for allocating court time to the case. The length of delay will vary from court to court but the longer the case, the longer the wait is likely to be.

It is possible to go to court to obtain an injunction within a matter of hours in an emergency, for example, to prevent assets being sold. However, in other situations even where the judge considers that the matter should be heard quickly it can still take three or four months to have a full hearing. Normally it will take at least more than six months for a case to be heard in the County Court and even longer in the High Court. The court diary revolves around the availability of the judges rather than the requirements of the litigants.

In July 1996 Lord Woolf published his report on the civil justice system in England and Wales. He put forward over 300 recommendations for reform. At the heart of his proposals is to give judges a more active role in the management of cases, with the aim of speeding up the whole process. The proposals were to be implemented by July 1998 but are being reviewed by the new Lord Chancellor.

SELECTED READING

Berlin, M. and Dyer, C. (1994)
Foulkes, D. (1995)
Ruff, A. (ed.) (1995)
Sparke, A. (1996)
Woolf, H. (Lord) (1996)

6   The legal framework

Anne Ruff

INTRODUCTION

Businesses in the United Kingdom operate in an environment regulated by legal rules. Therefore they need to be familiar with the legal context of their operations. This chapter examines six areas of English and European Community law which are of particular relevance to business organisations operating in the UK. These areas are:

- the law regulating business organisations;
- contract law and practice;
- product liability and the law;
- the workplace, the environment and the law;
- industrial relations and the law;
- competition and the law.

THE LAW REGULATING BUSINESS ORGANISATIONS

The law provides an organisational framework within which businesses function. From a legal point of view businesses in the United Kingdom usually fall into one of three legal categories:

- sole trader;
- partnership;
- limited company.

A sole trader is not subject to any specific legal requirements. A partnership is usually regulated by a partnership agreement made by the partners, which rests on legislative foundations. A limited company is subject to extensive and detailed legislative regulation which depends to a certain extent upon the type of limited company.

There are two other categories of business organisation of limited legal importance. First, corporations, which can be established by royal charter such as the BBC, or by statute such as British Gas. Such corporations are often in effect public or private monopolies. Second, European Economic Interest Groupings (EEIE) which were recently introduced by the European Union in order to encourage cooperation between businesses in different member states.

Businesses need to consider not just their own legal status, but also the legal status of the organisations with which they trade. This is because the legal rights, duties and obligations of a business as well as those of individuals involved with the business will vary according to its legal status.

Legal status

A sole trader as an individual has legal personality and is personally liable for the activities and all of the debts of the business. Since 1992 a sole trader can create a single member private limited company. This enables sole traders to limit their personal liability.

A partnership, on the other hand, does not have legal personality under English law. This means that each partner, as an individual, has legal personality and is 'jointly and severally liable' for the activities and all of the debts of the partnership. A partnership is the form usually taken where the business involves the provision of skills and expertise. Professionals such as solicitors or accountants, are normally organised in partnerships.

The most important characteristic of a limited company is that it has 'legal personality'. This means that the company, as opposed to its directors, shareholders or employees, can sue and be sued for breaches of the law. Directors, shareholders and employees may also be liable for breaches of obligations they owe as individuals but the company is liable for actions done on its behalf. The courts are rarely prepared to lift the 'corporate veil' to examine the actions of the individuals or the parent or holding company who may in fact control the company.

The owners of the company are the shareholders who own shares in the company. Shareholders may be individuals or other companies. The shareholders share in the profits and the losses of the company, but their liability for losses is limited to the value of their shares. Unlike sole traders or partners they do not own the business's assets such as its buildings, nor are they liable for its debts. Commercial ventures are most likely to take the form of a limited company, although they often start their existence as a partnership or sole trader.

There are several reasons why a sole trader or partnership may decide to become a limited company. The main reasons are:

- so that the owner or partners will in future benefit from limited liability as they will only be personally liable up to the value of their shares in the company;
- to produce a lower tax bill because a company is only liable to pay corporation tax, whereas sole traders and partners are assessed for income tax and capital gains tax on their profits and gains;

- it is easier to raise capital for the business by, for example, selling shares in the company;
- to separate the ownership of the business from its management. Shareholders, unlike partners or sole traders are often not involved in the day-to-day running of the business.

There are disadvantages in setting up a limited company. These include:

- satisfying the legal formalities required under the Companies Acts;
- being required to publish the company's accounts;
- the owners of the business may have less control over the management of the business.

Name of the business

One way of discovering whether a business is a limited company or not is by finding out its corporate name which may be different from its trading or business name. A limited company must have the words 'Ltd' or 'Limited', or 'plc' or 'public limited company' at the end of its name. The corporate name and the address of its registered office for example must be printed on all the company's letters and displayed at the company's registered address and any other business premises.

The use of the words '& Co.', or 'Company' alone means that the business is not a limited company and that it is run as a partnership or by a sole trader. However, both types of businesses are also required to identify the partners or owner of the business on their business correspondence and at their business premises.

Management responsibilities

If the business is a run by a sole trader then that individual will be responsible for the organisation, management and development of the business. No legal formalities have to be satisfied for the establishment of such a business. Sole traders can recruit employees to assist them in the business. However, it is the sole trader who will normally be personally liable if the business breaks the law, whether the liability is for breach of contract, for negligence, for breach of statutory duty or a breach of the criminal law.

If the business is a partnership then the law requires there to be between two and twenty partners. Although certain professional partnerships, such as solicitors, are allowed to have more than twenty partners. Each partner has the authority to enter into contracts on the partnership's behalf. Equally each partner is potentially liable for all the debts and other legal obligations of the partnership. This includes liability for breaches of the civil and criminal law. Although the partnership does not have a separate legal personality, the partnership can sue and be sued in the partnership's name, or the firm's name if that is different to the names of the partners.

The partners' rights and obligations are found in the partnership agreement which is in effect a contract entered into by all the partners and which is based on mutual trust and good faith. The Partnership Act 1890 provides a statutory backdrop to this agreement. The agreement need not be in writing, but it is advisable to put it in writing so as to avoid any disagreements in the future. The agreement should deal with the establishment, management and dissolution of the partnership as well as its financial and administrative arrangements.

The agreement may provide that a particular partner is responsible for the management of the partnership. Whether or not there is such a partner the agreement should clearly set out any limitations on any partner's authority to act on behalf of the partnership. For example, an agreement may provide that junior partners do not have the authority to enter into contracts worth more than £1,000. Such a limitation should also be made known to third parties who have dealings with the partnership. If it is not, the partnership may well find itself liable irrespective of the limitation in the partnership agreement.

Management responsibilities in a limited company are subject to considerably more legal regulation than in a business run by a sole trader or as a partnership. The extent of the regulation depends upon the precise legal form of the limited company (see Figure 6.1) rather than its commercial and financial size and importance. A small family run company can be subject to the same amount of legal regulation as large private companies such as those owned by Richard Branson and Andrew Lloyd Webber. A limited company must be registered under the Companies Act 1985 which is the principal Act regulating the governance of companies. There are just under one million registered companies in Great Britain.

Commercial companies are limited by shares. A shareholder acquires shares in a company and has a share certificate which indicates the number of shares owned. A profitable company will pay dividends to its shareholders which are calculated according to the number of shares owned. A company can raise money by issuing more shares as well as by raising loans from financial institutions or from individuals.

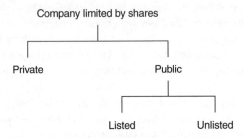

Figure 6.1 Legal forms of limited company

Most limited companies are private companies and will have 'Ltd' or 'Limited' at the end of its name. A private company normally has two or more shareholders and a company secretary. An auditor will also have to be appointed. It can be set up with one director and a company secretary but is subject to special rules. A private company does not need to have a minimum amount of capital, but it will need to issue at least one share which must have a nominal value of at least one penny. Its shares cannot be sold to the public. They can be sold or given to existing shareholders, employees or family members and to venture capitalists under the Venture Capitalist Trust Scheme. It can begin trading once it has received its certificate of incorporation from the Registrar of Companies. It will be required to publish its accounts but small and medium-sized private companies can take advantage of the option of filing abbreviated rather than full accounts. In September 1996 the Department of Trade and Industry published a consultative paper on the requirements of small companies to produce their accounts in standard formats, as part of the Government's reform programme to assist small businesses.

Public companies on the other hand can offer their shares for the public to buy. However, when selling shares to the public the company must provide to potential purchasers detailed written information about the company in a prospectus. A public company must consist of at least two shareholders and a qualified company secretary together with a professionally qualified auditor. A public company must have a minimum authorised share capital of £50,000. As well as a certificate of incorporation, a trading certificate must have been issued by the Registrar of Companies before the public company can start trading and borrowing money. A public company would have 'plc' or 'public limited company' at the end of its name.

Not all public companies are listed companies. Listed companies are those whose shares can be purchased on a recognised market such as the London Stock Exchange. To be admitted to the Stock Exchange a company would have to satisfy additional stringent requirements as to its financial probity. There is also an Unlisted Securities Market but its future is under discussion.

As already indicated a limited company must be registered with the Registrar of Companies. The incorporation procedure is more straightforward than in most EU member states. It is possible for the procedure to be carried out in one day and it is also possible to buy 'off-the-shelf' companies which have already been incorporated but which are dormant. Once the company is incorporated it becomes a separate 'legal person' which is the fundamental principle of English company law. The 'veil of incorporation' is lowered and the identity of the shareholders is generally but not always irrelevant to legal liability.

To register a company certain formalities have to be gone through including producing two documents which underpin the operation of the company. These two documents are: 'The Memorandum of Association' and 'The Articles of Association'.

The Memorandum of Association sets out the constitution and powers of the company. Usually such powers will include the power to borrow and raise money. It must also deal with certain matters, such as the precise name and registered address of the company as well as stating that it is a public company (if it is). Most importantly it will contain the objects clause of the company. This restricts the transactions which the company can legally and validly undertake to those listed in the clause. Therefore it is important that the management of the company does not develop new ventures without first ensuring that such ventures fall within the existing objects clause.

The Articles of Association set out the rules under which the company must operate, in addition to those laid down in the Companies Acts. The rules are agreed by the shareholders and will usually include, for example, the delegation by the shareholders of the day-to-day management of the company to the Board of Directors. The articles should be regularly reviewed to take into account changes in the law and in business practice. The articles may be supplemented by shareholders' agreements which have a wider scope than the articles and can, for example, confer certain rights on shareholders which cannot be conferred by the articles.

The Board of Directors will normally include the following people:

- chairman;
- managing director;
- finance director;
- company secretary;
- director of human resources;
- other executive directors;
- non-executive directors.

A small company is likely to have a much smaller Board of Directors. While policy decisions are usually taken by the whole board, the power to take other decisions is usually delegated to one or more directors. Directors are not automatically paid for being directors so usually directors have a contract of employment with the company which entitles them to receive a salary.

However, all the directors are responsible to the shareholders for the management of the company and can be dismissed by the shareholders on a majority vote of the shareholders at the Annual General Meeting (AGM) or at an Extraordinary General Meeting (EGM). The directors are often also shareholders themselves. To avoid a conflict of interest, the law imposes rigorous duties on directors to prevent them using information and opportunities acquired as directors for their personal advantage. In certain circumstances a director may be held criminally liable for a breach of such a duty. In addition directors owe duties to creditors and the company itself not to continue trading when the company is unable to pay its debts. Despite these rigorous duties it is not certain whether a director would be liable to shareholders for negligence in the management of the company.

Unlike other EU member states, company directors under English law, only have a very limited duty to consider the interests of their employees. There is currently no requirement to have active worker participation in the boardroom. However, some multi-national companies such as BAT Industries have voluntarily introduced European Works Councils.

In practice the control of a company often rests with its senior managers (not all of whom will be directors) rather than with its shareholders or even its board of directors. The interests of managers and shareholders do not always coincide, and this led to concern about the role and accountability of managers to shareholders. Managers can manipulate the information which they are required to disclose to shareholders. The requirement of shareholders' approval is often a formality, and shareholders often have to overcome practical and financial difficulties if they wish to challenge the behaviour of directors. In October 1996 the Law Commission provisionally recommended that the law and procedures by which shareholders can enforce their right against, and obtain compensation for the company from directors should be streamlined.

In the United Kingdom the Cadbury Committee on the 'Financial Aspects of Corporate Governance' was set up to examine the above concerns in relation to listed companies. It was a non-governmental committee and in 1992 it published its recommendations and a Code of Best Practice, which it hoped would be adopted by all, not just by listed, companies. In 1995 the Greenbury Report made recommendations on the disclosure of directors' remuneration. The Hampel Committee is reviewing the recommendations of the Cadbury and Greenbury Committees.

Briefly, the Cadbury Committee recommended that the board of directors should control the company and monitor senior management. The board would be able to do this more effectively if a number of non-executive directors were appointed to the board. The majority of these directors should be independent of, albeit appointed by, the management. In addition the committee proposed the establishment of audit and remuneration committees where the non-executive (but not necessarily the independent non-executive) directors would be in control.

It should be noted that none of these provisions are legally binding or enforceable by any professional bodies. However, the Cadbury Code and the Greenbury Code are of practical importance. For example, the London Stock Exchange requires directors of listed companies to state in their companies' reports and accounts whether they comply with the codes. Since 1995 statements on internal controls and on being a going concern also have to be included by the directors in their annual report.

Nevertheless the recommendations and code have been criticised for being bland and vague as well as unrealistic in expecting so much of the non-executive directors and imposing costly management structures on smaller companies. It remains to be seen whether the recommendations and code will be effectively implemented on a voluntary basis or whether legislation will be required.

Who is liable for the acts of the company?

As a separate legal person the company can enter into contracts, commit torts and criminal offences. In practice such acts are, of course, carried out by persons who are the agents or employees of the company.

Directors and other authorised agents of the company, such as employees, can enter into contracts on behalf of the company and normally the company will be liable for any breaches of contract and will be able to enforce the contract against the other party.

The company will be vicariously liable for torts committed by its employees during the course of their employment. A company and its directors can be found guilty of criminal offences. In practice such offences are likely to be breaches of statutory regulations such as health and safety, consumer protection and environmental provisions. It is possible for a company to be charged with an offence such as manslaughter. However it is usually difficult to prove that the company had the necessary 'guilty mind'.

Reorganisation and liquidation of the company

A company can be reorganised with the consent of the shareholders and creditors. This is the case where the reorganisation is merely internal and where it involves amalgamation with another company. If however, the company is subject to a takeover bid by another company there are a number of provisions regulating such a takeover including the Companies Act 1985 and the City Code on Takeovers and Mergers. The existence of a company can be voluntarily liquidated or ended by its shareholders. The procedure usually followed is described as a 'voluntary winding-up'.

Financial difficulties are more likely to bring the existence of the company to a premature end. Detailed provisions relating to insolvency are contained in the Insolvency Act 1986. Company directors who allow an insolvent company to continue trading are in breach of both the civil and criminal law. They may be ordered to compensate the company and thereby its creditors. A company is considered insolvent when it is unable to pay its debts.

There are various methods of dealing with an insolvent company including: winding up the company, which can be done voluntarily or compulsorily, on the order of the court; putting the company into receivership; entering into a voluntary arrangement with creditors; or obtaining an administration order from the court. These last three options do not automatically result in the liquidation of the company, although that may well be the outcome in practice. Only licensed insolvency practitioners can carry out these procedures.

Summary

Limited companies are subject to much more legal regulation than partnerships or sole traders chiefly because of the risk of abuse arising out of the limited liability of the shareholders. The law is concerned not just with regulating the creation and operation of the company but with making the directors accountable to the shareholders, however, despite extensive regulation UK company law has not yet responded adequately to the problems raised by groups of companies nor to the demands for worker participation.

CONTRACT LAW AND PRACTICE

Contract law is of crucial importance to all businesses whether they are sole traders, partnerships or limited companies. Contract law is the legal mechanism which regulates the supply of goods and services. Arguably, for managers it is the most important area of law because many of their daily activities are regulated by it. However, research has shown that many people in business try to avoid becoming entangled with contract law. Sales managers, for example, are more concerned with trying to strike a bargain in the commercial sense than with being sure that a legally enforceable contract has been made. However, larger organisations will normally have taken legal advice on their contracting procedures either from a firm of solicitors or from their own in-house legal department.

The aim of contract law is to uphold 'the reasonable expectations of honest men' and the courts will try to give effect to agreements wherever possible. Contract law has two functions. First, it has a planning function. Second, it has a dispute resolution function in that it provides remedies where there has been a breach of contract.

Planning function

A contract can be used to lay down the rights and obligations of the parties to the agreement. The contract can define the subject-matter of the agreement, agree delivery dates, price, and what will happen if certain eventualities occur such as late or short delivery, or if the goods are defective. The contract can also as a general rule limit or exclude the liability of one party so long as the particular limitation or exclusion clause is reasonable. Therefore a business should adopt contract terms which protect the financial and commercial interests of the business.

There are two main legal problems which businesses are likely to encounter in practice when entering into contracts. They are at what point and on whose terms they have entered into a contract.

The law states that a contract is entered into when one party in effect makes a clear and precise offer which is accepted without qualification by the other party. It is not always easy to identify the 'offer' and 'acceptance' when there has been a long period of negotiation.

A legally binding agreement, or contract, does not usually have to be in writing. A business can be bound by an oral agreement, or by an agreement which is partly oral or partly in writing whether in letters or in a more formal document, as well as by a written contract. The most important contracts which must be in writing are those for the sale or transfer of an interest in land, such as the ownership or tenancy of business premises.

Therefore, it is not unknown for a business to think that it has entered into a contract when it has not, or for a business to think that it has contracted on its own standard terms when it has in fact contracted on the other party's standard terms. If there is a dispute about these matters the courts adopt an objective approach in determining from the evidence what was the intention of the parties.

The disadvantage of supplying or obtaining goods and services when there is no contractual obligation to do so is that, for example, as the supplier you would only be able to obtain a reasonable price for the goods or services which may be less than the 'contract' price. As the purchaser of the goods or services you would not have a contractual remedy for late delivery or defective goods. Therefore, it is advisable for a business to make sure that long-running negotiations crystallise into a legally binding agreement before work is carried out on the assumption that there is or will be such an agreement.

The second problem can arise where, as is common, businesses use standard form contracts. Although contracts do not have to be in writing, businesses often use standard terms of business known as standard-form contracts. These may, for example, be contained in an invoice or referred to in a letter or contained on an acknowledgement of order form. The difficulty arises when both parties to the contract have their own standard forms which contradict each other. For example, the manufacturer of industrial equipment may use standard terms which contain a price escalation clause so that the price can be increased between the placing of the order and the delivery. The buyer may order the equipment on its terms and conditions which provide that the price at which the goods are ordered is the contract price. A dispute may well arise if the seller wishes to increase the price in accordance with the price escalation clause. A business should try to ensure that its standard form contracts are phrased in such a way that its terms and conditions prevail, although this may not always be possible if the other party to the contract does likewise.

A further problem that can arise in contract formation is that the law tends to consider contracts as just involving two parties. In practice many contracts are, for example, part of a series of sub-contracts branching out from a main contract, but each contract is viewed separately rather than as part of a whole. English law, unlike European law, distinguishes between contractual obligations and tortious obligations such as liability for negligence.

Dispute resolution function

The second function of contract law is to provide remedies where there has been a breach of contract. Under the doctrine of privity of contract only the parties to the contract can normally sue or be sued for breach of contract. However, it is possible for one or both of the parties to act through an agent. In practice many contracts are made through agents acting on behalf of their principals who are regarded as being the party to the contract. If company A enters into a contract with company B then the agreement would in fact have been made by the agents or employees of the company, but it is the two companies which are the parties to the contract. Similarly one partner can act on behalf of the partnership as a whole.

There are two possible remedies where one party is in breach of contract. If the term broken is a particularly important term or the breach has serious consequences then, as a general rule the innocent party can choose to regard the contract as terminated by the breach. There is no need for the innocent party to obtain a court order although their intention to regard the contract as terminated must be made clear to the party in breach. The second remedy is to claim damages, which the innocent party will be able to recover, for any foreseeable loss which has arisen from the breach.

If the term broken is less important or has less serious consequences then the innocent party will only be able to claim damages. Such damages may include compensation for the loss of any profit which may have been made on, for example, sub-sales. However, the innocent party is under an obligation to take reasonable steps to minimise the loss suffered.

A party to a contract can also be liable for misrepresentation. Like breach of contract this too can lead to the termination of the contract and liability for damages. Misrepresentation occurs where a party to the contract has made a false statement of fact which induces the other party to enter into the contract.

PRODUCT LIABILITY AND THE LAW

A business's commercial survival depends upon the success of its product whether that is the provision of goods or of services. If the product is defective or does not live up to the claims made for it then this can have legal as well as commercial repercussions for the business. A retailer will be liable to the purchaser for breach of contract if the goods or services supplied are defective. However, privity of contract limits contractual liability to the parties to the contract. Traditionally, the tort (civil wrong) of negligence could provide the purchaser with a remedy against, for example, the manufacturer of goods which harmed the purchaser, but recent statutory developments have supplanted the tort of negligence in this context.

The main provisions in UK law on product liability are now to be found in the Consumer Protection Act 1987 and the General Product Safety Regulations 1994 both of which implement EC Directives. In addition to being aware of these provisions, businesses operating in the United Kingdom need to ensure that:

• their advertising and sales strategies are not misleading because this could result in civil and criminal liability as well as being in breach of the

Advertising Standards Authority's requirement that advertisements should be legal, decent, honest and truthful;

- their products comply with any particular contract specification in order to avoid liability for breach of contract;
- any guarantee which they provide does not exclude or restrict their liability to a consumer under the tort of negligence;
- their business does not engage in trading practices regarded as unacceptable by the Office of Fair Trading and complies with any relevant code of practice.

The Consumer Protection Act 1987 imposed a new form of civil liability on producers of defective products, and criminal liability on the suppliers of unsafe consumer goods. A producer of defective goods will be liable to pay compensation for any loss or damage caused by a defective product. Liability is not dependent upon the plaintiff establishing that the producer was negligent. 'Producers' includes manufacturers, industrial processors, importers and 'own-branders'. A 'product' covers all goods and electricity. 'Defect' means that the product is not safe bearing in mind, for example, who is likely to use it and the use to which it will be put. If a product is found to be unsafe then the producer should be able to withdraw it from sale. This means, for example, that the producer should mark the products so that an unsafe batch can be easily identified and withdrawn. The producer's liability is limited to 'loss' or 'damage' to an individual or to their private property which amounts to at least £275.

The producer has various defences. The most important one in practice is that because of the state of scientific and technical knowledge at the time the particular product was supplied, producers generally would not have been expected to discover the defect. It is questionable whether, by allowing such a broad defence, the UK legislation complies with EC law.

The 1987 Act also imposed criminal liability on suppliers of unsafe consumer goods in an attempt to prevent accidents occurring by making suppliers face criminal prosecution if they do supply such goods. The general safety requirement introduced by the Act has been supplemented if not replaced by the General Product Safety Regulations 1994 which requires producers and distributors to place only safe products on the market.

'Producers' include manufacturers, own-branders, and can include importers. A 'safe' product means any product which under normal or reasonably foreseeable conditions of use, does not present more than a minimal acceptable risk which is considered to be consistent with a high level of protection for the user. Producers are under an obligation to provide consumers with relevant information about any such risks and to adopt a system to enable such products to be withdrawn from the market.

'Distributors' include wholesalers and retailers who are required to exercise due care in ensuring that only safe products are supplied, as well as being under an obligation to monitor their safety. In 1994 'consumer goods' was replaced by the term 'products' which includes products intended for use by consumers or likely to be used by consumers and would, for example, cover food. However, certain products are excluded, for example antiques, or goods sold for the purposes of repair or reconditioning.

Criminal liability can also arise from breach of the safety regulations made under the Act. These regulations apply to specific types of goods. However, if a product is subject to specific EC safety legislation or if it complies with UK health and safety requirements then it is not also subject to the general safety requirement.

The supplier has a variety of defences including the due diligence defence which means that the supplier took all reasonable steps and exercised 'due diligence' to avoid committing the offence.

Any prosecution is usually brought by a local authority's trading standards department against an individual or, where appropriate, against a company and its directors. In addition an application can be made for an order that the goods be forfeited.

THE WORKPLACE, THE ENVIRONMENT AND THE LAW

In addition to liability for their products, businesses operating in the UK are legally required to ensure that they provide a safe system of work for their employees and that their processes comply with environmental protection laws.

Health and safety at work: criminal liability

The Health and Safety at Work etc Act 1974 introduced a unified and integrated system of health and safety at work applicable to all employees. In addition it established the Health and Safety Executive (HSE) and the Health and Safety Commission (HSC). They are responsible for providing advice and information to employers. The Health and Safety Executive is normally responsible for investigating and enforcing the legislation as well as for bringing criminal prosecutions where there has been a breach of its provisions.

The aim of the 1974 Act is to prevent accidents rather than merely to provide sanctions for breach of the Act. The Act imposes general duties on employers to ensure the health and safety of employees by, for example:

- providing and maintaining plant and systems of work that are safe and without risk to health;
- providing the necessary information, instruction, training and supervision.

In addition, specific duties are placed on employers, such as providing a written general health and safety policy, bringing that policy to the attention of all employees, and consulting safety representatives appointed by recognised trade unions, or other employees on health and safety matters. Employers must also carry out, record and respond to a risk assessment.

Detailed legislative requirements are to be found not in the Act but in regulations which are often supplemented by practical guidance in codes of practice. Businesses need to be familiar with the regulations and codes of practice relevant to their sphere of operation. For example if a business provides work equipment for use in its business or on its premises then the business must comply with the Machinery (Safety) Regulations 1992 which implement an EC Directive as well as the Provision and Use of Work Equipment Regulations 1992 made under the 1974 Act.

The Act also imposes obligations on businesses to ensure that persons on their premises (other than employees) are not exposed to risks to their health and safety; and on employees to take reasonable care for their own health and safety and for that of other people.

Health and safety inspectors have wide-ranging powers to enter and inspect premises. They can also issue improvement notices requiring any breach of the legislation to be remedied within a specified time. If any of the activities occurring at the workplace involve a risk of serious personal injury then the inspector can serve a prohibition notice forbidding the continuance of those activities until the breach has been remedied.

In addition the inspectors can prosecute employers in the magistrates' court or in the Crown Court. An employer can raise the defence that it was not reasonably practicable to do more than what was in fact done to make the workplace safe and remove the risk of harm. A fine (normally limited to £20,000 in the magistrates' court) is the normal punishment where a successful prosecution is brought. The HSE prefers to prosecute companies rather than individual employees.

The triple role of an HSE inspector as guide, investigator and prosecutor can be criticised on the ground that it can lead to a conflict of interest. For example, a breach of the legislation which should lead to a prosecution may also indicate that the first two roles were not satisfactorily carried out.

The European Union has been following a programme of harmonisation of the health and safety at work legislation of member states which started more than fifteen years ago. The programme is almost completed. The general duties imposed by EC law are similar to those in the 1974 Act. In the United Kingdom the EC provisions have been implemented to date by six sets of regulations in 1992 including the Management of Health and Safety at Work Regulations which establishes the principle that management should assess risks in the workplace, prioritise them and then take appropriate preventative action.

There are likely to be more sets of regulations in the future dealing with, for example, construction projects. However, these EC developments should be considered in the context of UK government policy which favours deregulation by, for example, repealing legislation which places unnecessary burdens on business and industry. The power to repeal such statutory burdens in certain circumstances has been given to ministers by the Deregulation and Contracting Out Act 1994.

Health and safety at work: civil liability

Accidents at work can lead to civil liability not just criminal liability. The Health and Safety at Work etc Act 1974 does not create any new forms of civil liability. However, in certain circumstances a breach of the regulations made under the Act will amount to the tort known as breach of statutory duty and give rise to a damages claim by any person who has suffered loss or injury as a result of the breach.

The main provisions relating to an employer's liability under the civil law to pay damages are derived from common law principles developed case by case in the courts, which are now encompassed within the tort of negligence. An employer has a duty to make reasonable provision for the safety of his employees. There are three aspects to this duty:

- to provide competent staff;
- to provide adequate material, premises and plant;
- to provide a proper system of work and effective supervision.

Employers owe their employees a duty to take reasonable care. They will be liable to pay compensation to an employee if they (the employers) are negligent and as a result reasonably foreseeable injury, loss or damage is caused to that employee. This now includes psychiatric damage as well as physical injury. Businesses also owe a duty of care to any visitors (including trespassers) to their premises.

Environmental protection and the workplace

During the last ten years environmental issues have become increasingly important, both commercially and legally. Businesses have been forced to take account of the effect their activities and products may have on the environment. Although there has been a mass of EC and UK legislation, there is still more to come and businesses need to make sure that they keep up to date with changes in the law.

The European Commission has been and will continue to be at the forefront of recent developments. Certain principles underpin the EU's approach, in particular:

- the polluter pays;
- prevention is better than cure;
- precaution rather than risk;
- integration of environmental issues;
- the concept of sustainable development.

However, even before these recent developments the United Kingdom had a well-established system of town and country planning which had often been used to protect the environment. Businesses operating within the United Kingdom must ensure that their activities comply first of all with local planning requirements, and second with any relevant environmental legislation.

Planning policy is normally determined by the Department of the Environment. Policies are set out in departmental circulars and policy guidance notes which are implemented by local planning authorities who are responsible for:

- drawing up plans for the local area – forward planning;
- granting or refusing applications for planning permission – development control;
- enforcing planning controls.

The planning powers of a local planning authority are based on the Town and Country Planning Act 1990 which gives the local authority considerable discretionary powers. However, these powers mainly relate to preventing new developments rather than controlling existing activities which may harm the environment. Nevertheless central government is encouraging local authorities to take into account environmental considerations when making planning decisions.

Although the environment is a material consideration which should be taken into account by the planning authority, the planning system is not suited to the control of pollution. However, a system of pollution control runs alongside the system of planning control and the planning authority should, and in certain circumstances must, consult with the relevant authority responsible for controlling pollution. Pollution control is chiefly concerned with:

- regulating the use of prescribed processes and substances;
- regulating air, water and noise pollution;
- the management and control of waste.

It is worth noting at the outset that any person has a right of access to any information on the environment held by public authorities or by subordinate organisations with public responsibilities for the environment. Such a right is aimed at achieving better environmental protection, but certain important categories of information are exempt from this requirement.

The use of prescribed processes and substances is governed by the Environmental Protection Act 1990 which established a system of regulation called Integrated Pollution Control (IPC). Processes used by the metal and chemical industries, for example, are likely to be subject to IPC. Prescribed substances whose release is regulated include sulphur (air), mercury (water) and certain pesticides (land). If a business uses a prescribed process or substance, then as a general rule the business must obtain authorisation to use that process from Her Majesty's Inspectorate of Pollution (HMIP). Failure to do so is a criminal offence.

Air pollution is covered by IPC where appropriate, but in other cases it is regulated by the Clean Air Act 1993 which provides that where a business plans to discharge certain substances into the air it must notify and obtain authorisation from the local authority. Failure to do so amounts to a criminal offence.

The grant of an IPC or an Air Pollution Control (APC) authorisation is subject to an implied requirement that the Best Available Techniques Not Entailing Excessive Costs (BATNEEC) are used to control pollution. Where a discharge will affect two or more aspects of the environment, such as air and water, then the Best Practical Environmental Option (BPEO) should be adopted.

Water pollution is regulated by the Water Resources Act 1991. If a business discharges trade or sewerage effluent into controlled waters, which includes rivers and the sea, then normally the business should obtain a consent from the National Rivers Authority. This is not necessary where an IPC authorisation has been obtained. The procedure for obtaining an NRA consent entails more publicity than for IPC and APC consents. Where trade effluent, whatever its nature, is discharged into a sewer a consent must be obtained from the local sewerage undertaker. Failure to obtain the necessary consents is a criminal offence.

Noise pollution is governed by a variety of both civil and criminal provisions including the Environmental Protection Act 1990 which created a statutory nuisance. This arises, for example, where the activities of a business create an unacceptable degree of noise, or smoke or fumes which are prejudicial to public health or a nuisance. 'Noise' includes vibration. An abatement notice can be issued by the local authority, or by a magistrates' court on the application of an aggrieved person. Failure to comply with an abatement notice is a criminal offence.

Under the Control of Pollution Act 1974 a local authority can issue a noise abatement order which designates a specific area a noise abatement zone. Noise pollution can also amount to the common law tort of private nuisance as well as the crime and tort of public nuisance.

The management and control of waste is regulated by the Environmental Protection Act 1990 which has been supplemented by regulations and a code of practice. The Environment Agency was established by the Environment Act 1995. It aims to adopt a holistic and integrated approach to environmental protection and enhancement. It is taking over key functions of environmental protection and resource management from existing authorities, e.g., HMIP, NRA.

Businesses operating in the United Kingdom need to ensure that they have the necessary specialist insurance cover if their activities may possibly cause pollution. Difficulties may arise where the pollution is historic, but such an action is easier to defend so long as the business had a good environmental management system in place at the time of any incident. Contaminated land can cause considerable financial problems because banks are unwilling to lend money to the owners of the land. Apart from obtaining adequate insurance cover businesses would also be well advised to appoint an environmental standards manager to ensure that the business complies with the legally imposed environmental standards. In 1992 BS7750, the standard for environmental management systems, was issued. Although it is not legally binding it sets the standard which environmentally friendly businesses should aim to achieve.

Despite a massive increase in pollution-control law there is some doubt about the Conservative Government's will to enforce the measures, when it was actively pursuing a policy of deregulation. Even with a Labour Government new initiatives are more likely to come from within the European Union which since 1992 has adopted a much more proactive approach particularly in the areas of agriculture, energy, industry, tourism and transport.

Industrial relations and the law

Workplace safety is one area where trade union safety representatives have a legally recognised role. Generally however, since 1979, UK legislation has restricted the traditional role of the trade union in the workplace as the recognised representative of the workers negotiating their terms and conditions of employment. On the other hand, EU law tends to favour an expanded role for workers' representatives whether in the boardroom or on safety committees. UK law is primarily concerned with two aspects of industrial relations:

• the relationship between the employer and the employee's trade union;
• the relationship between employer and employee.

The relationship between the employer and the employee's trade union

The law relating to trade unions has undergone a major transformation in the last fifteen years as a result of government policy. The trade unions were perceived as having too much influence in the workplace which prevented innovation and change and caused economic decline. The purpose of much of the trade union legislation in this period has been to reduce the power and influence of trade unions. In addition employers in some industries have negotiated single union deals or no union representation agreements with their employees.

The current legislation is concerned with the status of trade unions, the legal immunities which apply to claims in tort arising out of a trade dispute, the requirement to hold secret ballots, and the provision of legal machinery and practical guidance for the promotion of good industrial relations.

Independent trade unions are registered with the Certification Officer, who is an official employed by ACAS, who maintains a list of trade unions and a list of employers' associations. Strictly speaking a trade union is legally classified as an unincorporated association. This means that a trade union, unlike a limited company, does not have legal personality. However legislation has provided that a trade union can enter into contracts, sue and be sued in its own name, and effectively own property.

Where there is a trade dispute between employees and their employer certain torts may be committed by the employees, or by other trade union members employed by another employer, or by the employees' trade union officials. Such torts include interference with an existing contract, intimidation and conspiracy. Any person, including a trade union, is immune from liability in certain circumstances where the action is done in furtherance of a trade dispute. However, a trade union's liability to pay damages is limited by reference to the size of its membership. The extent of a trade union's immunity has been restricted by legislation during the 1980s, particularly in the context of secondary picketing. It is also worth noting that the judiciary has always tended to regard trade union immunity with suspicion.

Picketing is regulated by detailed legislative provisions. Practical guidance can be found in the Code of Practice on Picketing issued by the Secretary of State for Employment in 1992. Picketing an employer's place of business and intimidation may also amount to a criminal offence.

The use of secret ballots by trade unions was encouraged by legislation in 1980. Legislation in 1984, 1992 and 1993 imposed additional detailed obligations on trade unions. In certain circumstances trade unions must hold a postal secret ballot of their members, for example, to find out whether the members are prepared to strike. If the union does not hold a ballot then it will lose its immunity from liability in tort. In 1995 the Secretary of State for Employment issued a Code of Practice: Industrial Action Ballots and Notice to Employers. In practice industrial action is often unballoted because it is an immediate response to particular circumstances.

Employees' contracts of employment are frequently based on a collective agreement drawn up by an employee's trade union and the employer or employers' association as a result of collective bargaining. An employer is under a legal duty to disclose relevant information to the trade union recognised by the employer as being entitled to represent the employees for collective bargaining purposes. ACAS published a Code of Practice in 1977 on the disclosure of such information.

Since 1991 it has in effect been unlawful for an employer to operate a closed shop whereby all employees must belong to a particular trade union. If an employer attempts to operate a closed shop then an employee can bring a claim before an industrial tribunal. In an unfair dismissal claim the employer may be required to pay compensation over and above that normally ordered. Furthermore any term or condition in a contract for the supply of goods or services is void if it requires the contract work to be undertaken only by union members or requires the recognition of a trade union by one of the parties to the contract.

Nevertheless terms and conditions of collective agreements are frequently negotiated at a local or national level by trade union officials on behalf of their members. Collective agreements are usually not legally binding as between the employer and the trade union. English law and industrial relations practice does not generally acknowledge that employees have a role to play in the organisation of the business either through their trade unions or through worker participation. As indicated above, worker participation is not recognised in English company law nor are works councils common in practice. Furthermore some large employers have introduced personal contracts for employees which tend to reduce the influence of trade unions at the workplace.

The machinery established for resolving disputes whether between employers and employees or between employers and trade unions has largely been removed from the ordinary court system. Generally the law is only turned to as a last resort. The emphasis is on conciliation and arbitration. ACAS and the industrial tribunal system deals with the former type of dispute. Trade disputes are normally resolved without recourse to the courts, sometimes with the assistance of ACAS or the Central Arbitration Committee (CAC).

Practical guidance is to be found in the codes of practice emanating from ACAS, the Department for Education and Employment, the Health and Safety Commission, the Commission for Racial Equality and the Equal Opportunities Commission.

The relationship between the employer and the employee

This is regulated by the employee's contract of employment. The express terms of the contract are supplemented by various rights and duties which the law implies into the contract. The law also provides remedies additional to those normally available for breach of contract. Therefore, if an employee is sacked then that employee could sue for breach of contract but in practice is more likely to bring a claim for unfair dismissal.

An employee must be distinguished from an independent contractor who is employed under a contract for services. An employee includes a person:

- who works under the control of the employer in the sense that the employer decides how and when a particular task will be carried out;
- whose work is an integral part of the business.

An independent contractor provides services as a person in business on her own account. Factors which the courts would take into account in deciding this question include who is responsible for the provision of equipment, who hires any assistants, who takes the financial risk and profits, if any, and who is responsible for management and investment. If the answer to these questions is the employer then it is most likely that the employee is engaged under a contract of employment.

Certain consequences flow from businesses engaging an employee rather than an independent contractor. The employer is vicariously liable for any torts committed by an employee in the course of their employment, and is obliged to provide an employee with a safe system of work. In addition employers are liable to pay income tax and social security contributions on their employees' earnings. Employers in the construction industry have been known to try and avoid the tax and social security liability by claiming that particular individuals are self-employed, that is independent contractors, rather than employees, despite the fact that the individuals work full-time for the employer.

The terms of the contract of employment can be found in any or all of the following:

- an express agreement between the employer and employee;
- terms implied by the common law;
- terms implied by legislation;
- collective agreements;

Terms implied by the common law or legislation include:

- the right of the employee to an itemised pay statement;
- the provision by the employer within two months of the start of the employment of written details of the main terms and conditions of the contract of employment;
- an obligation on the employee to obey the employer's lawful orders;
- a duty of fidelity whereby the employee will not divulge trade secrets or confidential information to other employers;
- a duty not to discriminate against employees on the ground of their sex, marital status, colour, race, nationality, ethnic or national origins;
- an obligation to pay men and women equal pay for equal work;
- the right of an employee to receive guaranteed payments where there is short-time working or temporary lay-offs;
- the right of an employee to statutory sick pay;
- the right of a female employee to have time off for ante-natal care, to statutory maternity pay, to maternity leave, to return to work at any time up to twenty-nine weeks after the birth of the baby, and not to be dismissed on account of her pregnancy or the birth of the baby;
- the right of employees not to be victimised because of their trade union membership or activities;
- the right of employees to have time off work to carry out official trade union duties or activities;
- certain rights which protect employees on the insolvency of their employer, for example, to recover from the Secretary of State for Employment wages due, or to have priority over other creditors where certain debts, such as guarantee payments, are owed.

Many of these provisions are regulated by EC law as well as by UK law. EC law has been particularly important in the area of sex discrimination and equal pay, although it is interesting to note that EC law unlike UK law does not prohibit racial discrimination except in the limited context of freedom of movement for workers. The EU is proposing a maximum working week of 48 hours.

Where an employee resigns or is dismissed the employer may also be entitled to claim damages for breach of the contract of employment. In practice this rarely occurs because the employee is not usually worth suing. However, the employer may wish to obtain a court order which would forbid the employee from working for or passing on confidential information to the new employer, if this was in breach of the contract of employment. The new employer may also be liable to pay damages to the old employer if it can be shown that the new employer induced the employee to break the contract of employment.

Alternatively the employee may consider that the dismissal or resignation was a breach of the contract of employment by the employer. The employee may sue the employer for wrongful dismissal in the County Court or the High Court. This is unusual except where the employee does not fulfil the requirements necessary to bring a claim for unfair dismissal or where the damages sought exceed the maximum award which can be made by an industrial tribunal in a successful unfair dismissal claim. However, in July 1994 industrial tribunals were given the jurisdiction to hear breach of contract employment cases, but there is a compensation ceiling of £25,000.

In practice employees who consider, for example, that they have been ill-used by an employer are more likely to bring a claim for unfair dismissal against their employer. Such a claim is heard by an industrial tribunal and must be brought within three months of the dismissal. In this area of law there is an emphasis on resolving disputes by conciliation which is facilitated by ACAS.

The privatisation of public services provided by local government or local health authorities has caused considerable problems in the law of unfair dismissal because the Transfer of Undertaking (Protection of Employment) Regulations 1981 (TUPER) as amended provide that the employees automatically transfer to the employment of the new employer. Frequently existing employees are taken on by the new employers but with lower wages and poorer terms and conditions. The difficulties relate to whether or not the employees have been dismissed, and if they have been whether by the old or by the new employer.

Where a case is heard by a tribunal the employee must establish the fact of dismissal. Then the onus is normally on the employer to show that the dismissal is fair, that is it was for an acceptable reason. Finally the tribunal must decide whether the employer's action falls within the band of reasonable responses of a reasonable employer.

Normally an employee should be warned rather than immediately dismissed. Employers should be familiar with and comply with the provisions of the ACAS Code of Practice 1 on disciplinary practice and procedures in employment. ACAS has also published a handbook entitled *Discipline at Work*.

The usual remedy for unfair dismissal is compensation which is made up of a basic award and a compensatory award. The basic award is calculated by reference to the age of the employee, the number of years employed and the weekly salary. The maximum basic award possible is normally £6,300 (1997 figure). The compensatory award is aimed at compensating the employee for the actual loss suffered as a result of the dismissal and is normally subject to a ceiling of £11,300 (1997 figure). There is no ceiling where the claim is based on sex or race discrimination.

In addition an employee can ask the industrial tribunal to order reinstatement in his or her old job or re-engagement in a different job. However, these remedies are rarely used in practice. It is not unusual for tribunal cases to be settled at or before the hearing. This has a financial advantage for the employee because social security benefits will not have to be repaid whereas they would have to be if compensation was awarded by the tribunal.

Industrial tribunals have a wide jurisdiction and can, for example, also hear claims for redundancy payments, as well as sex and race discrimination and equal pay claims. Legal aid is not available for either party, but employers are often legally represented at the hearing.

Employers should note that while they are not legally obliged to provide their employees or ex-employees with a reference, if they do so they should make sure that it is truthful and accurate. If it is not, they could be liable to compensate the employee for any loss suffered if the reference defamed the employee or was negligently prepared and as a result, for example, the employee was not offered a job.

Finally it is worth noting that although the relationship between the employer and the employee is based upon contract with the implicit assumption that the parties are of equal status it is arguable that the judiciary still tend to favour the employer over and above the employee.

Competition and the law

Freedom of the market supposedly encourages competition, and freedom of contract is one of the legal tools used to achieve this economic end. However, contracts or agreements can be used by businesses as a way of attempting to limit the effectiveness of competitors. This can be done, for example, by:

- limiting the freedom of current or former employees to work for other employers in the same line of business;
- agreeing with other businesses operating in the same market to restrict the supply of goods, or information, or services to a limited number of suppliers;
- agreeing with other suppliers to fix the prices at which retailers can sell particular goods;
- the merger of two businesses which results in the new organisation having a substantial share of a particular market.

Neither English nor EC law allows such agreements to operate without restriction. In addition both EC law and English law are concerned with outlawing anti-competitive practices generally whether or not they are based upon an agreement.

The aim of the law is to protect the public interest by ensuring free competition between the manufacturers and suppliers of goods and services. Free competition is thought to lead to greater efficiency, lower prices and better services for the customer. The principle of free competition is enshrined in Article 3 of the EC Treaty which provides for: the institution of a system ensuring that competition in the common market is not distorted. The EC Treaty also provides for free movement of goods, workers, businesses, services and capital.

However, it should be noted that both UK and EC law permit businesses to protect their trade secrets. In particular, the law can be used to limit or prohibit the use by competitors of the ideas underlying a business's goods, services and packaging. Original ideas can be of immense financial value. The law describes these ideas as 'intellectual property' which includes, for example, the law relating to patents, copyright, trade marks, goodwill and confidential information.

Competition law is a complicated area of law partly because in certain circumstances only EC or only English law applies, whereas in other situations both may apply. In 1989 the UK Government published a White Paper proposing reform of the UK law on restrictive trading agreements to bring it into line with the approach adopted by EC law. However, the reform has not yet been implemented, although some changes were introduced in 1994. The main provisions of UK and EC competition law are summarised below.

Employees

An employer can include an express term in the employee's contract of employment, which will limit the range of employers for whom the employee can work in the future. Such terms normally provide that on leaving the employer's employment the employee should not work in the same type of employment for a fixed period of time and in a defined geographical area. These terms are found in many contracts of employment and are of most practical importance where the employee has technical knowledge, or personal contact with the employer's customers, or where the employee holds a senior position. The English courts treat such terms as potentially invalid because they are in restraint of trade. For the term to be valid the employer would have to show that the term:

• protected the employer's trade secrets or confidential information; or
• prevented the employee from soliciting the employer's customers; and
• was reasonable.

An employer will not be able to enforce such a term if its primary aim is to stop the employee working with a competitor or setting up a business in competition with the employer. If the term is valid an employer can obtain an injunction ordering the employee not to work for another employer in breach of the contract of employment, as well as claiming damages for any loss suffered. The careful drafting of such terms is of crucial importance: if they are too wide they will be unenforceable; if they are too narrow they will not adequately protect the employer's interests. However, what is reasonable will depend partly upon current employment conditions and practices.

EU law on the other hand is concerned with protecting an employee's freedom of movement. A member state cannot restrict the immigration of workers from other member states, even where there is high unemployment in that member state, because Article 48 of the EC Treaty provides for the free movement of workers. This right can be limited on public policy, public security or public health grounds, but not on grounds of nationality.

Restrictions on goods and services

UK legislation, in particular the Restrictive Trade Practices Act 1976, requires the registration of any agreement between two businesses operating in the UK, which tries to restrict, for example, the price, the quantity, or the supply of goods or services or information. The parties to such an agreement should apply to the Director General of Fair Trading to have the agreement registered. The Director General can refer the agreement to the Restrictive Practices Court which can declare that the restrictions are valid or invalid in accordance with well-established principles. Normally alterations to the agreement are made with the approval of the Director General. In addition third parties can bring actions for damages.

Certain types of agreement are exempt from these provisions, such as those providing for the supply of goods or services outside the United Kingdom. The Deregulation and Contracting Out Act 1994 has introduced the concept of the non-notifiable agreement. It is likely that small companies will no longer have to register restrictive agreements unless they are price-fixing agreements; and that agreements which fall within the block exemptions granted under EC law will no longer also have to comply with the requirements of UK law.

A business may be in breach of the legislation even where they expressly and repeatedly forbid their employees from entering into restrictive trading agreements but nevertheless an employee does enter into such an agreement. The business may ultimately be liable to pay a heavy fine.

Unlike UK law which concentrates on the form of the agreement, EC law is chiefly concerned with the effect of the agreement on trade between member states. Therefore many small UK businesses will only be subject to UK law.

Article 85 of the EC Treaty prohibits and declares invalid any agreement between businesses and any concerted practice which may affect trade between member states and which has as its object or effect the prevention, restriction or distortion of competition.

An example of an agreement falling within Article 85 is an agreement by two or more businesses to share their markets or sources of supply. In November 1994 the European Commission fined forty-two companies and associations in the cement industry £200 million because of agreements just to supply their own home markets. Blue Circle, one of three British companies involved, was fined £12.3 million. The Commission can impose a fine of up to 10 per cent of a business's turnover.

The European Commission can grant block exemptions to types of agreements, such as franchising agreements, or negative clearance to otherwise invalid agreements if they will result in commercial advantages which also benefit the consumer.

Anti-competitive practices

The Competition Act 1980 provides for a two-stage investigation by the Director General of Fair Trading and the Monopolies and Mergers Commission into anti-competitive practices which has the effect of restricting, distorting or preventing competition in any market in the United Kingdom. A business with less than a 25 per cent share of the market whose turnover is less than £5 million will be exempt from the provisions of the Act. If an anti-competitive practice is found to exist then the business can be asked to give an undertaking to the Director General or the Secretary of State can make an order prohibiting or restricting a practice to prevent its adverse effects.

EC law also regulates anti-competitive practices. Article 86 of the EC Treaty prohibits the abuse of a dominant position by a business within the common market which affects trade between member states. A business is in a dominant position where it knows that its actions can affect the market significantly. The 'market' does not mean all trade within the European Union; it is defined by reference to the market for the particular product and to the relevant geographical area. An economic analysis of the market would have to be carried out to establish whether or not a particular business is dominant.

A business with a market share of less than 30 per cent is unlikely to be regarded as being in a dominant position. However, the European Commission tends to define 'market' narrowly in individual cases. If a business considers that a competitor is abusing its dominant position the business can, for example, complain to the European Commission which may then investigate the competitor's activities. Examples of such practices include refusing to supply a particular customer, and 'tying' pubs to particular breweries.

Resale price maintenance agreements

Manufacturers of goods use these agreements to try and control the retail price of their manufactured goods. Usually there is one agreement between the manufacturer and a wholesaler; and a second agreement between the wholesaler and a retailer. However, under the Resale Prices Act 1976 it is unlawful for suppliers and dealers of goods to refuse to supply goods unless the purchaser agrees to resell the goods at a specified price. The Restrictive Practices Court can, but rarely does, grant an exemption to a particular agreement where, for example, it would be in the interest of customers to do so because the variety of goods available would otherwise be substantially reduced.

Other forms of price-fixing can come within the Restrictive Trade Practices Act 1976. EC law does not have specific provisions relating to resale price maintenance agreements but price-fixing, or excessively high or low prices, or price discrimination between customers potentially fall within Articles 85 and 86.

Free movement of goods, businesses, services and capital

Article 30 of the EC Treaty prohibits member states from imposing quantitative restrictions on imports and from introducing any other measures which would have the same effect in practice. Such measures would include a requirement that a fruit liqueur should have a minimum alcohol content of 25 per cent. Any such restriction would have to be justified on the grounds, for example, of public health. In England and Wales retailers argued that the legislative ban on Sunday trading was in breach of Article 30. However, the European Court of Justice held that the UK Government could justify the ban on the grounds of public policy. Nevertheless the Government amended the Sunday trading laws in 1994. In practice the continued drive towards harmonisation of technical requirements and standards will reduce inadvertent breaches of Article 30.

The EC Treaty provides for the gradual abolition of restrictions imposed by member states on the freedom of:

- the nationals of other member states to set up a business there;
- the nationals of other member states to provide services there;
- residents of member states to move capital between member states.

The first two freedoms, unlike the third freedom, have not yet been fully implemented.

Monopolies and mergers

Monopolies are regulated under English law by the Fair Trading Act 1973. The Director General of Fair Trading can ask the Monopolies and Mergers Commission to investigate and report on the existence of an alleged monopoly. A monopoly would usually exist where a business or a group of linked companies supplies 25 per cent or more of particular goods or services in the United Kingdom. Since the beginning of 1995 the Director General can propose that the Secretary of State should accept an undertaking which would deal with any adverse effects of the monopoly rather than a monopoly reference being made.

Under EC law monopolies are regulated by Article 86 of the EC Treaty. Mergers between two or more businesses are also regulated both by English law and by EU law. Which law applies will depend upon the combined turnover of the merged businesses. However, both sets of law only apply in practice to relatively large businesses, or businesses with a large market share.

The UK law relating to mergers is based on the Fair Trading Act 1973. There are different provisions depending upon whether it is a 'newspaper' merger or a 'non-newspaper' merger. In the case of 'non-newspaper' mergers the legislation only applies where either the value of the assets taken over exceeds £70 million, or where one business increases its market share to more than 25 per cent. The Secretary of State may require such businesses to give undertakings which will ensure that the public interest is not adversely affected by the merger. Alternatively the Office of Fair Trading can refer such a merger to the Monopolies and Mergers Commission which may investigate and prohibit the proposed merger.

Under EC law mergers like monopolies are regulated by Article 86, but are also subject to the Mergers Control Regulation 1989. EC law will only apply where the EU turnover is more than ECU 250 million (£175 million) or where the world-wide turnover is more than ECU 5,000 million (£3,500 million). In any case if two-thirds of the EU turnover is in one member state then the EU provisions will not apply. Any merger subject to the legislation must be notified to the European Commission which may grant an exemption. If the Commission is not notified then the merger may be void and the businesses may be subject to financial penalties.

CONCLUSION

Two key themes dominate this chapter. First, the dramatic impact of EC law, and, second, the UK government's policy of deregulation of business and industry to promote competition and encourage the private sector. This has so far involved reducing the influence of trade unions and a partial deregulation of employment protection legislation in order to remove barriers to job creation, as well as the break up of public sector monopolies and the privatisation of public services.

The Deregulation and Contracting Out Act 1994 gives ministers potentially wide powers to reduce or remove statutory burdens on businesses where that would not affect any necessary protection. This policy could be regarded as being at odds with the European Union's agenda which often favours the legislative regulation of businesses' activities whether by extending employees' rights, extending health and safety requirements or ensuring protection of the environment. However, the Labour Government elected in May 1997 is likely to be more sympathetic to the EU's proposals.

SELECTED READING

Clarke, A. (1996)
Cooper, J. (1996)
Cotter, B. (1996)
Freshfields Environment Group (1994)
Griffiths, M. (1996)
Ruff, A. (ed.) (1995)
Schilling, H. and Sharp, I. (1996)
Singleton, E. S. (1992)
Slade, E. (1993)
Stranks, J. (1996)

7 UK management and human resource management

Stephen Fox

Human Resources. While hardly an original observation, it must be emphasized that Britain will not regain innovation-driven status without a world-class education system encompassing all socioeconomic and ability levels. The rate of social investment must rise substantially, standards must be raised and enforced, and technical fields must be stressed. This is perhaps the most pressing issue facing Britain and the area in which current policies provide the least comfort. (Porter 1990: 720)

INTRODUCTION

The purpose of this chapter is to describe the nature of UK management and to discuss current issues about the future development of managers in Britain. Three major periods of time will be considered: pre-1980s, the 1980s and the 1990s. When one considers that most senior managers are, broadly speaking, in their mid-forties and fifties and therefore began their careers in the 1960s and early 1970s, then it is important to look back to that period in order to understand the social and corporate formation of those who are currently top managers, who are arguably among the most influential people in Britain today.

SCENE-SETTING: THE LATE 1980S WATERSHED

In an early survey, Mangham and Silver (1986) reported that more than half of British companies made no provision for training their managers. Even the larger companies (those with over 1,000 employees) were in this group, 20 per cent of them not train their managers at all. Of the 80 per cent of large companies which did, the average expenditure was £600 per head, the equivalent at the time of the price of a packet of cigarettes a day. This survey raised a warning bell and shortly afterwards a number of further investigations were carried out which informed public and corporate policy. The two main ones being Handy *et al.* (1988, originally published as Handy 1987) and Constable and McCormick (1987).

A wide public debate ensued and the national Training Agency (now disbanded – see Keep and Mayhew's Chapter 8 in this volume) drew the main points together in a major discussion document: *Management Challenge for the 1990s: The Current Education, Training and Development Debate* (Training Agency 1989). This reported that there were almost 2.4 million managers out of a total working population of about 23 million, (17.8 million of them in organisations employing ten people or more, see Figure 7.1). This 2.4 million British management population roughly breaks down by age as follows: 31 per cent (0.7 million) were under 35; 20 per cent (0.5 million) were between 35 and 44; and 40 per cent (0.9 million) were over 45 years old. The breakdown by seniority was as depicted in Figure 7.2. The implication is that there were about one-third of a million senior British managers managing the rest of the working population, running the nations' largest employing organisations, responsible for the nation's wealth generation and public services. If we widen this group to include middle managers then we can say that there were just over 1 million managers in Britain managing the rest of the population, served by 1.3 million junior managers and 3.2 million professionals of various types. Out of a working population of 23 million, 1 million managers seems like a very small proportion. At the time of the Handy report, new entrants to management were running at 90,000 per year, of whom 35,000 were expected to enter middle management, and 17,500 senior management. Of the 90,000 only 10,000 received any formal education in management up to degree level or its equivalent, with a further 15,000 picking up some management education from their studies for professional institutions (Handy *et al*. 1988: 167).

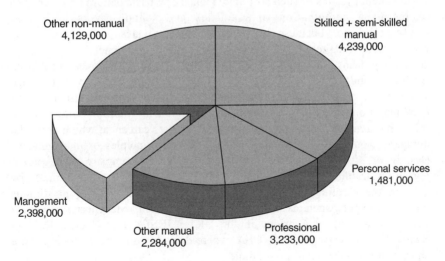

Figure 7.1 How many managers are there in the UK?

Source: Training Agency 1989: 4

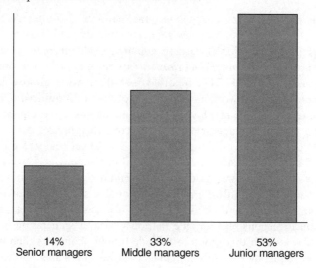

Figure 7.2 Levels of managers in the UK

Source: Training Agency 1989: 5

Handy *et al*. (1988: 169) also reports that there are three basic approaches to developing managers in Britain: the corporate, the academic and the professional, which are not mutually exclusive. The corporate approach has been exemplified by the top thirty or so British firms, ICI, BP, Shell, Unilever etc., although many other large firms aspire to the internal training and development systems of such corporate giants. The basic pattern here has been to recruit a combination of graduates and school-leavers each year (traditionally *not* business or management graduates – compare Perks reference in Chapter 4 of this volume, to the preference of the major accounting firms for recruits with Oxbridge arts degrees, over accounting graduates) and to provide them with 'a mix of training and early experience geared to a long-term career in the organization', the experience usually being confined to one specialist management function. The 'tradition being that the move into general management comes late in one's career' at which point the company would provide training in the 'general principles of management' (Handy *et al*. 1988: 169) either internally, via in-company management education, training and development (METD) programmes, or externally by sending the carefully chosen prospective general managers to prestigious business schools such as London Business School, Manchester Business School, Cranfield or Ashridge in the UK or INSEAD in France, IMD in Switzerland, or Harvard in the USA, where they would in most cases attend a short senior management programme.

During the 1980s more firms adopted this pattern, the larger firms increased the number of graduates and reduced the number of school-leavers in their annual intake and, over the years, many of them have over-recruited in the expectation that some would leave the company to go elsewhere. The larger companies would attempt to retain the best and those who left would nevertheless be of good quality and well trained, by more average standards, thus benefiting the wider business community. Also during the 1980s, the proportion of business graduates in the corporate intakes has increased.

The academic approach 'is a broad imitation of the American tradition' (Handy *et al.* 1988: 169) except it has never reached the same critical mass in the UK, only covering about one in ten new entrants to management, whereas in America 'the great majority of aspirant managers acquire a grounding in business and management concepts at a university business school before joining or soon after' (ibid.). Also, whereas in the USA a Master of Business Administration (MBA) is regarded as an essential prerequisite for a managerial career, and only MBAs from the top schools (e.g. Harvard, Yale, Stanford) can command premium salaries; in the UK there is no such 'industry standard', for reasons to be explained in the next section. Instead there has been a plethora of different types of qualification, with the MBA regarded as the best (although the UK was producing only about 3,000 per annum in the late 1970s), but with BA Business Studies, being common at undergraduate level, and with a very similar content. The 'post-graduate' Diploma in Management Studies, (DMS) is usually taken part-time by practising managers, the BTEC and the Higher National Diploma being a shorter version of the BA Business Studies (BABS). In addition to these, all of which teach a very similar syllabus, regardless of the apparent differences in academic level and status, there are a number of more specialist degrees at undergraduate and masters level, such as BA Textiles and Marketing or MA Accounting which adds to the credential confusion in British management education, while also enhancing its relevance to some employers. Nevertheless, most undergraduate business or accountancy courses are more sought after than any other university degree, suggesting that students at least perceive them to be worth something in the job market.

The professional approach allows one to earn as one learns and has been the traditional way of being educated into the older professions. The approach 'is a mixture of tutored work experience (articles) with formal study leading to a graded series of qualifications, normally ending with membership of an institution' (Handy *et al.* 1988: 170). Of the professional institutes relevant to management, the accounting institutes are probably the most prestigious (covering 168,000 people). These figures are, however, illusory in the sense that the 168,000 accountants are not all practising auditing accountants, as Perks observes. The real position is that 'accountancy has long been regarded by young people and by employers as an appropriate, high standard and high status preparation for a wide variety of jobs in business' (Handy *et al.* 1988: 171). None the less, the figures for the accounting professional bodies are followed by the members of the Consultative Council of Professional Management Organisation (CCPMO), which collectively cover over 200,000 people, see Table 7.1.

Table 7.1: Members of the Consultative Council of Professional Management Organisation

- Institute of Chartered Secretaries and Administrators
- Chartered Institute of Management Accountants
- Institute of Marketing
- Institute of Purchasing and Supply
- Institute of Personnel Management (now Institute of Personnel and Development, having merged with the Institute of Training and Development)
- Institute of Bankers
- Chartered Insurance Institute
- Institute of Industrial Managers (now Institute of Management, having merged with the former British Institute of Management)
- Institute of Administrative Management

The accountancy professions have been responsible for training many of those who have entered general management or the internal accounting functions of firms, with a smaller proportion of their members actually practising as independent high street accountants or as members of the larger accounting firms (such as Arthur Andersen, Coopers & Lybrand, Price Waterhouse, KPMG, Touche Ross, etc.). Thus the accounting professions, and firms, like the larger British companies, have provided a national training ground for many UK managers.

The number of specialist management professions in Britain matches the tendency of the larger companies to leave their junior and middle managers in one management function from the point of recruitment, until either retirement or the late move into general management. The professions provide an additional avenue of training, within corporate functional 'chimney stacks', to that provided by the companies. Often leading edge management practice in specific functional areas would be performed and developed in the larger companies, and the professions would learn from them and provide a vehicle for the dissemination of 'best practice' to smaller, less well-resourced firms by means of professional journals. For example the Institute of Management disseminates best practice in *Management Today* and the Institute of Personnel and Development does so through *People Management*. Both also organise conferences and a central advisory function as well as some form of training syllabus and examination.

The debate on the *appropriate number* of educated, trained and developed managers in Britain, at times overshadows the debate on what kind of education should be regarded as the most *appropriate form*. The question – what size of critical mass of educated managers is necessary to cause a discernible improvement in the performance of British business? – is important. However, the question is almost meaningless unless we also ask *what form should this education take?* The current, confusing, patchwork of provision has emerged out of many battles and compromises among those with a vested interest in the form of British management education – employers, government, educationalists, the relevant professional institutes and associations, and the alumni of MBA, DMS, BABS and other programmes, each of which have championed their own credential as the most appropriate, not wishing its market value to diminish.

In order to understand and assess the 'post-Handy' compromise it is necessary first to look back to get a feel for British business culture and its relationships with government, academia and the professions. For it is this historic culture which has most shaped the incumbents of the current most senior managerial positions. Therefore having broadly outlined the position found in the watershed years of 1986–89, we will now proceed through the following three sections:

- the pre-1980s;
- the 1980s and 1990s;
- the 'corporate approach' to management development in the 1980s and 1990s.

THE PRE-1980S

Thomas (1980) provides one of the most insightful accounts of the history of the development of management education in Britain during the 1960s and 1970s. His account may be contextualised by Hannah's (1980) brief historical account of the rise of the multidivisional firm in corporate Britain with some international comparisons with the USA, France and Germany (for a fuller account see Hannah 1976). The latter argues that the idea of the professional manager was closely allied to the rise of the large multidivisional firm and that this species of private company did not emerge in Europe until the 1930s, which is earlier than the American business historian, Alfred Chandler, dated it but still fifty years behind the emergence of professional management in America during the 1880s (see Perkin 1989: chs 1 and 7, for a related discussion).

The issue of firm size and structure is of relevance to the character of British management, for as we saw in the previous section, the corporate approach to management development, described by Handy, takes place largely within the largest firms where multiple specialised managerial functions thrive. These companies are also the breeding grounds for leading edge 'professional' practices disseminated more widely via Britain's diverse managerial professions. Hannah argued that the USA experienced a first wave of mergers and acquisitions from 1880 to the turn of the century which accounted for the early increase in size of American firms and the divorce there between ownership and control. 'Ownership capitalism' or 'family capitalism' (where the firm is run by the founding owner and family) has steadily given way to 'managerial capitalism' (where the firm is run by salaried managers on behalf of diverse shareholders, rather than a dominant family) in the larger American firms over the course of the twentieth century. Hannah argues that a similar wave of merger and acquisition took place in Britain during the 1920s and 1930s, 'when modern corporations such as Imperial Chemical Industries (ICI), Unilever, and English Electric were formed ... and the creation of more extensive managerial hierarchies to coordinate, monitor, and allocate resources to the component companies or operating units' (Hannah 1980: 43).

However, by 1948 there were still only a dozen clearly multidivisional firms based in Britain:

> in 1930 the looser holding company arrangement with only an embryonic managerial hierarchy was still dominant in Great Britain; in the United States during the same period, the centralized, functionally departmentalized structure predominated. In 1948 the federated holding company was still strong in Britain, while the multidivisional organization had made more headway among the leading firms in the United States. (Hannah 1980: 53)

Also, family influence over even the largest firms in Britain continued, if outright control had begun to shift to salaried managers. In 1919 55 per cent of the largest 200 firms in Britain had family board members, which actually increased to 70 per cent by 1930 and was about 60 per cent in 1948. However, it was now the exception rather than the rule for them to own the majority of the capital (see also Table 3.5 in Chapter 3 of this volume). In some sectors, notably brewing, shipbuilding and food, founding families 'retained their directorial prerogatives' (Hannah 1980: 53). Also many multi-unit holding firms which appeared to be large multidivisional combines actually remained as 'federations of family firms', such as Imperial Tobacco and the Metal Box Company (ibid.: 54)

Hannah notes that the persistence of family capitalism and family management in Britain, into the 1940s and 1950s, may have caused a 'brake on the development of modern management' in Britain, but that this was controversial at the time and remains so. He cites the Dunlop Rubber Company as one case where the family was ousted and replaced by professional managers in the crisis of 1921–22, and contrasting cases such as the Pilkingtons (glassmakers) where the family managers were actually very skilled and innovative, not at all a brake on managerial professionalism. Others such as the Kenricks (hardware manufacturers) were 'merely skilled at obtaining enough credit to survive even when their firms deserved to go under on general grounds' (ibid.). This is one early example of the problems besetting the adequacy of auditing practices in the UK (see Chapter 4 this volume).

By the 1950s there were two types of large British firm, those still dominated by their founding families and those fewer firms now controlled by salaried managers. The latter tended to be more professional and influenced by management ideas from America, such as mass-production techniques, especially in the more technological business sectors. However, it was not simply the desire of families to hang on to power in their firms, but the actual structure of British capital markets which encouraged this tendency. In Britain, as Piesse (Chapter 3 this volume) discusses, unlike the USA and Germany, there were no real equivalents to the investment banks and industrial banks, respectively, which controlled new capital for transportation and industrial enterprises. Instead capital came from many sources: reinvested profit, stock exchange issues, stockbrokers, insurance companies, merchant banks, the business families and managers themselves. It was thus more difficult to distinguish among a founding entrepreneur and his family, the financial interest, from the managerial interest, since these roles were not so clearly and institutionally defined. The families behaved as financiers to each other as well as managers of their own enterprises.

Another factor peculiar to the British economy was the role of retailing and distribution (Napoleon gibed that the nation was one of shopkeepers). Unlike the USA, these types of firms tended to grow big on economies of scale, dominating the high street and other distribution outlets, but then began to integrate backwards, gradually buying up their suppliers and controlling production as well as distribution via large managerial hierarchies. Boots the chemist, thus became ICI's major competitor in the fine-chemical trade; GEC, now a major manufacturer, began as a wholesaler and retailer of electric-lighting equipment in the 1880s; both the British Shoe Corporation and Burtons, the mass clothing retailer, grew to large managerial hierarchies on the strength of their chains of high street shops. In this respect it was the retailers in Britain which grew in scale to the size that required many layers and functional specialisms of managerial staff, whereas it was manufacturers that did so in the USA and Germany. The early dominance of large retailers, is reflected in the growth of the advertising and marketing profession in Britain, as Michael Thomas argues in Chapter 2 of this volume.

Hannah also notes that cartels (price-fixing among firms within an oligopoly) remained legal in Britain, as elsewhere in Europe, until the late 1950s. This meant that takeovers among firms were not necessary to gain monopoly-style advantages, such as the charging of high prices. Consequently firms could stay smaller and remain under family control, while enjoying the price-fixing benefit usually associated with large monopolies.

Writing in the late 1970s, Hannah was equivocal about the effects upon the economy of the persistence of family capitalism in post-war Britain. However, his general view indicates more than a suspicion that the overall effect was probably deleterious to the modernisation of British industry, and the development of British management, which has tended to be initiated by foreign-owned companies in Britain (e.g. American firms, such as Ford, which introduced scientific management and mass-production in the 1960s and 1970s, and Japanese firms, such as Nissan, which introduced quality control and 'just in time' methods in the 1980s and 1990s). As Hannah puts it:

> The family firm was not symptomatic of an entirely irrational approach to industrial policy; rather, a case can be made for it on the basis of the alternative resources available for management. Although little is known

about changes in the recruitment and training of managers in the twentieth century, the lack of professional development in the field cannot be traced solely to the low demand for managers. Business in Britain was proverbially less prestigious than politics or the professions; although the universities gradually responded to the needs of industry, a substantial gap in the supply of technically trained manpower for management probably remained. Britain's earlier heavy reliance on its market-based industrial organization also led to an underinvestment in managerial talent in the early stages of corporate development. As a result, patronage had to replace professionalism. A young man who wished to learn the business of management could often envisage no better training than in the family firm, where many potential managers both within and outside the family sought it. (Hannah 1980: 69)

Hannah observes that, by the late 1970s, about 17 per cent of British manufacturing was foreign-owned and 'uses imported technology and managerial techniques and, less frequently, non-British managers', the proportion of non-nationals being none the less 'higher than in any other European country' (ibid.). This was broadly the position when Thomas analysed the emerging role of British management education and its detractors. In the late 1960s the corporate route into management, controlled by owning families in the vast majority of British firms, predominated. The managerial professions enjoyed low status, in contrast to the older professions, and in any case augmented rather than challenged the idea of the family firm as training ground. The practice of long-burn, functionally specialised managerial careers with late, and therefore rare, transitions into general (i.e. 'top') management kept technical specialists in their functional places, preserving general management posts for the gifted amateurs who had the benefit of a broad public school and/or Oxbridge classics or arts degree, and who were generally the male children of Britain's owning families.

Thomas (1980) notes that the foundation of the London and Manchester Business Schools (LBS and MBS respectively) in 1965, backed by business itself, which subscribed over £5 million, matching the level of government funding, and supported by higher education, (although the universities of Oxford and Cambridge refused to accept that management and business could be a suitable subject for academic study), constituted a 'revolution' (Wheatcroft 1970) and an 'explosion' in management education (Thomas 1980: 71). The 'traditional skepticism of the businessmen about the need for, or possibility of, formal education for management seemed finally to have been dispelled' and 'management, it seemed, was at last to join the ranks of the most exalted professions, blessed henceforth by its association with the most exalted sector of the education system' (ibid.).

The founding of university management education in 1965 was in fact the result of a much longer battle between the business community at large, which tended to believe that management was an 'art' that could not be taught and that good managers were born not made, and the various advocates of the 'management movement' which tended to believe that management could be a rational science and were influenced by the 'scientific management' principles of F. W. Taylor in the USA and Quaker social ideals in the UK as exemplified by Cadbury, Rowntree and Lever Bothers (Child 1969).

The 'management movement' had to battle to persuade both business and the universities of the merits of a formal management education. Until the mid-1960s the universities did not want to entertain this idea, fearing it would taint them with the world of vocational education and training, and business did not want to entertain the idea because it did not trust the possibility that management could become a science and it did not want to lose control of the ways in which its managers were trained and selected for top jobs. But as Thomas shows, from the end of the war in 1945, British management had a new-found receptivity towards American management methods, since the war effort had forced them to consider every possible means of improving production.

In 1947 the British Institute of Management (BIM, now the Institute of Management – IM) was founded at the instigation of the Board of Trade and replaced the Institute of Industrial Administration which had been set up by the management movement in 1920 and still had only 517 members in 1939. In 1945 the Ministry of Education set up a committee to advise on management education, chaired by a long-standing member of the management movement, Colonel L. Urwick. This led to the establishment in 1949 of a 'National Scheme of Management Studies' originally under the auspices of the BIM which was run by the technical and commercial colleges and eventually taken over and administered by the Council for National Academic Awards (CNAA) which was set up to be the generic awarding body for the polytechnics (as noted by Keep and Mayhew, Chapter 8 this volume, the polytechnics became universities in 1992). The National Scheme was attacked for the poor quality of its teachers and calibre of its students and underwent several revisions which resulted in the establishment of a range of credentials from the Higher National Certificate (HNC) to the Higher National Diploma (HND) and the Diploma in Management Studies (DMS) all of which survive today. This scheme included a mix of 'background' and 'tool' subjects in specialist areas such as business control, personnel and industrial relations. It was estimated that about 11,000 students a year were in need of initial management training, but the courses were again attacked by business and in 1950 there were only 847 entrants, which dropped to 564 in the following year, very few of which were sponsored by private companies. A survey conducted in 1978, covering nine previous years' intakes to the DMS, found that private industry was still most reluctant to support management education and that most of the students were in fact employed by the nationalised industries in the public sector.

Thomas quotes the survey's conclusions which indicate some of the reasons for the situation described in the above paragraph:

The private sector (manufacturing and service) did not appear as enthusiastic about the DMS as the much maligned government sector. This difference in support may result from the supposedly more bureaucratic and larger government agencies placing higher value on promotion by qualification and examination, while the private sector still perhaps visualises itself as entrepreneurial, with the emphasis on experience rather than level of education (Sibbald 1978, cited by Thomas 1980: 80)

Thomas concludes that the scheme was not instituted at the call of business but as the result of the State's initiative and was formulated by Urwick, whose views, although a leading management intellectual, were far from representative of the business community at large. Consequently business reacted by 'verbal criticism, a reluctance to sponsor students, and a refusal to recognise the credential as a qualification', yet the courses survived until the late 1970s due to the support of the State employment organisations (Thomas 1980: 81).

While state-initiated courses survived due to state support, the private sector continued to favour the corporate approach to management development, which could be controlled by the boards of directors and the founding families. Hooper's (1960) book *Management Survey,* summarises the gist of this philosophy. It still regarded management essentially as an art, particularly an art of judgement, an indefinable ability which was mainly in-born, but which could be refined by the right kind of liberal education (e.g. Oxbridge arts degree or attendance at public school – cf. Perks's comments in Chapter 4 of this volume on the major accounting firms).

Apart from judgement, 'acceptability to others' was highly important and depended upon the following qualities considered to be 'in the grain of the man' (Hooper 1960: 155): 'general personal appearance; absence of unpleasing mannerisms; the existence of pleasing ones; the absence of disturbing or flamboyant traits of character ... whether he has poise and is at ease in company'. Such social graces were more a consequence of class than in-born characteristics, and indicated the 'clubable' type of man (women never entered the discussion at the time) which private firms preferred to see rising to their top echelons. Hooper conceded that there was now a place for management *as a science*, mainly at the bottom end of the corporate ladders and recommended three stages and kinds of education and development for the aspiring manager, be he 'ranker, technician, graduate or proprietor's son' (ibid.: 171–2). These were: a general training in the science of management which could be gained in a technical or commercial college; followed by practical training related to the type of business being entered which should be acquired within a particular firm, and developed to a more specialised degree by working for the examinations of an appropriate professional institute; and finally a training to develop 'the whole man' in order to gain the 'larger view' necessary for entry into top management and the practice of management *as an art*, which could be gained by attendance at the Administrative Staff College,

Henley (a private management school founded in 1947, arguably Europe's first such school).

Against Hooper's prescriptions, the new business schools might appear to have been a breakthrough for the management as science movement, however, despite the large amount of money raised to found them, at the behest of the Foundation for Management Education (FME), Confederation of British Industry and British Institute of Management, it was not long before they were being criticised as roundly as the previous institutional innovations, such as the National Scheme. The problem was the postgraduate MBA, not the post-experience senior and middle management executive programmes, which were run along the country club lines of the Henley Administrative Staff College and later Ashridge. Business did not like the MBA because it had no veto over the programme entrants; because it was a credential that might lead to a management profession, with the danger of becoming a management union; because the credential might increase the possessor's ability to move jobs and demand higher salaries; and because it did not like the attitude of some MBA graduates: 'described by one Deputy Chairman as the "I am trained to be a Managing Director syndrome" ... It is industry's belief that this attitude tends to be fostered in the business schools' (BIM 1971: 11 i.e. the 'Owen Report', cited by Thomas 1980: 95).

Instead of MBAs, Thomas says that what industry wanted was a quick injection of expertise into middle management (Thomas 1980: 94–5). Their disapproval was shown when a second appeal for funding the business schools in 1970, fell £1.25 million short of target, and evaluation studies of even the post-experience courses approved of by industry showed that they were predominantly supported by nationalised industries, financial services and government agencies. However, regarding the MBA, studies of LBS and MBS graduates in the 1970s, showed that despite its words big businesses (i.e. those employing over 2,000) did recruit MBAs, did pay a premium for them even though they never requested an MBA in job advertisements. Yet MBAs tended to be employed in staff and advisory functions rather than line management and with no automatic right to join top management.

By the end of the 1980s, the two original business schools were fifteen years old, many other universities had opened management schools or departments (e.g. Bradford, Lancaster and Warwick, among others) and, despite the criticisms voiced by the business community, the employment prospects of MBAs, and holders of other types of business credential (e.g. BA Business Studies and the Diploma in Management Studies) was becoming an advantage in entering the managerial labour market. Industry's bark was perhaps worse than its bite.

For Thomas in 1980, the conclusions were that management as science and technique meant that the mystique of management as art was under threat, and this was good for meritocracy. The new forms of knowledge (sociology, psychology, organisation theory, operations research, market research, etc.) were scientific, therefore universalistic and suggested that wholly new technical criteria might be used for selection into management and for advancement within the occupation, instead of 'experience' as recognised by practising managers and their bosses. 'Experience' could be criticised as being mere time-serving, and a codeword for being socially 'acceptable'. However, employers still tended to resist these new meritocratic criteria, especially at the top, where the art of management still counted for a great deal, and deflected the new technically professional managers into functionally specialised staff roles. In short, the birth of formal management education in late twentieth-century Britain was an achievement of government and the management movement, both of which looked to American examples, in the teeth of opposition and resistance from UK manufacturing industry.

THE 1980S AND 1990S

The culture of the 1980s actually began in 1979 with the election of the Thatcher Conservative Government, which brought considerable change to the market-place 'consuming' management education. In the 1980s knowledge and education themselves became 'commodities' to be bought and sold as the idea of 'the market' was gradually applied by government to many of the institutions previously comprising the public services (Fox 1989a, 1989b). Such trends generated a new managerial culture in Britain and the previous differentiation between private and public became less clear-cut. Many managers from the big privatised former public utilities (such as British Steel, British Airways, British Gas, British Telecom) were pushed out in the name of managerial efficiency and streamlining and many of them found jobs in the private sector. Senior managers who remained, took the credit for turning around the fortunes of the former public sector organisations and demanded, and received, salary increases and perks on a par with the traditional private sector, much to the disgust of the press and the public.

As the former public sector organisations and those remaining in the public sector continued to introduce market-based reform, they increased their demand for recruiting managers from the traditional private sector. For example, in 1984–85 the top 200 district administrators in the National Health Service (NHS) were replaced by district general managers, 66 per cent of whom came from outside the NHS. Thus the 1980s saw much more movement in managerial labour markets than previous decades and many revolving doors between private and public sectors, as well as the erosion of this distinction, leading to a homogenisation of British managerial culture and practices. This shake-up of the corporate managerial labour market was part of a national recognition that the manufacturing sector was in severe decline. Britain began importing more than it exported in manufactures for the first time in its history in 1983 and this was possible in the 1980s because of North Sea oil revenues (see Ingram, Chapter 1 this volume). It was thought that services, especially the former public services (in telecommunications and transport), were a potential source of revenue in the national balance of payments if they could be made more competitive, hence the increased fluidity in managerial labour markets between broad business sectors from the mid-1980s on. As in many things, Britain learned from the previous experience of the USA.

Dissatisfaction with the American economy in the 1970s had led some influential commentators there to blame the widespread application of certain management techniques, taught in the business schools, such as ROI-based (return on investment) financial controls, portfolio management concepts and market-driven strategies (Hayes and Abernathy 1980). It was argued that these techniques were damaging to long-run innovative product/market development and tended to encourage short-run profitability at the expense of long-run business development. It was also argued that these techniques were part of a collective corporate mind-set or group-think due to the domination of American boardrooms by 'people with financial and legal skills and to the widespread acceptance of the doctrine of pseudoprofessionalism' (Hill, Hitt and Hoskisson 1988: 51). This doctrine was blamed upon American management education which was attacked for its over-analytical orientation, which placed too much emphasis on quantitative analysis, business forecasting and accounting and too little emphasis upon qualitative and people skills involving moral and interpersonal skills (Finney and Siehl 1985–86; Rehder 1982; Leavitt 1975a, 1975b) – in the terms of the British debate on management education discussed above: too much science and not enough art. Whether this accusation was true or not as an explanation of America's balance of payments problems, the argument had more credibility there than it could do in Britain, because management education had controlled access to most managerial posts there for many years, so there was a possibility of a dysfunctional national managerial group-think. The same could not be said of Britain, even though the British curriculum is closely modelled on the American one, since management education only controlled about 12 per cent of management entrants in the mid-1980s. If the UK suffered any similar kind of national 'groupthink', it is more likely to be due to the dominance of the accounting profession (noted by Handy *et al.* 1988: 2; and see Perks, Chapter 4 this volume) and its world-view, which focuses upon short-term, bottom-line results.

The arguments in America were powerful enough for them to make a serious attempt at reforming management education; Richard Boyatzis of McBer Consulting was commissioned to investigate the competencies of successful managers, which he did, surveying over a thousand managers and producing various lists of discrete competencies which individually or in combination were taken to account for managerial effectiveness (Boyatzis 1982). It was thought that American management education could be reformed by adding the teaching of these competencies to the analytic techniques already taught, but simultaneously blamed for the short-termist mind-set of top managers in America. Albanese (1989) describes the lengths to which the competency-based approach was pushed on to recalcitrant American management academics.

By the mid-1980s the idea of 'competence' was catching on in the UK and initially applied to vocational occupations such as ambulance driving. About the time of the Handy and Constable/McCormick reports, policy-makers in the Government's Department of Employment came to believe that the competency approach could be applied to management and that this would find more favour with UK employers than academic management education had so far. This government department funded several large projects, similar to the Boyatzis study, although adopting somewhat different methodology (called 'functional analysis'), and placed the management of these projects into the hands of what it called 'Industry Lead Bodies'. The lead bodies were staffed with volunteers and nominees from Britain's leading companies, and the professional institutes, and commissioned consultants and researchers to produce the sets of competencies which, it was hoped, would then be 'owned' by, taken seriously and adopted by the industries concerned. The lead body for management became known as the 'Management Charter Initiative' (MCI – see Day 1988 for an early account).

In many ways the competency approach was similar to the 'management as art' philosophy of Hooper's, but it was also a way to 'scientifically' legitimate experience over education, a way to provide existing managers with a credential without going back to university for an MBA. The MCI vision was to provide a professional route into British management, which would encourage management education at junior levels, but would recognise other experience at middle and senior levels. The 'new architecture' and the new 'ladder of progression' (see Figures 7.3 and 7.4) clearly positioned all business degrees as *prior to* entry into junior management (Day 1988: 31). It is possible to interpret this as industry's response to the 'I am trained to be a Managing Director syndrome' allegedly 'fostered in the business schools' (BIM 1971: 11). Whether this move on the part of employers was an attempt to preserve the class-based access to most senior managerial jobs in most top companies, or whether employers simply believed that only they could select good middle and senior managers is unclear. It is certainly possible to read the MCI movement as being in line with Thomas's (1980) thesis. Either way, not only did the new 'ladder of progression' put management education in its place, on the lowest rung of the ladder, but it also sought to add a competency dimension to the early education of potential managers by adding training in management skills and operations, closely following the American experiment with the competency approach.

However, the underlying reason for the adoption of the competency approach in Britain was that British, like American, manufacturing was in decline, having slumped gradually over forty post-war years. As noted above Britain began for the first time to import more than it exported in manufactured goods in 1983 (see Smith 1984, for a critical analysis at the time and see Cairncross 1992, and the Trade and Industry Committee 1994, second report on the *Competitiveness of UK Manufacturing Industry,* for more recent analyses). The ability to import

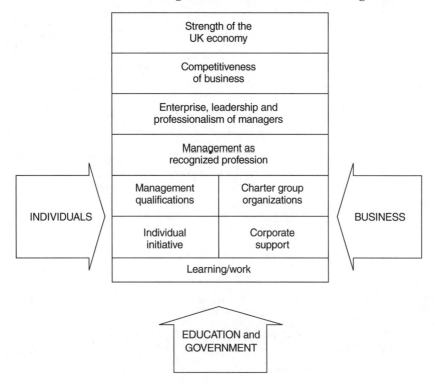

Figure 7.3 The new architecture
Source: Day 1988: 31

more than it exported was temporarily provided for Britain by North Sea oil revenues, which hid the balance of payments problem facing the country (see Ingram's Chapter 1 in this volume). The Thatcher Government precipitated a wide-scale reform of British manufacturing in the early 1980s with corporate cost-cutting shaking out many layers of middle managers. Increasingly, managers could not expect to work in one functional area, in one company, or in one sector of business for their entire careers. Instead they could expect to be made redundant and to have several 'careers' in several firms, over the course of their working lives. Handy (1985) summarised these trends, and discussed their implications.

One of the consequences was that British management at last began to see the need for credentials; since they no longer expected to spend their careers in only one firm, a widely recognised credential would help them move from one employer to the next, rather like a passport. This led to an expansion in all kinds of MBA in higher educational institutions, but this model was being challenged in the late 1980s by the MCI competency approach which was based on the accreditation of a manager's experience, rather than analytical skills tested by

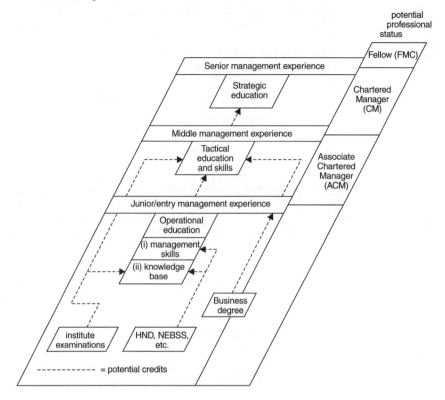

Figure 7.4 Ladder of progression

Source: Day 1988: 31

academic examinations. The competency approach was tied to a new system of national vocational qualifications (NVQs – and Scottish vocational qualifications (SVQs), see Keep and Mayhew's Chapter 8 in this volume) which was welcomed by some as a more credible qualification than the theory-based MBA. On the other hand the new credentials were regarded by others to be academically inferior, a mere rubber stamp on existing experience, a distraction from the real need for a better *educated* management population.

The attempt to integrate the competency approach with the academic approach, in ways outlined in theory by Day (1988) never happened in practice. Rather the two systems now exist side by side, the competency system adding to the general confusion, rather than clearing it up. The NVQ system was heavily criticised (see Keep and Mayhew's Chapter 8 in this volume) and the MCI has gradually distanced itself from this form of credential and has begun encouraging some higher education (HE) institutions to experiment with the design of the traditional MBA. Some academics welcome this move, hoping that by courting the MCI, their educational activities would acquire importance in the eyes of employers. Others worry that academic standards will be eroded and that the management schools will become even more technicist than before (as argued by Leavitt 1975a, 1975b; Rehder 1982), devoid of the capacity to offer any critique of the managerial and organisational world (Grey and Mitev 1995; Reed and Anthony 1992; Wilmott 1994). Others have examined the theoretical assumptions underlying the competency movement and found it wanting. It is ironic that after years of berating the management educators for being over-analytical, the employers themselves adopted an over-analytical methodology for reforming them, perhaps in the hope of convincing the management scientists among them. However, there has been a growing body of management academics in the UK who are themselves critical of the over-scientistic and technicist nature of much management research and education (Anthony 1987; Carter and Jackson 1989; Fox 1994a 1994b; Grey and Mitev 1995; Salaman and Butler 1989; Willmott 1994). Such writers variously argue, within the management education and research community, for qualitative research, critical perspectives and alternative educational methods. Accordingly, some academics argued the theoretical case against the scientism of the competency approach (Burgoyne 1989; Collin 1989), while accepting the need to provide a system of credentials which meets employers' requirements, as well as being academically rigorous.

Considering that the competency approach is the most concerted attempt in decades to radically re-shape the way managers are made in Britain and since the MCI management competency approach is, in the mid-1990s, still being heavily promoted by government with mixed support from employers, it is worth looking at this debate more closely. On the optimistic side, the approach aims to improve the educational support available to small and medium-sized firms (SMEs) in Britain. The MCI cites the IBM–LBS 'Made in Europe' study, which compares Britain's overall competitiveness with Germany, Sweden and The Netherlands and concludes that large British companies are as competitive as large firms in other nations, but that Britain's overall competitiveness is held back because it has a longer 'tail' of poorly performing SMEs than other countries (MCI 1995a). Therefore the solution MCI currently argues for, is to find ways of providing such firms with low-priced, high quality education, consultancy and expertise. It aims to do this via the Training and Enterprise Council (TEC) and Local Enterprise Councils (LEC) network (see Keep and Mayhew, Chapter 8 this volume) and by reforming management education to make it more accessible and user-friendly to SMEs. The emphasis on 'competency' in the NVQ system and in the reform of management education is intended to accomplish this. But the approach is marred by intrinsic problems, which many employers recognise and express by not rushing to adopt it, despite the heavy promotion of it by government, industry lead bodies, and TECs, and problems which some academics articulate in publication. These arguments are summarised below.

The competency approach generally assumes that 'a managerial competency is a skill and/or personal characteristic that contributes to effective performance' (Albanese 1989: 66). It further assumes that:

1 managerial competencies can be identified;
2 managers and potential managers can be trained to acquire and perfect managerial competencies; and
3 competent managers make a difference in the level of organisational performance (ibid.).

All of these assumptions can be challenged; (1) and (2) are in this section and (3) is in the next section on human resource management (HRM). More specifically, the UK's Training Commission defined competence as 'the ability to perform the activities within an occupational area to the levels of performance expected in employment' (Training Commission 1988). Collin (1989: 22) points out that the Training Commission document refers to Boyatzis for whom competency was 'an underlying characteristic of a person which results in effective and/or superior performance in a job', and that for him, such 'underlying characteristics' included 'motives, traits, skills, aspects of self-image or social role, or a body of knowledge'. Nearly all of these assumptions are challengeable in principle as well as in empirical detail, despite the plausibility of the Boyatzis study, as we will see below.

Burgoyne (1989: 56) summarised 'eight underlying problems or issues which any specific competency based scheme must face up to', namely:

1 The divisibility of competencies and their reintegration for performance.
2 The measurability of competencies, and appropriate methods.
3 How universal or generalisable a listing is over different categories of manager.
4 The ethical/moral content of professional management, and their representation in competency listings.
5 The permanence of competency listings given the changing nature of managing.
6 Accommodating different styles and strategies of managing.
7 How managerial competencies relate to the whole person.
8 How individual competence contributes to and integrates into collective or organisational competence.

These above points overlap with many of the points made in Collin's (1989) paper and we will briefly discuss each. The issue of the *divisibility of competence* challenges assumption (1), that competencies can be identified. The analytic process of identifying competencies is a reductionist one which Collin points out may be more the projection on to the data of the researcher's preferred categories than a meaningful exercise in the eyes of the managers being studied. The resulting lists of discrete, separate competencies may be more of a reification of an abstraction than anything relevant to managers' experience and categories of sense-making. The argument here is similar to the point made against 'intelligence' and 'personality' tests, i.e. that they do not measure a pre-given innate characteristic, nor a socially meaningful concept, but that they create the phenomena which they are seeking to measure. Thus one definition of 'intelligence' is that it is *whatever* 'intelligence tests' test; at most this may be an aspect of what intelligence means in our culture, abstracted in some way by psychologists, but certainly not the full cultural meaning of it.

A second way in which the divisibility of competence is an issue is that even if, for the sake of argument, we accept that competency can be analytically divided into identifiable discrete competencies which have some kind of objective reality beyond the researchers' formulations of the cultural 'phenomena', this still leaves the problem of how the individual possessing them actually reintegrates them *in action,* i.e. in *the performance* of her/his managerial work. As Burgoyne (1989: 57) puts it 'managing is not the sequential exercise of discrete competencies' and 'learning separate aspects of managerial competence one at a time does not guarantee integral managerial performance' (ibid.: 58). Expressed in this way the issue also challenges assumption (2) that managers can be trained to acquire and/or perfect the individual managerial competencies.

The problem of *the measurability of competencies* is connected to the above problem of their divisibility and as Collin shows is a similar problem to that facing 'intelligence' and 'personality' testing among psychologists (for a thorough debunking of 'personality tests', see Heritage 1974). She points out that research into the latter has been going for over eighty years without a consensus emerging on the results, in contrast research seeking to measure managerial competencies, is more recent, more limited, and yet subject to exactly the same type of problems; she concludes that the very idea of measuring managerial competence opens 'a Pandora's box of research problems' (Collin 1989: 23).

The issue of *universality or generalisability* over different categories of manager challenges the idea that competencies can be identified and then taught or applied, because the very abstraction of the competencies as listed makes it difficult to translate into practice in specific cases. For Burgoyne (1989: 58)

all managerial jobs are different at a detailed level of resolution, and all managerial jobs the same at a high level of abstraction. Competency is, of course, exercised in discrete and specific situations, and each competent action will have its own mixture of idiosyncratic and shared elements.

As a consequence, 'the more universally true any given list of competencies is, the less immediately useful is it to making any particular choice about how to act and conduct oneself in a specific situation' (ibid.).

The problem of universality is related to the problem of *the permanence of any competency listing.* Not only are all situations idiosyncratic, but they change over time; organisations are becoming flatter, branch managers have changing responsibilities vis-à-vis the centre, previously entrepreneurial decisions tend to become routinised and systematised over time, but then revolutionary innovations in systems can destroy and replace established routines (e.g. the introduction of 'just in time' management has radically changed systems of production that had become taken for granted). This changeability over time makes all but the most general or universal competency listings rapidly obsolete, and as Burgoyne notes above: the more universal a list, the less useful it is. The very project of identifying competencies is therefore caught in a 'catch 22' paradox.

Apart from different and changing situations, there is the problem of *accommodating different styles and strategies of managing.* There are two aspects to this. First, the competency approach tends to presume that all managers operate as managers on a principally cognitive level. Collin points out that 'it may be that managers perceive what they need to do to be effective not just cognitively, but also affectively ... the strong intuitive experience of managers cannot be denied, although it is often played down' (Collin 1989: 23). This point relates to the management-as-art versus management-as-science debate, and the experience versus education debate. It is ironic but inescapable that the competency approach which was devised to counteract the over-scientific approach to management education, is itself subject to the biases of science and education towards the cognitive over the affective and intuitive.

Second, competency is rarely exercised or recognised in a social vacuum, competent action is therefore rarely purely individual, but is often a concerted collaborative effort, sometimes involving 'teamwork', but not necessarily since not all social groups can be described as 'teams'. Instead, it is increasingly recognised by some learning theorists that learning, intelligence and competent action itself is a function of situated social relationships and interaction (Goody 1995; Lave and Wenger 1991; Resnick *et al.* 1991; see also Fox 1996 for a fuller discussion of 'situated leaning' and 'social intelligence').

The issue of *different styles and strategies* is further linked to the problem of *how managerial competencies relate to the whole person.* Being a competent person as Burgoyne (1989: 60) points out 'is different from having competencies' and raises questions about who is the person deploying the competencies and how does that person develop? This is also connected to the problem of *the ethical/moral content of professional management* as that relates to personal ethics and morality. The two issues connect because the tendency is for lists of competencies to emphasise the technical over the ethical, as if discrete competencies were simple repertoires for dealing with known contingencies. But, as we saw above, specific situations are often too idiosyncratic to be covered by general rules/repertoires and in any case change over time; moreover different managers can be equally effective using different styles and the acceptability/appropriateness of their style or strategy is, in any case, socially and morally defined rather than cognitively defined in the abstract. All of these issues are at stake in the eighth problem of *how individual competence contributes to and integrates into collective or organisational competence.*

These arguments indicate some of the fundamental problems with the competency approach, which undermine its credibility with employers as well as management educators. They all result from an overly reductionist and overly scientific approach to defining management practice, the very problem that the competency approach was set up to change in management education in the first place. Much of management education is currently as technicist as the MCI in its research paradigm, being based on pseudo-scientific assumptions about cause and effect which are highly dubious predictors for the control of social behaviour. Not that the cause–effect paradigm should be thrown out, but that it needs to be balanced with analyses of the social and cultural life of managers, firms and industry networks

A potential solution might be for management educators to give more weight to the qualitative disciplines which aim to research management practices *from the manager's viewpoint*, on the model of Kotter (1982), Mintzberg (1973) and Stewart (1967). For some this should be modified in accordance with Wilmott's (1987) labour process critique. For others, even on the left, this critique has been found lacking (Hall and Jacques 1989) and requires wholesale rethinking. For me, it is the lack even of a debate over alternative paradigms which is the problem with management research and education, outside of organisational analysis (Burrell and Morgan 1979), since this leaves the whole system uncritically wedded to a functionalist, technicist paradigm which is widely seen to be irrelevant even by the managers and employers who share the management scientists' desire to predict and control the social world in order to make it perform 'better' according to classic economic yardsticks. If management schools were to begin to debate their foundational paradigms of research and teaching this would shift them in the direction of the rest of the social sciences. It is interesting and optimistic to note that even the MCI appears to support this shift, for it summarises the critique of British management education on two grounds – its irrelevance to policy-makers in government and business and its lack of esteem in the eyes of academics in cognate areas: 'management research plays little part in the decisions of policy makers in government and is held in low esteem by academic peers in cognate areas' (MCI 1995b). However, if this is the situation in Britain, it is very unclear whether this pattern is similar across Europe (see Calori and De Woot 1994; Fox 1992; for some comparative indications).

THE 'CORPORATE APPROACH' TO MANAGEMENT DEVELOPMENT IN THE 1980S AND 1990S

One of the areas where managerial practitioners have had a great deal to prove about their contribution to a firm's competitiveness is human resource management. This area of managerial practice has been central to the restructuring of British manufacturing in the 1980s, presiding as it did over waves of redundancy and later the outsourcing even of aspects of its own functional specialism, such as recruitment processes which have been outsourced to the expanding head-hunter business, and training and development which has also been outsourced to a considerable extent. The HRM function left inside the companies is often focused more sharply on rewards and remuneration systems, performance appraisal systems and career planning for the upper echelons, the people the company believes it cannot afford to lose. The changing nature of HRM (it used to be, and is still sometimes, called 'personnel management') in Britain is inescapably connected to the question of how firms identify and develop their middle and senior managers. As Handy said in 1988, the corporate approach to developing managers has long been favoured by employers. In the previous two sections we have examined the academic route and the professional route, especially as these have begun to come together under the auspices of the MCI, since the Handy and Constable/McCormick watershed. Accordingly, the present section will look at the changing nature of the corporate approach itself.

In this regard we are hampered by the lack of empirical studies of this area of managerial life in Britain. For most of the literature on HRM is of the prescriptive variety, as written by internal or external consultants with a particular technique to promote or assess. One research programme funded under the ESRC (Economic and Social Research Council) Competitiveness of British Industry initiative included a strand of research on managerial labour markets in the late 1980s and attempted to provide empirical description of company practices. The two case studies which follow are derived from this study and are illustrative of corporate HRM practice in the late 1980s when they were conducted (see Fox and McLeay 1992; Fox, Tanton and McLeay 1991).

Case 1: Tesco PLC

Tesco is one of Britain's three top food retailers with about 70,000 employees and had a turnover of £4,119 million, 100 per cent of it earned in the UK, back in the late 1980s. The total management population was 2,000 people with a board of ten directors, twenty-seven functional heads and six regional managing directors with responsibility for retail operations throughout the country. Reporting to the six were thirty-two Retail Executives and 370 branch managers. These 450 staff comprised the top and senior managers and most of the remaining 1,550 managerial staff were spread out across the group's 335 branches (i.e. an average of four to five managers per branch) of which nearly half had over 25,000 square feet of sales area.

Tesco had a reputation as a fast-growing, highly competitive food retailer which had competed mainly on price during the 1970s and early 1980s until it grew to the operational size of its main competitor Sainsbury PLC, which is still regarded as the market leader. In the late 1970s Tesco began to position itself 'up market' by improving quality and its store design and layout, increasing its number of larger stores, increasing the range of its home label goods and improving service. The capacity to pursue this strategy depended upon their 1977 'Operation Checkout' which was a fundamental change in its marketing strategy, away from the price emphasis, towards quality and nearly doubling market share from 7 per cent to 13 per cent over a ten-year period. This strategy involved widening the aisles in the stores and upgrading the furbishments, taking price-range and stock-control decisions away from branch managers and making them centrally, thus changing the role of branch managers significantly.

By the late 1980s this strategy had paid off with a marked increase in turnover and profits, and the central staff had just reached a point of stability after about a decade of fast change and increased responsibility. Key to the success of these strategic changes was the way in which the top management handled the HRM issues particularly regarding the 2,000 management staff. Prior to the strategic changes begun in 1977, they had a policy of recruiting what they called 'born entrepreneurs' to run their branches, that is, people who worked up from junior posts or were recruited from competitors to manage each branch almost in its entirety. After 1977, more decisions were taken centrally and many general systems were put in place to make each branch conform to a common blue-print, a managerial marketing and operations formula decided at head office. Consequently, the majority of managers had to take on a more standardised role, which allowed the centre to compare individuals more accurately for the purposes of performance appraisal, reward and promotion/'plateauxing'/ redundancy decisions.

The management development department became important in managing the change of culture. It set up four management development programmes, each one as a staging post in a vertical career path. At the first (lowest) level they had a Retail Manager Trainee Programme recruiting 200 people per year (graduates and A level school-leavers) into the regional branch network and about sixty into head office posts. The former could expect to become Assistant Branch Managers within eighteen months, the latter could expect an equivalent promotion at head office functions such as 'Buying', 'Merchandising' and 'Accounting'. After a few years in these 'deputy' roles, such managers could then attend the second staging post programme, a four week Management Development Programme at the company's in-house management development centre (Ponsbourne) covering such subjects as: 'business awareness', 'people management', 'personal development', using traditional classroom methods, an outdoor management development element and various 'introspection instruments' for assessing how one is perceived in the eyes of one's peers.

Assuming the individual carried on up the ladder after this programme s/he would become a manager of a large store or a manager in a head office function (e.g. Marketing Manager) at almost senior level. At this level the next staging post programme was the Senior Management Programme (again at Ponsbourne). This was a three-week course accepting about sixty people per year and covered similar themes to the previous programme, but in more depth and at a higher level in the company politics. Attendence at this programme would mark a managers' entry into senior management (i.e. the top 450), for those who were successful on it. Beyond this was the top programme – the Executive

Management Development Programme – a two-week course run at the Ashridge Management Centre. Here the bottom half of the top 120 managers would learn similar skills to before, plus skills for dealing with city analysts and wider communication skills. They would be evaluated all of the time, both formally and informally by their seniors and peers, and the successful ones would enter the top fifty to sixty posts in due course.

By 1988, 70 per cent of the head office functional heads were home-grown in the above ways and 100 per cent of the Regional Managing Directors, Retail Executives and Branch Managers were similarly home-grown. Research conducted in the late 1980s showed that many of Britain's larger firms adopted a similar approach to the internal management development of their senior people, i.e. a hierarchy of internal programmes teaching many of the softer skills such as communication, interpersonal skills, personal development and harder-edged skills such as business awareness. Companies with such management development 'ladders' include GKN, ICI, ASDA, Cadbury-Schweppes, Boots, among others (see Fox *et al.* 1989). Such companies manifest what Handy described as the 'corporate approach' in which those who the company has earmarked for career advancement are selected for custom-designed management development, of varying degrees of sophistication, depending upon the company, industry and level of manager. Unlike the image presented by Thomas in 1980, the corporate programmes of the late 1980s involved a risk of failure for the managers concerned. The courses were not only 'educational' and 'developmental', but also functioned like very long and intensive assessment centres, especially at the highest levels, and not everyone attending them could be guaranteed a promotion; some might 'plateau-out' or even be invited to leave the company rather than rise up the ladder.

While those selected for the management development programmes were carefully picked and therefore least at risk, their peers not selected for such high profile treatment would be at a higher risk of being made redundant as companies in the 1980s shed posts from top to bottom in pursuit of cost-cutting strategies. At Tesco those managers who were not part of the centralising change process, were likely to be perceived by top management as either surplus to requirement or even as blockages to change. Branch managers who resisted their changing role could be invited to leave. Tesco, in common with many of the large firms made use of professional 'out-placement' consultants who would counsel redundant managers and assist them to find new jobs in the retail industry, or to seek new careers in other industries or within managerial functions other than their own. Such 'derecruitment' practices increased the demand for vocational masters programmes in higher education among middle managers and increased the general turnover rate in the British management labour market. For the first time in generations the major British corporations also began recruiting their top managers from outside sources (competitors for instance) using the growing number of head-hunting agencies, rather than entirely home-growing their top teams. At Tesco about 30 per cent of head office functional heads were brought in from outside, although the majority were home-grown. Those functions in which most turnover developed tended to be the ones in which the specialism is most transferable from company to company, even industry to industry, such as accounting, IT and marketing. Retailing skills *per se* were less in demand among manufacturing, chemicals, engineering, etc. firms, whereas the general managerial functions, such as personnel, marketing, IT and accounting, were.

Case 2: Memec PLC

Memec (Memory and Electronic Components) PLC was founded in 1974 and grew to nearly 500 employees by 1988, with a turnover of £81 million and profits of £8.3 million. The group comprised two lines of business – components and systems – providing marketing, sales and distribution services to manufacturers of high technology electronic products. The company had 70 per cent of its operations in the UK, 11 per cent in the USA, 17 per cent in Germany and 2 per cent in South-East Asia and these operations were set up as a series of subsidiaries. The size of the management population of this SME was sixty-five plus 100 sales managers. The sixty-five comprised a main board of five directors, including the founder who was also the Chairman and Chief Executive, ten managing directors and ten financial controllers, one in each main subsidiary, and forty production managers. The two main product groups handled by the company were semiconductor components and computer peripherals.

Over fourteen years the business had grown from a small business to an SME within the electrical engineering sector. It faced five or six major competitors, some of which had been set up by its own ex-employees – about twelve of Memec's key people had left over the last ten years to establish new businesses which now competed with it. Not all of these had been equally successful, but all had survived and a few had become genuine competitors running at turnover in the £1–10 million region. The sector was regarded as a growth sector with expanding world markets. The foreign operations had all been established in the last three years: in 1985 they bought a company in the same business in Germany, in 1985–86 they started up from nothing in the USA and in 1988 they bought a business in Hong Kong and were beginning to examine other countries such as Australia and France.

Memec was the opposite kind of employer to the large British corporation discussed by Handy and illustrated by the Tesco case study. It was small, relatively young, and still managed by its owner-founder, a manufacturer and retailer, with the emphasis on the latter. So how did this company grow and develop its management? First, it recruited managerial staff from its competitors as its business grew, in both the sales and production areas, recruiting people with at least two years' experience. Second, it promoted its own people where it felt they had a good 'grasp of the overall business'. Third, it had a graduate intake of three or four people per annum – two financial types and two with technical backgrounds in electronics but with an interest in the commercial aspect of the business – who would become ripe for promotion, into financial control, production or selling, in due course. Before a graduate such as this could become a managing director of a subsidiary, they had to gain at least five years' experience and the top management team could specify the skills they were looking for in such people. They needed to be good at communicating, negotiating, managing people, spotting problems before they arise, logical thinking, selling and be ambitious.

The process of identifying people with the above characteristics was fairly informal, but systematic, and relied heavily upon the Chief Executive's personal judgement. He would travel around the subsidiaries and stores, talk with the staff, as well as the Managing Director and Financial Controller, and on the basis of this make judgements about who was promotable. In addition to this informal process, the company ran a central training scheme, with a four-day selling course for the sales managers, 75 per cent run by the senior sales people for those below them and 25 per cent by hired specialist sales trainers. On the production side they ran a three-day course twice a year which were problem-focused, each production manager bringing real problems to the course to work on. At the end of the course, they would each identify four new goals and return six months later to report on how far they had achieved them. This learning design had been devised at Memec and was run by the Chief Executive, the Finance Director and the Production Director. As with the larger corporations like Tesco, Boots, ICI and GKN, the courses provided an extra vehicle through which the top team could assess which of their junior colleagues were suitable for promotion. On the operations side the Financial Controllers, Data Processing Managers and Store Managers all spent a day per annum on technical updating in their respective fields.

The processes for promoting managerial staff were systematic and regular and yet heavily based on the subjective judgements formed by the top team and Chief Executive in particular. Like the larger firm, Tesco, there was a preference for promoting internally rather than recruiting from outside, except when buying a whole company overseas or setting up a new business overseas. This preference was justified in terms of past experience; with external people they could only be 80 per cent sure of their decision and had recruited some people who turned out to be problematic – one resigned and one overseas recruit had to be dismissed. The company found that it had more confidence in and control over home-grown people, when making promotion decisions.

CONCLUSION

Standing back from the two cases, we can make some general points about the way British companies develop their managers – the 'corporate approach' as Handy called it. First, there is a preference for organisationally home-growing managers rather than for hiring them 'ready-made' either direct from a business school, a competitor or elsewhere. The areas where this preference is sometimes waived are the functionally specialised ones of IT, accounting and finance, marketing, selling, personnel and training etc.; in most business-specialised areas of management, (such as retailing, engineering, chemicals production, etc.) if a promotion is likely to work the individual seems to require a depth of knowledge of the actual company itself, its politics, people, culture and ways of doing things – at least it is required of him or her in the eyes of the recruiters/ promoters/developers who make decisions about who will be developed to what level and post. The 'cultural chemistry' of the firm is of crucial importance, affecting the social and technical viability of the selection decision.

Second, the study from which the two cases are drawn (Fox *et al.* 1989, partially reported in Fox and McLeay, 1992) did not set out to test the Thomas (1980) suggestion that British firms decide who to educate and develop on the basis of class. However, it is clear that cultural chemistry is an important ingredient in such decisions, as indicated in the previous paragraph. It seems likely that this 'cultural chemistry' is, to some extent, class based in some older companies where the founding families have either always been upper class, as is the case in some of the British banks and city institutions (see Ingram 1984), or have entered the upper classes by the purchase of cultural capital from the profits of their business as in some of the manufacturing and retailing families where generations of family members are still prominent on the boards of directors (such as Cadbury-Schweppes, and Sainsbury). But it is also clear from the two cases discussed that 'cultural chemistry' need not be related to class, as defined by the acquisition of 'cultural capital' (attendence at a major public school, Oxbridge etc.), but that it is also important in younger companies, succeeding commercially without the benefit of 'cultural-capital-rich' top management teams.

Third, whatever the nature of the culture of a British company, it remains true that the corporate approach involves the company in: (a) deciding who is most promotable, and (b) designing developmental pathways for those individuals, involving both formal training courses and planned career moves. The pattern tends to be that as the company grows, rationalises or otherwise changes, in accordance with its business strategy, it uses management development as a vehicle for both developing and selecting some managers in line with that strategy. Frequently the management development programmes were delivered in-house but lately the trend has been to commission business schools and/or management staff colleges to run programmes. In the late 1980s and early 1990s after the full-time MBA expansion of the mid-1980s had plateauxed, there was still considerable growth in the market for part-time executive MBAs, where companies could nominate and sponsor their own serving managers on public programmes run by the business schools. In-company MBA programmes customised by a business school and run for an individual corporate client were also expanding, as were consortial MBA programmes (run for a region or an industry). All of these forms of MBA demonstrate that business schools in Britain are increasingly prepared to accept corporate control over who gets educated and developed at MBA level. Full-time public MBA programmes still run, attracting individual students who perceive the credential to be useful in either helping them switch career from one functional specialism or industry to another, or into consultancy. Also many British full-time MBA programmes attract a high proportion of international students with similar career goals but also seeking to switch from one national culture to another. However, the main point about British MBA programmes is that they collectively educate and develop only a few thousand new entrants or existing managers per annum, 1–3 per cent of the 90,000 per annum new entrants to management posts in Britain.

Fourth, the corporate approach, illustrated by the two cases, remains the typical route by which managers are developed. Although the approach may be sufficient for developing the high-flyers within companies and for making promotion decisions, the question remains as to its overall adequacy as an approach to developing both the firm's and the nations' overall stock of managers. The system in general may be good at selecting the best of a batch, but not good at developing the batch as a whole. This point was made by Handy *et al.* (1988: 168) when he observed that:

> The conclusion is inescapable that in Britain management education and training *is too little, too late for too few.* The British have rationed something which should be universally available and turned a potential common good into a special reserve. What should be a prerequisite of all managers has become a perk of the minority. The result is, in some areas a spurious elite. The scarcity of MBA graduates, for instance, has created an artificial market with artificial salaries leading many to argue, possibly correctly, that no training can possibly be worth that much more money but then to go on to argue, probably incorrectly, that the training is therefore of no value at all. This has made the MBA course a more contentious issue than it needs to be [original emphasis].

The overall quality of the managerial stock in any company, or across the nation is much more difficult to determine, although the international comparisons suggest British managers are much less well educated than American, Japanese, French and German ones, in the round (Handy *et al.* 1988).

Further research is undoubtedly needed into the *formation* of British managers and into conceptualising the nature of management in both its technical and social aspects according to dimensions such as industry, sector, age, location, size, structure, strategy, form of ownership and company culture, i.e. the demographic details of the British management population.

SELECTED READING

Grey, C. and Mitev, N. (1995)
Handy, C., Gordon, C., Gow, I. and Randlesome, C. (1988)
Reed, M. and Anthony, P. D. (1992)
Thomas, A. B. (1980)
Willmott, H. (1994)

8 UK vocational education and training

Ewart Keep and Ken Mayhew

INTRODUCTION

The system of vocational education and training (VET) in Britain has undergone a profound transformation in the last fifteen years. Given the scale and pace of these changes, and the often transitory nature of many developments in education and training, this chapter cannot cover all aspects in detail. The aim is to map the current system and to focus on the most significant trends in the developing structure of education and training policy-making and supply. It should also be noted that the system being described here applies only in England, Wales and Scotland; Northern Ireland has a separate and different education and training system, which limits of space preclude us from considering.

In terms of structure, the chapter opens with a consideration of developments in the sphere of vocational education. It then examines the changing institutional structure of training provision, the programmes through which training is delivered and the changing methods by which it is delivered. Discussion then turns to the quantity and quality of training, and its distribution across the workforce. The chapter concludes with a brief overview of the overall effectiveness of the British VET system.

Before commencing this review of British VET, it is perhaps worth highlighting two issues which have underlain the nation's VET policies. The first is that the debate has traditionally been bound up with a general ideological controversy about the role of the State. As the first industrialised nation, Britain initially left the provision of education to religious charities, and training to employers. While an involvement by the State in education slowly and haltingly evolved, training continued to be organised on a voluntary, *laissez-faire* basis, with minimal state involvement, funding and legislative underpinning. This approach was in marked contrast to that adopted by other industrialising countries. In Germany, France and Japan, the state took a direct and leading role in stimulating industrial growth, and as an integral part of such efforts invested in the development of vocational education and training systems (Gospel and Okayama 1991; McCormick 1991). More lately, many other European states have chosen to provide some form of statutory backing to training activity.

The second issue, in part, springs from the first. Britain's divergence of approach to the supply of VET and its apparent effects upon economic competitiveness, has led to periodic discussion about the need for reform which has spanned the last one hundred and fifty years (Perry 1976; Reeder 1981). Rising levels of unemployment have, more recently, added urgency to this recurring debate, which has been framed around comparisons between British VET provision and that found in competitor nations. During the 1980s, comparative studies (IMS/MSC/NEDO 1985; Prais 1990) indicated that British employers provided less training than their counterparts elsewhere in the developed world and that, as a consequence, the skills base of the British workforce was relatively weak, particularly with regard to what are termed 'intermediate skills', i.e. those possessed by craft workers and technicians (Ryan 1991).

These general international comparisons, as well as company-commissioned studies of overseas competitors (for example, Brown and Read 1984) have provided the backdrop to management and government policy debates about the need to improve VET provision (Keep 1991). From these debates a broad consensus has emerged that strengthening the nations's skills base is a fundamental requirement for economic success. The best means by which to secure improvement, unfortunately, has not been subject to the same level of consensus, and the role of the State and degree to which the supply of VET can be left to market forces has remained a focus of controversy.

THE DEVELOPMENT OF THE EDUCATION SYSTEM

Before turning to employer-based training, we consider the contribution of the education system to Britain's VET performance.

James Callaghan's Ruskin College speech in 1977 is often regarded as the symbol of a major change in official thinking. The speech emphasised the need for education to make a greater contribution to the country's economic well-being, expressing doubts about the 'relevance' of what was being taught and about the acceptability of attainment levels. On entering office in 1979 the Conservative Government initially moved slowly but towards the end of the 1980s embarked on a radical transformation of the system, which was seen as playing a vital role in the National Education and Training Targets set by the Confederation of British Industry (CBI) and approved by the Government in 1991. This section describes how the education sector is evolving and considers the impact of government policy.

Schools

Children are legally required to attend school from the age of 5 until 16 (until 1972 the school leaving age was 15), moving from primary to secondary schools at the age of about 11. The vast majority of children are in state schools, with 7 per cent being privately educated. Tuition is free, but there is no maintenance support. In England and Wales until recently there were two main state examinations taken at about the age of 16. These were Ordinary (O) levels and Certificates of Secondary Education (CSEs). The former were taken by the academically more gifted. The latter were taken very much less seriously. Both were academically, rather than vocationally, orientated. For those who carried on at school, a further two of years study led to Advanced (A) levels, usually in three or four subjects. It was (and is) largely on the basis of A level results that pupils were selected for entry into higher education. In 1988 O levels and CSEs were replaced by General Certificates of Secondary Education (GCSEs). The intent was to remove the élitism of O levels and to provide a unified set of qualifications. The cost was an inability to discriminate as finely as before at the top end of the ability range. In 1989 the Advanced Supplementary (AS) level was introduced. Its aim is to provide a broader set of subjects than is available under A levels alone. The system of qualifications in Scotland is different. The two main exams are the Standard and Higher levels of the Scottish Certificate of Education. The Certificate of Sixth Year Studies allows pupils to progress beyond the standards set by Highers and provides the bridge between school and university study.

Within the limits of preparing their pupils for these exams, schools used to be left largely free to determine the mix of subjects and the allocation of time to them. This all changed with the introduction of the National Curriculum which started in 1989. English, maths and science are the core subjects.

History, geography, technology, music, art, physical education and (for secondary school pupils) a modern foreign language are the other foundation subjects. It was envisaged that the National Curriculum would take up to 70 per cent of class hours. At the same time a greater stress was put on fostering 'economic and industrial awareness'. Similar initiatives are being taken in Scotland. It was also announced that attainment targets were to be instituted. These would define what should be known at the ages of 7, 11, 14 and 16, and national tests would be conducted on pupils at these ages.

Traditionally the Department of Education (from 1992 the Department for Education) and the Scottish Education Department had responsibility for the provision of resources and for the overall direction of policy. It was the job of local education authorities (LEAs) in England and Wales to supervise and manage schools, further education colleges and institutions providing 'advanced further education' – the polytechnics, for example. In Scotland the local authorities managed most state schools, though the Scottish Education Department had direct control over the grant-aided ones as well as over the Higher Education Central Institutions and Colleges of Education. By contrast, all UK universities were independent bodies to whom funding was directly channelled via the University Grants Committee (UGC).

Dissatisfaction with school governance dates back some time. For example the Taylor Committee was set up in 1975 to investigate the role of school governing bodies. The Education Act of 1980 very much reflected its deliberations when it insisted that parents and teachers should be represented on all governing bodies. However, it was only with the 1986 Act that radical reform started. It ensured that LEAs could not override the views of other members of a governing body. It also rearranged the respective duties of head teacher, governors and LEA. The latter retained the final say on appointments and dismissals. It had to provide a budget which the governors could spend as they wished on books and equipment. Budgets could also be devolved for other items of expenditure, while governors were obliged to present an annual report to parents. There were also provisions to appraise teacher performance.

A whole array of themes were entangled in these changes. There had grown up a massive distrust of LEAs. This was partly a political matter – in some areas of the country, the Government believed, the LEAs were 'leftist' and too concerned with pursuing partisan political objectives. There was also a view that too often they had been 'captured' by an educational establishment which had grown self-indulgent as a semi-monopolistic, largely self-regulating profession. This led, some suspected, to inefficiency and abuse. It was argued that the profession should be subject to more external controls. These controls would be both administrative (for example, teacher appraisal) and market related (for example, the enhanced power of parents).

These themes reverberated even more noisily in the Education Reform Act 1988. There were to be regular assessments of school performance. A policy of more open enrolment was declared. This means that parents can attempt to send their children to schools they believe to be the best and avoid those that they perceive to be the worst – though in the absence of funds for capital investment inevitably there would be rationing problems. Schools were required to manage the major part of their budgets; this initiative was dubbed the 'local management of schools'. But the Act went further than this; schools could choose to 'opt out' of LEA control altogether and become 'grant maintained'. In this case they received their budgets directly from central government. With this Act an additional theme was coming to the fore – the belief that local self-management increased teaching motivation and efficiency.

In 1991 the Government-established 'Parents' Charter' went further to shift the balance of power to the consumer from the supplier. The Education (Schools) Act of 1992 insisted on the publication of information about performance and attendance in every school and for inspection reports every four years. In similar spirit the National Record of Achievement was introduced in England and Wales. This was meant to furnish a simple record of achievement in education and training through working life.

Traditionally inspection of schools had been the responsibility of Her Majesty's Inspectors (HMI). New arrangements were now made for private inspection teams. These had to contain at least one lay member. A massively increased inspection rate was announced in the 1992 White Paper, *Choice and Diversity*.

Government clearly hoped that in due course all schools would become grant maintained. In the process the role of the LEAs would be much reduced. In their place a Funding Agency for Schools would take on the role of providing budgets and ensuring standards.

These reforms, however, attracted considerable criticism. At the most general level there were severe doubts about the ability of a market-based model to achieve the efficiency gains officials claimed were possible. First-year economics textbooks tell us that perfectly competitive markets will produce the socially best use of resources. But they also tell us that markets can easily fail. The presence of monopoly elements is one cause of market failure. Others are lack of information, economies of scale and externalities. Many believe that, despite the Government's efforts to improve the information made available to consumers, ignorance is an inherent feature of the sector. By this they mean that the consumers (or their parents) are not only ignorant of their own needs, how these might be fulfilled and about their progress towards fulfilling them, but that they are reliant, at least in part, on the supplier for providing them with such information. Economies of scale may also be important. To give two examples. Specialist subjects which require cooperation between schools may suffer in an era when each school must be cost-effective. There is already evidence of diseconomies of scale in administration now that LEAs have a reduced capacity to play a coordinating role. The fear that monopoly and asymmetric information will prejudice the market-based approach is the explanation for the apparent paradox of a government simultaneously stressing the market and at the same time introducing controls and checks which are almost Gallic in their *dirigisme*. To the extent that the teaching profession is a self-regulating monopoly, there always was scope for the abuse of this position.

However, if the introduction of a market changes teaching motivation – which it is meant to do – then dangers of such abuse may be all the greater. Motivation may become much more narrowly selfish and self-protective. Externalities occur when trading between a consumer and a supplier has effects on others of which the two agents do not take account. For instance, it is important that the teacher is willing to reveal to potential employers a *balanced* judgement about the qualities of his pupil. However, the more the teacher–pupil relationship starts to resemble a commercial one, the more likely the teacher is to be unwilling to make such information available – in other words the more serious the externality problem is likely to be. Here there is a parallel argument to the one made by Perks (see Chapter 4 in this volume) regarding auditors whose commercial interests scarcely assure their independence from the firms whose accounts they assess.

At the less theoretical level there has been a complex of interrelated complaint. Teacher morale, it has been argued, has been badly damaged. Testing requirements have imposed massive burdens on schools to the detriment of the main teaching function. Attempts at the performance measurement of schools, pupils and teachers are at best unrevealing because crude summary measures are bound to be an inadequate way of capturing a sophisticated and multi-dimensional process. At worst they can damage the education process itself. The National Curriculum is too restricting and, like other reforms, has been introduced with insufficient regard having been paid to the views of the experts.

Dissatisfaction came to a head in the spring and summer of 1993 specifically over the issue of pupil testing. In the light of a report from a committee, headed by Sir Ron Dearing, the Government announced several modifications to its plans. These included: dropping school league tables of test results on 7 and 14 year olds; reducing the compulsory element of the curriculum; giving fewer and shorter tests to pupils.

Post-school education

The late 1980s also witnessed major changes in arrangements for post-school education. A distinction used to be made between further and higher education, with the latter providing qualifications of degree standard. The major institutions were colleges of further education, polytechnics and universities. The Education Reform Act of 1988 announced a number of important initiatives. The system of funding was altered. For universities the University Grants Committee (UGC) was replaced by the University Funding Council (UFC), the latter effectively being more under the sway of central government. Local authorities lost control of the polytechnics, for which boards of governors were appointed with half of the governors coming from 'business and the professions'. The Polytechnics and Colleges Funding Council (PCFC) was set up to operate in much the same manner as the UFC. Colleges of Further Education remained under the control of local authorities, but the colleges were given greater budgetary independence.

Subsequent government White Papers heralded further reform. In 1992 the so-called binary divide between universities and polytechnics was ended. The previously separate UFC and PCFC were abolished and replaced by the Higher Education Funding Council (HEFC) which now funds the whole of higher education (HE) but not further education (FE). In 1993 LEAs finally lost control of the colleges of further education, which henceforth were to be financed and monitored by the Further Education Funding Council (FEFC).

As with school reform, a recurrent theme was obtaining 'value for money'. Only thus could the desired increase in throughput be achieved without unacceptable increases in government spending. This was to be achieved by introducing greater competition for funds from the public authorities. Thus comparative ratings of research and teaching effectiveness were becoming of ever greater importance.

Links to the world of work

Throughout the 1980s there was a renewed emphasis on taking steps to encourage the education system to make a greater direct contribution to preparation for the world of work and to vocational courses. This is reflected in the content of the National Curriculum and in official encouragement of a shift towards the sciences and technology in the post-compulsory sector.

At the school level an early initiative was the Technical and Vocational Education Initiative (TVEI). Apart from stressing the need to improve skills and qualifications, especially in science, technology and modern languages, it was concerned to ensure that pupils were equipped for working life by ensuring that the school curriculum related to the working environment. The Government now insisted that all children have a period of work experience before leaving school. The Certificate of Pre-Vocational Education (CPVE) caters for those continuing in full-time education for a year after compulsory school-leaving age (i.e. 16). It is meant to give a broad preparation for work or for further vocational courses. The City and Guilds of the London Institute are currently attempting to improve the CPVE. The introduction of General National Vocational Qualifications (GNVQs) as part of the of the NVQ system (see discussion later) is, at least in spirit, the most radical attempt in Britain to date to provide and stimulate vocational courses in schools. GNVQs are meant to offer a vocational route to run in parallel with A levels. They are being developed to cover five areas – business, manufacturing, art and design, health and social care, and tourism and leisure. An underlying theme is emphasis on promoting equality of status for academic and vocational qualifications. In this spirit, it was planned to introduce Ordinary and Advanced National Diplomas (ONDs and ANDs). There would be 'equivalence scales' for these diplomas; for example a certain number of GCSE passes or NVQs would merit the award of the OND.

This stress on links with business was not confined to the content and availability of courses and qualifications. Many steps were taken to enhance the direct influence of businesspeople on the educational process. They were having the single biggest influence on the content of NVQs and GNVQs. The Government insisted on the presence of such 'lay persons' on the new-style school inspection teams. Their presence on school and polytechnic governing bodies was increased. There were many attempts to stimulate links between school, college and industry, for example, the Education Business Partnership (EPB) and LINK. The latter is designed to stimulate research contacts between business and the education sector. Compacts involve employers promising jobs with training for schoolchildren once they have finished school, in return for which the employer has some input into the content of what the pupil is taught at school. The attempt to encourage the establishment of City Technology Colleges was also a move made in the same spirit.

What has the education system delivered?

What has all this produced in terms of outcomes? Before considering this, it is important to point out that there appear to have been conflicting official visions about what was wanted from the system. One vision stresses not only links between school and work, but new syllabuses, examinations and teaching methods in order to bring on the less able. This involves a modular- and competencies-based approach and an exam system (GCSEs) capable of being coped with by those who are less academically gifted. By contrast, the other vision suggests a return to a more traditional curriculum and to traditional learning values (reading, writing and arithmetic). Thus recent high success rates in GCSEs have been seen, by those of this second vision, as a dilution of standards. Such disagreements make it difficult to achieve substantial progress towards enhancing educational attainments for the broad mass of the population.

Over the years education expenditure has increased only slowly. In 1989–90 it was 9.4 per cent higher in real terms than it had been in 1974–75. The increase was more than accounted for by recurrent spending. Capital spending fell in real terms. Spending fell slightly as a percentage of GDP and as a share of government spending. Least favoured in expenditure allocations were the polytechnics and the universities. Spending constraints continued into the 1990s and are accompanied by official statements appearing to suggest that much can still be achieved by productivity gains. However, such statements are made on the slenderest of evidence. The other side of the coin is reduced teacher morale, reflecting both the strains imposed by the drive for efficiency and the perception that salaries in education are insufficient.

Against this background of restricted spending the numbers of pupils in the education system have been increasing. In 1979–80, 66.7 per cent of 16-year-olds were enrolled in post-compulsory education (be this at school or elsewhere) – 42.1 per cent were full time and 24.6 per cent were part time. The corresponding figures for 17-year-olds were 52.7 per cent (26.8 per cent full time and 25.9 per cent part time) and for 18-year-olds 37.4 per cent (14.8 per cent full time and 22.6 per cent part time). In August 1990, participation was higher for all three age groups. For 16-year-olds it was 81.7 per cent, for 17-year-olds 61.7 per cent and for 18-year-olds 40.4 per cent. Encouragingly, the proportion of full-timers also increased. Accompanying this was an increase in staying-on rates at school, with a particularly dramatic rise recently. In 1979–80 staying-on rates were 28.6 per cent, 17.5 per cent and 1.9 per cent for 16-, 17- and 18-year-olds respectively. A decade later, in 1990–91 the corresponding figures were 40.6 per cent, 25.5 per cent and 3.8 per cent. As an indicator of how rapid progress has been recently, between 1987 and the spring of 1991 the full-time staying-on rate for 16- and 17-year-olds increased from 41 per cent to 58 per cent. The qualifications of school-leavers have also been improving. In particular the percentage of those leaving school with no qualification at all declined markedly.

Similarly, there was an increase in those engaged in higher education. Between 1974–75 and 1989–90 numbers in all forms of higher education rose from 705,000 to 1,094,000. The increase was massively greater in the polytechnics than in the universities. In recent years the trend has accelerated.

Summary

In conclusion, in return for very restricted expenditure increases, more people are going through the educational system and emerging with qualifications. The Government takes pride in a more cost-effective and efficient system whose relevance for the business world is increasing. However some doubts have to be voiced.

Many worries used to be expressed about declining standards in reading, maths and science among average and below average pupils. Whilst such concerns were probably exaggerated, it is true that there is limited evidence of positive improvement at the very bottom end, following the reforms described above. Further, it may be that the impact of spending constraints on teaching morale and quality has yet to be fully felt. Severe doubts are also beginning to be expressed about the effects of government *dirigisme* on the content of school education. Similar concerns are being voiced about the impact of funding and inspection on the content, quality and balance of post-compulsory education. More generally the new system of NVQs may be aiming too low when compared with foreign qualifications and at the same time is in danger of diluting educational quality at the higher end of the ability range.

The new market-based model, accompanied by heavy regulation, is an untested one for which the theoretical arguments are not overwhelming. Thus it is necessary to suspend judgement about its ultimate impact. Finally one has to ask the question, what use will be made of the products of this extended education system once they enter the world of employment? Later in this chapter we argue that Britain's VET problem is as much a problem of lack of employer demand for skills as of lack of supply of them. If this diagnosis is correct, then will the developments we have described in this section make any difference? At the lower level more employees will have IT skills and what are generally described as social skills, but will this persuade employers that they should upgrade their operations to utilise these qualities? Will the output of a massively higher number of 'university' graduates have a similar effect? Possibly so. Also it is possible that the higher aspirations of the workers themselves may force the hands of employers. It is also possible that British employers will act in much the same way as before. In this case education will act as an important queuing device for its recipients, waiting to enter work, but will lead to little social gain in terms of extra productivity. In other words a job currently done by, say, a person with A levels will in future be done in just the same way by a person with a degree. If this happens then the economic returns to government expenditure on education will be very low indeed.

THE DEVELOPMENT OF THE NATIONAL TRAINING SYSTEM PRIOR TO 1979

As outlined above, until the 1960s the peacetime role of the state in training was minimal, with responsibility resting with individual employers. However, a growing belief in the need for improvement in Britain's training performance, coupled with the slow pace of change being generated by voluntary training arrangements, led to the Conservative government's 1962 White Paper on training, which in turn led to indirect state intervention in the form of the Labour government's 1964 Industrial Training Act (see Perry 1976 for details). Ministers were given the power to create Industrial Training Boards (ITBs) – sectoral bodies made up of employers and trade union representatives which could impose a levy on firms within their industry. This levy funded the ITBs' operating costs, and sectoral training activity through training grants to firms whose training plans and provision met ITB standards. By 1969 there were twenty-seven ITBs covering 15 million employees (mainly in manufacturing) out of a national workforce of 25 million (Lindley 1983).

In 1972, following criticisms about bureaucracy and the inability of the ITB system to accommodate itself to the circumstances of small firms, the operation of the ITBs was reviewed. The resulting Employment and Training Act of 1973 replaced levy/grant funding with a new system based on exemptions from the levy for all small firms and for those companies whose training met criteria specified by the ITB. The State would in future fund the ITBs' operating costs (for details see Perry 1976; Senker 1992).

The Act also created a new national, tripartite body – the Manpower Services Commission (MSC) – to supervise manpower policies, the operation of government training schemes and employment services, and the activities of the ITBs. The MSC rapidly became involved in measures aimed at reducing persistent cyclical skill shortages in the economy, and in devising various special temporary employment measures and training schemes aimed at the unemployed (for details see Ainley and Corney 1990; Evans 1992).

THE CHANGING INSTITUTIONAL STRUCTURE SINCE 1979

Since the election of a Conservative government in 1979, the training system has undergone a revolutionary transformation. The Government's training policy has been shaped by a number of basic precepts. These include the assumption that market forces, rather than statutory rights and duties, are most effective in determining the type and amounts of training undertaken; that the role of the State in training should hence be limited to supporting provision for disadvantaged groups (such as the long-term unemployed), helping with pump-priming funding to aid innovation, and exhortation. The message is that it is the responsibility of employers and, to a lesser extent individuals, to determine their levels of investment in training and that VET should be employer-led and employer-controlled, with the influence of educationalists and trade unions being sharply reduced (for a concise statement of government beliefs on training see Department of Employment 1988).

The transition from Industrial Training Boards to Industrial Training Organisations

The first moves towards a training system embodying these beliefs came in 1981, with the Government's decision to abolish seventeen of the ITBs, and to replace them with voluntary sectoral bodies. Boards were retained in seven sectors – including clothing, engineering, and construction – where the Government felt that the ITBs were essential to securing wider national training objectives. Ministers made clear, however, that this reprieve was only temporary, and that the ultimate aim was the abolition of all the boards. In 1988, following a further review of ITB operations, all but the Construction Industry Training Board (and an associated body in Engineering Construction) were replaced by voluntary arrangements.

The voluntary sectoral bodies that have replaced the statutory ITBs were originally styled Non-Statutory Training Organisations (NSTOs), but have more lately retitled themselves Industry Training Organisations (ITOs). They are controlled and financed exclusively by employers and, in contrast to the ITBs, involvement in them by trade unions and educationalists is not guaranteed but is available only at the invitation of the employers. A company's membership of its sector's ITO is entirely voluntary, as is the decision to support or participate in its activities. The ITOs have no powers to raise a levy, or to compel companies to train or to cooperate with their plans. Their main roles have proved to be helping to define future sectoral skill needs, organising group training schemes, the dissemination of information on training, and encouraging and exhorting firms to do more training. About ninety NSTOs were established in the wake of the 1981 round of ITB abolitions, and there are currently about 120 ITOs operating. These cover 83 per cent of the national workforce (Berry-Lound, Chaplin and O'Connell 1991: 535).

How well have the new arrangements worked? Evidence about the performance of the ITOs suggests that they may not constitute a major improvement in the effectiveness of sectoral training arrangements in Britain. Government-commissioned research in the mid-1980s indicated that the majority of the ITOs were ineffective when judged against the MSC's targets for their activities (Anderson 1987; Rainbird and Grant 1985; Varlaam 1987) There is some evidence that their effectiveness has since improved (Berry-Lound and Anderson 1991), but significant problems remain. One is the limited resources available to the ITOs. For example, in the year 1990–91, of 78 ITOs, 54 per cent had annual incomes of less than £200,000 (Berry-Lound, Chaplin and O'Connell 1991: 539). Moreover, when the work of the ITOs is measured against the twelve-point list of 'ideal outcomes' which the ITOs have set themselves, it is clear that progress has been slow. By 1991 only two of these outcomes' had been achieved by more than 50 per cent of the ITOs covered in a HOST Consultancy survey (Berry-Lound and Anderson 1991).

A local focus for training policy

The second stage in institutional development of a new training delivery system was marked by a shift towards a local focus for training policy and activity. In September 1988, following a refusal by the Trade Union Congress (TUC) representatives to endorse the proposed Employment Training (ET) scheme for the long-term unemployed, the Government announced the abolition of the MSC (by the then renamed the Training Commission) and its intention to shift decision-making away from national and sectoral levels towards a new focus on local labour markets. The chief component of the new system was to be a network of Training and Enterprise Councils (TECs) in England and Wales, and in Scotland a broadly similar set of bodies to be styled Local Enterprise Companies (LECs).

In legal terms, TECs and LECs are limited companies. Two-thirds of the members of each TEC's board must be chairmen or chief executives of private sector companies. Trade union participation is by invitation. TEC board members serve in a personal capacity and are not deemed to represent their company or organisation. The role of TECs and LECs is to monitor and address skill requirements in the local labour market, to manage government training and work experience schemes for the unemployed, to encourage companies to invest in training and to act as a catalyst for local economic growth and regeneration. TECs and LECs have a contractual relationship with the Government, from whom they receive funding for training schemes for the unemployed, plus a small basic grant to cover operating costs and promotional activities. Eighty-two TECs cover the whole of England and Wales, with twenty LECs in Scotland.

It is important to emphasise that a distinctive feature of the TECs is that they were not constituted as representative bodies, and the composition of many TEC boards probably does reflect the sectoral and size distribution of the local employer community (Emmerick and Peck 1991). At the same time, TECs have been designed by the Government to be explicitly unrepresentative of other stakeholders in VET – educationalists, trade unions, community groups, local authorities and the unemployed. For example, in November 1991 trade union representatives accounted for just 5.1 per cent of all TEC board seats (Emmerick and Peck 1992: 13–14). Furthermore, the legal status of TECs as limited companies, and the lack of any compulsory requirement for formal linkages with representative bodies in the localities within which they operate, means that their accountability to their local communities remains at best uncertain.

It is also important to stress that any relationship between TECs or LECs and local firms is on a purely voluntary basis. Unlike the German chambers of commerce and handicrafts, which local employers are by law obliged to join, participation in TEC activities remains entirely at the discretion of the firm.

Information about the activities of TECs and LECs remains patchy (for studies of them, see Bennett and McCoshan 1993; Coffield 1992; IDS Study 485; Peck and Emmerick 1991, 1992), and it is too early to offer any definitive conclusions about their effectiveness. Nevertheless, some achievements and potential difficulties are already clearly identifiable.

To date, perhaps the TECs' greatest success has been to harness the enthusiasm of large numbers of senior private sector executives (National Training Task Force 1992; Wood 1992). As a form of 'action learning' the TECs provide a significant opportunity to improve knowledge about, and to alter attitudes towards, training among an influential segment of the business community.

On the debit side, problems have included reductions in government funding, conflicts with the Government over official supervision of their activities, and difficult relations with other parts of the training system, such as the ITOs. However, the greatest single difficulty faced by TECs is that nearly 90 per cent of the money they receive from government is devoted to schemes that are aimed at the unemployed, and which only cover entrants or re-entrants to the labour market rather than existing members of the workforce – a problem which has been sharply compounded by the recession and rising unemployment. It is thus open to question whether TECs can promote a step-change in training activity in Britain, or whether their main purpose will prove to be the management of measures for the unemployed. The chief executive of one TEC has commented that, 'we seem to be caught between, on the one hand, the need to increase the skill level of the labour force, and on the other, the requirement to remove individuals from the unemployment register at any cost' (*Guardian* 1991). The crucial issue is therefore the degree to which TECs will prove capable of enhancing training provision for those in employment.

A new qualifications structure

Underlying these institutional changes has been a revolution in the vocational qualifications structure in Britain, with the creation of a unified system of National Vocational Qualifications (NVQs). In 1986, an MSC-sponsored review of existing vocational qualifications concluded that the existing structure was complex, confusing to employer and trainee, offered patchy coverage, restricted access to training for adults, made inadequate provision for the accreditation of prior learning, and over-emphasised the testing of knowledge at the expense of assessing skills and competences (Manpower Services Commission/Department of Education and Science 1986).

A new, employer-led National Council for Vocational Qualifications (NCVQ) was established to address these issues through the creation of a system of NVQs in England, Wales and Northern Ireland. In Scotland an existing body – the Scottish Vocational Education Council (SCOTVEC) – was charged with creating parallel Scottish Vocational Qualifications (SVQs). The NCVQ adopted a radical approach, based on the formulation of an NVQ framework of qualifications at five (initially four) levels.

NVQs and SVQs are based on the standards of competence, as defined by employers, that are required to undertake specific jobs. NVQs must be modular, and be broken down into component 'units of competence'. The trainee acquires an NVQ by achieving the standards for each of these units, for which a credit is received. Credits can be accumulated either through undertaking training, and/or through the 'accreditation of prior learning' (APL). The competences required for an NVQ are normally assessed in the workplace, rather than the classroom or written examinations, and assessment is generally expected to be undertaken by the candidate's supervisor or other managerial staff. As a result of this competence-based approach, NVQs and SVQs are grounded on and specified in terms of the outcomes of learning, rather than the processes through which the learning is seen to take place, and are specified independently of any particular location, mode and duration of training delivery (Jessup 1991).

The NCVQ does not design the NVQs, it simply recognises and approves (kitemarks) existing and new qualifications that fit within its framework. The design of the qualifications for each industry rests with employer-led lead industry bodies (LIBs). Cross-sectoral bodies have been established to deal with areas of employment such as clerical and administrative work.

The system of competence-based NVQs is a radical innovation which gives Britain a vocational qualification structure unlike anything found elsewhere in Europe, where more traditional, knowledge-based qualifications are the norm. The official view is that NVQs will enhance the status of vocational awards *vis-à-vis* traditional academic qualifications, and encourage more training by enhancing the flexibility of provision (Debling 1991; Jessup 1991). Moreover, NVQs provide the glue that binds together the newly devolved training system. As the focus of policy has shifted to local delivery mechanisms, the role of national standards as a means of ensuring coherence has increased. NVQs form the chief means monitoring the success of national training policies, of individual Training and Enterprise Councils, and of companies' training efforts.

It should be noted that NVQs have not been without their critics. Some commentators have accused employers of defining competences in a very narrow, task-specific way, in contrast to their European counterparts who often specify a broader mix of training and general education (Callender 1992; CBI 1989; Prais 1989; Raggatt 1991; Steedman and Wagner 1989). It is alleged that some NVQs require the minimum level of skill needed to perform a particular job, rather than encourage broader-based learning in transferable skills (McCool 1991), and it is possible that there is an inherent conflict between the short-term needs of individual employers and the longer-term needs of trainees and the national economy (Callender 1992). Concern has also been expressed that the levels of skill being specified are sometimes low, particularly when contrasted with those required by overseas employers. Jarvis and Prais (1989: 70) suggest that NVQs may be creating 'a certified semi-literate under-class'. Doubts also exist about the status and credibility of workplace assessment (Prais 1989, 1991), and about the ability of the personnel and training systems within many workplaces to deliver the support that NVQ training and assessment will require

(Callender 1992). Finally, the capacity of the NCVQ to rationalise vocational qualifications is open to question (Keep and Mayhew forthcoming).

Key to the success of NVQs is the speed with which they are adopted by employers. Current indications are not particularly encouraging. A survey of 171 organisations employing almost 600,000 people, undertaken by the *Employee Development Bulletin* (*EDB* 1993a: 2–15), indicated that while 61.4 per cent of respondents had employees who were working towards or who had achieved NVQs, only 3 per cent of the people employed by the organisations were involved. The survey also revealed significant concerns about employers' over-reliance on workplace assessment; NVQs' failure to require more general educational attainment, such as proof of literacy and numeracy; low standards; bureaucracy within the NVQ system; and the apparent inability of NVQs to simplify the range of vocational qualifications on offer.

New schemes and targets

There are two further major elements of the new training system – Investors in People (IiP), and the National Education and Training Targets (NETTs).

Investors in People

The Investors in People initiative is a national standard for effective investment in employees. It was developed in collaboration with CBI members, the Association of British Chambers of Commerce (ABCC), the TUC, ITOs and other training organisations. IiP was launched in November 1990. The aim is to encourage organisations to invest in training, to help them to do so more effectively, and to reward this commitment with a nationally recognised kitemark of training quality.

In order to achieve IiP status an organisation's owner or chief executive must make a public commitment to develop all employees in order to achieve business objectives; the organisation must regularly review the training and development needs of all its employees; demonstrate action to train and develop individuals on recruitment, and throughout their employment; and provide evidence that the organisation regularly evaluates and reviews its investment in training. Assessment of most organisations in England and Wales applying for IiP status is made by their local TEC, though large companies can deal with a national Employment Department unit. In Scotland IiP assessment is undertaken by a national body – Investors in People (Scotland). The award of IiP status is made for three years, after which it is necessary for the organisation to provide evidence of continued achievement and development.

The importance of IiP rests with the fact that it provides the TECs with their chief lever for attempting to improve the training of the employed workforce. Unfortunately, to date, the speed with which organisations have achieved IiP status has been extremely slow. By September 1992 just seventy-six companies had become IiPs, with a further 1,100 organisations committed to achieving the standard (*EDB* 1992: 16).

National Education and Training Targets

The final element of the new training system is the set of National Education and Training Targets (NETTs), which form a series of performance objectives for British vocational education and training to the year 2000. These were formulated by the CBI following bilateral talks with other employers' groups, trade unions, and educational bodies. The NETTs were launched in the summer of 1991 with endorsement from the TUC. The Government subsequently decided to offer its support for the targets.

The main targets set by the CBI are as follows (CBI 1996):

Foundation learning
1 By 1997 at least 80 per cent of young people to attain NVQ/SVQ Level 2 or its academic equivalent in their foundation education and training.
2 All young people who can benefit should be given an entitlement to structured training, work experience or education leading to NVQ/SVQ Level 3 or its academic equivalent.
3 By the year 2000, at least half of the age group should attain NVQ/SVQ Level 3 or its academic equivalent as a basis for further progression.
4 All education and training provision should be structured and designed to develop self-reliance, flexibility and broad competence as well as specific skills.

Lifetime learning
1 By 1996, all employees should take part in training or development activities as the norm.
2 By 1996, at least half of the employed workforce should be aiming for qualifications or units towards them within the NVQ/SVQ framework.
3 By the year 2000, half of the employed workforce should be qualified to NVQ/SVQ Level 3 or its academic equivalent as a minimum.
4 By 1996, at least half of the medium-sized and larger organisations should qualify as 'Investors in People', assessed by the relevant TEC or LEC.

An employer-led organisation called the National Advisory Council on the Education and Training Targets (NACETT) is responsible for monitoring progress towards the targets. As part of this remit, NACETT produces an annual report outlining trends in VET.

The NETTs are important in the running of the training system. They establish strategic goals, and rates of progress towards their achievement provide a set of performance indicators for TECs and LECs. They also, 'offer a framework that binds together a wide range of other initiatives in the education and training field and gives them coherence' (*SEB* 1992). Finally, the actual process of achieving the targets is hoped to foster a 'learning culture' among British employers and employees (*LMQR* 1992: 16).

It should be noted that the targets are ambitious, particularly those relating to the adult workforce. They are predicated on the use of the NVQ system by all employers, and their achievement would require major increases in employer expenditure on training, and a radical improvement in the planning and evaluation of in-company training activities. How achievable they are remains unclear. The hotel and catering sector have already concluded that the targets of half the workforce aiming for NVQs by 1996, and half the workforce qualified to NVQ level 3 by the year 2000, are unattainable in their sector, and have set themselves targets at half the national level (*EDB* 1993a: 3). If sufficient significant sectors of the economy follow suit, the achievement of the targets will prove difficult.

The New Institutional System

In overall terms the structure of the training system is currently as shown in Figure 8.1.

DELIVERY MECHANISMS AND THE NEW TRAINING INITIATIVE

Having reviewed the new institutional structure in British training, it is necessary to take a brief look at a few of the most important programmes through which training is delivered. These programmes are best viewed within the context of the strategic goals for training which were established in 1981 by the MSC's New Training Initiative (NTI).

The development of skill training

This first objective covered the reform and modernisation of the traditional route to a skilled job in industry – the craft apprenticeship. As a result, apprenticeships have moved away from a fixed traineeship period, towards more flexible formats and training to set standards of occupational competence. Unfortunately, despite these changes, the number of apprenticeships has fallen rapidly. Between 1970 and 1983 the number of apprentices fell from 218,000 to

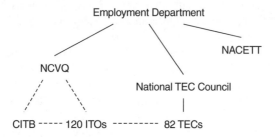

Figure 8.1 Training system in England and Wales

102,000, and by 1990 had further declined to just 53,600 – less than 25 per cent of the 1970 figure (see Keep 1994).

Equipping all young people for work

This objective meant the introduction of structured programmes of initial vocational education and training for all those not on apprenticeship schemes. In the past, the vast mass of young entrants to employment (i.e. all those not on apprenticeships) had received little or no training.

In 1981, partly in response to rising youth unemployment, and partly in order to meet this second NTI objective, the MSC introduced the Youth Training Scheme (YTS) to provide broad-based work-related training for both the young unemployed and employed (for further details of YTS see Chapman and Tooze 1987; Jones 1988). In 1988, YTS moved from a one-year to a two-year scheme, and subsequently its name was changed to Youth Training (YT). YT is now gradually being replaced by locally based systems of 'training credits', which are essentially financial credits or vouchers given to young people to be used to obtain education and training (see Keep 1994).

Widening opportunities for adults

The NTI's final objective related to the need to provide training and retraining opportunities to the vast mass of the adult workforce, for most of whom training provision tended to be minimal. During the 1980s employers evolved a wide variety of attempts to improve adult training provision for those in employment (see Rainbird 1994), while government efforts were directed at tackling the training and work experience needs of the long-term adult unemployed through a complex succession of schemes and programmes (including the Community Programme, the Job Training Scheme, Employment Training, and Employment Action).

Management training

One other area of activity, not mentioned in the NTI, that has undergone profound change has been management education and training. As with most other aspects of British VET, international comparisons of management training in the mid-1980s showed British provision in a poor light. British managers tended to be less well educated, and less well trained, than their counterparts in countries such as Germany, France, America and Japan, and the systems of management education, training and development in many large British companies were found to be often both weak and patchy (Constable and McCormick 1987; Handy 1987; Mangham and Silver 1986 – see also Chapter 7 by Fox, in this volume).

As a result of these revelations, the Management Charter Initiative (MCI) was launched by a group of leading companies under the auspices of the Council for

Management Education and Development (CMED), with the aim of raising the profile of management qualifications and increasing the amount of training taking place. The MCI has promoted a charter of good practice to which companies are encouraged to subscribe, and has sought to develop a coherent set of general competence-based management qualifications, akin to NVQs. At the same time, there has been a substantial expansion in the provision of management education, chiefly through the growing provision of MBA qualifications. This growth, including MBA programmes, has been increasingly tailored by higher education institutions to meet the needs of individual companies or groups of companies.

Although the volume of management education and training in Britain has undoubtedly increased substantially in recent years, problems remain. Provision remains patchy, with many smaller companies still offering their managerial employees little systematised training, and with training often being restricted to supervisory and junior management, with limited provision for more senior managers (MCI 1993). Moreover, of 510 organisations surveyed by the MCI in 1993, only 39 per cent of respondents had even heard of the Management Charter Initiative (MCI 1993).

Methods of training delivery

While the national framework of training provision has been changing, both in terms of institutions, and national programmes and qualifications structures, so too have the means by which training is delivered. In general terms, there has been a move away from lengthy off-the-job training courses and classroom-based learning, and moves towards new, more flexible forms of training delivery, such as open learning, computer-based learning, computer-assisted learning, and more systematised forms of on-the-job training, as well as the provision by some employers of general, non-vocational education for workers, as for example with the much publicised Ford EDAP scheme (see Hougham, Thomas and Sisson 1991).

Having examined the structural changes through which the mechanisms of training policy and delivery have been going, we now turn to survey the overall scale of training activity, and to see whether the new system is delivering improvements in the volume and quality of training being delivered.

THE SCALE, QUALITY AND SCOPE OF TRAINING

The volume of training

In terms of the general volume of training activity in Britain, the most comprehensive survey was undertaken in 1987 (Training Agency 1989), and this showed that in 1986–87 employers offered 64.7 million days off-the-job training and 60.7 million days on-the-job training (a total of 125.4 million days). The average duration of training per trainee was 14.5 days.

There is evidence that there has been a quite significant increase in the overall volume of training in recent years. Thus the Employment Department's Labour Costs Survey data indicated an increase in the proportion of employers' total labour costs (excluding wages and salaries) accounted for by training, from 0.3 per cent in 1981, to 0.5 per cent in 1988 (Janes and Roberts,1990). Labour Force Survey (LFS) data reinforce the view that training has increased. In spring 1984 the LFS showed that just under 2.6 million people had received some form of job-related training in the four weeks preceding the survey. By spring 1991 this had risen to 4.3 million – an increase of 73 per cent (Turner, Dale and Hurst 1992: 379). Another major survey (Gallie and White 1993: 29) also reported 'a dramatic increase' in the proportion of the workforce being trained since 1987. While there are signs that the recession has caused some falling back in the amounts of training (Keep and Mayhew forthcoming), the figures suggest that employers have placed an increased emphasis on improving the skills of their employees.

How far these increases can be related to changes in the structure of the training system and delivery mechanisms is unclear. Other factors that may have contributed to the rise in training volume include the removal of the most inefficient firms in the economy during the recession of the early 1980s; the pressures generated by increases in international competition; structural shifts in employment, with the service sector demanding new levels of social and customer care skills; the spread of new technology (Gallie and White 1993); and the gradual education of employers to the value of training via government and CBI exhortation, and the popularisation, via the media and management textbooks, of academic studies pointing to training's role in boosting productivity.

The quality of training

While the total volume of training is important in assessing performance, the quality of what is being provided also influences the state of progress. Unfortunately, the evidence on the quality of training is less encouraging than that on the volume. One indicator is the qualifications towards which trainees are working. Labour Force Survey data from the summer of 1992 showed that only a minority of trainees (37 per cent) were aiming for qualifications, and that of those, 43.4 per cent of men and 44.1 per cent of women were working towards qualifications equivalent to or below GCSE level (*LMQR* 1993a: 7). Moreover, LFS figures from the autumn of 1992 suggested that 36 per cent of training for male workers, and 38 per cent of training for women, lasted for three days or less (*EDB* 1993b: 16). Finally, the quality of training on government-funded training schemes, as measured by qualifications gained, has not been impressive. To take the example of YT, which in various forms has now been running for about a decade, and which is supposed to provide foundation level vocational training for all entrants to the workforce, the national average of trainees achieving qualifications has fallen from a peak of 41 per cent in December 1990 to just 31 per cent (*LMQR* 1993a: 8).

The distribution of training

Another note of caution that needs to be sounded concerns the distribution of training opportunities. While the overall amount of training may be increasing, access to training still varies greatly. Put briefly, those employed in small firms, part time workers, the less well educated and qualified, the self-employed, older workers, and manual workers, are all less likely to receive training. Because certain groups of people are more frequently concentrated in types of employment where training is weak, for example women in part-time employment, disadvantage in access to training disproportionately affects some sections of the working population. There are also significant sectoral differences. Those employed in the public sector are more likely to be trained than those in the private sector, and, in the private sector, those employed in services are more likely to be trained than those in manufacturing, and to be trained for longer periods (Training Agency 1989).

The weakness of training provision for some groups of workers, and its patchiness across the economy is an important problem. In the 1987 Training in Britain survey, 51.7 per cent of employees received no training, and 20 per cent of firms offered no training whatsoever to their employees. Gallie and White (1993: 35) underline the 'great differences in virtually every aspect of training and development as between qualified and unqualified people, or as between those in higher-level jobs and those in jobs at the lower skill levels'. They point out that this 'excluded group' of 'the educationally unqualified, or those in the lowest job segment' amount to about a third of the total workforce (ibid.).

BRITISH VOCATIONAL EDUCATION AND TRAINING: CONCLUSIONS

The British VET system provides a context for the supply of skilled labour that is quite distinct from that existing in most other European countries. Various factors have all tended to mark Britain out from its major continental rivals: in education, the normal school-leaving age has been 16, until recently; the use of a school-leaving examination (GCSE) at 16; the lack of any substantial vocational element in the period of compulsory schooling; the high degree of subject specialisation for academic pupils between ages 16–18 via A levels; the absence, until very recently, of any coherent vocational alternative to A levels; and the apparently low levels of attainment by the majority of pupils in subjects such as mathematics and foreign languages.

In the area of training, the absence of any legislative compulsion to train; the lack of any training tax or levy (except within the construction sector); and the essentially voluntaristic relationship between companies and the major institutional elements of the system, such as TECs and NCVQ, coupled with what is now the most deregulated national labour market in Europe, provides firms with a great degree of freedom in fashioning labour market and training policies that suit their individual requirements. With the exception of a limited duty to provide training in support of health and safety requirements, training is not forced upon employers by legislation – they are free, unlike say French employers who face a training tax (Oechslin 1987), to do as much or as little as they choose. In marked contrast to the rest of the European Union, where legislative underpinning for training and the active involvement of the social partners are more often the norm. British training policies since 1979 have represented a decisive rejection of legislative backing for training, and for any notions of social partnership and tripartite control of training design and delivery. At the same time, relatively few forms of employment arrangement, such as part-time working, use of casual labour, and overtime working, are regulated by legislation. The results, unsurprisingly, are very diverse employment practices, and great variations in training effort and quality between firms.

A second point to be noted is that, while there undoubtedly has been progress in increasing the amount of VET that takes place within the British economy, doubts remain concerning the quality of what is being provided. In particular, progress at the level of intermediate skills, where many have argued Britain's skills gap compared to its overseas competitors is most acute (Ryan 1991), has not been very marked. Indeed, the very sharp decline in the craft apprenticeship system (see Keep 1994) suggests that, in the long term, the outlook for the supply of intermediate skills in manufacturing industry may actually be set to worsen.

Finally, the underlying thrust of policy has been to undertake institutional reform in the belief that such reform and the creation of a market-based, employer-led training-system can, of itself, deliver a fundamental change in the quantity and quality of British training. It can be argued that the pace and scale of institutional change have focused attention on the supply of training, to the detriment of more fundamental questions concerning the often relatively weak demand for skills in Britain, and the structural forces within the wider economy which may limit the need for and utilisation of skills. These structural forces include weak personnel management systems in many companies, short-termism in the British economy, the poaching of skilled labour, the dwindling importance of the domestic economy both as a production base and as a market for many large companies, and the nature of domestic consumer demand. Indeed, some commentators (Finegold and Soskice 1988) have argued that the British economy, or at least parts of it, may be trapped in a 'low skills equilibrium'. The failure of policies to adequately address these issues is a matter for concern. There is little point in expending considerable amounts of time, effort and money in creating skills within a national workforce, when the call for them by private sector employers may ultimately be limited (see Keep and Mayhew forthcoming).

NOTE

*Parts of this chapter draw on material prepared for Keep and Mayhew's forthcoming volume *The British System of Vocational Education and Training: a Critical Analysis*.

This chapter was written in 1993 but the key issues and scope of research make it highly relevant to this text and Ken Mayhew and Ewart Keep have kindly given permission to include it in this work.

SELECTED READING

Bennett, R. J. and McCoshan, A. (1993)
Confederation of British Industry (1991a)
Jessup, G. (1991)
Keep, E. and Mayhew, K. (forthcoming)
Prais, S. J. (1991)
Ryan, P. (ed.) (1991)

9　Industrial relations in the UK

Alan Whitaker

INTRODUCTION

There are few commentators who would dissent from the view that over the last decade and a half, the system of industrial relations (IR) in the United Kingdom has experienced dramatic change. As the authors of the most recent, authoritative survey of workplace industrial relations concluded 'there were major changes in employee relations during the 1980's', so much so that 'the traditional distinctive "system" of British industrial relations no longer characterized the economy as a whole' (Millward *et al.* 1992: 350). It is not the intention of this chapter to debate whether such changes should be regarded as irreversible or not, nor to explore in any depth the factors driving such a transformation. Rather the chapter begins with a brief overview of the so-called traditional system of industrial relations, before moving on to review the broader factors stimulating recent change. It then considers what change has meant for management and unions, and reviews some of the important features of change. (Space precludes any consideration of the changing role of the State either as an actor or an agent of change, but the reader is referred to the relevant chapters in Edwards 1995, where excellent, short accounts of the State's role in terms of economic management, legal regulation and as a major employer are to be found.) Finally this chapter seeks to address the key question of whether we are witnessing the emergence of a 'new' industrial relations, one based more upon cooperation within the workplace, representing what some might see as a marked shift in the 'culture' of industrial relations from adversarialism and confrontation towards consensus.

THE TRADITIONAL SYSTEM

Until the 1980s industrial relations between employees and employers in Britain were characterised in terms of a system of collective representation focused upon the 'institutions of job regulation' (Clegg 1979; Flanders 1965), whose central function was to contain the conflict which was inherent within the employment relationship. Industrial relations is defined here, following Gospel and Palmer (1993: 3) as 'processes of control over the employment relationship, the organization of work, and relations between employers and employees'. The key mechanism for achieving this was said to be 'voluntary collective bargaining' between employers, employers' associations and trade unions. Although not the only source of 'rules' governing employment (see Clegg 1979 ch. 1) it was regarded as the most important; the defining characteristic (and, perhaps, justification) for the British system. Collective bargaining covered a broad range of issues but in the main worked through voluntary procedures. Negotiations were adversarial, reflecting the wider socio-historical development of British IR (see Fox 1985). Although the twin characteristics of 'voluntarism' and the 'abstentionism' of the law (Flanders 1974; Kahn-Freund 1954) had been perceived as important stabilising influences, the inadequacies and shortcomings of the system had long been recognised. For example, the Royal Commission on Trade Unions and Employers' Associations, 1965–68 (the Donovan Commission, Cmnd 3623) in its 'two systems in conflict' analysis (the 'formal' and the 'informal') identified some of the negative consequences and weaknesses associated with the 'traditional' liberal collectivist style of IR, in particular, the 'problem' areas of pay, performance and industrial action. Its proposed solution included procedural reforms and the restructuring of collective bargaining (formalizing the 'informal'), but without the kinds of changes in labour law that might undermine the voluntaristic bases of British IR. Acknowledging the continuing weaknesses of the system, the 1970s saw further attempts to encourage reform by both Conservative and Labour administrations, albeit in different ways (see Coates 1989; Davies and Freedland 1993: chs 7, 8; Fox 1985: ch. 8; Lewis 1991). However, this picture of the system of industrial relations in Britain, briefly outlined above, remained a 'reasonable portrayal' as late as 1984, applying to large parts of manufacturing, the whole of the public sector and to large organisations in private services (Millward *et al*, 1992: 351). Since then change has been both widespread and marked.

THE AGENTS FOR CHANGE

The election of a radical, reforming Conservative Government in May 1979, committed to free market economics, 'rolling back' the frontiers of the State, and curbing what it perceived as the abuses of union power through a programme of labour law reforms, ushered in a period of radical change. In Gospel and Palmer's (1993: 23–25, 29) terms what we have witnessed is the implementation of a 'liberal individualist' policy in the arena of industrial relations, the full consequences of which are still being worked out. At the same time it is necessary to recognise that more deep-seated and fundamental shifts have also made their presence felt in a more acute form since 1979. It is to these that we now turn, if only to place in proper perspective the view that so much of what we have seen can be simply attributed to the election of a Conservative government with an ideological agenda offering a dramatic break with previous consensus politics, including 'traditional' approaches to IR and its reform. In Crouch's (1982: 119) words, a government determined to achieve a 'reversal of the post-war compromise'.

Many authorities have remarked upon the significant changes now affecting the world of work, (for example, Castells 1989; Harvey 1989; Hyman 1991; Martin 1988). There is not the space here to offer anything other than the briefest outline (see Whitaker 1992 for a more detailed analysis), but it is certainly the case that the United Kingdom has not been immune from the structural changes which have been radically impacting upon the world economy and the advanced industrialised nations, in particular. As Martin (1988: 216) remarks, what this country has been experiencing is the outcome of a number of 'intersecting forces or processes' which have come together to provide the break-up of the social, economic and political structures of post-war Britain. In Hyman's words (1991: 261) we can recognise a 'coincidence of elements' in operation in the 1980s, and their combined effects upon the system of industrial relations have been dramatic. For Hyman (1991: 260–4), the key elements include the following:

- the instability and disruption which has been a characteristic feature of western economies over the last twenty years;
- a complex realignment of international capital;
- significant changes in the internal control mechanisms of corporations necessitating, among other things, the need for new initiatives in industrial relations;
- the persistence of long-term trends in the structure of the economy and the working population, for example, the continued decline of numbers employed in manufacturing industry and the growth of the services sector;
- in political terms the 1980s also saw a shift to the right in many countries with all that this has entailed in terms of market 'deregulation' and the privatisation of state enterprises and services;
- the dramatic increase in the power, sophistication and application of micro-electronic technologies, bringing with it new applications for the reorganisation of production and utilisation of labour;
- the changing relationship between technology, production systems and product markets offering the potential for new market opportunities;
- the impact of production strategies characteristic of major Japanese corporations which have both reinforced the competitive threat to Western management while embodying a 'model' to be imitated and emulated, if possible.

Whether and to what extent all of these interrelated factors can be identified as a part of recent experience in the United Kingdom is a matter of debate, but some were recognised by the 1990 Workplace Industrial Relations Survey (WIRS 90) as being especially important.

In its discussion of the sources of change WIRS 90 (Millward *et al.* 1992) cited the changing composition of workplaces, particularly the decline in the numbers of large, highly unionised plants that occurred in the recession of the early 1980s. These are clearly linked to more fundamental structural changes in the economy and for Millward and his colleagues are likely to be 'enduring and mostly irreversible'. The effects of these have been felt by the trade unions, in particular the steep decline in membership (see Table 9.1). The shift in employment from private sector manufacturing and public sector industries to private sector services, the rise in overseas owned workplaces, the increase in part-time employment (the majority of which is done by females), all have impacted adversely on trade union membership. Traditionally well-organised groups (male, full-time manual workers) have declined, and in their place we have seen a rise in groups with traditionally lower union density (female, part-time and white-collar workers, often found in smaller workplaces). As an explanation for the fall in union membership in the 1980s, and since, such compositional changes have been questioned (Kelly 1990) and, though important, it is clear that other factors have been influential. Amongst these

Table 9.1 Trade union membership in the UK

At end of year	No. of unions	Total membership (000)	Per cent change on previous year
1979	453	13,289	+1.3
1980	438	12,947	−2.6
1981	414	12,106	−6.5
1982	408	11,593	−4.2
1983	394	11,236	−3.1
1984	375	10,994	−3.2
1985	370	10,821	−1.6
1986	335	10,539	−2.6
1987	330	10,475	−0.6
1988	315	10,376	−0.9
1989	309	10,158	−2.1
1990	287	9,947	−2.1
1991	275	9,585	−3.6
1992	268	9,048	−5.6

Source: Bird and Corcoran 1994

Notes: 1 In 1992 there was a decline of 5.6 per cent in trade union membership in the UK. This was the largest fall since 1981, resulting in a cumulative loss of 4,241,000 since 1979, or 31.9 per cent.

2 Women now account for 39.5 per cent of the total union membership (3,576,000).

3 All figures include trade unions which are not affiliated to the TUC.

4 The 22 unions with a membership of 100,000 or more accounted for 80.3 per cent of the total membership.

5 TUC membership at the end of 1993 was 7,296,052, the lowest level since 1945. In the 1980s the TUC has suffered particularly badly compared to its counterparts in other advanced economies. OECD estimates (1992) indicate that union density ranges between 12 per cent and 15 per cent in the USA, France and Spain; it is around 26 per cent in Japan, and between 75 per cent and 85 per cent in the Nordic countries of Sweden, Finland and Denmark. The TUC figure comprises 64.7 per cent men (4,717,306) and 35.3 per cent women (2,578,746).

Millward *et al.* (1992) identify changes in the legal environment seen in the UK in the 1980s. In this regard there can be no doubt that the sheer volume and complexity of legislation combined with the ideological zeal which has underpinned the changes has contributed much to the changed shape of industrial relations, (see Davies and Freedland 1993; Kessler and Bayliss 1992: ch. 5; Wedderburn 1991: ch. 8). As one authority has remarked 'the law now plays an increasingly important role in regulating the employment relationship' (Lewis 1991: 72). Another has described it as a 'legal revolution' (Hendy 1993: 1). Nothwithstanding the difficulty of establishing the actual role of law in the conduct of IR (Lewis 1991: 60) it does seem the case that the law has been used to strengthen the employer's hand in their relationship with both individual employees and trade unions. Perhaps equally important has been its use as an instrument of government economic policy. Following Wedderburn (1991: 212–24) the themes of the Conservative labour law programme can be summarised as:

- disestablishing collectivism;
- the deregulation of employment law;
- union control and ballots for individuals;
- enterprise confinement;
- sanctions without martyrs.

Government action of a different kind is another source of influence identified by Millward *et al.* Here it stems from the programme of privatisation which has been pursued with determination. This has achieved a major switch from public to private ownership of commercial monopolies and among the consequences of this has been the weakening of the statutory obligations to recognise trade unions and consult employees through various mechanisms. WIRS 90 found little evidence that trade union negotiating rights had, in practice, been extensively withdrawn, but conceded that less extensive changes than wholesale derecognition may have occurred (Millward *et al.* 1992: 359). Other government initiatives which have sought to replicate the discipline of the market within the public sector include compulsory competitive tendering, often leading to the contracting out of services, within local authorities and health authorities, and the introduction of 'cash limits' as a way of containing increases in public sector pay levels coupled with the encouragement of, not to say insistence upon, local at the expense of national bargaining. Moreover, as an employer, the Government's behaviour has reflected its changed approach to IR. In a variant of 'privatisation', functions of central government have been transferred to semi-independent agencies (for example, the Benefits Agency); pay claims and other challenges such as over closures and job losses among nationalised industries and public sector services have been resisted, often at the cost of major disputes, and performance-based reward systems have been extensively implemented, reinforcing the tendency towards individual-centred employee relations practices (Millward *et al.* 1992: 361).

The sources for change, then, have been powerful and insistent, what this has meant for unions and management and the relationship between them is the focus of the next section.

UNIONS AND MANAGEMENT: THE CHANGING SHAPE OF WORKPLACE INDUSTRIAL RELATIONS

As Tables 9.1 and 9.2 demonstrate the period since 1979 has been an extremely difficult one for British trade unions as regards membership and density, both of which are important indicators of the strength and organisational capacity of trade unions to act as a 'voice' for the workforce in their dealings with management. From a peak of 13.3 million members in 1979 membership has fallen to 9.05 million by the end of 1992 (Bird and Corcoran 1994). Moreover,

Table 9.2 Union presence, membership density and collective bargaining coverage in 1984 and 1990

Percentages	1984	1990
Per cent of establishments with union members among:		
All employees	73	64
manual employees	68	58
non-manual employees	58	51
Union membership density:		
All industries		
all employees	58	48
manual employees	66	53
non-manual employees	51	43
Private manufacturing		
all employees	56	48
manual employees	70	60
non-manual employees	32	22
Private services		
all employees	30	27
manual employees	40	32
non-manual employees	23	24
Public sector		
all employees	80	72
manual employees	82	72
non-manual employees	79	72
Per cent of employees covered by collective bargaining:		
All establishments	71	54
Private manufacturing	64	51
Private services	41	33
Public sector	95	78

Source: Millward *et al.* 1992: 58–9, 94.

more recent figures issued by the Trade Union Congress (TUC) reveal that the decline continues. Over the ten year period to January 1994 total TUC-affiliated membership fell by some 27.6 per cent, from 10.8 million to 7.3 million (TUC 1994). It is a picture reinforced by the findings of the Autumn 1994 Labour Force Survey which revealed that of the 21.5 million employees in Great Britain only 7.1 million (33 per cent) reported that they were members of a union or staff association (Labour Research 1995: 15).

The concomitant decline in compulsory union membership, the closed-shop, is even more marked. As WIRS 90 reveals, such union membership arrangements covered 5 million employees in 1980, but by 1990 this figure had dropped to 500,000 (Millward *et al*. 1992: 102). Alongside this there has been a substantial decline in trade union recognition since 1984, with the figure for all workplaces and all employees falling from 66 per cent to 53 per cent in 1990. Put another way, it means that employer recognition of trade unions for joint determination of rates of pay – a key indicator of the role of unions in IR – has fallen considerably in recent years. That the decline has been very much concentrated in particular sectors, such as engineering, printing and publishing, and among smaller establishments (those with fewer than 200 employees), and is more pronounced in independent establishments than in those that belonged to larger organisations (Millward *et al*. 1992: 72), can only be of cold comfort to the union movement, as can the finding that there has occurred a much smaller decline in union membership in larger workplaces, given that the number of such workplaces has reduced dramatically. Likewise, recognition of the point that the influence of unions may still go beyond simple membership figures needs to be set against the reality of major variations in the prevalence of union recognition between different sizes of workplaces and economic sectors (Corcoran 1995). Perhaps as important for the future growth and vitality of the union movement are the findings that newer workplaces were less likely to recognise trade unions than older workplaces, and that the lowest levels of recognition were to be found in those private sector workplaces that were set up in the early part of the 1980s. Similarly, the fact that formal derecognition of unions has not occurred on any scale (just over 1 per cent of all workplaces) according to the WIRS 90 authors, has to be set against their comment that there is some evidence to suggest that it may be a 'growing phenomenon', especially when the findings of the WIRS trading sector 'panel' are taken into account. Here a matched sample of industrial and commercial establishments, which were surveyed in both 1984 and 1990, revealed that nearly a fifth of those which recognised unions in 1984 no longer did so in 1990 (Millward *et al*. 1992: 74). More recent research adds weight to these findings while arguing that it is not yet a major problem facing the unions (Gall and McKay 1994).

If one turns to the scope and coverage of collective bargaining, the scale of decline revealed by WIRS 90 is equally marked. Between 1984 and 1990 the aggregate proportion of employees covered by collective bargaining dropped from 71 per cent to 54 per cent (8.4 million employees out of a total population size of 15.3 million covered by the WIRS 90 sample). However, given that the 6.6 million employees excluded from the survey because they work in establishments employing fewer than twenty-five people are much less likely to be covered by collective bargaining than those in the sample, it is reasonable to conclude that collective bargaining now directly affects only a minority of employees in Britain. In private sector manufacturing there was a fall from 64 per cent to 51 per cent and in private services from 41 per cent to 33 per cent, which means that in the private sector as a whole the coverage of collective bargaining fell from 52 per cent to 41 per cent. Neither has the public sector remained immune, with a fall from 95 per cent to 78 per cent over the same period, though much of this can be attributed to the loss of negotiating rights by the teachers in state schools in England and Wales and by nurses in the NHS which occurred during this time, as well as similar changes in local and central government. For the WIRS 90 researchers, such reductions represented 'one of the most dramatic changes in the character of British industrial relations that our survey series has measured' (Millward *et al.* 1992: 93). Nor was pay determination the only matter affected by this contraction in the coverage of collective bargaining. The 1980s and 1990s have seen employers pushing through concessionary agreements allowing changes in working practices and greater flexibility, and seeking to reduce collective bargaining as a constraint on their freedom to manage (Elger 1990; Millward *et al.* 1992). Moreover, bargaining agendas have been squeezed, often to exclude topics such as employment/manning levels and other closely related aspects.

A MANAGEMENT OFFENSIVE?

In a sense what the changes cited above reflect is the pressures British management have encountered since the 1980s to review and adapt their industrial relations policies. As product markets have intensified so have the requirements to be more responsive and versatile in the organisation of production and the use of labour. To this can be added, as mentioned earlier, the political and legal changes which have been hostile to collectivism within the management of industrial relations, and have sought to cajole and encourage management into putting their house in order and assuming responsibility for the conduct of their relationships with unions and/or individual employees. One consequence of this has been a growing interest in ideas about human resource management (HRM). This will be discussed below in terms of whether we are witnessing the emergence of a 'new industrial relations'. Another has been the consuming interest in flexibility, particularly labour flexibility (Pollert 1991; Whitaker 1992), which has been in evidence in Britain recently. A third has been the continuing shift in the level of bargaining, away from (multi-employer) national bargaining to single employer bargaining, and within the latter there have been important changes in the level at which it takes place in large, multi-establishment companies. These shifts are well documented and have been discussed at length elsewhere (Millward *et al.* 1992; Storey and Sisson 1993). They have lead to speculation that what we have seen in the 1980s has been an employers' counter-offensive aimed at regaining and/or restructuring workplace control. In certain respects we have, although the much publicised examples of aggressive 'macho' management (Mackay 1986), in the private and public sectors in the 1980s, such as British Leyland, British Airways, British Steel and British Coal, are not typical (Legge 1988).

As was pointed out above, formal derecognition of unions is rare although it may be increasing. Moreover, the WIRS 90 survey, while cataloguing the decline of union membership and a reduction in the scope of coverage of collective bargaining, also alerts us to the fact that in workplaces where trade union representation and collective bargaining persisted, 'surprisingly little altered' (Millward *et al.* 1990: 350) However, as others have recognised 'in workplaces where unions continue to be recognised, there is also evidence that managements have exploited the economic and political situation to limit their scope' (Edwards *et al.* 1992: 28; also see Elger 1990, 1991).

THE MARGINALISATION OF TRADE UNIONS?

In many respects it is far too early to pronounce on whether British unions have entered into a period of terminal decline. Certainly a broad historical perspective would cast doubt on this (Kelly 1990), in the sense that unions have experienced and survived membership loss and this kind of hostile environment before. However, few would doubt that since the end of the 1970s the decline of union power has been dramatic. Kelly (1990) notes, following Lukes (1974), that employer/union power is revealed in a number of ways: who wins industrial actions; who succeeds in controlling the industrial relations agenda (for example, the scope of collective bargaining); and who is best able to mould employees' definitions of their interests and ideological stance. On each of these, the recent record of the unions has been generally poor. As Table 9.3 indicates their ability to mobilise the countervailing bargaining power of employees through strike action has been weakened as recession and the fear of unemployment has impacted upon employees. At the time of writing the provisional estimates compiled by the Department of Employment (now amalgamated with the Department of Education) reveal that in 1994 the number of working days lost was 255,000, compared to 649,000 in 1993 and the number of strikes was 178 compared with 211 in 1993. These are the lowest calendar totals since 1891 when records began.

Furthermore, the image of declining union power in the eyes of members and the public at large has been reinforced by the highly visible and publicised defeats of strong unions in the 1980s, particularly the National Union of Mineworkers in 1985. As the bargaining agenda shifted to rationalisation and job losses, many unions found themselves unable to stem the tide of events. Likewise, faced with the heightening of international competition and the need

Table 9.3 Strike trends in the United Kingdom, 1946–93 (annual average)

Year	All industries			Non-coal industries		
	Strikes	Workers involved ('000)	Days lost ('000)	Strikes	Workers involved ('000)	Days lost ('000)
1946–52	1,698	444	1,888	625	228	1,318
1953–59	2,340	790	3,950	608	551	3,407
1960–68	2,372	1,323	3,189	1,451	1,189	2,872
1969–73	2,974	1,581	12,497	2,723	1,447	9,881
1974–79	2,412	1,653	12,178	2,141	1,555	11,147
1980–85	1,276	1,213	9,806	1,022	1,046	5,830
1986–89	893	781	3,324	656	705	3,166
1990	630	298	1,903	543	283	1,844
1991	369	177	761	340	170	729
1992	253	148	528	243	145	520
1993	211	385	649	206	371	622

Source: Years 1946–73 – Durcan *et al.* 1983; subsequent years – annual articles on stoppages of work in *Employment Gazette*

for organisations to adjust rapidly if they were to survive, unions also found themselves unable to resist or challenge effectively the work intensification experienced by many of their members. As management shifted the terms of the effort bargain in its favour, workers have found themselves working harder (Edwards and Whitston 1991). It is hardly surprising that the demoralisation of unions (and their members) was the result of the erosion of the reputation and credibility of unions as bargainers and independent sources of workplace power.

If one focuses on the industrial relations agenda it is clear, again, that unions have fared badly. At a national level they have been systematically excluded by successive Conservative administrations, determined to abolish corporatist structures and bargaining over the economy. At a microlevel, in both the private and public sectors joint procedures have been weakened or eliminated, and unions have been by-passed or marginalised if necessary as management has sought to increase direct employee involvement (Millward *et al.* 1992; Sisson 1993; Storey 1992).

The question as to whether one can discern a 'new realism' among union members and leaders (and, indeed, the workforce more generally) is more problematic, but for Kelly (1990: 42) 'could signify a more profound, ideological weakening of union power' if it is occurring. Whether it is or not, has been linked to the emergence of what Guest (1991) has termed the 'new orthodoxy' of human resource management and with it the possibility of a 'transformation' of industrial relations. It is to these related issues that we now turn in the concluding section of this chapter.

A NEW INDUSTRIAL RELATIONS?

Following Beardwell (1992: 1–2), the ongoing debate as to the emergence of a 'new' industrial relations in this country can be conveniently divided into two lines of argument (and, perhaps, practice), both interrelated. The first has focused on the restructuring and reshaping of the system and processes of workplace IR which has taken place, especially since 1979. It stresses the 'significance of the decline of formal union membership, the reshaping of bargaining arrangements and the intensification of work as the reassertion of a managerially driven industrial relations agenda'. Its main concern has been with making the existing system work in a different – and more effective – way. The second has encompassed a different philosophical approach, emphasising particularly the rise of individualism at the expense of collectivism; an individualism which has been encouraged and reflected in many public policy initiatives in the political, social, economic and industrial spheres initially under a Prime Minister (Margaret Thatcher) who could assert in October 1987 that 'there is no such thing as society'. The rise of this 'acquisitive individualism' has come to constitute, in Phelps Brown's (1990: 1) words, the 'counter revolution of our time' and has, it is said, made itself felt in many, if not all, areas of public and private life. Whether this is so or not is not our concern here, but within IR it has been identified with the growing interest in and emphasis upon the individual employee as an integral element in the emergence of what has been viewed as an alternative to the pluralist (liberal collectivist) tradition of British industrial relations, namely 'human resource management' (Guest 1989). For many of its supporters this line of argument offers the prospect of 'more profound changes to the collective relationships which will radically reshape the agenda' and substance of industrial relations, transforming the employment relations landscape. It is a formulation which has also been closely associated with what has been described as the rise of the 'enterprise culture' in the 1980s, provocatively characterised by Keenoy and Noone (1992: 562) as the 'scripted design for a new social consciousness'.

It is only intended to comment upon these ideas at stake in the term HRM, in so far as they have been viewed as a possible blueprint for a 'new industrial relations'. Suffice it to say though, that it is a topic which has attracted much interest and comment of late from both researchers and practitioners, and opinions seem to be sharply divided as to its theoretical status, conceptual parameters and empirical character. Criticisms have been levied at it because of its imprecision and ambiguity, not to mention its contradictions (see, for example, the collections edited by Blyton and Turnbull 1992; Storey 1995). The fact that it appears to have become the 'shorthand to describe almost any apparently new employee relations development in these "new times"' (Keenoy and Noone 1992: 565), only makes the need to address its rhetoric, realities and hidden agendas (Legge 1995) all the more pressing.

Given the changes to industrial relations which have been outlined above it is appropriate to ask whether we are now witnessing the emergence of a new, more cooperative approach to the management of the employment relationship along both its individual and collective dimensions. In seeking to answer this, one has to recognise that company responses to the pressures they are facing are diverse, although there do appear to be common developments which have challenged the traditional model of managing IR through collective bargaining – the search for flexibility, the adoption of human-resource type policies and practices and the restructuring of relationships with trade unions where necessary. Likewise, the trade unions are far from united on how best to adjust to an environment that has changed dramatically and in ways which are hostile to their existence (for an analysis of union approaches to HRM see Lucio and Weston 1992; and for a sympathetic but critical assessment of the future of unions see Taylor 1994). This diversity inevitably makes generalisations difficult. However, in a valuable recent research publication which draws upon the WIRS survey data and other sources, Millward (1994: 2–3) has sought to explore this question. He suggests that the term 'new industrial relations' can be seen as referring broadly to three patterns of employee relations arrangements: (a) the Japanese model; (b) complete and continuing avoidance of trade union involvement; and (c) the replacement of traditional IR with integrated HRM to encourage employee commitment, flexibilty and quality. For Millward, Japanese-style IR can be broadly equated with what has come to be designated 'new-style' agreements in British IR (Bassett 1986; Lewis 1990). For some commentators (e.g. Oliver and Wilkinson 1992) this would be too simplistic, nevertheless the existence of a 'package' of features, comprising single union deals, no strike agreements, greater consultation and employee participation and a move towards single status can be regarded as a novel approach to the restructuring of IR. However, the conclusion Millward reaches is that such agreements are rare, notwithstanding the publicity and interest they have generated. If they have had any impact 'it cannot have been by their spreading into more and more workplaces'. In his opinion, quantitatively they 'do not form the starting-point for a "new industrial relations" in Britain' (Millward 1994: 126–7).

As to whether there has been a retreat from trade unionism, much of the answer to this for Millward (1994) turns on the issue of union recognition and derecognition. Here the evidence is not easy to interpret, but the WIRS 90 data does seem to suggest that the derecognition of unions in both large and small organisations since 1984, added to the reduced likelihood of newer establish-ments recognising unions, have been largely responsible for the overall decline of the proportion of workplaces and employees covered by collective bargaining (Millward 1994: 119–20). The absence of unions is not uncommon, of course, as Millward points out. In much of the private sector, especially those areas where small independent firms predominate, unions have nearly always found it difficult to establish a foothold. Two other points are worth making here. First, that while clear cases of wholesale derecognition remain rare, according to WIRS 90, it is not necessary to withdraw recognition in order to achieve significant changes in relationships with trade unions. Furthermore, as was remarked earlier, although there is growing evidence that the nature of derecognition may also be changing, as well as increasing, it does not, as yet, amount to a major problem for unions in the view of Gall and McKay (1994). Second, that in this matter, as in the adoption of HRM, the evidence of employers behaving strategically is very thin. Pragmatism and opportunism seem to be dominant characteristics rather than anti-union principles (Kelly 1990: 57).

The third possible blueprint for the 'new industrial relations' considered by Millward i.e. integrated HRM practices, is equally disappointing, with the findings indicating 'modest change and development rather than a sea change' (Millward 1994: 127). The measures taken by him as evidence of an HRM approach were changes in methods of communication and consultation between management and the individual worker, with the aim of increasing involvement; the harmonisation of terms and conditions of employment, and the absence of formal measures to check work start and finish times of employees, indicating the existence of 'trust-based' rather than adversarial industrial relations. Millward recognises that what constitutes HRM is a matter of controversy, and that for many of its advocates what matters is its strategic dimension, rather than practice. Nevertheless, he has sought to identify and explore three aspects of practice that 'could reasonably be regarded as indicative of an HRM approach'. However, the question of the relationship between HRM practices and trade unionism was of especial interest, all the more so given the view that the existence of such practices might challenge and undermine the position and role of unions (Guest 1989). In the event this was found not to have happened, indeed, the 'fragments of HRM', where they existed, were more likely to be in workplaces with recognised unions, as opposed to those without them (Sisson 1993). 'Thus the arrangements at workplace level which managements had put in place to consult, communicate with and inform employees were more widespread and highly developed in unionised workplaces than in the non-union sector' (Millward 1994: 129). It leads him to the conclusion that the movement – or lack of it – in the elements of HRM practice he identifies are not associated with the substantial spread of non-unionism revealed by the WIRS survey, nor has the latter change been accompanied by a growth in HRM or other more 'progressive' management practices. To many informed commentators and researchers the last-mentioned will not come as a surprise. Others, for some time, have questioned whether the reality of HRM has been able to match the rhetoric of its enthusiasts (Evans, Ewing and Nolan 1992; Guest 1991; Kessler 1993; Legge 1989). As the General Secretary of the TUC, John Monks (1993: 231) suggests, in Britain HRM has not advanced beyond individual market leaders with strong positions, the management agenda being dominated by more money.

Overall, then, there appear to be few signs that a 'new industrial relations' has taken the place of the old. As yet, no new pattern of employee representation has emerged to replace that provided by trade unions. Perhaps, even more important is the consequence that non-managerial employees are increasingly being treated as a 'factor of production'. According to Millward:

> Britain is approaching the position where few employees have any mechanism through which they can contribute to the operation of their workplace in a broader context than that of their own job ... There has been no spontaneous emergence of an alternative model of employee representation that could channel and attenuate conflicts between employer and employees. (Millward 1994: 133)

Moreover, the relative lack of legal protection for individual workers in Britain compared to other developed economies, coupled with the recent growth in economic and social inequalities only serves to exacerbate this situation. It is perhaps useful to conclude by commenting on what this might mean for the character of IR and the prospects for a shift towards a more cooperative approach. In this regard one cannot be optimistic. The 'frontier of control' may have shifted in management's favour (Purcell 1991), but there are few signs that the employment relationship has been 'refashioned' or 'remade' for the long term. Nor is it clear that the antagonistic 'them and us' attitudes which have been viewed as a deep-seated characteristic of British IR have disappeared (Kelly and Kelly 1991). The Thatcher years produced a radical upheaval in British IR and have left a significant legacy, whose consequences are still being worked through but, as Evans, Ewing and Nolan (1992) argue, they have done little to tackle the fundamental problems of the British economy. The view that excessive trade union power was a prime cause of 'disorderly' IR and economic decline, although popular and easy to accept, was always too simplistic, as was the solution, that *if* union power was constrained by legislation, freeing-up market forces and other ways whereby management might be encouraged to manage, *then* all would eventually come good.

The market solution to IR difficulties has yet to produce the pay-off in terms of macro-economic performance (Metcalfe 1993). Evans, Ewing and Nolan (1992) comment that in fact adversarial-pluralist strategies still dominate British IR, which is not surprising given the inherently conflictual nature of the employment relationship. Its regulation remains a 'continuing preoccupation and a permanent problem for contemporary management' (Keenoy 1992: 93). If Millward is correct in his view that workers are increasingly being treated as a factor of production today it merely reflects the continued short-termism and opportunism which have been such prevalent features of British management's approach to IR. Essentially it means that little has changed, despite the large-scale shifts documented by the WIRS 90 researchers. In itself this is not surprising. The adversarial nature and traditions of the British IR system are very much a consequence of the distinctive characteristics of British society. The heritage of the past still exerts a profound influence on contemporary employment relationships (Hyman 1995: 48).

SELECTED READING

Beardwell, I. (1992)
Evans, S., Ewing, K. and Nolan, P. (1992)
Gospel, H. F. and Palmer, G. (1993)
Storey, J. (ed.) (1995)
Whitaker, A. (1992)

10 Volume editor's conclusions

Stephen Fox

In conclusion we will examine the main ways the British business environment could possibly change in order to integrate more efficiently with other European business environments. This will summarise some of the main themes detailed in the book as a whole.

ECONOMIC POSITION AND POLICY

Britain sought to avoid the high social costs of most EU member states by opting out of the Maastricht social chapter and avoiding a statutory minimum wage. This policy allowed Britain to compete on wage costs and to attract inward investment to assist in the reconstruction and modernising of her manufacturing base. However, the reasons behind this are that UK firms operate within a stock market culture which demands high returns to investors in the short term, which is one of the reasons why the British government was reluctant to pay the same social costs as other EU member states where firms do not face such demanding investors. In this context, the question is whether Britain should increase the social cost burden upon its employers in line with the rest of the EU, or whether the EU as a whole should move towards the UK position. It is not the issue of social costs alone which is at stake, but the structure of European capital markets. At the moment UK companies are heavily dependent upon equity raised via the stock market (rather than loans payable to banks or reinvested profits); this is in common with the financial structure of American companies, a continent with which Britain trades as much as within Europe. If world-wide international business is financed in the American way by equity capital raised on the major world stock exchanges, then it would make sense for Europe to shift in this direction also in order to become increasingly competitive. This policy might benefit some EU states more than others, especially those which lack local capital resources and which are in a strong position to compete internationally on wage costs.

The UK's long-term, comparative, economic decline is well documented. The question facing UK policy-makers *vis-à-vis* the EU is twofold: how to avoid worsening its position and how to turn the economic performance around. There are short-term and long-term strategies here. It is universally recognised that the UK needs to educate more of its working population, both vocationally and academically, in the long term. Since the late 1980s the UK has practically doubled its student population, although in the process the higher education system has been put under intense strain. Most of the other short-term measures have already been attempted, including the private sector cost-cutting and delayering of the 1980s, the privatisation of 'lame-duck' public industries, the 'roll-back' of the State, the weakening of workforce bargaining power via legislation to obtain maximum cooperation and flexibility, the benefits of North Sea oil, and the attraction of inward investment and managerial skills. In short, most of the obstacles that were held, in the 1970s, to be holding UK entrepreneurship and management back have now been removed and some windfall factors, such as North Sea oil have been of additional help. In these circumstances the continuing decline of UK economic fortunes may be due to:

1 Entrepreneurial failure i.e. under-investment or bad investment decisions; of these the former is more likely since the UK stock market requires high short-term paybacks and the high level of public scrutiny of firm's investment plans by city analysts mitigates against bad investment decisions but may also depress the overall rate of investment. It is estimated that in the 1980s about 15 per cent of British R&D investments were in the defence business, a figure comparable to the USA; this sector has been declining since the collapse of the former USSR in the late 1980s and it may be that UK defence firms are finding it difficult to diversify but can no longer invest as they used to.

2 Entrepreneurial redirection i.e. UK entrepreneurs may be investing outside the UK and not repatriating the profits. As business internationalisation continues apace, UK firms may necessarily need to invest abroad to build alliances and joint ventures and this outflow may not be offset by even the high levels of inward investment. For example, in the late 1980s ICI, one of the UK's oldest and largest companies, employed about 120,000 world-wide of which some 55,000 were UK based. In line with its international business strategy, the UK headcount is now down to about 15,000–20,000 and ICI's expanding operations are mainly outside the UK.

3 Management failure i.e. sufficient investment in good areas but weak pay-offs because of poor management and implementation; it is difficult to assess the extent of management failure since managements provide most of the information on which to assess themselves and have very close relations with the independent auditors whom they also appoint. It is clear, however, that UK managers are less well educated than most of their overseas counterparts and speak fewer foreign languages.

4 Workforce skills failure i.e. entrepreneurs and management could not invest, or their investments failed, because of a persistent lack of key skills in the workforce, e.g. electrical engineering, one of the UK's main business sectors suffered skills shortages in the late 1980s despite facing buoyant growth

prospects at the time. This must be seen as a political failure, since education and training policy and most delivery mechanisms are under government control within the public sector.

The UK's dependence upon international trade, not only within Europe, means that the structure of its capital markets are unlikely to change, therefore UK employers are likely to remain focused on short-term profitability and therefore low labour and welfare costs. However, it could be that after seventeen years of Conservative cost-cutting pressures, even UK employers would no longer resist a minimum wage.

BUSINESS CULTURE

In the UK about 1 million middle and senior managers run the economy within the legal and policy framework established by government. We know from international comparisons that these managers are comparatively poorly educated, and like the rest of the UK population are generally weak in languages, maths and science. As late as the 1960s and 1970s a good arts degree was the preferred credential for the future 'captains of industry' and a culture of 'amateurism' was common in British business. Britain's international trade still follows the colonial patterns established by its empire, although most of its former colonies have become independent states, loosely connected via the 'Commonwealth'. British management abroad tends to be of the ex-patriot variety and is highly interwoven with the diplomatic culture of the British foreign office, especially beyond Europe and America.

In the UK itself, there is a long-standing educational gap between the university educated top 15 per cent and the rest of the population which has contributed to the maintenance of a 'them and us' culture between management and workforce, which the politics of class-division have also maintained. Since the late 1980s the UK has doubled the student numbers going through higher education, but it is indicative of the extent of class divisions in the UK that John Major, on becoming Prime Minister, could actually make serious political capital out of his working-class family background, his lack of a university degree and his promise of a genuinely class-free society. The latter must have been some sort of admission that despite Thatcher's upwardly mobile 1980s, social class remained an impediment to success in 1990's Britain.

Since the oil shocks of the 1970s, the retail sector, defence industry, petro-chemicals and pharmaceuticals have remained strong, whereas textiles, automobiles and many primary industries (e.g. steel, coal, shipbuilding) have all declined in the UK. These trends are indicative of substantial industrial restructuring and this, in turn, reflects a recognition by the UK's political and business élite that its fortunes are determined more by global markets than domestic ones. It is unclear how many other EU member states are as subject to the vagaries of international trade and capital markets as the UK is, but it is this factor which is most influential upon Britain's policy on European political union and social policy.

MARKET KNOWLEDGE

Perhaps because of the UK's long-standing strength in retailing, as well as the London art market and the British music industry, the UK marketing and advertising business is among the most creative and sophisticated in the world, as Michael Thomas's chapter shows. However, the UK advertising industry has less market knowledge about consumer populations in countries which are UK export targets.

FINANCE AND ACCOUNTING

In addition to the structure and culture of UK financial markets (discussed above) there are questions over the independence of auditors from the managements they audit as Bob Perks writes. In comparison to some other countries this might however appear to be less of a problem. However, this is one area in which the British tradition of voluntarism and amateurism may be in conflict with traditions of public scrutiny elsewhere in Europe in countries where the role of the State, and its public bureaucracies, is seen to be wholly legitimate rather than an encroachment upon individual entrepreneurial freedom, as it sometimes is in the UK. This is more of a cultural matter than of the technical transparency of actual company accounts.

The sheer numbers of accountants and accountancy-trained managers in the UK, may be an issue for Britain. Senior managers in Germany tend to have higher degrees, even doctorates, in the technical and scientific fields central to their industry, be this engineering or chemicals, whereas managers in the UK tend to be trained in acountancy or one of the other management functions (e.g. marketing, IT, personnel) and there is a sharper divide between business operations and corporate strategy within the UK. UK corporations, especially holding companies, tend to think about strategy as if it were mainly a matter of acquisitions and divestments, rather than a matter of organic business growth. However, it could be that the holding company structure with a slim head office staffed mainly by accountants and financial analysts overarching a portfolio of operating companies is the pattern for international business management. So again it is unclear whether the British tradition should change even if it could. Much more research is needed into the structure of international business, but Britain may well be unusual within Europe for the extent of its *intercontinental*, as well as international business links.

BUSINESS LAW

There are two major features of the UK legal system, as it applies to business, which might need to change if the UK business environment were to move closer to Europe as a whole. The UK tradition of voluntary codes of conduct, rather than statutory regulation, ranges from the control of advertising standards, to consumer protection, to corporate governance; there may be a case for increasing statutory controls and professionally administered public watchdogs. This would probably be seen in the UK as an unacceptable increase in bureaucratic red tape, however, the extension of public regulations might benefit the professionalism of UK management, as it does to some extent in the area of health and safety at work.

The second area in which the legal system might be expected to change could be the UK's reliance on expensive and time-consuming verbal court proceedings, which could be replaced by a more administrative approach to settling cases, more reliant upon written arguments than the simultaneous presence of the parties to dispute in the court or tribunal.

HUMAN RESOURCES

The two main areas here are the climate of industrial relations and the level and quality of educational and vocational standards among the working population. In the UK the Conservative backlash against corporatism and worker participation has been stronger than in most other European countries; management, assisted by government legislation, has the unilateral right to manage with minimum union and workforce input and has had for nearly two decades. The UK no longer suffers the damaging strikes of the 1970s, in either the public or private sectors, but as we noted under 'economic position and policy' above, UK manufacturing performance and overall economic position still follows a pattern of comparative decline. While some of the cause for this is the short-termism of UK capital markets, a wider cause is the comparative under-investment in human capital by the national authorities over the entire post-war period. Since the late 1980s student numbers entering higher education have almost doubled but this may have been at the expense of the quality of individual student attention which the British system is still famous for. Although student numbers have recently increased, it is still doubtful whether industry gets the right kind of graduate and, on the other hand, whether industry knows how best to use good graduates.

Overall, it would appear that the UK business environment is highly open to international and intercontinental trade and competition, that its sources of capital are notoriously light-footed and that this creates a climate of short-term results, under-investment and cost-cutting. UK firms in the holding company structure model are best adapted to this environment and even the large multinationals such as ICI, BP and British Aerospace are under pressure to restructure themselves as a portfolio of separate businesses underneath a slim head office managed by accountants. Takeover and divestment culture predominates, and increasingly this culture is less a simple feature of the UK business environment but characterizes international business also. This poses a major strategic dilemma to the European Union, which, as an economic common market, was created in order to improve European competitiveness in world trade, not simply to check the outbreak of further European wars.

Glossary

A level	Advanced level
AA/NTC	Advertising Association/NTC Publications Limited
ABC	Audit Bureau of Circulation
ABCC	Association of British Chambers of Commerce
ACAS	Advisory Conciliation and Advisory Service
ACCA	Associate of the Chartered Association of Certified Accountants
AGM	Annual General Meeting
AND	Advanced National Diploma
APC	Air Pollution Control
APL	accreditation of prior learning
AS level	Advanced Supplementary level
ASA	Advertising Standards Authority
ASB	Accounting Standards Board
BABS	Bachelor of Arts in Business Studies
BATNEEC	Best Available Techniques Not Entailing Excessive Costs
BIM	British Institute of Management
BPEO	Best Practical Environmental Option
BT	British Telecommunications plc
CAC	Central Arbitration Committee
CBI	Confederation of British Industry
CCPMO	Consultative Council of Professional Management Organisations
CIMA	Chartered Institute of Management Accountants
CIPFA	Chartered Institute of Public Finance and Accountancy
CMED	Council for Management Education and Development
CNAA	Council for National Academic Awards
CPVE	Certificate of Pre-Vocational Education
CRE	Commission for Racial Equity
CSE	Certificate of Secondary Education
CSO	Central Statistical Office
DEG	*Department of Employment Gazette*
DMS	Diploma in Management Studies
EAT	Employment Appeal Tribunal
EC	European Community
ECRE	European Consultation on Refugees and Exiles
EDB	*Employment Development Bulletin*
EFTA	European Free Trade Association
EGM	Extraordinary General Meeting
EMS	European monetary system

EOC	Equal Opportunities Commission
EPB	Education Business Partnership
ERM	exchange rate mechanism
ET	Employment Training scheme
EU	European Union
FE	Further education
FEFC	Further Education Funding Council
FME	Foundation for European Management Education
FRED	Financial Reporting Exposure Draft
FRS	Financial Reporting Standard
GCSE	General Certificate of Secondary Education
GDP	gross domestic product
GNP	gross national product
GNVQ	General National Vocational Qualifications
G7	Group of Seven leading industrial nations (USA, Japan, Germany, France, UK, Italy and Canada)
HE	higher education
HEFC	Higher Education Funding Council
HMI	Her Majesty's Inspectors
HMIP	Her Majesty's Inspectorate of Pollution
HNC	Higher National Certificate
HND	Higher National Diploma
HRM	Human resource management
HSC	Health and Safety Commission
HSE	Health and Safety Executive
ICAEW	Institute of Chartered Accountants in England and Wales
ICAI	Institute of Chartered Accountants of Ireland
ICAS	Institute of Chartered Accountants of Scotland
ICC	industrial and commercial companies
IiP	Investors in People
IM	Institute of Management
IMF	International Monetary Fund
IOD	Institute of Directors
IPD	Institute of Personnel and Development
IPC	Integrated Pollution Control
IR	industrial relations
ISE	International Stock Exchange
IT	information technology
ITB	Industrial Training Board
ITC	Independent Television Commission
ITO	Industrial Training Organisation
ITS	Industrial Trends Survey
LBS	London Business School
LEA	local education authority
LEC	Local Enterprise Councils
LFS	Labour Force Survey
LIB	lead industry body
MBA	Master of Business Administration
MBS	Manchester Business School
MCI	Management Charter Initiative
METD	management education, training and development
mfg	manufacturing

MP	Member of Parliament
MSC	Manpower Services Commission
NACETT	National Advisory Council on the Education and Training Targets
NAIRU	non-accelerating inflation rate of unemployment
NAO	National Audit Office
NASDAQ	National Association of Securities Dealers Automated Quotations
NCVQ	National Council for Vocational Qualifications
NEDO	National Economic Development Office
NETT	National Education and Training Targets
NHS	National Health Service
NSTO	Non-Statutory Training Organisation
NTI	new training initiative
NVQ	National Vocational Qualification
O level	Ordinary level
OECD	Organisation for Economic Cooperation and Development
OFFER	Office of the Electricity Regulator
OFGAS	Office of Gas Supply
OFTEL	Office of Telecommunications
OFWAT	Office of Water Services
OND	Ordinary National Diploma
OTC	over-the-counter
P/E	price–earnings
PCFC	Polytechnics and Colleges Funding Council
PSBR	public sector borrowing requirement
PSDR	public sector debt repayment
QC	Queen's Counsel
SCOTVEC	Scottish Vocational Education Council
SEAQ	Stock Exchange Automated Quotation System
SIB	Securities and Investment Board
SMEs	small and medium-sized firms
SRO	self-regulatory organisation
SSAP	Statement of Standard Accounting Practice
SVQ	Scottish Vocational Qualification
TEC	Training and Enterprise Council
TGI	Target Group Index
TGWU	Transport and General Workers Union
TOPIC	Teletext Output of Price Information by Computer
TUC	Trades Union Congress
TUPER	Transfer of Undertaking (Protection of Employment) Regulations
TVEI	Technical and Vocational Education Initiative
UFC	University Funding Council
UGC	University Grants Committee
UITF	Urgent Issues Task Force
VET	vocational education and training
WIRS 90	Workplace Industrial Relations Survey 1990
YT	Youth Training
YTS	Youth Training Scheme

Bibliography

Advertising Association/NTC Publications Ltd (1993) *The Marketing Pocket Book*, London: NTC Publications.

Advertising Association/NTC Publications Ltd (1993) *The Marketing Pocket Book 1993 and 1997*, London.

Ainley, P. and Corney, M. (1990) *Training For-the Future: the Rise and Fall of the Manpower Services Commission*, London: Cassell.

Albanese, R. (1989) 'Competency-based management education', *Journal of Management Development*, Vol. 8, No. 2: 66–76.

Albert, M. (1991) *Capitalisme contre Capitalisme*, Paris: du Seuil.

Anderson, A. (1987) *NSTOs: their Activities and Effectiveness*, London: Manpower Research.

Anthony, P. D. (1987) *The Foundation of Management*, London: Tavistock Publications.

AP Information Services (1993) *The Marketing Manager's Handbook,* London: AP Information Services.

AP Information Services, *The Marketing Manager's Handbook 1993*, London.

Bacon, R. and Eltis, W. (1976) *Britain's Economic Problem: Too Few Producers*, London, Macmillan.

Bain, A. D. (1992) *The Economics of the Financial System,* 2nd edn, London: Blackwell.

Bairam, E. (1988) 'Balance of payments, the Harrod foreign exchange multiplier and economic growth: the European and North American experience 1970–85', *Applied Economics,* December.

Baker, M. (ed.) (1991) *The Marketing Book,* 2nd edn. Oxford: Butterworth Heinemann.

Baker, M. (ed.) (1994) *The Marketing Book,* 3rd edition. Oxford: Butterworth Heinemann, Oxford, 2nd edition.

Bassett, P. (1986) *Strike Free. New Industrial Relations in Britain*, London: Macmillan.

Beardwell, I. (1992) 'The "new industrial relations"? A review of the debate', *Human Resource Management Journal*, Vol. 22: 1–7.

Bennett, R. J. and McCoshan, A. (1993) *Enterprise and Human Resource Development: Local Capacity Building*, London: Paul Chapman.

Berlin, M. and Dyer, C. (eds) (1989) *The Law Machine*, 8th edn, Harmondsworth: Penguin.

Berry-Lound, D. and Anderson, A. (1991) *Review of the Industrial Training Organisation Network*, Sheffield: HOST Consultancy/Employment Department.

Berry-Lound, D. Chaplin, D. and O'Connell, B. (1991) 'Review of Industrial Training Organisations', *Employment Gazette*, October: 535–42.

Bird, D. and Corcoran, L. (1994) 'Trade unions: membership and density', *Employment Gazette*, Vol. 102, No. 6: 189–97.

Blanchflower, D. and Oswald, A. (1989) 'Self employment and the enterprise culture', *British Social Attitudes Survey,* London: SCPR, pp. 127–143.

Blyton, P. and Turnbull, P. (eds) (1992) *Reassessing Human Resource Management,* London: Sage.

Boyatzis, R. E. (1982) *The Competent Manager: a Model for Effective Performance*, New York: Wiley.

British Institute of Management (BIM) (1971) *Business School Programmes: the Requirements of British Manufacturing Industry,* London: BIM (the Owen Report).

Brown, G. F. and Read, A. R. (1984) 'Personnel and training policies: some lessons for Western companies', *Long Range Planning,* Vol. 17, No. 2: 48–57.

Buckle, M. and J. L. Thompson (1992) *The UK Financial System in Transition: Theory and Practice,* Manchester: Manchester University Press.

Burgoyne, J. (1989) 'Creating the managerial portfolio: building on competency approaches to management development', *Management Education and Development* Vol. 20, No. 1: 56–61.

Burrell, G. and Morgan, G. (1979) *Sociological Paradigms and Organisational Analysis: Elements of the Sociology of Corporate Life*, London: Heinemann.

Business Statistics Office, *Business Monitor (Retailing)*, London: HMSO.

Callender, C. (1992) *Will NVQs Work? Evidence from the Construction Industry,* IMS Report No 228, Sussex: Institute of Manpower Studies.

Cairncross, A. (1992) *The British Economy since 1945: Economic Performance, 1945–1990,* Oxford: Blackwell.

Callaghan, J. (1976) address to the Labour Party Annual Conference, Blackpool, 28 September.

Calori, R. and De Woot, P. (eds)(1994) *A European Model: Beyond Diversity,* New York: Prentice-Hall.

Carter, P. and Jackson, N. (1989) 'The emergence of postmodern management', *Management Education And Development*, Vol. 21, No. 3: 219–28.

Castells, M. (1989) *The Informational City,* Oxford: Blackwell.

Caves, R. E. and Associates (1968) *Britain's Economic Prospects,* Brookings Institution, Washington, DC, and London: Allen and Unwin.

Caves, R. E. and Lawence, B. K. (1980) *Britain's Economic Performance,* Washington: Brookings Institution.

CEPR, (1994) *Independent and Accountable: a New Mandate for the Bank of England,* report of an independent panel chaired by Eric Roll,

Chapman, P. G. and Tooze, M. J. (1987) *The Youth Training Scheme in the United Kingdom*, Aldershot: Gower.

Child, J. (1969) *British Management Thought: a Critical Analysis*, London: Allen and Unwin.

Christopher, N., Payne, A. and Ballantyne, D. (1993) *Relationship Marketing,* Oxford: Butterworth Heinemann.

Clarke, A. (1996) *Business Entities: a Practical Guide*, London: Sweet and Maxwell.

Clegg, H. A. (1979) *The Changing System of Industrial Relations in Great Britain*, Oxford: Blackwell.

Coates, D. (1989) *The Crisis of Labour. Industrial Relations and the State in Contemporary Britain*, Deddington: Philip Allan.

Cobham, D. (1992) *Markets and Dealers: the Economics of the London Financial Markets*, London: Longman.

Coffield, F. (1992) 'Training and Enterprise Councils: the last throw of voluntarism?', *Policy Studies*, Vol. 13, No. 4: 11–51.

Collin, A. (1989) 'Managers' competence: rhetoric, reality and research', *Personnel Review*, Vol. 18, No. 6: 20–5.

Confederation of British Industry (CBI) (1987) *Investing For Britain's Future: the Report of the City/Industry Task Force,* London: CBI.

Confederation of British Industry (CBI) (1989) *Towards a Skills Revolution*, London: CBI.

Confederation of British Industry (CBI) (1991a) *World Class Targets: a Joint Initiative to Achieve Britain's Skills Revolution*, London: CBI.

Confederation of British Industry (CBI) (1991b) *Competing with the World's Best: the Report of the CBI Manufacturing Advisory Group*, London: CBI.

Conservative Party (1979) *The Conservative Manifesto, 1979*, April, London: Conservative Central Office.

Constable, J. and McCormick, R. (1987) *The Making of British Managers*, London: CBI/ BIM.

Cooper, J. (1996) *Disability Discrimination Act 1995*, London: HMSO.

Corcoran, L. (1995) 'Trade union membership and recognition: the 1994 Labour Force Survey, *Employment Gazette*, May.

Cotter, B. (1996) *Defective and Unsafe Products: Law and Practice*, London: Butterworth.

Crouch, C. (1982) The Politics of Industrial Relations, 2nd edn, London: Fontana.

Davies, J., Easterby-Smith, M., Mann, S., and Tanton, M. (eds) (1989) *The Challenge to Western Management Development*, London: Routledge.

Davies, P. and Freedland, M. (1993) *Labour Legislation and Public Policy*, Oxford: Clarendon.

Day, M. (1988) 'Managerial competence and the charter initiative', *Personnel Management*, August: 30–4.

Debling, G. (1991) 'Developing standards', in P. Raggatt and L. Unwin (eds), *Change and Intervention: Vocational Education and Training*, London: Falmer, pp. 1–21.

Department of Employment (1988) *Employment for the 1990s*, Cm 540, London: HMSO.

Dorey, P. (1993) 'One step at a time: the Conservative government's approach to the reform of industrial relations since 1979', *Political Quarterly*, January–March.

Drucker, P. (1954) *The Practice of Management*, New York: Harper and Row.

Durcan, J., McCarthy, H. and Redman, G. (1983) *Strikes in Post-War Britain*, London: Allen and Unwin.

EDB (1992) *Employment Development Bulletin*, No. 33, September.

EDB (1993) *Employment Development Bulletin*, No. 40, April.

EDB (1993a) *Employment Development Bulletin*, No. 42, June.

Edwards, P. (1995) *Industrial Relations. Theory and Practice in Britain*, Oxford: Blackwell.

Edwards, P. Hall, M., Hyman, R., Marginson, P., Sisson, K., Waddington, J. and Winchester, D. (1992) 'Great Britain: still muddling through', in A. Ferner and R. Hyman (eds), *Industrial Relations in the New Europe*, Oxford: Blackwell, pp. 1–68.

Edwards, P. K. and Whitston, C. (1991) 'Workers are working harder: effort and shop floor relations in the 1980s, *British Journal of Industrial Relations*, Vol. 29, No. 4, December: 593–601.

Elger, T. (1990) 'Technical innovation and work reorganization in British manufacturing in the 1980s: continuity, intensification or transformation?' *Work, Employment and Society, Special Issue: The 1980s: A Decade of Change*.

Elger, T. (1991) 'Task flexibilty and the intensification of labour in UK manufacturing in the 1980s', in A .Pollert (ed.), *Farewell to Flexibility?* Oxford: Blackwell.

Emmerick, M. and Peck, J. (1991) *First Report of the TEC Monitoring Project*, Manchester: Centre for Local Economic Strategies.

Emmerick, M. and Peck, J. (1992) *Reforming The TECs: Towards a New Training Strategy*, Manchester: Centre for Local Economic Strategies.

Evans, B. (1992) *The Politics of the Training Market: From Manpower Services Commission to Training and Enterprise Council*, London: Routledge.

Evans, S., Ewing, K. and Nolan, P. (1992) 'Industrial relations and the British economy in the 1990s: Mrs Thatcher's legacy', *Journal of Management Studies*, Vol. 29, No. 5: 571–89.

Fallick, J. L. and Elliott, R. F. (eds) (1981) *Incomes Policies, Inflation and Relative Pay,* London: Allen and Unwin.

Finegold, D. and Soskice, D. (1988) 'The failure of training in Britain: analysis and prescription', *Oxford Review of Economic Policy*, Vol. 4, No. 3: 21–53.

Finney, M. and Siehl, C. (1985–86) 'The current MBA: why are we failing?', *Organizational Behaviour Teaching Review*, Vol. 10, No. 3: 1–11.

Flanders, A. (1965) *Industrial Relations: What is Wrong with the System? An Essay on Its Theory and Future*, London: Faber.

Flanders, A. (1974) 'The tradition of voluntarism', *British Journal of Industrial Relations*, Vol. 12, No. 3, November: 352–70.

Foulkes, D. (1995) *Administrative Law*, London: Butterworth.

Fox, A. (1985) *History and Heritage, the Social Origins of the British Industrial Relations System*, London: Allen and Unwin.

Fox, S. (1989a) 'The panopticon: from Bentham's obsession to the revolution in management learning', *Human Relations*, Vol. 42, No. 8: 717–39.

Fox, S. (1989b) 'The production and distribution of knowledge through open and distance learning', *Education and Training Technology International*, Vol. 26, No. 3: 269–80.

Fox, S. (1992) 'The European learning community: towards a political economy of management learning', *Human Resource Management Journal*, Vol. 3, No. 1: 70–91.

Fox, S. (1994a) 'Debating management learning: I', *Management Learning*, Vol. 25, No. 1: 83–93.

Fox, S. (1994b) 'Debating management learning: II', *Management Learning*, Vol. 25, No. 4: 579–97.

Fox, S. (1996) 'Management learning: programme and project', in J. G. Burgoyne and M. Reynolds (eds.), *Management Learning*, London: Sage.

Fox, S., Tanton, M. and M., McLeay, S. (1991)'Smoothies, trendies and sharpbenders: human resource management in financially distinctive firms', paper presented at EIASM workshop on 'Strategy, Accounting and Control', Venice, 1990.

Fox, S. and McLeay, S. (1992) 'An approach to researching managerial labour markets: HRM, corporate strategy and financial performance in UK manufacturing', *International Journal of Human Resource Management*, Vol. 3, No. 3: 523–54.

Freshfields Environment Group (1994) *Tolley's Environment Handbook: a Management Guide*, Croydon: Tolley's.

Gall, G. and McKay, A. (1994) 'Trade union derecognition in Britain 1988–94', British Journal of Industrial Relations, Vol. 32, No. 3, September: 433–48.

Gallie, D. and White, M. (1993) *Employee Commitment and the Skills Revolution*, London: PSI.

Gilbody, J. (1991) *The UK Monetary and Financial System,* London: Routledge.

Goody, E. N. (ed.) (1995) *Social Intelligence and Interaction: Expressions and Implications of the Social Bias in Human Intelligence*, Cambridge: Cambridge University Press.

Gospel, H. and Okayama, R. (1991) 'Industrial training in Britain and Japan: an overview', in H. Gospel (ed), *Industrial Training and Technological Innovation: a Comparative and Historical Study*, London: Routledge, pp. 13–37.

Gospel, H. F. and Palmer, G. (1993) British Industrial Relations, 2nd ed, London: Routledge.

Gower Report (1986) *Review of Investor Protection,* Cmnd 9125, London: HMSO

Gowland, D. (1990) *The Regulation of Financial Markets in the 1990's*, Cheltenham: Edward Elgar.

Grey, C. and Mitev, N. (1995) 'Management education: a polemic', *Management Learning*, Vol. 26, No. 1: 73–90.

Griffiths, I. (1987) *Creative Accounting*, London: Unwin.

Griffiths, M. (1996) *Law for Purchasing and Supply*, 2nd edn, London: Pitman.

Guardian (1991) 4 November.

Guest, D. E. (1989) 'Human resource management: its implications for industrial relations and trade unions', in J. Storey (ed) *New Perspectives on Human Resource Management*, London: Routledge.

Guest, D. E. (1991) 'Personnel management: the end of orthodoxy?', *British Journal of Industrial Relations*, Vol. 29, No. 2, June: 149–75.

Haldane, A. G. (1991) 'The exchange rate mechanism of the European Monetary System: a review of the literature', *Bank of England Quarterly Bulletin,* February: 73–82.

Hall, S. and Jacques, M. (eds) (1989) *New Times: the Changing Face of Politics in the 1990s*, London: Lawrence and Wishart.

Handy, C. (1985) *The Future of Work: a Guide to a Changing Society*, Oxford: Blackwell.

Handy, C. (1987) *The Making of Managers: a Report on Management Education, Training and Development in the United States, West Germany, France, Japan and the UK*, London: National Economic Development Office.

Handy, C., Gordon, C., Gow, I. and Randlesome, C. (1988) *Making Managers*, London: Pitman.

Hannah, L. (1976) *The Rise of the Corporate Economy*, 2nd edn, London: Methuen.

Hannah, L. (1980) 'Visible and invisible hands in Great Britain', in A. Chandler and H. Daems (eds), *Managerial Hierarchies: Comparative Perspectives on the Rise of the Modern Industrial Enterprise,* Cambridge, MA: Harvard University Press.

Harvey, D. (1989) *The Condition of Postmodernity*, Oxford: Blackwell.

Hayes, R. H. and Abernathy, W. J. (1980) 'Managing our way to economic decline', *Harvard Business Review*, July-August: 67–77.

Hendy, J. (1993) *A Law unto Themselves. Conservative Employment Laws: a National and International Assessment*, 3rd ed, London: Institute of Employment Rights.

Her Majesty's Stationery Office (HMSO) (1992) *Her Majesty's Guide to the UK Privatisation Programme,* London: HMSO.

Heritage, J. (1974) 'Assessing people', in N. Armistead (ed.), *Reconstructing Social Psychology*, Harmondsworth: Penguin, pp. 260–81.

Hill, C. W. L., Hitt, M. A. and Hoskisson, R. E. (1988) 'Declining US competitiveness: reflections on a crisis', *Academy of Management Executive*, Vol. 11, No. 1: 51–60.

Hirsch, F. (1977) *Social Limits to Growth*, London: Routledge and Kegan Paul.

Hobsbawm, E. J. (1968) *Industry and Empire,* London: Weidenfeld and Nicholson.

Hooper, F. (1960) *Management Survey*, Harmondsworth: Pelican.

Hougham, J., Thomas, J. and Sisson, K. (1991) 'Ford's EDAP scheme: a roundtable discussion', *Human Resource Management Journal*, Vol. 1, No. 3, 77–91.

Howells, P. and Bain, K. (1990) *Financial Markets and Institutions*, London: Longman.

Hyman, R. (1991) 'Plus ca change? The theory of production and the production of theory', in A. Pollert (ed.), *Farewell to Flexibility?* Oxford: Blackwell.

Hyman, R. (1995) 'The historical evolution of British industrial relations', in P. K. Edwards (ed), *Industrial Relations: Theory and Practice in Britain*, Oxford: Blackwell.

Independent Television Commission (ITC) (1991) *The ITC Code of Advertising Standards and Practice*, January, London: ITC.

Ingram, G. (1984) *Capitalism Divided? The City and Industry in British Social Development*, Houndmills: Macmillan.

Institute of Manpower Studies/Manpower Services Commission/ National Economic Development Office (IMS/MSC/NEDO) (1985) *Competence and Competition*, London: NEDO.

Jameson, M. (1988) *A Practical Guide to Creative Accounting*, London: Kogan Page.

Janes, M. and Roberts, B. (1990) 'Labour Costs in 1988', *Employment Gazette*, September: 431–7.

Jarvis, V. and Prais, S. J. (1989) 'Two nations of shopkeepers: training for retailing in Britain and France', *National Institute Economic Review*, Vol. 128: 58–74.

Jessup. G. (1991) *Outcomes: NVQs and the Emerging Model of Education and Training*, Brighton: Falmer.

Jones, I. (1988) 'An evaluation of YTS', *Oxford Review of Economic Policy*, Vol. 4, No. 3: 54–71.

Kahn-Freund, O. (1954) 'Legal framework', in A. Flanders and H. A. Clegg (eds) *The System of Industrial Relations in Great Britain*, Oxford: Blackwell.

Keenoy, T. (1992) 'Constructing control', in J. F. Hartley and G. M. Stephenson, *Employment Relations*, Oxford: Blackwell.

Keenoy, T. and Noone, M. (1992) 'Employment relations in the enterprise culture: themes and issues', *Journal of Management Studies Special Issue*, Vol. 29, No. 5: 561–70.

Keep, E. (1991) 'The grass looked greener: some thoughts on the influence of comparative vocational training research on the UK policy debate', in P. Ryan (ed), *International Comparisons of Vocational Education and Training for Intermediate Skills*, London: Falmer, pp. 23–46.

Keep, E. (1994) 'The transition from school to work', in K. Sisson (ed), *Personnel Management in Britain*, 2nd edn, Oxford: Blackwell.

Keep, E. and Mayhew, K. (forthcoming) *The British Vocational Education and Training System: a Critical Analysis*, Oxford: Oxford University Press.

Kelly, J. (1990) 'British trade unionism 1979–89: change, continuity and contradictions', *Work Employment and Society Special Issue: The 1980s: A Decade of Change?* pp. 29–65.

Kelly, J. and Kelly, R. (1991) 'Them and us: social psychology and the "New Industrial Relations"', *British Journal of Industrial Relations*, Vol. 29, No. 1: 25–48.

Kessler, S. (1993) 'Is There Still a Future for the Unions?', *Personnel Management*, July.

Kessler, S. and Bayliss, F. (1992) *Contemporary British Industrial Relations*, London: Macmillan.

Kotter, J. (1982) *The General Managers*, New York: Free Press.

Labour Research (1995) 'Work changes take toll on unions', *Labour Force Survey*, Vol. 84, No. 5: 15–16.

Lave, J. and Wenger, E. (1991) *Situated Learning: Legitimate Peripheral Participation*, Cambridge: Cambridge University Press.

Leavitt, H. J. (1975a) 'Beyond the analytic manager: part I', *Californian Management Review*, Vol. 17, No. 3: 5–12.

Leavitt, H. J. (1975b) 'Beyond the analytic manager: part II', *Californian Management Review*, Vol. 17, No. 4: 11–21.

Legge, K. (1988) 'Personnel management in recession and recovery', *Personnel Review*, Vol. 17: 3–69.

Legge, K. (1989) 'HRM: a critical analysis', in J. Storey (ed.), *New Perspectives on Human Resource Management*, London: Routledge.

Legge, K (1995) 'HRM: rhetoric, reality and hidden agendas', in J. Storey (ed.), *Human Resource Management. A Critical Text*, London: Routledge.

Lewis, R. (1990) 'Strike free deals and pendulum arbitration', *British Journal of Industrial Relations*, Vol. 28, No. 1: 32–56.

Lewis, R. (1991) 'Reforming industrial relations: law, politics and power', *Oxford Review of Economic Policy*, Vol. 7, No. 1: 60–75.

Lindley, R. (1983) 'Active manpower policy', in G. S. Bain (ed.), *Industrial Relations in Britain*, Oxford: Blackwell, pp. 339–60.

LMQR (1992) *Labour Market Quarterly Report*, February.

LMQR (1993a) *Labour Market Quarterly Report*, February.

LMQR (1993b) *Labour Market Quarterly Report*, May.

Lucio, M. M. and Weston, S. (1992) 'Human resource management and trade union responses: bringing the politics of the workplace back into the debate', in P. Blyton and P. Turnbull (eds) *Reassessing Human Resource Management*, London: Sage, pp. 215–32.

Lukes, S. (1974) *Power – a Radical View*, London: Macmillan.

Mackay, L. (1986) 'The macho-manager: it's no myth, *Personnel Management*, January.

Martin, R. (1988) 'Industrial capitalism in transition: the contemporary reorganisation of the British space economy', in D. Massey and J. Allen (eds) *Uneven Re-development: Cities and Regions in Transition*, London: Open University/Hodder and Stoughton.

Management Charter Initiative (MCI) (1993) *Management Development in the UK 1993*, market research report, London: MCI.

Management Charter Initiative (MCI) (1995a) Management research seminar, held at Regent's College, London, 25 October 1995.

Management Charter Initiative (MCI) (1995b) *Seminar Report*, London: MCI.

Mangham, I. L. and Silver, M. S. (1986) *Management Training: Context and Practice*, Bath: University of Bath, School of Management, ESRC/DTI report.

Manpower Services Commission/Department of Education and Science (1986) *Review of Vocational Qualifications in England and Wales*, London: HMSO.

McCool, T. (1991) 'Making standards work together', presentation to CBI conference 'Leading Standards Forward', London, 3 December.

McCormick, K. (1991) 'The development of engineering education in Britain and Japan', in H. Gospel (ed.), *Industrial Training and Technological Innovation: a Comparative and Historical Study*, London: Routledge, pp. 38–68.

Metcalf, D. (1989) 'Water notes dry up: the impact of the Donovan reform proposals and Thatcherism at work on labour productivity', *British Journal of Industrial Relations*, March: 1–33.

Metcalf, D. (1990) *Labour legislation 1980–1990: philosophy and impact*, Centre for Economic Performance Working Paper No. 12, September.

Metcalf, D. (1993) 'Industrial relations and economic performance', *British Journal of Industrial Relations*, Vol. 31, No. 2: 255–83.

Millward, N. (1994) *The New Industrial Relations?* London: Policy Studies Institute.

Millward, N. *et al.* (1992) *Workplace Industrial Relations in Transition*, Aldershot: Dartmouth.

Mintzberg, H. (1973) *The Nature of Managerial Work*, New York: Harper and Row.

Mishan, E. J. (1967) *The Costs of Economic Growth*, n. p. The Staples Press.

Monks, J. (1993) 'A trade union view of WIRS3', *British Journal of Industrial Relations*, Vol. 31, No. 2: 227–33.

National Training Task Force (1992) 'Draft copy of the Cleaver Report', London: NTTF (mimeo).

Newman, D. and Foster, A. (1993) *European Market Share Reporter*, London: Gale Research International Ltd and Manchester Business School.

Oechslin, J. J. (1987) 'Training and the business world: the French experience', *International Labour Review*, Vol. 126, No. 6, November–December: 653–67.

Oliver, N. and Wilkingson, B. (1989) 'Japanese techniques and personnel and industrial relations practice in Britain: evidence and implications', *British Journal of Industrial Relations*, March: 73–92.

Oliver, N. and Wilkinson, B. (1992) *The Japanization of British Industry: New Developments in the 1990s*, Oxford: Blackwell.

Pawley, M., Winstone, D. and Bentley, P. (1991) *UK Financial Institutions and Markets*, London: Macmillan.

Perkin, H. (1989) *The Rise of Professional Society: England since 1880*, London: Routledge.

Perks, R. W. (1993) *Accounting and Society*, London: Chapman and Hall.

Perry, P. J. C. (1976) *The Evolution of British Manpower Policy*, London: British Association of Commercial and Industrial Education.

Phelps Brown, H. (1990) 'The counter-revolution of our time', *Industrial Relations*, Vol. 29, No. 1,

Piesse, J., Peasnell, K. and Ward, C. (1995) *British Financial Markets and Institutions: an International Perspective*, London: Prentice Hall.

Pliatsky, L. (1982) 'Cash limits and pay policy', *Political Quarterly,* Vol. 4: 16–23.

Pollert, A. (ed.) 1991 *Farewell to Flexibility*, Oxford: Blackwell.

Porter, M. E. (1990) *The Competitive Advantage of Nations*, London: Macmillan.

Prais, S. J. (1989) 'How Europe would see the new British initiative for standardising vocational qualifications', *National Institute Economic Review*, Vol. 129: 52–4.

Prais, S .J. (ed) (1990) *Productivity, Education and Training*, London: NIESR.

Prais, S. J. (1991) 'Vocational qualifications in Britain and Europe: theory and Practice', *National Institute Economic Review*, May.

Purcell, J. (1991) 'The rediscovery of the management prerogative: the management of labour relations in the 1980s', *Oxford Review of Economic Policy*, Vol. 7, No. 1: 33–43.

Raggatt, P. (1991) 'Quality assurance and NVQs', in P. Raggatt and L. Unwin (eds), *Change and Intervention: Vocational Education and Training*, London: Falmer pp. 61–80.

Rainbird, H. (1994) 'Adult Training', in K. Sisson (ed.), *Personnel Management in Britain*, 2nd edn, Oxford: Blackwell.

Rainbird, H. and Grant, W. (1985) *Employers' Associations and Training Policy*, Coventry: Institute of Employment Research.

Reed, M. and Anthony, P. D. (1992) 'Profesionalizing management and managing professionalization: British management in the 1990s', *Journal of Management Studies*, Vol. 29, No. 5: 591–613.

Reeder, D. (1981) 'A recurring debate: education and industry', in R. Dale, G. Esland and M. MacDonald (eds) |*Education and the State: Volume 1, Schooling and the National Interest*, Lewes: Falmer.

Rehder, R. R. (1982) 'SMR Forum: American business education – is it too late to change?', *Sloan Management Review*, Winter: 63–71.

Resnick, L. B., Levine, J. M. and Teasley, S. D. (eds) (1991) *Perspectives on Socially Shared Cognition*, Washington, DC: American Psychological Association.

Robinson, C. (1992) 'Privatising the British energy industries: the lessons to be learned', *Metroeconomica*, Vol. 43, No. 1–2: 103–29.

Roy, D. J. (1987) *Economic Trends*.

Roy, D. J. (1989) 'Labour productivity in 1985: an international comparison', Paper presented to 21st Conference of the International Association for Research in Income and Wealth, Lahnstein, August.

Ruff, A. (ed.) (1995) *Principles of Law for Managers*, London: Routledge.

Ryan, P. (ed.) (1991) *International Comparisons of Vocational Education and Training for Intermediate Skills*, Brighton: Falmer.

Salaman, G. and Butler, J. (1989) 'Why managers won't learn', *Management Education and Development*, Vol. 21, No. 3: 183–91.

Schilling, H. and Sharp, I. (1996) *Corporate Governance*, London, Butterworth.

Scott-Quinn, B. (1990) *Investment Banking: Theory and Practice*, Euromoney

SEB (1992) *Skills and Enterprise Briefing*, 16/92, June.

Senker, P. J. (1992) *Industrial Training in a Cold Climate*, Aldershot: Avebury.

Sibbald, A. (1978) 'A case of education', *Management Today*, July: 19–22.

Singleton, E. S. (1992) *Introduction to Competitive Law*, London: Pitman.

Sisson, K. (1993) 'In search of HRM', *British Journal of Industrial Relations*, Vol. 31, No. 2, June: 201–10.

Slade, E. (1993) *Tolley's Employment Law Handbook*. Croydon: Tolley's.

Smith, K. (1984) *The British Economic Crisis*, Harmondsworth: Pelican.

Smith, T. (1992) *Accounting for Growth: Stripping the Camouflage from Company Accounts*, London: Century Business.

Sparke, A. (1996) *The Compulsory Competitive Tendering Guide*, 2nd edn, London: Butterworth.

Steedman, H. and Wagner, K. (1989) 'Productivity, machinery and skills in Britain and Germany', *National Institute Economic Review*, Vol. 128: 40–57.

Stewart, R. (1967) *Managers and Their Jobs*, Maidenhead: McGraw-Hill.

Storey, J. (1992) *Developments in the Management of Human Resources and Industrial Relations*, Buckingham: Open University Press.

Storey, J. (ed.) (1995) *Human Resource Management. A Critical Text*, London: Routledge.

Storey, J. and Sisson, K. (1993) *Managing Human Resources and Industrial Relations*, Buckingham: Open University Press.

Stranks, J. (1996) *Law and Practice of Risk Assessment*, London: Pitman.

Tanton, M. and Easterby-Smith, M. (1989) 'Is the Western view inevitable? A model of the development of management education', in J. Davies, M. Easterby-Smith, S. Mann and M. Tanton (eds), *The Challenge to Western Management Development*, London: Routledge.

Taylor, R. (1994) *The Future of the Trade Unions*, London: Andre Deutsch.

Thirlwall, A. P. (1992) *Balance of Payments Theory and the United Kingdom Experience*, 4th edn, Basingstoke: Macmillian.

Thomas, A. B. (1980) 'Management and education: rationalization and reproduction in British business', *International Studies of Management and Organization*, Vol. 10, No. 1–2: 71–109.

Thomas, M. J. (1989) *Pocket Guide to Marketing*, Oxford: Blackwell.

Thomas, M. J. (1994) 'Marketing: in chaos or transition?' *European Journal of Marketing*, Vol. 28, No. 3: 55–62.

Thomas, M. J. (ed.) (1995) *The Gower Handbook of Marketing*, 4th edn, Aldershot: Gower.

Thomas, W. A. (1986) *The Big Bang*, Oxford: Philip Allan.

Thomas, M. J. (1996), The Changing Nature of the Marketing Profession and Implications for Requirements in Marketing Education. Ch 9 in Shaw, S. A. and Hood, N. (eds) *Marketing in Evolution*, Macmillan, London.

3I Group plc (1993) *Plc UK: a Focus on Corporate Trends*, London: *3I* Group, April.

Trade and Industry Committee (1994) *Competitiveness of UK Manufacturing Industry*, London: HMSO.

Trades Union Congress (TUC) (1994) *TUC Information Sheet*, June.

Training Agency (1989) *Training in Britain: Employers' Activities*, Sheffield: TA.

Training Commission (1988) *Classifying the Components of Management Competences*, Sheffield: Training Commission.

Turner, P., Dale, I, and Hurst, C. (1992) 'Training: a key to the future', *Employment Gazette*, August: 379–86.

Ullman, L. (1968) 'Collective bargaining and industrial efficiency', in R. E. Caves and Associates, *Britain's Economic Prospects*, Brookings Institution, Washington, DC, and London: Allen and Unwin.

Varlaam, C. (1987) *The Full Fact-Finding Study of the NSTO System*, Brighton: Institute of Manpower Studies.
Wedderburn, W. (1991) *Employment Rights in Britain and Europe. Selected Papers in Labour Law*, London: Lawrence and Wishart.
Wheatcroft, M. (1970) *The Revolution in Management Education*, London: Pitman.
Whitaker, A. (1992) 'The transformation in work: post-Fordism revisited', in M. Reed and M. Hughes (eds), *Rethinking Organization*. London: Sage, pp. 184–206.
Willmott, H. (1987) 'Studying managerial work: a critique and proposal', *Journal of Management Studies*, Vol. 24, No. 3: 249–70.
Willmott, H. (1994) 'Management education: provocations to debate', *Management Learning*, Vol. 25, No. 1: 105–36.
Wood, L. (1992) '"Urgent need" found for government to examine TECs' funding', *Financial Times*, 25 March.
Woolf, H. (Lord) (1996) *Report on Civil Procedure*, London: HMSO.

Index

Abbey National 108
acceptance houses 111
accounting, financial reporting and corporate
    governance 122–40
    accountancy profession 127–9; accounting
    standards 130–1; auditing standards
    131–2; auditor independence 135–7;
    Cadbury Report 137–40; Companies Acts
    123–7; creative accounting 133–5;
    smaller companies 132–3; types of
    business organisation 122–3
Accounting Standards Board (ASB) 130, 135
ACORN (Classification of Neighbourhoods),
    CACI 46–7
acquisitions, corporate 37–42
adversial system 151
advertising 63–5
    expenditure 71, 73, 84; GNP 72; newspaper
    64–5, 73–4; top advertisers 72–83, 85–7
Advertising Association 97
Advertising Standards Authority 93–5
advocates 159–60
AEI 130
Agricultural Futures Exchange 101
agriculture 81
Air Pollution Control (APC) 178
Amstrad 135
anti-competitive practices 187
apprenticeship 235–6, 240
arbitration 155
Arthur Andersen 194
Articles of Association 166–7
ASDA 214
Ashridge Business School 192, 201
Association of British Chambers of Commerce
    (ABCC) 233
Association of British Insurers 36
Association of Cost and Executive Accountants
    129
Association of International Accountants 129
Association of Investment Trust Companies 36
Audit Commission 126

audit committee 138
auditing 124–6
    private sector 124–6; public sector 126;
    standards 131–2
auditor independence 135–7

balance of payments 8, 10
Baltic International Freight Futures Exchange
    101
Bank of England 107–8
    banker to government 108; banker to UK
    banks 108; management of national debt
    107; monetary supervision 107
banking
    commercial 110; retail 110
Banking Act 1987 107, 109
Banking Act 1989 108
banks
    and Bank of England 108; private 111
Barber, Anthony 6
barristers 158–60
BAT Industries 168
batting average effect 26
BBC 147
BCCI 108, 137
Best Available Techniques Not Entailing
    Excessive Costs (BATNEEC) 178
Best Practical Environmental Option (BPEO)
    178
Big Bang 113
Blue Circle 186
bonds 116
Boots 197, 214
BP 192
brand proliferation 90
British Aerospace 135
British Airways (BA) 89–90, 146, 250
British Coal 142, 250
British Code of Advertising 93
British Gas 142, 147
British Institute of Management 201
British Leyland 250

British Merchant Banking and Securities Houses
 Association 36, 109
British Rail 147
British Shoe Corporation 63, 197
British Steel Corporation 147, 250
British Telecommunications (BT) 19, 34, 147
broadcasting standards 92–5
brokerage 104
Brookings Institution 4
BS 5750 88, 93
BS 7750 178
building societies 108, 110
Building Societies Act 1986 110
Burgerliches Gesetzbuch (BGB) 156
Burton Group 60, 63, 135, 197
business culture 259–60
business environment and technology
 in 1980s and 1990s 29–42; capital markets
 and corporate ownership 35–42;
 corporate transition 29–35
business name 164
business organisations 122–3
 and law 162–70, 260–1; liability 169;
 management responsibilities 164–8; name
 164; reorganisation and liquidation 169;
 see also economy, business and
 technology;
Cabinet 148
Cable and Wireless/Mercury 34
Cadbury Report 122, 136–40, 168
Cadbury-Schweppes 214
Callaghan, James 6, 220
capital markets 35–42, 83
case law 157–8
CBI Manufacturing Advisory Group 17
central government 143–5
Chartered Association of Certified Accountants
 (ACCA) 124, 128–9
Chartered Institute of Arbitrators 155
Chartered Institute of Management Accountants
 (CIMA) 129
Chartered Institute of Marketing (CIM) 96
Chartered Institute of Public Finance and
 Accountancy (CIPFA) 129
Citizens Advice Bureau 96
City Code on Takeovers and Mergers 169
Civil Code 1896, Germany 156
civil courts 152–3
Clean Air Act 1993 177
clearing banks 109–10
clothing
 footwear 69; men's 60, 68; women's,
 children's 60, 69
club membership 54–6, 61
Code of Advertising Standards and Practice
 94–5
Code Civil 156
Code of Practice on Picketing 180

collective bargaining 243, 248–9
collective representation 242–3
collective responsibility 148
commercial banks 108
Commission for Racial Equality (CRE) 150
Committee of the Regions 143
Companies Acts 122–7, 130, 132, 169
 accounting 126–7; auditing 124–6
company
 advantages 123; insolvencies 41; liability
 169; private 123; reorganisation and
 liquidation 169; smaller 132–3
competency approach, management 204–11
Competition Act 1980 187
competition and law 184–5
conciliation 155
Confederation of British Industry (CBI) 143,
 151, 201, 220
constitutional framework 141–56
 central government 143–5; courts 151–4;
 dispute resolution 155–6; EU 142–3;
 government accountability 147–50;
 government agencies 146–7; local
 government 145–6; pressure groups
 150–1; privatisation 147; tribunals 154–5
Consultative Council of Professional
 Management Organisation (CCPMO)
 193–4
Consumer Credit Act 1974 95
consumer durables 54, 59
consumer profile 45–51
consumer protection 92–7
Consumer Protection Act 1987 95, 172–3
Consumers Association 95–6, 150
contract of employment 181–4
contract law 170–2
 dispute resolution 171–2; planning function
 170–1
contracting out 21
Control of Pollution Act 1974 178
Coopers & Lybrand 194
corporate governance 137–40
 see also accounting
corporate ownership 35–42
corporate transition 29–35
Council for Management Education and
 Development (CMED) 236–7
Council of Ministers 143
Council for National Academic Awards (CNAA)
 199
county councils 145
Court of Appeal 153
Court of Auditors 143
courts and tribunals 151–4
 civil courts 152–3; criminal courts 153–4;
 dispute resolution 155–6; tribunals 154–5
Coutts & Co 111
Cranfield Business School 192

creative accounting 122, 133–5
  techniques 134–5
criminal courts 153–4
cultural chemistry 217

Dearing Report 130, 224
debentures 116
deindustrialisation 13
denationalisation 147
Department for Education 221
Department of Employment and Productivity 4
deposit-taking institutions 108–13
  building societies 110; clearing banks
    109–10; investment institutions 111–12;
    merchant banks 111; non deposit taking
    wholesale banks 111; private banks 111
deregulation 102, 114, 189
Deregulation and Contracting Out Act 1994 175,
  186, 189
derivatives and new instruments 116–17
Diploma in Management Studies (DMS) 193
direct mail 71–2, 82
directors' remuneration 168
dispute resolution 155–6, 171–2
  arbitration 155; conciliation 155; mediation
    155; supervised settlement 155–6
distribution, market 60–3
district councils 145
do-it-yourself (DIY) 56, 63
Donovan Commission 4, 23–4, 243
Dunlop Rubber Company 196

economic developments since 1979 7–29
  employment 13–18; industrial relations and
    productivity 21–9; North Sea oil and trade
    8–13; privatisation and public sector 18–21
economic growth 2–7
  and GDP 3
economic position and policy 257–9
Economic and Social Committee 143
economic transition 1
economy, business and technology 1–45
  business environment and technology in
    1980s-1990s 29–42; developments since
    1979 7–29; economic growth,
    productivity levels, inflation 3–7; future
    prospects 42–4
ECRE (European Consultation on Refugees and
  Exiles) 150
Education Act 1980 222
Education Business Partnership (EBP) 225
Education Reform Act 1988 222, 224
Education (Schools) Act 1992 222
education system (VET) 219–41
  delivery 225–7, 235–7; development
    220–35; post-school education 224; scale,
    quality and scope 237–9; schools 220–4;
    and world of work 224–5

employee rights 185–6
employment 8, 13–18
  civilian 88; contract 181–4; government
    services 16; industrial 81, 88;
    manufacturing and services 15–17; and
    plant size 31–2; relationship 181–4;
    structural change 114
Enterprise Allowance Scheme 31
enterprise culture 252
Environment Act 1995 178
Environment Agency 178
Environmental Protection Act 1990 177–8
environmental protection and workplace 176–9
Equal Opportunities Commission (EOC) 150
equity markets 115
Eurobond 116
European Commission 143
European Court of Justice 143
European Economic Interest Groupings (EEIE)
  163
European Free Trade Association (EFTA) 143
European Marketing Confederation 96
European Parliament 143
European trade 8–13
European Union (EU) 142–3
European Works Councils 168
Eurotunnel 34
exchange rate mechanism (ERM) 120
expectations gap 122, 135–7

Fair Trading Act 1973 188
family capitalism 195–6
finance and accounting 260
finance and capital markets 37
financial and corporate sector, relationship
  100–1
financial institutions 107–17
  assets 112; Bank of England 107–8; deposit
    taking 108–13; securities market 113–17
financial intermediation 104–6
  maturity transformation 105; risk
    transformation 105; volume
    transformation 105
financial markets, structure 106
financial regulation and supervision 117–18
financial reporting, see accounting
Financial Reporting Council 130
Financial Reporting Exposure Drafts (FREDs)
  131
Financial Reporting Standards (FRSs) 131
financial sector 100–21
  financial institutions 107–17; financial
    intermediation 104–6; financial markets
    structure 106; flow of funds 102–4; future
    developments 120–1; institutional fabric
    100–2; UK and European monetary union
    118–20
financial services, retail stores 101

Financial Services Act 1986 118
fixed interest securities 116
flow of funds 102–4
food consumption 54, 57
    regional 58
Food and Drink Acts 95
Ford Motor Company 33, 237
foreign exchange markets 117
Foundation for Management Education (FME) 201
FT-SE 100 index 117
fuel imports and exports 10

gardening 56, 64
GEC 130
General Product Safety Regulations 1994 172–3
gilt-edged securities 116
GKN 214
Glaxo 34
global financial markets 101
GNP and population 87
goverment services, employment 16
government
    accountability 147–50; central 143–5; local
      145–6
government agencies 146–7
government banker, Bank of England 108
Gower Report 118
grant maintained schools 222–3
Greenbury Report 168
grocery
    brands and new products 91; multiples 60,
      67–8; shopping habits 66; trade structure
      67

Hampel Committee 168
Harvard Business School 192
Healey, Denis 6
health and safety at work 174–6
Health and Safety at Work etc Act 1974 174–6
Health and Safety Commission (HSC) 174
Health and Safety Executive (HSE) 174
Her Majesty's Inspectorate of Pollution (HMIP)
    177
Higher Education Funding Council (HEFC) 224
holidays 57, 65–6
Home Purchase Acts 95
House of Commons 148
household
    characteristics 55; expenditure 51–60
human resources 261–2
    definition 190; management 190–218

ICI 192, 214
IMD 192
income
    average 51, 79; distribution 53–4
income elasticity of demand 12–14
incomes policy 5

Independent Television Commission 94–5
individual freedeom 25
Industrial Re-Organisation Corporation 4
industrial relations 8, 242–56
    agents for change 243–7; changes 21–9; and
      law 179; management offensive 249–50;
      non-zero sum game 28; Prisoner's
      dilemma 28; trade unions 250–1;
      traditional system 242–3; transformation
      27, 252–6; unions and management
      247–9
Industrial Revolution 1
Industrial Training Organisations (ITOs) 229
inflation 3–7
information technology 90–2
innovation
    investment 35; research and development 26,
      33–5
inquisitorial system 152
INSEAD 192
insolvency 41
Insolvency Act 1986 169
Institute of Chartered Accountants 124
Institute of Chartered Accountants in England
    and Wales (ICAEW) 128–9
Institute of Chartered Accountants (ICAS)
    128–9
Institute of Chartered Accountants in Ireland
    (ICAI) 128
Institute of Financial Accountants 129
Institute of Management (IM) 194, 199
Institute of Personnel and Development 194
Institute of Practitioners in Advertising 97
institutional framework 142–56
    constitutional framework 142–6
Institutional Shareholders Committee 36
insurance companies 112
Integrated Pollution Control (IPC) 177
intellectual property 185
International Arbitration Centre 155
International Commodities Clearing House 117
International Petroleum Exchange 101
International Stock Exchange (ISE) 113–15
international trade 2
investment institutions 111–12
Investors in People (IiP) 233–5
ISO 9000 88, 93

Jaguar 90
Japan
    direct investment 32, 35; management
      practice 32–3, 253
Joint Stock Companies Act 1844 123
Jones, Jack 7
judicial precedent 157

Kenricks 196
KPMG 194

labour
    costs 43–4; quality 26–7
labour market 22
law and business organisations 162–70
    company liability 169; legal status 163–4;
        management responsibilities 164–8; name
        of business 164; reorganisation and
        liquidation 169
law of contract, see contract law
law sources 156–8
    case law 157–8; legislation 156–7
legal advice 159–60
legal aid 160
legal framework 162–89
    business law 162–70; contract law 170–2;
        product liability 172–4; workplace and
        environment 174–89
legal and institutional framework 141–61
    institutional framework 142–56; legal
        profession 158–60; UK law 156–8
legal profession 158–60
legal status, business 163–4
legislation 156–7
leisure, hobbies and personal care 54–6, 60, 62
liability, company 169
limited company 162–6
LINK 225
litigation 160
local education authorities (LEAs) 221–2
Local Enterprise Councils (LEC) 207, 230
local government 142, 145–6
London Business School (LBS) 192, 198
London Commodity Exchange 101
London Derivatives Market 117
London Gold Market 101
London International Financial Futures
    Exchange 117
London Silver Market 101
London Traded Options Market 117
London Underground 147

Maastricht social chapter 257
Machinery (Safety) Regulations 1992 175
Management Charter Initiative (MCI) 236–7
management development ladder 212–16
management education, training and
    development (METD) 192
management education, five-phase model,
    xviii-xix
management and human resource management
    190–218, 249
    1980s and 1990s 202–11; 1980s 190–5;
        corporate approach 211–16; pre-1980s
        195–202
management practice, Japanese 32–3, 253
management responsibilities 164–8
managerial capitalism 195
managerial revolution 26

Manchester Business School (MBS) 192, 198
manpower demography 18
manufacturing 17–18
    employment 15–16, 81; productivity 8,
        15–18; UK and Japan 17
market environment 46–99
    advertising 63–5; consumer protection 92–7;
        consumers' profile 46–51; direct mail
        71–2; distribution 60–3; future of
        marketing 97–9; household expenditure
        51–60; market research 72; marketing
        process 83–92; television 65–71; top
        advertisers 72–83
market knowledge 260
market performance, measurement 117
market research 72
    expenditure 83
Market Research Society 97
marketing
    future 97–9; process 83–92; relationship
        88–90; targeted 91–2
Marketing Society 97
Marks and Spencer (M&S) 89–90, 92
Master of Business Administration (MBA) 193
Maxwell, Robert 130, 135, 137
mediation 155
Memec 215–16
Memorandum of Association 166–7
merchant banks 111
Mergers Control Regulation 1989 189
Mnagement Charter Initiative (MCI) 204
monetary policy 108
monetary supervision, Bank of England 107
monopolies and mergers 188–9
movement of goods 188
multiple retailers 67

Napoleonic Code 1804 156
National Advisory Council on the Education and
    Training Targets (NACETT) 234
National Association of Pension Funds 36
National Audit Office (NAO) 126
National Coal Board 142
National Council for Vocational Qualifications
    (NCVQ) 231–3
National Curriculum 221, 224–5
national debt, Bank of England 107
National Economic Development Council 4
National Education and Training Targets
    (NETTs) 220, 233–5
    foundation learning 234; lifetime learning
        234
National Plan 4
National Power 147
National Rivers Authority 178
National Union of Mineworkers 250
National Vocational Qualifications (NVQs)
    231–3

nationalised industries 18
Nationalised Industry Consumers Councils 96
New Training Initiative (NTI) 235–7
  adult opportunity 236; delivery 237;
    equipping young people for work 236;
    management training 236–7; skill training
    235–6
newspapers 64–5
  advertising 73–4
noise pollution 178
nomination committee 139
non-accelerating inflation rate of unemployment
    (NAIRU) 8
non-deposit taking wholesale banks 111
non-executive directors 138, 168
non-traded sector 18–19
North Sea oil 8–13, 202
  production 8–9; tax revenues 8–9

OFFER (Office of the Electricity Regulator) 149
Office of Telecommunications (OFTEL) 34
Official List 115
OFGAS (Office of Gas Supply) 149
OFTEL (Office of Telecommunications) 149
OFWAT (Office of Water Services) 149
Ombudsman 148–9
options and futures 116
over-the-counter (OTC) trading 115
own-label brands 91–2
ownership capitalism 195–6

Parents' Charter 222
partnership 122, 162–5
patent registrations 31
pension funds 112
Pergamon Press 130
picketing 180
Pilkingtons 196
Police Federation 151
pollution 176–9
population and GNP 87
Post Office 147
post-school education 224
press, journals 75–7
pressure groups 150–1
Price Waterhouse 194
primary market 106
Prisoner's dilemma 28
private banks 111
private companies 123
private sector, auditing 124–6
privatisation 8, 18–21, 147, 246
  public asset sales and proceeds 20
Procter & Gamble 77
product liability 172–4
productivity 3–8
  growth 21–9; reasons for accelaration 26–9
public companies 123, 166–8

public sector 8, 18–21, 103–4
  auditing 126; bodies 146–7
public sector borrowing requirement (PSBR)
    20–1
public sector debt repayment (PSDR) 21

quality 89–92
  improvement 26–7
Queen's Moat Houses 132

racial equality 150
ratio decidendi 158
refugees 150
Registrar of Companies 166
regulation and supervision, financial 118
relationship marketing 88–90
remuneration committee 139
repackaging of funds 105
resale price maintenance agreements 187
research and development (R&D) 33–5
restrictions on goods and services 186
Restrictive Practices Court 186–7
Restrictive Trade Practices Act 1976 186–7
retail trades 70
retailers, multiple 67–8
risk insurance 101
risoner's dilemma 28

Safeway 89–90
Sagacity Life Cycle groupings 51–2
Sainsbury's 89–90, 212
schools 220–4
Scottish Vocational Education Council
    (SCOTVEC) 231
secondary market 106
Securities and Investment Board (SIB) 118
securities market 113–17
  equity markets 115; fixed interest securities
    116; foreign exchange market 117;
    International Stock Exchange 113–15;
    measurement of market performance 117;
    new instruments and derivatives 116–17
select committees 148
Selective Employment Tax 4
self-employment 29–31
services, employment 15, 83
share ownership 36
  by sector 115
Shell 192
shopping 48, 57–60
  grocery 66
Social Contract 5
social grade definitions 48–51
Society of Company and Commercial
    Accountants 129
Society of Motor Manufacturers and Traders 151
sole trader 122, 162–4
solicitors 158–60

South Sea Bubble 113
sport 60–2
Statements of Standard Accounting Practice
    (SSAP) 130
statutes 156
statutory minimum wage 257
stock exchanges, comparison 114
stop-go business cycles, xx 6
strikes 23, 250–1
supervised settlement 155
surpluses and deficits, matching 102–4

targeted marketing 91–2
Taylor Committee 221
technology 101–2
    see also economy, business and technology
television 65–71
    industry structure 77–9; ownership 68, 80;
        reach data 81; viewing patters 82
tendering 147
Tesco 212–15
total quality management 89
Touche Ross 194
Town and Country Planning Act 1990 177
trade
    EC 11; international 2, 12
Trade Descriptions Act 95
trade unions 7
    and employer 179–81; membership 245, 247;
        reform 24–5, 243–7; structure 23–5;
        workplace industrial relations 247–9
Training and Enterprise Council (TEC) 207,
    230–1
training, management 190–5, 236–7
    academic 192–3; corporate 192; professional
        192–3
training (VET) 237–9
    delivery 235–7; distributiion 239; prior to
        1979 227–8; quality 238–9; since 1979
        228–35; volume 237–8
Transfer of Undertaking (Protection of
    Employment) Regulations (TUPER) 1981
    183
Transport and General Workers Union (TGWU)
    7
travel 57, 65–6

Treaty of Rome 93, 119
trends, analysis 83–4
tribunals 154–5
    industrial 184
tripartism, xix
two-sector economy 102–4

UK and European monetary union 118–29
unemployment 24–5
Unilever 77, 192
unit and investment trusts 112
Unit Trust Association 36
unitary authorities 145
University Funding Council (UFC) 224
University Grants Committee (UGC) 221
Unlisted Securities Market 115
Urgent Issues Task Force (UTIF) 131

value delivery 98
Venture Capitalist Trust Scheme 166
vocational education and training (VET)
    219–41
    delivery mechanisms 235–7; development
        220–7; institutional structure since 1979
        228–35; prior to 1979 227–8; scale, quality
        and scope 237–9

waste control 178
Water Resources Act 1991 178
Weights and Measures Act 1878 95
Wellcome 135
Wilson Report 114
winding up 169
Woolf Report 161
workplace and environment 174–89
    anti-restrictive practices 187; competition
        184–5; employees 185–6; employer and
        employee 181–4; environmental
        protection 176–9; free movement of
        goods 188; health and safety 174–6;
        industrial relations 179; monopolies and
        mergers 188–9; resale price maintenance
        187; restrictions on goods and services
        186; trade unions 179–81
workplace relations 21–9